AMERICA'S HISTORY RETOLD

1400-2012 A.D.

America's History Retold

1400-2012 A.D.

Vol. 1

Conquests, Colonialism and Constitutions

Alfred de Grazia

AMERICA'S HISTORY RETOLD

1400 TO 2012 A.D.

Volume One

CONQUESTS, COLONIALISM AND CONSTITUTIONS

metron publications

ISBN: 978-1-60377-080-4

Library of Congress Number: 2011943961

Copyright 2009, 2011 by Alfred de Grazia

All Rights Reserved

METRON PUBLICATIONS

P.O. Box 1213 PRINCETON NJ 08540-1213

Cover by METRONAX – *Portrait of Benjamin Franklin*

by Joseph-Siffred Duplessis, Paris, 1778

It is my pleasure to dedicate these volumes of America's History Retold *to my helpful and courageous friend, Bruce Mainwaring*

I wish to thank my dedicated research assistant, tireless interlocutor, editor and beloved wife, Anne-Marie Hueber (Ami) for her help in writing this book; my always good-natured assistant Christoph Meyer-Rudolphi for his work on the layout and the illustrations; the Library of the University of Pennsylvania which opened its stacks to us; and the hospitality of the International House of the University of Pennsylavania which hosted us for several studious months.

AMERICA'S HISTORY RETOLD
TABLE OF CONTENTS

VOLUME ONE:
CONQUESTS, COLONIALISM AND CONSTITUTIONS

INTRODUCTION : *A fact is never just a fact* 14

Part One: INDIAN AMERICA: *Step backwards to leap forwards* — 23
Chapter 1: The Environment, *unleashed nature courts revenge* — 34
Chapter 2: Intercontinental diffusion, *people from everywhere, and before Columbus* — 52
Chapter 3: American Indian nations, *500 peoples, all different* — 73

Part Two: EUROPEAN INVASIONS: *The Age of Discovery* — 107
Chapter 4: Renaissance and Reformation, *ideas are riskier than exploring* — 112
Chapter 5: Portuguese and Dutch, *smart, small, powerful and rich in their hey-day* — 125
Chapter 6: Spaniards, *in the 'otro mundo' of the South* — 135
Chapter 7: French, *North and West with the Jesuits* — 160
Chapter 8: English, *the seaboard footholds* — 171
Chapter 9: Africans, *improbable survival* — 194

Part Three: EIGHTEENTH CENTURY CULTURES: *Going every which way* — 217
Chapter 10: Indian recessions, *a dozen factors of fatal decline* — 231
Chapter 11: Dependency and development, *too big for their britches* — 268
Chapter 12: Structures of Government, *social inventions and suppression* — 305
Chapter 13: Yankees, *doctrinaire elders in a crisis of love* — 317
Chapter 14: Pluralists, *people from everywhere* — 344
Chapter 15: Southerners, *planters, Blacks, and* hoi polloi — 363
Chapter 16: Frontier folk, *cultural minimalists* — 389

Part Four: REVOLUTION AND CONSTITUTION: *Violence and rare cunning* — 402
Chapter 17: Prelude to rebellion, *civil disobedience* — 405
Chapter 18: Seven-fold war, *independence, inevitable yet hard-won* — 430
Chapter 19: Continental Congress and Confederation, *better men than usually believed* — 453
Chapter 20: The Framers, *an elective king and the tax power* — 466
Chapter 21: Constitutional government, *the Bill of Rights and a centralizing nation* — 497

VOLUME TWO:
ORIGINATING AMERICAN WAYS OF LIVING AND WORKING

Part Five: DIRECT DEMOCRACY: *Omnipotence of the People* — 12
- Chapter 22: Jefferson's time, *buying Greater Louisiana* — 18
- Chapter 23: The War of 1812, *Washington is burning* — 36
- Chapter 24: Governance without power, *the usual issues and a Monroe doctrine* — 47
- Chapter 25: "Jacksonian democracy," *low-brow nationalism vs. Calhoun* — 56
- Chapter 26: Settlement and Infrastructure, *how they lived and moved about* — 69
- Chapter 27: Industrial and urban frontiers, *productive cities, immigrants, slums* — 85
- Chapter 28: Character and Speech, *several American languages and personality types* — 105

Part Six: EXPANSION AND INTEGRATION: *How the West was won* — 132
- Chapter 29: International transactions, *Americans turned up everywhere* — 135
- Chapter 30: The Hispanic Southwest and Texas, *fiercest ragamuffins win* — 144
- Chapter 31: The Mexican War, *a full war, including amphibious landings* — 155
- Chapter 32: California, *a world apart with wide world contacts* — 161
- Chapter 33: North and West, *an easy life, once you passed through* — 172

Part Seven: THE VOLUNTARY CULTURE: *Nothing people couldn't do together* — 188
- Chapter 34: Individualism and affection, *anxiously alone and incidentally love* — 196
- Chapter 35: Movements, *revivals, labor and utopias* — 208
- Chapter 36: Arts and sciences, *including games, Germans and transcendentalism* — 223
- Chapter 37: Women and feminists, *piety, protests, popular hatred* — 245
- Chapter 38: Political parties and legislatures, *the balancers, hobbling through history* — 258

Part Eight: CIVIL STRIFE, *Futile debate, a million guns and a century of terrorism* — 273
- Chapter 39: Constitutional law and States' rights, *much might be done that wasn't* — 277
- Chapter 40: Slavery and State sovereignty, *hidden in racism and paranoia* — 290
- Chapter 41: War among the States, *a grandiose horrid lesson unlearned* — 311
- Chapter 42: Civil War II: 1865-1965, *embracing a caste system* — 336

Part Nine: NATIONAL INDUSTRIAL DEMOCRACY: *The future arrives by steam and muscle* — 372
- Chapter 43: Entangled federalism, *pro-corporation courts, but a new civil service* — 376
- Chapter 44: Immigration, *where we all come from* — 401
- Chapter 45: Internal migration, *a people endlessly boxing the compass* — 443
- Chapter 46: Conversion to urban industrialism, *world champions and shameful cities* — 465

VOLUME THREE:
SHARING EARTH'S CULTURES AND POWERS

Part Ten: CULTURAL CHANGE: *The Celts conquer the cities* — 13
    Chapter 47: Religious practices, *Catholic ascendency* — 19
    Chapter 48: Popular cultures, *jazz, fads, and nobody spoke English* — 39
    Chapter 49: Sophisticated culture, *nude descending a staircase* — 73
    Chapter 50: Social turbulence, *terrorism North and South* — 90

Part Eleven: IMPERIALISM: *Catching up with world predation* — 106
    Chapter 51: Patterns of expansion, *Bible, guns, trade and emulation* — 108
    Chapter 52: The Caribbean, *America's bean bowl* — 118
    Chapter 53: The Pacific Sphere, *business and the Navy hand in glove* — 124
    Chapter 54: Finishing World War I, *a triumphant intervention but spoiled ending* — 128

Part Twelve: NEW POLITICAL FORMATIONS: *High creativity from hard times* — 136
    Chapter 55: Transforming society, *what won't they think of next* — 141
    Chapter 56: The Great Depression, *broke brokers singing 'Can you spare a dime'* — 160
    Chapter 57: The New Deal, *finally a welfare state and creative tide* — 174
    Chapter 58: Law and Constitution, *obstinate justices, centralized economy, bureaucracy* — 193

Part Thirteen: SUPERPOWER: *A great promise and meltdown* — 206
    Chapter 59: Diplomacy of 1919-1945, *wistful isolationists and bangabouts* — 209
    Chapter 60: World War II, *taking over Western civilization with the materiel of war* — 232
    Chapter 61: Postwar domestic politics, *buying the vote changed from person to public* — 251
    Chapter 62: World domination and Cold War, *hi-costs of being numero-uno* — 276
    Chapter 63: Peripheral wars, *Johnny on the spot* — 295

Part Fourteen: MODERNITY AND MALFUNCTION: *Skybursts of artifacts and ideas, and their fizzles* — 314
    Chapter 64: Agriculture, industry, technology, *hi-tech uniformly unifying* — 320
    Chapter 65: Consumerism and fiscal disorder, *downsizing future generations* — 347
    Chapter 66: Exploitation and crime, *2% jailed, but why so few?* — 366
    Chapter 67: Well-being and environment, *the donnybrook of people and nature* — 399
    Chapter 68: Modern culture, *let freedom ring* — 428

Part Fifteen: RE-CONSTITUTION: *All that's needed is highly Improbable* — 476
    Chapter 69: Leaders, *populist panjandrums* — 481

Chapter 70: A Revolution of Values, *americanizing world culture*   503
Chapter 71: World governance, *globality* versus *ethnicity*   535
Chapter 72: A decade for better or worse, *where did it take us?*   564

LIST OF WORKS OF ALFRED DE GRAZIA   578

An imaginary portrait of Betsy Ross, reputed
to have sewed the first American Flag

Introduction

As I finish writing this history
in my ninety-second year, I figure
that I have lived more than one-third of the life-time
of the United States of America.

When a child I listened to a loving old neighbor
tell stories about her father's service
in the Grand Army of the Republic.
I examined my little palm curiously
when she related how a bullet pierced a hole in his hand.

Her father might have had a grandfather
who served in George Washington's Revolutionary Army.
Going back in time by four hundred years,
I would need a lineage of only six more
old story-telling native American ancestors
to be able to recite to my audience an eye-witness account
of some of what was happening in the year 1400 A.D.
This period would be contemporary
with the late Middle Ages in Europe,
the Ming Dynasty in China,
the Aztec Empire in Mexico,
and the time of five hundred Indian nations
within the present boundaries of the USA.

The cultural pall of family and school
typically and early enveloped me,
allowing the curious eye of a child only a few peepholes
for objectivity and contrariness.
I was bathed in the Midwest atmosphere even in embryo,
Inasmuch as pregnant ladies were being told in those days
That they should become as fat as possible

and bear large babies...and so, weighing in at over nine pounds
I entered my Midwestern culture,
which then began to stretch in all directions.

I was regarded as one of the brighter pupils of Americana
at Franklin Elementary School in Chicago
between 1925 and 1932, wherefore and naturally I would come to believe
that the poor apprentice lad, Benjamin Franklin,
had grown to be greatest of Americans, George Washington not
withstanding. It was there I learned to set type by hand,
as Franklin had done.

Then came the linotype and monotype, with the right and left
adjusted lines still universally employed. Then came
the computer program, with the ability that a few poets had dreamt of
a centered and independent line, fitted to the meaning.
American history was my epic, so I considered it in the form of free verse,
largely metered, with a centered changing line.
Despite respectable criticism, I persisted and can
offer now my work in this unprecedented form.

I continued to soak in the culture,
even as I sought to become its critic,
which meant my own critic, too.
One Sunday afternoon
- the year may have been 1926 -
on Chicago's Navy Pier, stretched far out upon Lake Michigan,
a Bandmaster, who happened to be my father, was conducting
an aggregation of musicians through an elaborate concert program.
This allowed me and my brother, small boys, to slip out
and into the game-room that was behind the concert hall.
There, iron and nickel-plated slot machines stood,
formidable, colorful. "See through a high-powered microscope!"
one of them announced,
"Read the Lord's Prayer Carved on the Head of a Pin!"
We gave it our two pennies and peered, entranced,
at the prodigious microscopy.
It was true, just as advertised.

Already, you see, a conglomeration of American culture traits had

merged here, to which this child was serenely adjusted.
To begin with, he was a typical American individualist,
insufficiently dutiful to sit through the concert. Moreover,
he was now experiencing the American ideal, of a
happy blend of the Bible, Science, Entertainment,
and Profit - without realizing what an incongruent and squabbling set
of ideas they made up. Moreover, slightly puzzled, he wondered
"Why should so important a message be reduced to so small a space?
Did it not belong on huge billboards?"
(Billboards were the favorite medium of the age for urgent advertising).
A long decade later, while studying political representation,
linguistics, and the sociology of knowledge at the same time,
the unconscious intricacy of this cultural integration
of dissimilarities dawned upon me.

Maybe there is even something else that is also typically American:
for I am compressing the nation's history into three volumes.
Is it to be a sacred patriotic manual?
There is more than enough of that, nor is it nice or helpful.
Is it scientific reductionism to a compact set of principles?
I hope so. Handy practicality?
In a way. Entertainment?
Would that it were!
Profitability?
Not for me.
Time-saving?
Possibly for you.

I prefer to believe that it is fairly sized,
for a functional and humanistic exposition of what was,
what might have been, and what should be.
My perspective is of a world-citizen, an earthling, who,
although tempted to give an American slant to events,
appreciates that the welfare of America,
as well as of the rest of the world,
depends upon the largest appraisal of American history.

My intended audience is fully adult, and broad-minded,
with a capacity for indignation at what has happened in the past,
made tolerable by a sense of irony at our ancient follies.

My book affects to be scientific, even while brief.
Like any other general work in science,
it conveys only the knowledge required to stake a claim
for the validity of selected theories and hypotheses.
The author warrants that anyone else would agree with him
after searching for and applying homologous facts.
He claims that his individual statements fit into a larger scheme
of scientifically testable theory about American history.
Given so large a task to be performed in a mere three volumes,
clarification and proof of the principles must be
by reference to representative and salient cases and instances.

Thus, I might say,
"...Although Washington, Grant, and Lyndon Johnson
were heavy drinkers, they were not the only Presidents who were such;
actually, alcoholic beverages were regularly consumed
by most of the three-score Presidents
before, after and/or during their terms of office"...
Digging up all of the facts that might validate or nullify this statement,
weighing their nuances, and reporting them,
I think of the argument whether Richard Nixon was a heavy drinker,
would be beyond the energies of the author, and,
even if complete evidence were available,
could not be afforded space in print.
Besides, where could I find time to write
monographs on all of my propositions?
Critics are expected, therefore, indeed invited,
to revel among all such statements:
correcting, approving, carping, and enlarging.
In any event I would not use such a statement unless
it contributed to some larger understanding of history;
this is not to be a collection of gossip
or a reckless blaster of idols.
The "New History" prefers a cosmopolitan civilization,
as broad as it is deep,
global, and this has been good. History-telling
ought generally to be corrective and therapeutic,
by which I mean that it should be realistic, moral, and useful.
To see historiography as divorced from ethical principle
(except as an operational procedure)

mistakes science,
natural as well as social.
All pure science has an applied science attached to it,
and is indeed dependent ultimately upon it.
So it is perfectly proper and necessary to write history
as the application of the pure social sciences
to the applied science of bringing about a better world.
We take care to separate the fact from the preferences;
what is true is not *ipso facto* right,
nor is what is right whatever usually happens or must occur.
And we take care to be clear and open, never hypocritical,
about what we deem to be a preferable condition
of people and society, and about the good and bad consequences
of the same event. Often we hear people say,
people both of the so-called elite and *hoi polloi,*
that you cannot judge the men and morals of the past by
the standards of today, or by your own standards
whereupon people go to churches or proceed to swear by
some ancient holy testament
if not the Bible, then some constitution or ancient writer.
Thus they reveal themselves to be quite willing in their own case
to let ancient morals govern modern conduct.
Are we to believe that we must accept the past
whatever its crimes and stupidities, without judging it??
If we did so, we would be making a most important moral
judgement and set a low standard for our conduct.
We cannot- at least, I cannot - tolerate letting history be my model.
I say that we must study the past scientifically and
judge it ethically, if we are to derive from history its greatest gifts.
I dare to hope that I have in this retelling
of American History
set a precedent for the new Millennium
of the Twenty-first Century.

Truth is hard to establish and to support.
Then, to justify expressing it openly is often as hard.
There you have the problem of the historian;
just when returning from proving an event,

you are assailed by those who would deny it,
yet in warding them off, you are called upon to
say whom you've helped by vouchsafing verity.
Notwithstanding, I shall try to establish,
to defend and to justify many truths of American history.
And that amounts often to retelling it, perforce reconstructing it.
Whoever retells convincingly its history reconstructs the country.

Many new theories occur, and,
around them flock facts in all their guises.
No fact is merely a fact. It exists in all of its facets,
by virtue of its every use, while it is we who determine uses,
whether we know so or not. A reverence of fact,
like true love, must embrace its every facet, for better or worse.

When in 1999 the United States and
its North Atlantic Treaty Organization
partners were spoiling Serbia's drive to destroy the Kosovars,
they had to deal with an obsessed Serbian psychopath
with a compulsion to repeat a disastrous defeat of Serbian history,
four centuries earlier, who possessed sufficient charisma
to carry along with him on his path to suicide an effective government
and in consequence the whole Serbian people.
And he had been given leave by a large fraction
of the informed public and masses of the world,
dupes of the myth of "national sovereignty",
to wreak havoc upon two million people.

Psychology pervades history, and begs to be taken into account,
to enable deeper understanding -
of defined good people and beneficial events,
as well as of defined evil. Personal development results
from exercising one's deoxyribonucleic acid
upon multitudes of interpersonal transactions,
whereupon the multitude of persons interact to make history.

Examples close to home may stir up thought.
George Washington could not conceive a child by his wife,
who had borne four children to her former husband, Daniel Parke Custis,
deceased after seven years' marriage.

Does this help explain why Alexander Hamilton became a
"son" to him? And, in the end, how Hamilton, a bastard, became great?
Washington's paternalism does help to explain his sponsorship of young Hamilton,
but, also, the social and political genius of Hamilton were continually manifested,
and he was personally engaging, though snobbish.

The Marquis de Lafayette, a vital booster of the American Revolution,
was a friend and attaché of General Washington. The two men believed in
freeing the slaves. They went so far as pricing land upon which slaves could be settled in
the Caribeean region and what it would cost to free them. Washington himself may have
fathered achild by a young African-American named Venus, daughter of a well-respected
overseer slave of his brother. Down to this day among the extended family of
Ford and white acquaintances of the Mount Vernon community, the story has held fast.
With the development of DNA testing, the West family friends and family sought to
apply the test. At first refused access to tiny samples of Washington's hair, skin or nails
by the custodians of the Mount Vernon Ladies' Association, a plea to the Federal
Bureau of Investigation brought action; but the FBI claimed it could not differentiate
distinctly. The results were dubious and left the West Ford partisans considering what
next to do. Besides the DNA test, the logic of circumstances could not alone carry the
day. The case has great importance. Today's world is burdened with racial and ethnic
conflicts and the USA is in the thick of the fray, domestically and globally.
A mixed human family, of Black and white, slave and free, emerging from the "Father"
of the world's strongest country, would have symbolic power – without obfuscating the
injustices of history.

It will be recalled that the matter of Thomas Jefferson's founding
of a line of African-Americans was settled by the positive results
of a test of DNA relationships between Jefferson
and his contemporary African-American descendants.

George Washington was formal and careful in manner
(notwithstanding his outbursts of rage).
Does this help explain why he got along
with the polite and aristocratic French,
without whose help independence could not be won?

Yes, and the Marquis de Lafayette bridged the
larger relationship brilliantly for Washington.
Besides, Washington had combat experience,
stellar qualities as a manager; and

he had great personal wealth, including slaves.
If not a Duke, he was the next best thing.
Finally, from a perfunctory owner of an inheritance of slaves,
he became over two decades a believer in emancipation
(saying he could not lead abolitionism publicly
for fear of splitting in two the nation that he had helped to create).

The smallest fact connects with the infinite world.
Although I cannot chase my facts that far,
I aim to give them a good run.
Should you be inclined to keep going,
you might be perplexed to find yourself
perusing a vast epic poem.
You might, too, agree that the subject -
research into American essences -
is worthy of the infinite hypotheticals of poetry.

Six hundred years of American beliefs and practices
- intertwined processes - will be continuously scanned
for what they provided to everyone of *welfare; culture*; and *governance*
(playing with ancient Greek roots, I once called these
Emos, Pneumos, and *Dikeos*).
Defining, achieving, and distributing the contents of
welfare, culture, and governance in America are
the essence of its organic movement over ages.

Included in welfare are affection, well-being, diet, health,
housing, income, wealth, medical care, and working conditions.

Within our circumscribed idea of culture are contained
schooling, knowledge, religion,
science, travel, entertainment and the arts.

Governance refers to power and influence, authority,
respect, prestige, deference, warfare, politics, organization and law.

Welfare, culture, and governance are intakes and outputs,
of all people as they act by themselves

V1-INTRODUCTION

and through all institutions;
hence all institutions are pertinent:
churches, armies, football leagues, fraternal orders, political parties,
street corner gangs, courts, circuses, and more.

The three avenues of energy are perceived by us
as the constant concerns of everyone, greatly varying and differently distributed.
As I pave substantially the historical process,
I shall continually note how major values were sought and shared.
Even though statistics may not be forthcoming,
my style will often be quantitative, concerned,
for instance, with *how much* the people have cared for and loved,
and neglected and hated one another,
from their beginnings until now.

The answers may be provided by ancient voices dimly heard,
by anthropologists and psychiatrists,
by politicians and jurists,
by statistical trends of care of the old, of divorce,
of child labor, of sexual activity, etc. By censuses. By pictures.
They may be afforded by outside observers, foreigners.
Still, given all of this, historians usually must deduce and conjecture.

Alone and in throngs, humans have been motivated,
and their history may be traced, along the three paths
of welfare, culture, and governance.
A fairly large sum of the values, well-distributed,
might give us the measure of "A happy people!"
But have Americans been actually happy?

———————————

American Indian tribes of North and South (1901 painting)

Part One

INDIAN AMERICA

Not only have (the Indians)shown themselves to be very wise peoples and possessed of lively and marked understanding… prudently governing and providing for their nations… and making them prosper in justice, but they have equalled many diverse nations in the world, passed and present, that have been praised for their governance, politics and customs, and exceed by no small measure the wisest of all these, such as the Greeks and Romans, in adherence to the rules of natural reason.
BARTOLOMEU DE LAS CASAS, *Apologetic History of the Indies (1566)*

The large view of American history
may well sweep over six hundred years,
from pre-Columbian Indian cultures of the fourteenth century
to the end of the twentieth century and into the future.
Reculer pour mieux sauter, and too,
the farther back the start, the farther forward the leap.

The American people are considered here to be
the past and present inhabitants of the territory of the
fifty States, the District of Columbia, the

Commonwealth of Puerto Rico, and sundry tiny
islands of the Caribbean Sea and Mid-Pacific Ocean.
Several millions live and work abroad, too, globally,
and tens of millions emerge in any given year
to flit around Earth's continents.

The name of Americans came hard.
They called themselves by their colonies, or were
spoken of as British Americans, then plain Americans,
then by their states much more than now,
or "hailed from" some "neck of the woods".
George Washington called his troops "Americans"
on occasion, and used the term in a letter
to the Continental Congress and finally
in his so-called "Farewell Address" declared:
"The name of American
which belongs to you in your national capacity,
must always exalt the just pride of patriotism
more than any appellation derived from local discriminations."

Few were keen on "Indianans".
There was still talk of calling them "U.S.-ians",
to rhyme with "Hessians", and today, in the corridors of
world governance, one harks to the word "Use-yans".
Many proposed "Columbians", others "Freedonians".
But the USA was the first country to shake off the
authority of Europe, and had first call on the word "Americans".
Too, Canadians, Mexicans, Brazilians, and the others,
found well-sounding names for themselves,
and when they felt like it, or in special circumstances,
organized themselves into the Pan-American Union,
and called themselves "Americans".
But Americans have
never been officially
from an "America", as such.
The world's super-power, mused a recent author,
was "a country without a name".

The bounds of this nation of Americans have always been "unnatural",
though people are conditioned to the idea of some determined
geographical goal or get used to their boundaries after a while,
and regard them as natural, or even sacred, as
Dante chants of Italy's shapely shores and mountains,
Shakespeare exclaims at the lovely isolation of England,
French kindergartners read straightaway of the
perfect hexagonal shape of *La belle France;* so
Americans sing out, *"from sea to shining sea!"*

At first thought, the Atlantic and Pacific and Caribbean seas,
with the St. Lawrence River and Great Lakes and Rio Grande,
seem to mark off territories logically, but only a
weak logic allots two nations one side
each of a river, lake, or ocean,
when more good might come from serving people of both banks.
The Rio Grande seems bent upon helping two great nations.

Also Baja or Lower California could become California State,
or the American Southwest be Mexican as it once was.
Hawaii and Alaska, so typically American while distinct
sub-cultures, are far distant and climatically alien.
The USA is an ocean from Britain, but Canada worked well
with France and Britain for a long time.

If within the continental United States,
one were to seek natural boundaries
natural regions would not appear, while those
regions so important to us, like New England and Dixie,
formidable centers of attitudes, interests, and peculiar behaviors
over the years, are cultural artifacts,
bereft of nature's will of climate or race.
Blacks assigned to heat "by nature" fled to prosper in Milwaukee;
Italians dug in the Mesabi iron range of Northernmost Minnesota,
while Germans worked the hot cow ranges of Southern Texas.

New England is bounded by the Atlantic Ocean on the East,
the St. Lawrence River to the North, the Hudson River to the West,

and a swollen New York City metropolis on the South.
Its Southern boundary and early cultural crossing of the
Hudson to the North proves that no
natural internal region exists.
Its foreshortened Northern boundary betokens that a
natural boundary can mean little internationally;
the Webster-Ashburton Treaty of 1842 sliced off
a "naturally American" area and gave it to the British.
So, too, was Oregon Territory's boundary,
politically and peaceably determined,
but hardly natural, in 1846,
despite a clamor for war.

Moreover, numerous ways have been found to
divide the national domain to give
states and localities boundaries, and draw
regional boundaries for administrative purposes and analyses.
Thomas Jefferson was culpable for drawing all America
beyond the original colonies as an exercise in rectangles -
states, counties and townships - so far as possible.

Once it would have been logical to include the Philippines
as an important part of American history,
for the United States was providing the Islands
with American government, dictating their present and future.
The Filipinos, now grown in numbers from six to seventy millions,
strategically well-situated, and possessing great natural resources,
might have occupied in an American history book -
according to the egalitarianism of which Americans boast -
a quarter of its pages between 1898 and 1946.

However, historians conveniently considered
the Philippines to be a passing imperial fancy of
the American government, for which they,
the historians, would shirk accountability,
when highlighting, for instance, the liberties, rights,
and material comforts of the American people.

Unequal historiography was a prerogative of imperial power.
Great Britain would claim preeminence as a democracy
because at home it gave some freedoms and
opportunities to some of its people,
even while imposing sovereign restraints
upon hundreds of millions of people
in Ireland, India, the South Pacific, the Middle East,
Africa and other parts of the world.

One did not have to be dark or black or brown
or red or yellow for this kind of subjection;
the English ruling class and its generally deluded and
often miserable domestic minions were pleased
to impose the same rule upon their own ethnics
wherever these settled, from Newfoundland to New Zealand,
and not excluding ancestors of today's Americans.
Ditto Spanish, Portuguese, Dutch, French, Belgian,
Russian, German and Italian elites and their minions,
when these were conducting themselves imperially.

The 305 million Americans are affected by the
natural processes of past ages, some of which
forcefully impacted not long before the European-African influx.
Enhanced geographic attention to American history
illuminates the basic conditions affecting human activity,
both before and after 1500 A.D.

Natural processes are history, too.
So we begin by doing honor to the natural processes
of the country, which are always with us.
Hurricane "Andrew" - one of the first named masculine
instead of feminine - in 1992
destroyed scores of thousands of buildings,
disrupted the lives, work, and income of millions of people,
and inflicted billions in costs upon Florida State and the nation.
It would be hard to name a recent piece of federal legislation
whose effects were so prompt and prodigious upon so many people.

As for the people of America Medieval,
(for there was a more ancient American history beforehand)
they bred many cultures prior to the European incursions.
Where they came from, where their customs and artifacts originated,
in all or part, pose intriguing mysteries. American traditions
are being deciphered and assembled in new order
to accelerate fast-moving changes in USA-Indian relations
- also to recollect and reorganize the past in our minds.

HISTORICAL GENERATIONS AND PERIODS
A Tour de Force

Historians follow the process of events through time
as they would the course of a river.
Whenever a set of events occurs to change the course of history,
they mark it as they would the bend of a river,
calling attention to changed landscape and a new direction.
They designate a new period, calling it by a name.
And so we have divided American history into a number of parts,
each new part containing mostly more of the same events
that have been flowing all the while
but carrying enough of new directions and new events
to be labeled as a new period.

One could call the new period a new historical
generation, adding this to three other types of generations
that we can distinguish also:
the *biological, political* and *memorial* generation.

There is a *political* or *social generation* of about
33 years, between civically active parents and
civically active progeny, a typical
length of a political and work life,
say from 25 to 58 years.
The average age of top politicians has changed little
from 1780 to 2000, averaging mid-forties.

The clutch of historical interests leads politics,

from one social generation to the next,
and politics retards the future, so that
a two-generation gap separates determining
realities from social action. Well-typifying
all states, representatives of Ohio
localities for two centuries subtended from
outmoded interests of their parents' generation,
acted in consonance with immediate issues,
and left the future to their successors,
by which time the future had become history.
So the three-phase cycle would probably continue,
not only there but everywhere.

A *biological generation* may be set at *20* years,
between successive births of women on the same line of descent.
This varies as women bear children now earlier, now later.
Too, women of one generation will average later or
younger births than in another period.
If all memories and calculations are correct,
and Dr. Techeng Kong of Taiwan is the
seventy-ninth direct descendent of Confucius,
premier philosopher of all Chinese history,
the average of biological generations that
called him up was ~ 32 years.

A *memorial or mnemonic generation* connects the oldest
story-teller and a young listener, typically
extending for some *65* years.
The average length of life by 2000 increased to the
mid-seventies from the mid-forties in 1780,
but there had always been the old around and about
for remembering.
The three concepts of bio-generations,
poli-generations, and memo-generations help to
invigorate the bland uniform years-count
when shaping the historical record.

<u>*Timing History by Generations*</u>
Six centuries before us comprise, then, only
18 political generations, 30 biological

generations, and between nine and ten
mnemonic generations, say ten.

We can readily understand how history can be passed down,
even with some veracity, by word of mouth,
especially when the events being reported are sacred or disastrous.
We can understand also how the force
of a culture is conveyed, for better or worse.
The hardest job on Earth, indeed, is to crack
the cement of customary cultural force once
it has been laid down, yet needs to be reseated.

Myself, I extend well beyond one of the ten mnemonic generations.

This method of registering history is in desuetude,
but if one went back to the Revolutionary War
and switched to the Indian folk historians,
proceeding by mnemonic generations,
the method would be state-of-the-art and
it would require a mere six generations more
to hear of Indian affairs in the year 1400 A.D.
The Indians had little reason to measure time like now;
they played their own kind of chronological games.

Thus, a little Indian girl who was told by her grandmother
(born in 1427) to watch for the cannibals
who came by sea and ate children up
was amazed on the dawn of "October 12, 1492"
to see men rowing back and forth from a large boat.
And she lived to tell this tale to a little Spanish girl
who in 1552 was on her way to Cuba
who could have told this and more stories
to a little boy in St. Augustine, Florida, in 1617.
This little boy, grown old and moved to Albemarle Point,
South Carolina, could tell many more stories to a
little girl from England in 1682.
This child could, as a grandmother,
convey many a tale to her granddaughter in
Charleston in 1747, and the
next grandchild would be thrilled with stories of the Revolution,

while scared at the thought of a new British invasion
in the War of 1812.

Subsequently the chain had only to perpetuate itself
through four more memorial generations to be
passing among the tellers of tales about the railroad trains,
the tragedies of the Civil War and Reconstruction,
the infinite smoke stacks of the Northern States,
the splendors and stinking crowds of the "Empire City",
controlled nuclear fission, and
man's landing on the Moon.

If, upon each occasion, the child had been knocked on the
head (not too hard) to assist her recalling the
telling of the arrival of Columbus,
if the line of descent had not failed nor had there been
substitute nannies in attendance, and even if
the story had neither been heard or read elsewhere,
the woman today at the end of the chain of history
would picture for us the ship of Columbus
mysteriously interpreted, mythically so,
since an Indian girl learned to evoke its sight.

Putting Labels on Nine Memo-generations

The memorial generations can be tabulated,
with a phrase describing the essences so far
as the United States is geographically involved. Each memorial
generation, it was earlier noted, carries roughly 3 biological
generations and two political generations:

1.
1427-1492...
A country
of hundreds of Indian nations speaking hundreds of
languages, concentrate their more technologically
complex cultures in the Northeast "United States",
"Florida", "Virginia", "Missouri", the "Southwest", and Hawaii.

2.
1492-1557...
Beachhead.
Spanish, Dutch, French, and English
pass-bys and stop-bys of
total U.S. coastline and Caribbean Islands.
Spanish follow Indians to explore two-thirds of interior of USA.
Demographic decline of Indians everywhere.

3.
1557-1622...
First lasting Spanish and English settlements in "USA".
Africans begin to arrive in North America. Indian decline continues.

4.
1622-1687...
Prototypical U.S. cultures established in New England,
New York, Delaware, New Jersey, Pennsylvania,
Virginia, the Frontier, and Far Southwest.

5.
1687-1752...
Stabilization and expansion of colonial cultures.
Heavy immigration begins.

6.
1752-1817...
Stresses between colonies and imperial government
end in independence and constitutional synthesis.
Immigration continues.

7.
1817-1882...
Intense internal states development.
Full continental expansion.
Industrialization begins and flourishes.
War to confirm national rule and end slavery.
Heavy immigration.

8.
1882-1947...
Southern depression and
terrorist resistance to North and Blacks.
Northern agricultural and industrial revolution.
The economy nationalizes.
Heavy immigration.
A cosmopolitan culture emerges.
The USA becomes a world power, then super-power.

9.
1947-(2012)...
USA is dominant world
military, scientific, cultural and economic power,
but begins to lose pre-eminence because of
domestic and world problems.
All the world experiencing deteriorating values and benefits,
despite extreme technical virtuosity.
The world is governed as one, but badly,
while the USA is pulling together the
components of its cosmopolitan global culture.

———————

Albert Bierstadt: Valley of the Yosemite, 1864

Chapter One

The Environment

The history of the United States, as of all the world,
was determined in the first place by its natural constitution -
physiography, climate, flora and fauna.
These are not, nor have ever been, static features.
To this day, and probably much more in early human times,
North America has been a restless continent,
moving in its parts and mobile even as a whole. The
physical geography of the country and
its natural regions insistently relate to its history.

They work like the clauses of the federal and
state constitutions. Constitutional clauses will fashion
certain kinds of activity, inspiring the regulation of some
such as interstate and foreign commerce, forbidding some
(such as "cruel and unusual punishment"), limiting others
(such as the number of Senators from a State = 2),
demanding still others (that a bill pass through
both houses of Congress).

Similarly, a good harbor such as New York's
will dictate a busy port; a river valley like the
Ohio will provide a way for people to penetrate the
interiors and carry on trade; a Mississippi delta
climate will favor growing cotton.

Great natural events, usually disasters, can violate the
customary nature of places and even transform the landscape,
just as rampaging crowds, wars, economic crises, and forceful leaders
can sometimes alter the meaning of clauses of the constitution.
Extraordinary and catastrophic events can and have altered the
natural constitution of the Americas.

Horrified humans watched, when 5700 years
ago, by radiocarbon dating which may be off the mark,
huge mud flows from Mt. Rainier overwhelmed
Northwestern Washington State. Or again, if today's
Seattle-Tacoma-Olympia settlements, now holding
2.5 million residents, had stretched back in time to the
Norman invasion of England in 1066,
they would have suffered destruction in the earthquake
which occurred around then.

Some of the land there subsided, some rose.
Much of the area was struck by a giant tsunami,
engendered by a shifting of the floor of Puget Sound.
Mountains collapsed. Forests were drowned. Lakes were
created. Tall Douglass Firs are to be found standing in

200 feet of water beneath Lake Washington.
The campsites and settlements of the people were
buried by debris or silt from floods: evidence of
them is being dug up today.

Worse disaster can strike the same region at any time;
the good news is that the historical record of it
will be more complete.
Because the Indian Americans of the day kept only oral records
(so far as we know), the successive events that befell them
are estimable only by geology and folklore.

We are more informed about the situation in New England
where in the eighteenth century earthquakes were common,
and the region around East Haddam had to endure
frequent strong shocks. The noises were terrifying,
both Indians and Europeans imagining the subterranean
world to be full of devils. *Machemoodus*, the Indians
named it, the place of noises, and each accused
the other's god for causing the troubles.

Geology in the past socio-generation has revolutionized
by accepting the theory of continental drift. (Never mind
the T-shirts that sprouted in Texas in the nineteen-sixties
exclaiming "Stop Continental Drift!") According to this scheme, the
Americas were formerly part of an all-continents Earth,
called Pangaea ("All Earth" in Greek), or of a smaller Earth,
or of an Earth with a single giant island containing
all of today's continents. They were split off from Euro-Africa
by a deep fracture from which up-welling and
out-flowing lava pushed them apart.

The fracture has turned into a welt of mountains, like a
slow-bleeding wound, the Mid-Atlantic Ridge; this
runs down the middle of the Atlantic Ocean now,
swings around the Antarctic, and starts North again
near the middle of the Pacific Ocean. The Americas are
framed by the encircling towering underseas ridges.

America was connected to Europe and Africa in the
Age of the Dinosaurs, conventionally given at about
65 million years ago. Obviously, were there
humans in those days, their survivors would have been rafted
apart. They would have evolved human physiognomies and
cultures more varied than were found by Renaissance explorers.

The Pacific Coast doesn't fit China and Japan and the
South Pacific Islands so well, inclining us to believe
that there was always an ocean present or that some
large piece of Earth is missing, conceivably the Moon,
an idea of so many difficulties that it is
conventionally regarded as highly improbable.

The Hawaiian Archipelego was probably a product of the same
earth-shaking movement that parted the continents; its
islands are but the tops of huge volcanos.
Volcanos of the North Cascade Range relate to the edge of the
North American plate, which the continent rides on, as it
encounters the Juan de Fuca Plate, named after the Spanish
explorer, the earliest European known to have ventured into
the area. Many volcanos are extinct, some are active or
may reactivate, as did Mt. St Helens, near Seattle.
Alaska, part of the same system,
supports very many volcanos and its chain of Aleutian
Islands swings over to Asia as part of the
Pacific Basin's "Ring of Fire".

Earthquakes are generally associated with volcanos and with
the great rifts of the world, their branches, and the
movements along the edges of the tectonic plates. The
present continental area of the United States is
subjected to the threat of earthquakes the
full length of the West Coast, but has felt
destructive quakes, some of the worst in the world, in the
Lower Mississippi Valley, Charleston (S.Ca.), and elsewhere. The
earthquake of 1807-8, centered at the
Spanish colony of New Madrid, Missouri,
affected several nations of Indians, and, too,

French, Spanish, and English settlers and traders,
all lately become U.S. American
as a result of the Louisiana Purchase of 1803.
Lakes were drained and other lakes created.
Upheavals were so great as to reverse for
some hours the flow of the Mississippi River.

The Ice Ages, so-called, were a dropping, freezing, flooding,
and crawling of immense bodies of ice over much of
the Northern Hemisphere and Southern South America.
Mountain-tops everywhere collected snow,
and sent rivers of ice downward at glacial speed.
When ice gathers on the continents,
ocean levels become lower, and this, in the
view of conventional theory, could have occasioned a
dry-land-bridge between Siberia and Alaska, where
there is now Bering Strait (named after the Danish-Russian
Arctic explorer of the eighteenth century).

Here, in majority view, was the crossing-place into the
New World of the ancestors of American Indians and Eskimos,
at a time given as 12,000 to 30,000 years ago.
Soviet archaeologists, and others now,
hold to the older dates.

Today, the theory is widely doubted. Given
strong motive, humans have not been blocked by land,
sea, or ice in venturing afar. The archaeological
analyses of R. MacNeish at Orogrande Cave
in New Mexico indicate that humans were resident there
some 20,000 years ago. Charcoal specimens and
human hair were found and gave such dates when
subjected to radiocarbon dating. Hand prints and
stone artifacts were found at the same site. It is not the
carbon-14 dating that persuades one so much as a number of
archaeological, anthropological, logical and
geological observations, such as will be alluded to below.

Remains of accurate chronological fixation are scanty, disputes frequent. Radiometric dating has not quelled the disagreements. A group of experts, less numerous than the Bering Straits partisans, allows the likelihood of these Bering migrations whether by sea or land, but adds two possibilities, first, that humans could have come from Asia, Africa, and Europe long before then and are merged with the descendants of the newcomers from Asia, and, secondly, that humans were always here, never left the Americas, and were to varying degrees replaced or assimilated by later groups from out of Siberia (for there are many significant ethnic as well as cultural affinities between various Siberian groups and Amer-Indians). There is also the possibility that various Siberian tribes might have originated from America, and, later on, ventured into Siberia as the ancestors of peoples found there now. We shall say more in the next chapter on our medieval migrations.

Whatever their origins, the cultures of the Indians, as they came to be called in the wake of Colombo, could not but be broadly influenced by the morphology of America. It may be theorized, from large appearances, that the most recent and crushing event to befall the continent, was the End of the Last Ice Age, marking a region from Alaska down to the now-called Border States. A grand melt sent broken ice, floods of water, stone and a transported biosphere outwards to elaborate the lakes, rivers, valleys, hills, and soils of almost all of the continent Southward to the Mexican border. Recent geology and archaeology places this epochal event in the history of the American Indian people.

Most of North America, to observers who do not regard it cordially as home, seems post-catastrophic. Looking down upon the continent as from a spacecraft, one sees vast Northern wastes left by the ice,

composing most of present-day Alaska and Canada,
plus a part of the United States.

Next, off the Eastern seacoast of continental
USA, one notes a wide current of ocean waters
running North, the Gulf Stream, that warms all the coastal
waters beginning with the Florida Keys
(sub-tropical in any event).

The Gulf Stream makes human habitation more possible
and comfortable all the way up to Iceland and Scandinavia,
as well as moderating the climate of the British Isles
and Western Europe. Discovered in 1513 by Juan Ponce de Leon,
who is more famous for not having found a fabled
Fountain of Youth in the Florida region,
the Stream was put to work
shortly thereafter to help carry Spanish ships, and later
ships of other nations, in a great elliptical journey
Southward, Westward, Northward, and back,
Eastward, to home ports.

The American East Coast itself is humid, cool in winter,
hot in summer, home to hundreds of inlets and harbors.
Out of it move large rivers into great bays; the largest
bays are the Delaware, Chesapeake, Hudson, and Naragansett.

Off the Coast of the South from what is now Virginia to Georgia are
thousands of ponds and embayments of varying sizes, of
mysterious origins, usually referred to as the Carolina Bays.
They are thought by some to be remains of ice ponds, by others
exoterrestrial ice dumps, still others to be products of
peculiar winds, and by a few to have been dug by a train of meteoroids
and filled by sea water. They had the effect of
pushing inland major heavy settlement.

Northward one encounters Long Island, then many islands,
all of them except the tiniest once inhabited by Indians,
later by Europeans as well. The present-day State of Rhode Island
and Providence Plantations, part of it a real Island, has
waters largely bounding it. Before the revolution in

roads and land vehicles, even minute islands had their
quota of inhabitants whose movements were accomplished,
their needs traded, by sea.

Cut by the St. Lawrence River and Bay, both of which were
instigated by a huge fracture springing Southwestward from
the mid-Atlantic rift, is a mountain chain that emerges to the
North of the Bay on its way through Labrador to Greenland,
and exists in the South as the Allegheny Mountains,
containing the Appalachians and other ranges. Below
St. Lawrence Bay, this great chain swings down in a
Southwesterly direction through New England and the
western parts of the coastal United States,
then in a kind of crescent moving westward
all the way through Alabama, Mississippi, and Louisiana.

Once more the range disappears beneath a river valley, this time the
Mississippi, and comes up to pass, as the Ozark Mountains of
Arkansas and the Pecos Mountains of Texas, into Mexico, traversing
its third valley, the Rio Grande, and ending in Mexico.

(I sketch this vastly long mountain range as an
ontological probability, granting that many
observers would prefer to snip it into eccentric pieces.
In any event we profit simply from contemplating
the possibility of this great figure-S resulting
from a world-shaking, push-and-shove event.)

From Canada to Mexico, very different Indian peoples
occupied the whole length and opposite sides of the giant
crescent. In sixteenth century America, these mountains
were penetrated by Spanish explorers,
in the seventeenth century by French and then British,
but they remained securely in the hands of Indian nations,
until the American Revolution occurred, and in large part
for a long memorial generation afterwards.

Gaps through the Alleghenies are several, and they open upon rolling heavily forested land, which on the South borders hot and humid lowlands, deltas, and swamps of the Caribbean Sea (named for the Carib Indian Peoples), and the Gulf of Mexico. Recent geological speculation over the Gulf and Sea, because of their configuration, shallowness, vast undersea salt domes and oil deposits, ponders whether some meteoroid or comet may have struck off of Yucatan, bringing an end to the Cretaceous Period, the "Age of Dinosaurs".

Over the years, the remains of thousands of dinosaurs have been found in North America, ranging widely from Alaska, the Yukon, and Greenland, Southward throughout the United States. Increasingly, legal and even constitutional issues are arising over who owns such bones being dug from the rocks, and, for that matter, who is authorized by whom to dig up and buy and sell ancient human bones. Lately, judicial opinion has swung over to granting to representatives of Indian tribes the right to repossess the remains of their ancestors, wherever these may have been uncovered, carried away and preserved.
(Later a nice problem will be revealed.)

Archaeology has had to cope with numerous "finds". Mammal fossils are common and it is now acknowledged that early Americans knew mastodons and mammoths, probably saber-toothed tigers as well (just as their Argentine contemporaries knew giant sloths and turtles whose carapaces were so capacious as to provide humans with cozy cottages). The horse has gifted many a fossil hunter; yet, after believing that it extincted in America prior to the Spanish coming, expert opinion is no longer so sure. A variety of mustang may have persisted.

Creation scientists and quantavolutionists disturbed science. The Age of Dinosaurs would have been by conventional calculations some 65 to 100 million years ago, and the Earth obviously presented a different face to the Sun or was insulated by a thick atmosphere against cold. Highly controversial claims have been made that dinosaur footprints are to be found next to those of humans, and that drawings of dinosaurs on certain Western cliffs are the work of ancient Americans. Moreover, in mine shafts of West Virginia, a concurrence of human and dinosaur bones has raised a rancourous dispute.

The Northern boundary of the United States occurs two thousand miles above the Gulf of Mexico and the Rio Grande, and gives us a sweeping straight line from Puget Sound on the Pacific across mountains and dry plain until it approaches, then follows, Lake Superior, the other Great Lakes, the St. Lawrence River part-ways, and a further line to the Atlantic Ocean. It's the longest international boundary in the world. The topographies and climates along the western boundary are practically identical; there is no "natural" reason for the division between Canada and the United States, and precious little economic, demographic and social reason. The same holds true around the Great Lakes until one comes upon the St. Lawrence region and Francophone Canada. Even here the boundary is fudged by the presence of many Francophones as well as Anglophones on both sides of the River and Bay.

The Great Lakes are regarded conventionally as meltwaters, left behind when the Ice Caps that covered half of the present United States retreated, some ten thousand years ago. The grandiose Niagara Falls, which the Algonquin Indians showed to amazed French explorers of the seventeenth century, and which in the past century have constituted a ritual visitation for newly married couples, began to cut back from Lake Ontario only several thousand years ago.

Once again, one may allude to the fact that the waters bursting through Niagara into the St. Lawrence River Valley

were under the observation of Indian Americans. Such an
experience, necessarily involving a great rushing flood, would
make a profound impression on the human mind, inspiring
reverence, fear, and folklore. Such is the stuff of which myth,
legend, religion and, of course, history are made.

Through the near Midwest of the United States run
the Ohio River and several parallel streams,
draining off the Alleghenies into the
Mississippi River Basin, second largest in
the world after the Amazon of Brazil, but without the
floral and faunal abundance of the tropical Amazon.
The origins of the River and its vast system of
Eastern and Western tributaries are in the melting
or collapsing ice cap. Forests here are not
so all-covering as in the Eastern Woodlands.

And, as one moves westward from the Mississippi,
one encounters some of the broadest plains of the world,
that carry on, inclining upward,
until they are called the High Plains and are transformed
into the thrusted and folded Rocky Mountains,
a cordillera that starts in Alaska,
transects Canada and the United States, moves
down through Mexico and Central America,
snakes into South America and carries its spectacular
heights all the way down to the Southern tip of
South America, where, some say, it continues,
after a deep break caused by the global fracture,
in the mountains of Antarctica.

There would seem to be two possible causes of this
Cordillera of the Americas, although geologists are generally
in favor of the one and loath to accredit the other:
A slowly cracking Atlantic rift would have produced
a uniformly slow cracking and pushing and
equally slow rising of the Rockies over a
period of perhaps seventy million years.

Alternatively, if the cracking of the globe had been

the work of a passing or impacting celestial body,
a sudden quantavolution instead of an evolution
would have occurred. The Globe's rotation would have
decelerated briefly or permanently, and
the crust been pushed back and curled, like
a scatter rug when someone slips on it.
The immense force required would have been supplied
by a sudden Atlantic crustal fracture,
a rafting of the Americas' tectonic plates westward,
while Euro-Africa moved Eastward. .

One descends the Western slopes of the Rockies and
enters a huge barren desert and semi-desert area,
often exhibiting rugged features.
Major rivers work their way from here: the
Columbia River and Snake River flowing into
the Pacific Ocean, the Colorado also
via the Bay of Lower California, and the
Rio Grande, at the base of the region, moving
West to East and into the Gulf of Mexico.
The Colorado River valley comes out of the
Bay of Lower California and streaks North
through the Grand Canyon until it appears to
begin in the Rocky Mountains.

For quantavolution or neo-catastrophism
conceives the Colorado River Valley as a long branch of the
fracture that delineates the North American tectonic plate
along its West Coast, which,
having also created the Bay of Lower California,
provided a natural channel for the Rocky Mountain's
flood waters to rush down to the sea.

Westward, the land from Southern California to
Washington State carries up as its spine the
Sierra Nevadas, sharp, new, and tall, then
falling down and again abruptly upwards rising with the Coast
Range and down finally into the Pacific Ocean,
from which the continental plate precipitates
to great depths.

Much rain falls upon the Northern section of the coast,
little rain upon the Southern end, and
only two great bays, at Puget Sound in the
Northwest Corner of the nation, and San Francisco Bay,
indent deeply the coast. The ocean waters and winds
allow a Mediterranean climate to the South, and
grant to the North a climate resembling, but warmer than,
those of Ireland and Southern England.

Indians, in pre-Columbian times,
were of quantavolutionary or catastrophic persuasion,
even as were the Europeans themselves.
Post-Columbian Europeans were of the same belief.
In fact, even until now, most Americans have
believed in a catastrophic history of the natural world;
either they have believed in the Bible and the Apocalypse of
St. John in this regard, or they have been
scientific catastrophists or quantavolutionists, or
they have accepted both the evolutionary and
the quantavolutionary, unconcerned with the
contradiction so long as they could be docile to
both sets of authorities, the
religious and scientific establishments.

It was not until the mid-nineteenth century,
four centuries after our story begins, that a
gradualist, uniformitarian, evolutionary scenario
was adopted to explain the set-up of the present large
features of the world. Every tribe of Indians
had descriptions of ancient catastrophes,
many of them referring to ancestral memories,
most difficult to validate now, or even centuries ago,
and to myths and legends. The story
of a Great Deluge worldwide was universal to
American Indian nations; so too, were accounts of
great cometary visitations,
of an Age of Ice, of all-consuming fires.

Explanations of American landscapes were forthcoming as
tales of sudden local or global transforms.

Whereas geologists, except rare dissenters,
put such events tens of millions of years away when it can,
and assert that such changes occurred by trillions of
tiny increments, Indian explanations are
more in keeping with the Biblical notions of the time
of Creation and the time of the Great Flood and other
cataclysms. Not transmitted in formal writing like
the Hebrew Bible accounts, the American "bibles" were
carried through time orally, from old to young,
with, in some cases and little understood until now,
a symbolic language. In Mexico, among the Mayans and their
successors and relatives, an actual writing for transmitting
history flourished, perhaps as old as any other language.

Natural histories of the United States generally
accord with conventional theory of Ice Ages,
with Darwinian theories to explain the species, and with
uniformitarian gradualist theories of how continents grew.
Two noteworthy evaders of Darwinian steamrollers of the
generation after Darwin were American,
Ignatius Donnelly and Clarence King,
both of the latter half of the nineteenth century.

Donnelly was a "Renaissance man": he combined soaring ambition
and great imagination with unusual adventures.
From Philadelphia and a lawyer, he became a Congressman,
studied and wrote upon ancient catastrophes and comets, and
led settlers into a utopian community in Minnesota, then
still fairly wild. His work was highly popular and he
toured the country lecturing. But he was lauded for
his quantavolutionary or catastrophic theories
by only a small group of scientists and scholars.
He argued that the tillites and till, the hard rocky surface that
composes so much of the ground-cover of the Northern States,

descended from the tail of Donati's comet in recent pre-history, part of a universal frightful destruction by flood and fire. Thus he found the great ice sheets of America unnecessary to explain natural history, and dismissed them as fictions.

Clarence King graduated from Yale, turned to geology, then in time became the first Director of the United States Geological Survey. He was a scientific leader of renown, yet became one of an ever-diminishing minority who believed in catastrophism. He could not conceive of other means of erecting and sculpturing the fantastic Sierra Nevadas than by a recent devastation. Although the historical record was almost entirely absent, the story was not lost; it was "the survival of a terrible impression burned in upon the very substance of human memory".

Geology, land movements, and catastrophes join mythology, archaeology and contemporary anthropology to provide the best available sources of human history. Indian myth and legend have been found often to tell a historical truth, about an eruption, an earthquake, a human decimation, a tidal wave, a great flood. Certainly the Indian inhabitants of the Washington State Scablands never let it be said that the area had become so incredibly scoured and tortured in consequence of trickles and flows.

Geologists, however, assumed so, as consistent with their general theory. It required the lifetime of University of Chicago Professor J. H. Bretz in the twentieth century to convince most geologists that these hundreds of thousands of square miles of Washington State were the effects of a single flood coming out of the Northeast, when a huge natural dam broke and melted ice water crashed down the natural decline toward the Pacific Ocean hundreds of miles away. Thousands of people, with their settlements, together with a whole region of flora and fauna, must have been obliterated.
A much greater catastrophe than this is implicated by the presence in America of legions of fossils from species of a few thousand years ago. How were the innumerable mammoth, mastodon, bears, great elk, tigers and other large animals exterminated? Their bones are found in stupendous masses in Alaska and elsewhere, broken, shredded, packed in jumbles. The total

ecosphere, in fact, from Arctic to Mid-America,
was destroyed.

Sooner or later, human bone fragments or
artefacts will be picked out of the organic debris.
Meanwhile, evolutionary science has been forced into
irritably admitting what has been often termed
"the catastrophic end of the Ice Age",
when humans were flourishing.

One group of scholars has blamed extinctions upon the Indians:
the Indians engaged in overkill - never mind their primitive
weapons and despite their being dismounted;
as they came out of Siberia, they moved Southward,
systematically killing everything in sight.

A quantavolutionary theory is more plausible, that a natural
disaster, of exoterrestrial origin, befell all living things and
exterminated most of the species.
Whether American mankind was spared remains a large question:
there may have been non-Siberian aborigines,
tribes of humans might already have come from Siberia.
Did some few survive the terrible events?
Were these then joined by fresh contingents,
driven from Siberia?

We are fashioned even today, as were our Indian ancestors, by
these ancient events, involving the San Andreas fault,
Mt. St. Helens, Mt. Shasta, the freshwater of the huge aquifers of
the Ogalalla High Plains descending from the Dakotas to Texas,
the great Mississippi basin, the plains and buttes of the deserts
where the Pueblo and other nations housed, indeed
all of the striking natural features and monuments of the
United States - from the 'Old Faithful' geyser of Yellowstone in
Wyoming, to the Great Swamp of Florida where the alligator holds
sway, or as the trite but fervent speeches have it – "from the
rock-ribbed coast of Maine to the sun-kissed shores of California".

History needs to be processed through ever-improving historical
geography, volcanology, and meteorology, and via myth in
oral accounts and pictographs.

It is possible that a significantly larger supply of groundwater and
river-and-stream water supplied the continent during the century
that was to be climaxed by the arrival of the Spanish boats. The
Great Salt Lake, for instance, was substantially larger, and there
may have been water still in the Bonneville Sea, the huge fossil
basin next to Salt Lake. Elsewhere, most groundwater levels have
also been lowering, because of heavy usage. But possibly ground
waters were deposited in the aftermath of catastrophic floods and
are not in such an equilibrium as hydrological theory pictures, that
is, with a continuous balanced cycle of depletion
from use, evaporation and runoff,
accompanied by renewal from rain and snow.

Most of the region of High Plains reaching from South Dakota
Southward to Texas is naturally dry and unsuited to farming.
Like the lower prairies leading upwards,
the region lacked woodlands, so that housing as well as
farming proved difficult. Given the severe
climate of hot summers and cold winters,
life was for millions in the latter half of the nineteenth and
early twentieth century in these regions harder
than for the first settlers of the East coast two centuries earlier.

People lived in caves where they could find them,
and in dugouts preferably nestled against low cliffs,
just as paleolithic man thousands of years before.
Then they built huts of sod, like those of Russian serfs,
copies of what the immigrants knew from their East and
Central European homelands. Over a million
"soddies" dotted the country from Minnesota
down to Texas. Besides blocks of sod,
only a window frame, a door, a stovepipe,
and several boxes were needed for "Home Sweet Home".
Indians of the Southwest built better houses, the Pueblo, for instance.
"Togetherness" was not only required but vital for warmth.
Children and animals were welcome. Thus went part of the

American experience, until year by year conditions
could be improved or the households abandoned.

Much plains topsoil eroded from abusive agriculture and
blew away in the infamous "Dust Storms" of the nineteen-thirties.
But then it was found to be underlain by subterranean
aquifers intermixed with sediments washed down the Eastern
slopes of the Rocky Mountains and carrying along the
meltwaters and rainwater of the mountains.
The Ogallala Aquifer, holding 80% of the waters of the High
Plains, is supposed to operate on a 6,000-year cycle of renewal.
That is, the water will be replaced slowly and perhaps not at all
fully. In the 1950's, deep pumps first bore into and took water
from it. A peak of $20 billions annually was returned for the grain
crops and livestock grown with its water. Although its existence
was quite unknown to the Indians and the Spanish and other
European-American generations that succeeded them, it has been
rapidly depleted. Many of its wells have been voided and capped.

As little concerned about forests as their water supply, most
Americans still possess the illusion that vast forests
occupy much of the nation, whereas the present forest land
of the United States is a mere 7% of the forests which greeted the
first Conquistadors of the great Western and Southeastern United
States of today, and the first French, Virginians, Puritans, and
Dutch. American equipment and companies, having set a
horrendous example at home, are presently helping other nations'
companies to destroy, in much less time, the primeval forests of
Madagascar, the Philippines, and Brazil, where little will remain,
perhaps not even 7% for the next generation.

Meaningful and responsible American history-writing ought
before now to have recorded the cutting of the country's forests
year by year as meticulously as it has registered the money
received and paid out from one year to the next in the account
books of the Federal Treasury. Its neglect to do so is
one reason to rewrite history.

The USA

Chapter Two

Inter-Continental Diffusion

Ordinarily a book of American history will register a qualification to the discovery of the Americas by Cristoforo Colombo, to the effect that certain Vikings led by one Lief Ericsson, son of an earlier explorer of Greenland called Eric the Red, toured the coasts Southward in the year 1000, came by chance upon "Newfoundland", which they called Vinland, and there founded a settlement, whose ruins to this day are discernible on a windswept plateau above the sea.

Perhaps it was here that the baby boy, Snorri,
was born, first known European child of America;
he lived out his years in Iceland.

Adam of Bremen, a believer in a global earth, wrote in the
1070's of interviews at the Danish Court asserting a Viking
presence in Iceland, Greenland, and Vinland; he says that
just recently a Norwegian expedition of Harold Hadrada was
forced to turn back because of dreadful weather conditions
along what must have been the American Coast.
In a rare but confirmed instance, in Maine
in 1957, a Norse penny coined between
1066 and 1096 was unearthed. Again,
at Spirit Pond, on the Maine coast, a map stone,
a memorial stone, an amulet, and a Christian
marker were found, ostensibly Norse.

There are other indications in favor of the Vikings (or Norse),
other embarrassing misidentifications, too, such as
a "Viking" tower at Newport, Rhode Island, which recent
estimates have unhappily removed to the seventeenth
century. A stone carved in runic characters called the
Kensington Stone, has brought contention since it was found
in Minnesota in 1898; it bespeaks in Latin a
Norse gang of the year 1362, fighting its way to
nowhere. It is roundly dismissed from accounts of early
Viking journeys to America.

Yet the Stone could conceivably originate with men who had
abandoned a Western Greenland Settlement,
who sought haven toward the southwest,
rather than follow the roadstead back to Scandinavia.
They might then either have sailed into
and descended South from Hudson Bay or had gone up the
St. Lawrence River, thence through the Great Lakes to
present-day "Minnesota". In 1354 one Paul Knudsson is
believed to have led an expedition in search of a lost group.
Viking expeditions discontinued not long thereafter.

Several years ago, the fossil of an American soft-shell clam was

discovered in a sand bar off of Northern Denmark and placed
in the thirteenth century by carbon-14 dating;
most likely it had been a stowaway on the bottom of a Viking craft
coming from the New World; its species had not been Europeanized
before the sixteenth century.

In 1996 a conclave of scholars reconsidered
a suspect parchment map of the mid-fifteenth century that
pictured Newfoundland as Vineland, using a
cyclotron to beam protons through the material and
expose its chemical constituents.
They allowed that it was probably authentic.

Acceptance of Viking priority is due to much more than
Scandinavian-American pressure groups, and is not owing to
Protestant envy, because these Vikings were, if anything,
Roman Catholic, as the Kensington Stone, with its pathetic
pleas to the Virgin Mary, reveals. The Viking history gets
better as times go on, though it will always suffer from a
deprecatory: *"So what?"*

The Vikings were piratical rather than peaceful traders or
settlers. Homicide brought banishment, keeping the
peace at home, but spreading misfortune elsewhere.
To Iceland, thence to Greenland, then to Vinland, would be
one route for the wicked. Scholar Peter Mason thinks
that their own character as outlaws led the Vikings
to wreak mischief upon Skraelings and Einfoetingers,
"an Indian is an Eskimo, a barbarian, and a monster".
Later on, all Europe would be flooded with stories of
New World monsters, one-eyed, one-legged people,
Amazons, and cannibals. Sir Walter Raleigh would report
to his gullible Queen a nation of headless people,
"their eyes in the shoulders".

Still from time to time some group of Vikings or domesticated
variants thereof would disembark to stay, ruling or as
subjects, and merging with the population. This happened,
for example, in Normandy (to which they gave their name),
Ireland, England, South Russia, and, most strikingly, in

Sicily, where Frenchified Norman gangs of the eleventh century ousted a sophisticated Saracen elite and organized quickly an envied cosmopolitan culture. The juiciness of such targets would provide a reason why the Vikings would not have followed up on their American adventures. Too, they lacked the later invaders' explosive weapons to face down hostile Indians, who were not yet decimated by plagues of European diseases.

And the Norse were moving now into a century, the fourteenth, called the "Little Ice Age", for its bitter cold (due to sunspot irregularities), that caused the abandonment of numerous Northern settlements. It was a century further cursed by bubonic plague, which killed off vast numbers of people everywhere it struck
(and eased living conditions for the survivors.)

The story of the Vikings is old, and far from complete. Meanwhile many other histories, more or less fictional - it is hard to tell - have been written about other precursors of the Italian navigator. Candidates for earlier contacts with America - in some cases, earlier settlements of America - are numerous and should be borne in mind. Also worth remembering is the theory to which I alluded earlier: that the Indians were aboriginal Americans, who did not come from Asia but were always here, and may even have sent tribes 'the wrong way' across the Bering Straits!

A Calico Indian site has recently been dug up in the Mojave Desert, offering dates of 200,000 years ago, which should be taken as an indication of the problem and a warning, not as a true measure of time. More recently discovered and most remote is a 250,000-year dating accorded worked stone at a site in Bahia, Brazil.

Charles Darwin, later to sponsor the theory of the origin of species by means of natural selection, as he visited Tierra del Fuego aboard the Beagle (it was at the time of Jacksonian populism in the United States) imagined that the Fuegoans, the most "simple and backward" tribe yet encountered by Europeans, were a form later evolved into the humans of the North.

And fifty years later, Fiorentino Ameghino, a famous Argentinean paleontologist, who named more fossil large animals species than anyone else, dug up bones he thought were the primeval human, whom he called *Homo Sinemento* (mindless), and considered that this Homo had possibly spread to Europe via the great continental bridge of Atlantis (generally regarded as only mythical). For his troubles he fell into disgrace and was relieved of his University position.

The clues from around the world are tantalizing. People from everywhere have been thrust into the act. A century ago, a distinguished French physician and savant, Jean Rivet, a founder, too, of the Musée de l'Homme, lost some of his reputation when he detected salient resemblances between Australoids and Polynesians of the South Pacific and the peoples of the South American Andes; he felt constrained to depict for them a journey along the rim of the Antarctic Continent, conventionally considered to have been under an immense burden of ice for long ages.

In 1513 a Turkish Admiral and author of
many maps put together a world map, now
called after him the Piri Rei's Map.
Only recently recovered from Turkish archives,
the map is believed to show outlines
of the Atlantic Coast in advance of the knowledge of its time,
Persistent conjecture is therefore allowable
on questions concerning the ability of ancient peoples,
including ancient Americans, to traverse
oceans and continents.

Even though most anthropologists and archaeologists resist such ideas, we must suspect that, prior to a few thousands of years ago, humans were able to arrive upon and get a foothold in the Americas. It seems even reasonable to portray the Americas as a residence of the earliest humans, when they spread from their point of earliest origin, wherever that might be. In such a case, the absence thus far of remains of earliest forms of humanity could be attributed to the effects of epochal disasters or to small original numbers, or to a disposition of remains totally defying paleontologists.

If, at most, homo sapiens is granted 150,000 years of history since humanization, there must be something wrong with the Bahia and Calico dates above. They are too old for mankind anywhere. More in line with the main evidence are findings dated between 10,000 and 30,000. But any dates over 12,000 years serve as threats to the Bering Straits Ice Age theory and also to the theory of unique Siberian origins.

And there are more and more of these dates. There exist sites in Monte Verde in Chile dated to be 13,000 years old; Clovis in the U.S. Southwest, dated 11,500 years; Meadowcroft in the Northeast, dated at 16,000 years; and several much older sites in Pennsylvania and Brazil, not so well documented, as well as the Orogrande Bahia site already mentioned. Nor are their implements strikingly Siberian - meaning a long preceding development occurred.

In 1994 studies by Antonio Torroni of genetic diversity of widely distributed Indian peoples of North America revealed that their degrees of relationship increased when calculated backwards, until it appears that they were all of a similar high degree of consanguinity some 29,000 years ago. This could mean, however, that they had already been separated genetically before they crossed the Bering Strait.

The announcement in 1993 of findings on the Northern slopes of the Brooks Range in Alaska called "Mesa", with a date of between 9,700 and 11,700 years, highlights a dilemma of American anthropology today. This site is paleo-Indian. A second site in Alaska contains the Nenana Complex, which is similar to the Siberian of the time. The two cultures here appear to be of the same age although very different. Either the dating is wrong or the Indians came from the South and encountered a Siberian-type culture in the region. But there is no counterpart to the paleo-Indian in Siberia. Hence it might conceivably have originated in the South and finally come North.

Such would suggest an ancient proto-American people and culture, of unknown origins and from somewhere in the South, probably Central America. Could the Indians have been in America all the time and gotten a late infusion from Siberia, which was then wrongly claimed as the sole source under the Bering Strait theory? This appears probable. Warlike tribes from Asia could have driven out and decimated aboriginal nations, just as the same types had brought ruin to the Middle East and Europe over the ages: I remind you of Medes, Celts, Teutons, Huns, Arabs, Tartars, Turks, and Mongolians.

The history of a scientific theory may reveal its Achilles Heel (as would have been the case if Achilles' medical history had been on file with the Trojans). Jesuit José de Acosta, a Jesuit traveler and scholar of the stature of Alexander von Humboldt, but two and a half centuries earlier, theorized as early as 1590 that the Indians had come to America by means of the Bering neck. Not until 1728 did the Danish-Russian Captain Vitus Bering discover the actual water connection between the Pacific and Arctic Oceans.

So disrespectful of tribal cultures were Europeans, that they needed the help of the Ice Age theory to project the American Indians from Siberia. The Theory argued that an Ice Age could lower oceanic levels to a point where a land-bridge would connect Asia and North America, a conception not unlike the biblical solution for getting the Hebrews under Moses out of Egypt. Louis Agassiz, a Swiss-American and Harvard Professor, popularized and won scientific belief in the Ice Ages in the mid-nineteenth century.

The theory was politically as well as geographically convenient, because it would assist American historians and public opinion to suppress guilty feelings for the treatment accorded Indians; they could think, absurdly, that Indians had not been truly aboriginal but were also newcomers, who had appropriated the land somewhat earlier.

Too, the Bering Strait idea came before the discovery of abundant fossils of a great many large animal species including tigers, elephants, camels, and horses, mammoths, and then, much earlier, dinosaurs. How these all came over to America and then were wiped out in at least two giant catastrophes was difficult to explain.

Strange that a cordial land-bridge should appear when ice-caps were melting and waters rising; queer, too, that iced-overed seas should not be traversable. Shortest distance was a mere 64 kilometers, with islands between. Unless there were a great mountain of ice that sloughed off suddenly.

Time, receding to dinosaurs, became a complex set of guesses. A succession of Ice Ages, great and small, of Intermediate Periods, of evolutionary periods and of extinction periods entwined with one another. Yet the idea of a recently collapsed Ice Age, that permitted an old Siberian race to cross over to a continent empty of humans and fan out over a great hemisphere, was stoutly maintained. It still dominates education below the rarefied air of a rare scholar.

But meanwhile a host of special interest groups rose up to snatch the honor of breeding American Indians away from the "Siberian School". Many major and minor cultures of the world have been pictured, with more or less evidence, as contributors to the Indian population and culture-mix. Operating under historiographical conditions of near total uncertainty, many of them nevertheless exude the supreme confidence that accompanies learned ignorance.

Most such writers used as background contemporary gradualist geography, or the Ice Age Bering Strait idea, but a mythical, religious, catastrophic or quantavolutionary natural history has also been employed. The last date when American and Euro-African land masses were united in the single continent of Pangaea is said by most geologists to have been 65 million years ago at the close of the Cretaceous Period, the Age of Dinosaurs.

Therefore a completely different, practically Biblical, or Atlantean, short chronology would have to be supported in order to get the peoples of the world to America by land or brief sea voyages. This appears to be impossible. Still a very short-time or micro-chronology figured in much thought about the origin of the American Indians until the uniformitarian evolutionists won their case.
So now we go to sea.

A courageous nautical scientist from Norway, Thor Heyerdahl, has shown how to sail as Polynesians did long ago to remote Pacific Islands, such as the Polynesian Island of Puka Puka and Easter Island, from Peru. His vessel was a model of an ancient Peruvian balsa boat. Thus could the South Americans have settled Polynesia. The presence in Polynesia of the sweet potato, of megalithic cultures, and stepped pyramids, and to a minor degree linguistic usages and legendary adversions common to both regions, helped his case, although not enough to bring conviction. In 1970 also, Heyerdahl constructed a papyrus reed boat of ancient Egypt, *Ra II*, then sailed it to Barbados in the West Indies.

Manual and wind power, and water currents, with expert seamanship, can work wonders. So can nature. In May of 1990, at 48 degrees N, 161 degrees W, (around the Middle North Pacific) a storm dislodged a container of 80,000 pairs of Nike-brand shoes from the goods ship "Hansa Carrier", bound from Korea for the United states. Within six months thousands of shoes began to wash ashore between the Queen Charlotte Islands and Southern Oregon. Some months later, many shoes had turned heel and followed the California Current Southward and then westward back to the Big Island of Hawaii.

What is even more remarkable, Gérard d'Aboville, a sturdy Breton, who had rowed across the Atlantic Ocean alone in 1980, in 1991 rowed his 26-foot kayak with a convertible cockpit from Japan to the State of Washington, averaging 7000 strokes a day and accomplishing the journey in 134 days. The kayak, basically the same boat, if not so finely-tuned as d'Aboville's, was the common Eskimo fishing and hunting boat since time immemorial.

With respect to the Atlantic Ocean, Alain Bombard crossed it in a rubber raft in 1952, and Guy Delage, a 42-year-old Frenchman, swam and accompanied a 15-foot raft (for resting) from the Cape Verde Islands to Barbados in the West Indies, 4,000 kilometers, half of it spent in the water, in 55 lonely days. Single-man sailings around the world were achieved in the 1990's, too. Whether the Bering Strait was ice or water or dry land would have meant little to the settlement of America.

The physiques and faces among the thousands of Indian-American tribes, not to mention their correspondingly numerous cultures and languages, differed greatly, attested by the first Europeans to arrive after 1492, and by the thousands of sculptures and drawings that have survived. Negro African features are common in pre-Columbian civilizations of Central America, among the Olmecs, Mayans, Guatemalans, and Caribbean folk. Japanese features are not absent there, either, nor are European features indistinguishable among the Indians of Northeastern North

America. Historian Vine Deloria thinks that Cro-Magnon man, found in France, might have been of the Indians of Northeastern North America.

Generally, Indians hardly presented a pure type or closely-related set of types; they were as different amongst themselves as the Caucasians, to whom belong all the Europeans, the North Africans, East Indians and Near Easterners, as well as most North and South Americans today. Lacking the theory of the Bering Crossing, scholars would probably not have lumped the Indians into a single American sub-race of the Siberian sub-race of the Mongolian Asian Race.

When "Kennewick Man" was found sticking out of an embankment of the Columbia River in Kennewick, Washington, in 1996, by college students at a boating festival, then turned over to anthropologists, who identified him as a Caucasian, and released him to a radiocarbon dating laboratory at the University of California, that estimated him as 9,300 years old, and then became subject of a lawsuit by Indians who claimed his bones as an Indian under the 1990 Native American Graves and Repatriation Act, so that he could be given a proper sacral burial, one could imagine the next step to be the script for a musical comedy.
Had Indians the right to a "white" man's bones, or was "finders, keepers" the rule?

If the facts be as attested, it becomes apparent that either more than one race found its way to America - a contention of this chapter - or that radiocarbon dating is often far off the mark - which I also contend, or both - to which I say amen.
Anyhow, the U.S. Corps of Engineers seized the bones, to the despair of both Indians and anthropologists, then relented to allow anthropologists to make the final determination of race. If adjudged mongoloid, the bones would be transmitted to the Department of the Interior for deciding which of five claimant tribes should receive them.

Evidence is scant, we insist: anthropology has not systematically resurveyed the comparative evidence; archaeology has yet to dig in the right place. And maybe a human population was eradicated in a catastrophe, a flood truly of Noachian proportions, with super-hurricanes and mega-fires and meteoroid falls. Of course, if all of mankind were young and the separation of the continents were recent, then the Indians that we have come to know as part of us were the original and perpetual residents. We ought to rescue these hypotheses from the wastebasket and place them on the table for future studies.

A favorite topic of debate among early anthropologists and historians, never fully settled, was the relative contribution of diffusions of invention and independent inventions in the acquisition of culture. Did various peoples invent their own languages? Or did language originate in one people and one spot and diffuse with them or from them among the whole human race? Alphabets - and writing systems, too: Are all of these descended from a single proto-system, as John de Francis proposed in 1989? Certain inventions seem so complex and peculiar that diffusion is to be preferred in explaining their presence at two widely separated points in space.

Furthermore, no design, practice, or myth is so simple as to evade the fecund differentiation brought about by the mathematics of permutations and combinations. A few sounds can make a thousand languages; similarly, a few differences of construction materials, weather, habits, perceived needs and learning techniques will prevent any two walls in the world from being identical, and therefore any two walls that seem to be almost identical will almost surely have originated at the hands of closely connected people, no matter where they may be at the time of construction. Now let us direct inquiries to pre-Columbian American history. Pan pipes are found in America and Asia. Corn is found abundantly in America, but also discovered in Africa and India. Palms and gourds crossed the Pacific Ocean, sweet potatoes may have, too. Cotton may be New World or Old World in origin. The pig, dog, chicken, and rat seem to have originated in Asia before transfer to America. The specialized fishing technique using cormorant birds as assistants probably crossed the Pacific at some point in time. The magnetic compass of China had its counterpart in Olmec Mexico, and one cannot say which was the older, both well over 2000 years. Once more we note: overall and through the ages, many different peoples take turns at being innovative at long-distance traveling and exploring.

Myths, symbols, even religious practices from the Old World and the New can resemble one another closely. The couvade, a custom whereby the husband goes to bed on the eve of his wife's *accouchement* and acts as if the pains of childbirth were his own, was found both in the new world and the old. The swastika, the pentagram, and the eight-pointed star were old world and new world symbols. Sacred ball-games were played all over the world.

Gods of Meso-America resembled in key instances divinities of Greco-Roman and Egyptian religion; the gods that correspond to planets even share behavioral peculiarities. The Roman god Mars is the same brutal warrior operating under different names among the Aztecs, Assyrians, Greeks, and Romans, and is identified as connected to the planet Mars.

Traditions of a world flood that left unique survivors are found everywhere. Various forms of writing are to be found in America. The Cuna proto-writing of Panama, an ideographic scrawling on wood and bark, resembles the writing of Easter Island and the ancient script of the Indus Valley of India. The Grand Traverse stone, an inscribed piece of slate, found in Michigan in 1877, has recently been expertly translated to reveal a money transaction written in Latin of the period 100 B.C. to 100 A.D.

In Mexico, representing the ancient Central American civilizations, there were to be found pyramids, of both the stepped ziggurat type and the smoothly ascending kind. Could these have been designed in ancient times both by Americans and Near East peoples, Egyptians and Babylonians? Or were they so close intrinsically, mathematically, and in time that there would have been most likely a mutual or diffused invention? Should the Cambodian pyramid puzzle be entered here, too? No answer is yet acceptable. On a Mayan dig at Acajutla, Mexico, of 1914, statuettes of the Egyptian divinities Osiris and Isis were found, and remain as embarrassments to conventional theory.

Central Americans seemed to have been expecting the coming of white-skinned strangers; they said some of these had once come out of the sea to help them; they might even have come from the sky, it was believed. A white-skinned hero or god was prominent in Central American millennialist thought, like the expectation in some quarters throughout European-American history later on, especially among Protestants, of the Second Coming of Christ. Some scholars have discovered that the god-hero may have been black- and yellow-striped in color, or a Black American god, who is the god of the planet Venus (and one recalls the Black Hindu goddess Kali, also representing Venus).

The expected event was dreaded, it must be added. The Mexican Aztec King Montezuma half-believed and feared that Hernan Cortez was the heroic embodiment of this god, a delusion that damaged greatly his nation's ability to resist the Spanish conquistador.

Many writers have exploited irresponsibly this god-trait and god-belief, implanting it upon their favorite candidate for early arrival in America. The legendary sinking of Atlantis, indicated as a continent of Caucasian race, would have allowed proto-European survivors to escape both to Egypt and Greece, as Plato reported, and to America, as Brasseur de Bourbourg and many another would have it.

In Brazil were found artifacts and inscriptions of indubitable Phoenician origin. A Phoenician origin has been claimed, too, for the Melungeon tribes of the United States, whose appearance was allegedly Semitic, and who claimed to have come from across the seas, but this is most likely incorrect. At Fort Benning, Georgia, inscriptions in Cretan along with a picture of a distinctive double-headed Cretan axe have been uncovered.

Cotton Mather, the illustrious Puritan elder, wrote in 1690 that the Indians, descending from the Canaanites who were begat by the disreputable Ham of the Bible, were affected by his Biblical curse, hence had a dubious future even in this New World - just one more example of the infinity of historical falsehoods that have encouraged genocide, in America as elsewhere.

Ham (probably a tribe) begat the Canaanites, the Canaanites begat the Phoenicians, the Phoenicians begat the Carthaginians, and these, equally good sailors, sailed to Britain and Sierra Leone (this we think we know) and, if to there, why not to America? Peralta, writing before the Plymouth landing, deplored the cannibalism and idolatry of many Indian cultures and thought they must be sprung from Canaanites, driven from the Promised Land by conquering Jews. Later, other writers believed the Carthaginians, who also practiced child sacrifice and idolatry, became disaffected when compelled by Greeks and Romans to desist in their religious practices, and departed for America in search of freedom of religion, setting an unflattering precedent for certain later dissenters.

In Tennessee, Jewish inscriptions and Roman coins have been found together, leading some to believe that the scattering of the Jews by the Romans after their incessant rebellions had led a band of Jews here. (Actually the Diaspora or spreading of Jews to far-flung homes had begun voluntarily long before this, through preceding Hellenistic and Roman times.) A burial ground at Bat Creek, Tennessee, was considered by the expert American semiticist, Cyrus Gordon, to contain Hebrew inscriptions, which may relate to the nearby Roman coins.

The Jewish experience in legendary American history is extensive. In the 1580's Peralta was also bringing the Ten Lost Tribes, driven from Jerusalem in 583 B.C. by Nebuchadnezzar the Assyrian, to Central America. They spread throughout the Americas afterwards: so the story goes. In 1775 James Adair, who had consorted intimately with the Chickasaw Indians and fought with them against the Cherokees, published a discourse to claim Hebrew origins for the Indians.

The idea was big in Colonial New England. Joseph Smith, the founder of Mormonism in the early nineteenth century, was a Vermonter, and so was his successor as President of the Church, Brigham Young. Perhaps his Yankee ancestry might help to explain why the Book of Mormon declares that the Indians are descended from survivors of the Assyrian holocaust. Since the Mormons later became one of the most powerful and progressive religious sects of America, and Jews have been associated with America from its dreamlike origins in Spain, Portugal, and the Low Countries up through the first settlements and into the present, our allusions to these theories of pre-Columbian events seem to be pertinent.

Tennessee appears to have hosted other remarkable peoples in times past. One large group of burials conveyed to the grave-digger the bones of little people, too battered by the rigors of life to be children, and therefore a race of pygmies, the least unlikely source of which would have been the Aetas tribe of the Philippine Islands. The Cherokees, a highly remarkable Indian nation, held a tradition that a pygmy people existed nearby at one time.

Connections have been made with the Hindus and Indo-Chinese. These, too, had been building stepped pyramids of colossal size. And in India, 700-year-old temples were found to contain representations of ears of corn.

Other resemblances between Southeast Asia and Mexico include the trefoil arch; sanctuaries built inside temples, the sacred tree and cross; a god holding a lotus flower; certain pillar constructions; a method of vaulting; diving gods; serpent gods; wire bells; and phallic ornaments. Von Humboldt, in his early-nineteenth-century travels, found many coincidences, among them similarities between Mexican and Hindu calendars. A triple-headed Amer-Indian vase, found in 1820, was claimed to represent the triple Hindu deity - Brahma, Vishnu, and Shiva.

A fine story has been concocted of the enormous fourth century fleet of Alexander the Great, intended for the invasion of India and points East, which was left stranded by his untimely death in 323 B.C., and disappeared from history. We are left to imagine that, lacking better to do and believing like Ptolemy and his later follower Columbus in a small round world, its admirals might have sailed it Eastward through the South Seas, ultimately entering upon the Pacific Ocean and encountering Polynesia, leaving there strains of Caucasian blood, and passing thence to the Americas. Additional hints of veracity: similar peaked helmets; similar metal-working techniques; the close identity of the Indian game of *pachisi* and the ancient Mexican game of *patolli*.

Lately, as I mentioned above, tests of blood types and blood chemistry - blood is a veritable encyclopedia to the knowledgeable reader - have been used as indicators of degrees of racial affinity among persons and groups. (A startling example was the offering of genetic proof in support of the theory of the origin of mankind from central African prototypes.) In connection with the Americas, Japanese blood chemistry has been shown to relate strongly to

Ecuadoran, Mayan and Zuni (United States) peoples. And Japanese and Ecuadoran artifacts dated to 3000 years ago closely resemble each other.

Further, there exists a strong Chinese cohort that plausibly finds the story of American West Coast explorations in the voyages and accounts of a renowned surveyor, Shu-Hai, sponsored by the Chinese Emperor. Around 220 B.C. another Chinese explorer, Hsu Fu, is supposed to have settled in America. Even earlier, a group of Buddhist monks is said to have carried its religion to Fusang, another name for America, and made converts there.

The Roman case is fairly strong, especially when abetted by the several Romanized peoples, evidence of whom is to be found in the New World. At least forty-one finds of Roman coins have been publicized, beginning in 1533, these in places as far apart as Tennessee, Panama, and Venezuela. Pompeiian house walls, uncovered in modern times from their burial by Vesuvian ash of the first century, carry paintings of New World pineapples. Roman bronze and iron pieces were dug up in Virginia in 1943.

Digging far South in the Toluca Valley of Calixtlahuaca, José Garcia Payon found a bearded Roman head of terra cotta dated back to about 220 A.D. Whether it had arrived by way of the Orient or the Occident is not known, but its authenticity is not disputed.

The earliest claims for African settlement are more logical than evidential. Ivan Van Sertima has argued that the Nubian conquerors of Egypt in the seventh and eighth centuries B.C., one of whose kings, usually called Ethiopian, appeared on the battlefield of Troy, were explosively expansive for a brief period, and probably crossed the ocean, entered the Caribbean Sea and merged with the Olmecs of Gulf Coast Mexico. Olmec statues, I have adduced above, are

distinctly Negroid of features, and could readily have
coincided in time with this Nubian period.

Much later on, Mandingo and Songhay expeditions of trade
and colonization across the ocean are legendary. Skeletal
similarities, the importation of cotton to Africa from the
Americas, and a few other indications, all uncertain, have
been introduced to the discussion. A strong legend has Abu
Bakr II, Emperor of Mali, despatching two
expeditions to America in the years between
1307 and 1311. Their fate is unknown.
The Gulf Stream, with its potential for assisting
westward travel, was well-known to the
West African peoples.

Perhaps a kind of prejudice has led scholars to credit Polynesians with
having reached and settled islands over thousands of miles of
the Pacific Ocean, while they have usually resisted the
idea that Africans would have had many occasions to reach
the Americas as readily. We should not be surprised to hear one day
of Central African expeditions, unconnected to the later slave trade.

Slightly better documented than the expeditions of Abu Bakr II
is the story of St. Brendan whose *curachs* left Ireland in the
Fifth century with the Holy Cross to explore a large maritime
region that included Barbados, the Bahamas and the Azores.
We have his "Navigatio" to peruse.
From 1275 to 1759
various maps circulated, bearing the "mythical"
Island of St. Brendan, some of them drawn by an
Irish monk working in Northern Europe.

Other Celtic brethren from Wales claim that in the same age
as St. Brendan, the explorer Madoc voyaged to America,
from which came an epic poem as supporting evidence (it is
well to remind oneself that modern "science" had written off
the Trojan war to Homeric legend, until Schliemann, an
amateur archaeologist, uncovered what was a reasonable

facsimile of a Trojan-Achaean conflict). Perhaps it was from such Fifth Century Celtic sources that a Merovingian Gaul of the 600's who called himself Aethicus told of a round-the-world trip, traversing the Atlantic Ocean. His fanciful story inspired many a would-be explorer for a thousand years.

Harvard scholar Barry Fell, a New Zealander by birth, built up over many years a Celtic-Iberian case, involving copper mines, institutional correlations in laws and practices among Celts and Algonquins, architectural similarities, and a script called "ogam" said to be commonly used in ancient times on both sides of the ocean. Far to the West of Ireland there began to appear with Dalorto's map of 1325 an Island of "Brazil". Where it came from and went no one knows.

More famous in historical cartography was the Island of Antilles (perhaps the same?) and this island, too, was far to the West and during the 1400's was reputed to be the haunt of Portuguese fishermen. It was drawn in Vizzigano's Map of 1424 and Bianco's Map of 1436. The renowned mapmaker Toscanelli recommended to Columbus that he use it as a stopover on his way to the Far East, and Columbus planned to do so.

For the years 1380 to 1433, customs records from England show the importation of beaver skins - they could only be American, probably Canadian Micmac, given their peculiar packaging - brought in by Basques of the Iberian peninsula, who wandered far and wide as fishermen and traders. It is claimed that the Bretons, famed for seamanship, fished off the shores of America, but the first hard evidence of a French-Breton presence there is Jacques Cartier in 1504. Bristol merchants poked around the Western seas regularly before Giovanni Cabotto was hired by the King to do the job right. Before him by a few years, Henry Sinclair, Earl of Orkney, is said to have reached the American coast.

But not even many a swallow can a summer make. It is important to give a special meaning to geographical discovery. Like a scientific discovery, or, I should say, like other scientific discoveries, a geographical discovery is to be understood as a recorded event that is replicable, here by a deliberate, successful, follow-up voyage. Such was the voyage of Columbus, well-recorded, and then promptly emulated by other voyages. Like some other scientific discoveries, such as penicillin, the discovery may be serendipitous: Columbus thought that he was reaching the Old Indies.

But this still does not make an "Age of Discovery", no more than a single scientific discovery makes a "Scientific Age". For this we need a large diverse set of cultures prompted to act by the initial successes. And we need a large lasting effect upon both sides of the discovery, the discoverers and the discovered. It is scarcely to be doubted that the Vikings discovered and reported to their confined culture their American findings, so that their directions could be successfully followed by a subsequent expedition.

However, the Norse world, and its connecting links with the European World, and the European World itself, were not ready to treat such discoveries as big news, full of promise, revealing a great set of cultures ripe for exploitation by the new technology of the Europeans. That is why
"Christopher Columbus discovered America".

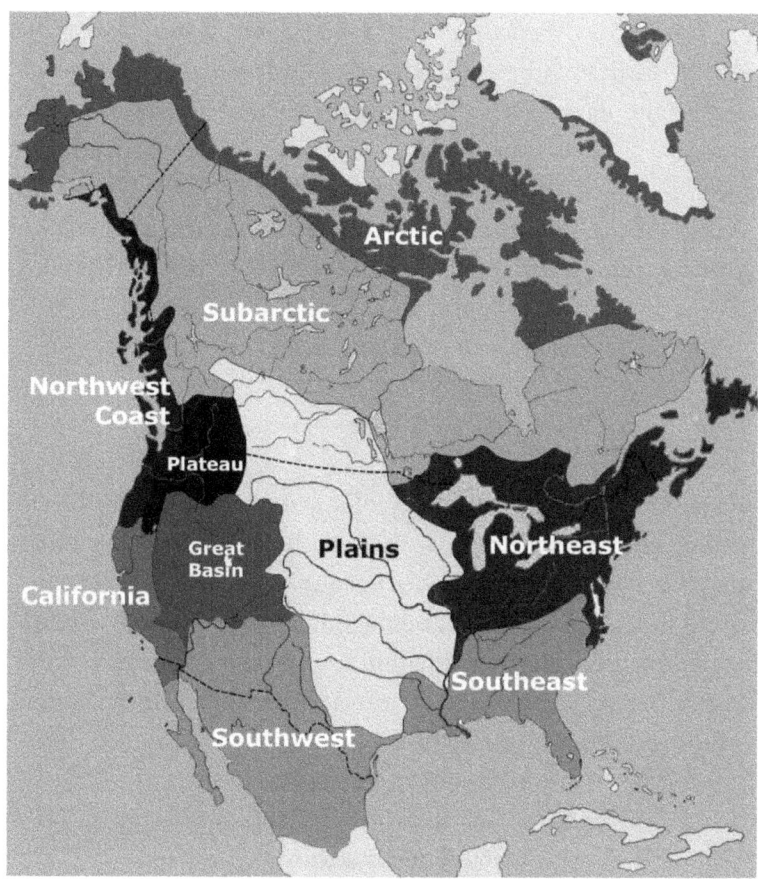

North American Cultural Regions

Chapter Three

American Indian Nations

To exterminate a people, erase its history and language.
Its archaeological ruins can go only so far, and belatedly, to
restore its past, and then not its people. To a few
cultural heroes - Vespucci, Oviedo, de las Casas, von
Humboldt, Wissler, and Levy-Strauss setting examples over a

stretch of 500 years - is owed the survival in our minds of hundreds of Indian nations of the New World. Most European invaders and their descendants have tried to submerge them by suppressing their past as well as by physical suppression. That the Indians, like the Africans in America, relied upon oral media for the transmission of their history from one memorial generation to the next, meant that the dissolution of their social structure would destroy their history, and therefore complete the erasure of their existence.

Possibly the greatest specific achievement of the Northern Indians in the century or so before the Columbus landings was the story of the Iroquois League and Hiawatha. This is legend in its highest sense, but would appear to many a hard-headed historian to be disqualified as history. It lacks written record. And to the modern anthropological historian, it lacks the substantiation that comes from controlled systematic interviews with tellers of the tales and witnesses of the events. Furthermore, archaeological evidence is scanty.

What we have are hundreds of people over two centuries of time telling foreigners about a prophet and dreamer, Deganawidah, who sought to unite all the Indian nations in peace, who had a heroic disciple named Hiawatha (meaning "the comber"), who combed the evil thoughts from the hair of the terrible chief of the Onandagas, Atotarho, and persuaded him to accept the new philosophy and join with his people the new League of Universal Peace that the Iroquois were trying to establish. Atotarho was to become the keeper of the eternal fire of the League of the Iroquois.

The five central tribes of Iroquois thereupon assembled and arrived at a constitution, under the leadership of Hiawatha and Deganawidah. They set up a Grand Council to deliberate and legislate, numbering fifty sachems, with varying members apportioned to the five tribes. Honorary members could be added to the Council. Much later the Tuscarora Indians were voted in as a sixth Nation. The fire keeper was always to be named Atotarho and could be considered the President. Each tribe had one vote. Hiawatha and Deganawideh would always have, in absentia, seats provided them.

Legislative procedure was simple but exhaustive. Mohawk delegates could open discussion on a question. They with the Senecas sat on one side of the fire. Agreement reached on the issue, the two tribes would hand the matter across the central fire to the Oneidas and Cayugas, who would consider it, and if they agreed to it, the "bill" was declared passed. If they disagreed, the issue was handed to the Onandagas, who sat between them as moderators, and they compromised the matter or voted for one or the other side. The "bill" went back to the first side for reconsideration, then to the other side for the same, and if in harmony, it became law. If still not agreed to, the Onandagas would decide the matter, and their decision would be final.

The Council was all-male, but women had the right to participate in the election of its members and to depose them on occasion of misrepresentation and misconduct.

The Iroquois Confederation was a sophisticated system of representative government, so similar to the Venetian constitution that some have considered it to have been brought to America in some mysterious way. (The Venetian election system was older; it was much admired in Europe and around the world for some centuries.) In the nineteenth century, the creators of the Tammany Hall organization of New York City Democrats would look for inspiration and its colorful offices to the Iroquois Confederation. The Confederation symbol of an eagle clutching five arrows for the original five nations was adopted later on for the Great Seal of the United States.

The Confederation proved successful in practically eradicating cannibalism among its members and affiliated tribes (exceptions were made for a bold enemy's heart, that was believed to convey his spirit to the eaters.) A large measure of peace among members of the League was achieved, and the League often reconciled conflicting tribes outside the League. It disallowed the death penalty for murder, which had been exacted by relatives before, and put a system of fines in its place.

Upon the departure of Deganewideh for the unknown, Hiawatha took up full leadership and with companions visited the tribes of most of America East of the Mississippi, persuading many to support the principles of the League. Enforcement was hardly available, no more than in most confederations, except among the central nations. Yet the Iroquois could on occasion take the field with an army of a thousand warriors, more than other tribes or alliances could manage, and sufficient to meet in battle a French or English colonial army. The Iroquois also used the Confederation as a means and an excuse for imperialism, much as Athens had done two thousand years earlier with its Amphyctyonic Council. The situation became especially unprincipled when the extensive fur trade developed, and the stronger Indian force could arrange and demand the best deals with foreign traders.

The United States, when it achieved its full continental girth, occupied territory previously held by some five hundred tribes that came to be called American Indians but that were denominated each by its own tribal name, regularly with subordinate clan names, and often with a larger affiliation added. Today, the United States recognizes the limited sovereignty of 554 nations.
Dividing the large area among the many nations, we arrive at a situation rather like that prevailing over most of European history, ancient, medieval and modern.

The Indians were neither cooped up
nor impossibly fragmented.

Estimates of the total inhabitants of the Western Hemisphere around the year 1492 have ranged unbelievably from 8 to 112 millions. This compared with a European population of the time of perhaps 85 millions and an African population of about the same number. Estimates of the Indian population then dwelling within today's U.S. boundaries have ranged from 900,000 to 11, even 18, millions.

"Nations" refer to organized peoples, in the language of the eighteenth century Enlightenment social theorist, Giambattista Vico of Naples, and in this sense there should be no reluctance in referring to Indian *nations*, granted a nation may be a single tribe.
A tribe was observed to be and might be defined as a (mythically and actually) blood-related collection of clans, speaking a common language. The clans were made up of extended families, usually termed sibs, descending into what we call today nuclear families. Mothers and fathers were universally important, but nuclear families were closely bound to tribal custom and rule. All in all, the system resembled extant Celtic social organisms of the British Isles of the same day, a homology provoking wonder whether the myriad encounters of Celt and Indian in America compacted to shape and stress various American behaviors and ways of thought.

Some tribes numbered as many or more people than the smallest dozen of recognized nation-states of the world. Several of the latter, such as the Arabian Gulf states, are essentially tribal. Since Indian tribal territories were in some cases larger than the territory possessed by Switzerland or Israel or a score of other modern states, there seems little reason not to call them all nations, or even states, for that matter. They possessed, after all, a sovereignty (in fact and international law) that no state of the USA can claim.

All of these tribes spoke their own languages. In the Americas
North and South, the two thousand languages estimated to
have been employed in the fifteenth century were (and are)
as complex in structure as those of the rest of the world.
Some of the languages seem to be able to communicate
thoughts that are difficult or awkward to express in English,
or the Frenchified Latin and Saxonized Teuton from which
English has largely descended. (Indian, Gaelic, Scottish,
Welsh, Cornish, and Scandinavian words and usages, plus a
great many others from other languages such as Spanish,
Italian, Greek, Hebrew, and modern German and Yiddish,
came to enrich the English and especially the American
language, together with a flood of scientific and technical
language, and with syntactical, phonetic and verbal creations,
on the part of African-Americans, the demi-monde, youth,
and grammatically undisciplined talkers -
of which more later.)

American varieties of English
came to sound from all quarters of the ultimate nation,
but it should be understood that
language spreads by power over people;
it is the voice of authority, even if the authority
is anti-authoritative, and egalitarian.
Possibly any one of the hundreds of Indian languages,
propelled by Cherokee power or Sioux power, say,
would have served today's America, given the appropriate
acquisition of terms in the beginning for appliances that the
Indians lacked: whiskey would be perhaps called fire-water.

Benjamin Whorf, the most inventive of American linguists,
believed that certain languages of the Indians whom he
studied - he comments specifically on Nootka and Hopi -
can express views of reality inaccessible to
speakers of Indo-European languages
(including the major languages of Western Europe).
Whorf pointed out how language and thought are so related that
one people will lean on vocal expression to
connect ideas while another people will have to

build a logical or conventional superstructure upon their words in order to express ideas. He wrote that in the Hopi language were embedded meanings that did not need to and did not appear in their word combinations. The Hopi, he declared, had no word for 'time,' but were quite able to elaborate a profound world-view that incorporated time differences.

Poetry was widely delivered and in many forms. There were lyrical love songs and lullabies, war-songs, death-songs. Hark to this couplet of death:

*"Toward me the darkness comes rattling,
In the Great Night my heart will go out".*
(A poem of the Papago of Arizona.)

Other poem-songs break into narratives as incantations, exclamations, laments. Still others deal with religious ritual; they heal, they propitiate the gods and spirits. There was no more break between poetry and prose than in, say, the work of Walt Whitman or even of this book.

Understandably, communication between 'Whites' and 'Reds' suffered from language differences, not just once upon landfall, but through five hundred years and to this day. One obvious, yet suppressed, source of friction, was the failure or refusal of the Whites, particularly British Isles immigrants, to learn Indian languages. (This peculiar lameness of the Britons descended among Americans down to the present day, no matter what their ancestry.) The twentieth century institutionalized the learning of some Indian languages, both by encouraging Indians to preserve them and by subsidizing university scholars. Possibly more Whites know Indian languages today than when Whiteskins lived next to Redskins.

As with language and nations, so with the concept of civilization. The aboriginal, at least the then resident

Americans, possessed very different cultures -
ways of living, sharing, ruling, dressing, eating,
working, playing, loving, fighting, and learning.
Americans, organized into their States,
have often thought that their personal State was different
from all others, Virginia from Massachusetts, Idaho from
Utah, and so on. Indian nations, say the Sioux and
the Kwakiutl, or the Seminoles and the Zuni,
or any other randomly chosen pair, were
much more different among themselves.

Indians were often engaged in warfare, and one
has to weigh this conduct against that of the "United" States,
which were quarreling continually, and fought a terrible Civil
War over their differences, after having sternly and
contemptuously criticized the Indians for being
disunited and incapable of overall integration.

Civilization refers to a culture capable of
creating and working with intricate things and ideas.
Rarely does someone block the definition, to exclaim,
"The highest art of man is peacemaking!
Nations at war cannot be ranked as civilized".
Also, most people think,
"The more and better of everything, the higher the civilization".
Simplicity of customs and ideas,
which some great philosophers, such as the
line of Stoics, thought the summit of civilized or
at least human conduct, would then be a
contradiction of civilization.

Since the name of civilization is given by authors and media,
and any people to whatsoever culture they please, but
generally excludes almost all tribal groups and is
justified by a record of continuous instrumental innovation,
of long-term incremental changes in living conditions
in the direction of complexity and by the
ability to live in permanent aggregates,
it would be difficult, indeed, to affirm that these criteria,

which were not possessed to a significant extent by the
"USA Indians", actually produced a
level of life-satisfaction or "happiness" equaling or
surpassing that of Indians in general, whether we speak
of the sixteenth century or the twentieth century.

We must therefore re-define civilization as a more subtle
concept. We have to admit warfare as a historical fact, of a
practice occurring on the average half the time everywhere. If
we do insist upon permanent peace, then, by definition, no
civilization has ever existed for very long. We can, of course,
in ranking civilizations as worthwhile, demote the warlike
ones. Apart from this, we should say that civilization is a way
of life that encourages and transmits to its members as an
organic whole an abundant facility and creativity
with regard to things and ideas.

The definition still contains problems. Is this what the
Whites wanted to bring to the Indians? Not at all. Most
Whites had no intention of providing the Indians with
anything except what would obtain cheaply
various desirable goods and services - land, women,
labor, tobacco, a canoe, and footgear.
Nor did the Indians want White civilization.
Indeed it is to the credit of the Indians that most died
rather than accept the kind of civilization tendered them.
The 'common man,' however undistinguished,
believes his culture to be civilized.
The concept of the White man's being civilized,
the Indian not, hardly appealed to the Indian,
any more than to a philosopher.
It was an insulting epithet.
It was a war-cry of the Whites.
Indians were "savage", "primitive", "backward" and "uncivilized".

Differences among Indian tribes in the nineteenth century
were larger than any that came to characterize the occupants
of the country one, two, or three centuries later, given even
the exceptional variety of immigrants who came from the

earliest days onwards. This is not to diminish the weighty distinctions among the earliest and later Europeans, Africans and Asians - of which we shall have much to say - but to stress that the Cigar Store Indian statue that boys and girls passed on the street every day for a century and more conveyed an utterly limited notion of the race.

Think instead of what must have come before the arrival of the Europeans, which in many cases was even lost to the Indians, as much as the monuments and learning of Athens were lost to the very Greeks of several centuries later. And then think, too, of the multitude of distinctions among the tribes as they faced up to the invaders. We must give some idea here and now of the variety of the Indian nations.

At the time of the early dynasties of Egypt, there dwelled in the Vera Cruz region of Mexico the Olmec nation. It may have been several nations. Even today there scowl at us most impressive human heads of many tons weight, and one finds increasingly Olmec burials, their myths, their artifacts, and, later on, a written language only now lending itself to decipherment. The civilization seems to have evolved into the Mayan, farther South.

The Mayan civilization of Central Mexico, the Yucatan Peninsula and Guatemala was also partly in ruins and in decline by the time of the Spanish intrusions. Compare it, if you will, to the Middle Age civilizations of Europe from 500 to 1000 A.D. It had a high order of culture with grand monuments, sculptures, paintings, clothing, numerous domesticated plants, writing, and institutions of government on a comparably high level. Its mathematics and astronomy were well advanced. It was a congeries of kingdoms, each with upper, middle and laboring classes.

The Aztec Civilization, centered at present-day Mexico City, appears to have replaced the Olmecs. Its ancestor was the culture of Teotihuacan, centered North of Mexico City, where for a thousand years, until the eighth century A.D., great pyramids were constructed, and a sprawling city of hundreds of apartment buildings, each sheltering some 50 to 100 people of related families, flourished. Its supreme deity was a goddess, probably connected with the planet Venus, often depicted as a feathered serpent, and portrayed, too, as the source of floods and fire and of the arts and plant life.

The Aztecs were obsessed with human sacrifice and annually killed many thousands of prisoners of war in the name of their god. Indeed, around the world in ancient times, worship of the goddess or god of the planet Venus, under her various names, was typically accompanied by sacred murder. An instance from the USA is afforded by the Pawnee Tribe's periodic sacrifice of a maiden on the close approach of the planet, a practice that continued into the nineteenth century.

Far to the South was the Andean civilization of the Incas, warrior cliques, presiding over a well-knit empire stretching for thousands of miles from Ecuador through Peru to Chile, who themselves were much later successors of the ancient civilization centered around Lake Titicaca at Tihuanacu, in westernmost Bolivia.

All of these high civilizations, from the Rio Grande down to Southern Chile, succumbed within a generation to the onslaughts of the Spanish conquistadors. They were reconstructed then in Hispanic forms.

Their descendants often moved back and forth, North and South, in and out of "United States territory". Today probably 10% of the American population is descended in all or part from the great Central Indian civilizations, another 5% (if Puerto Ricans at home and on the continent are counted) from the Caribbean Indians in some degree. Aside from the nearly one million Americans identifying themselves as Indians today, there are probably two million who are descendants of USA tribes but miscegenated unrecognizably with Caucasian, Black, and Oriental inhabitants.

Puerto Rico and Alaska momentarily aside, North of the Rio Grande were the Indian cultures and nations whom we intend now to describe. In some cases they stood above the realms and remains of pre-existing cultures, which we shall mention in passing. The enormous disparity in population estimates has been stated. There is no simple route toward reconciling them. One authority warns that another generation of research may help, but only to bring the estimates to within 30 to 50% percent of reality.

The basic study was done by Mooney in 1928; it was a thorough and expert investigation of all sources and of consultations with outstanding scholars in the field. He set a figure that was somewhat reduced by another distinguished student, Kroeber, in the nineteen-thirties. Other scholars agreed, though they stressed that the figures were conservative.

But figures have escalated amazingly since 1940. Despite their great number and diversity, the tribes of the United States and Canada, embracing half the total land area of the Americas, counted only a million souls according to the Mooney-Kroeber tally; this was an estimated 7% of all American-Indians. A fifth of a million were in Canada, leaving less than a million for the USA, with 9.4 million square kilometers or one-quarter of the land area of the Americas. This comes to an average of one person for every 10 square kilometers.

One wonders at the grossly enlarged figures that have been advanced more recently. They do help expand the enormity of the European "crime" of genocide of the Indians, just as the expansion of the number of Jewish Holocaust victims, when given as 7,000,000 say, rather than 4,500,000, allows for greater indignation in some quarters.

Regardless, in both cases, the gravity of the collective crime is far greater than can be conveyed by statistics.

The student of the Trojan War, that magnificent drama of an ancient multinational war of which Homer sings, feels let down upon learning that the ruins of Troy as discovered by Schliemann, if indeed this site called Hisarlik was that of Troy, were retrospective of a town of some 5000 Trojans, men, women, and children. Lately, a large outer wall has been uncovered, stretching far around the site, that could accommodate a considerably larger population. The Roman Empire was the best administered in ancient history, yet scholars have never been able to come close to agreeing on its population at its peak, estimates varying from 50 to 150 millions. Destruction of records is the main problem there.

Regarding America, I am ready to lend tentative support to the figures arrived at by William M. Denevan at the close of several studies of the problem. He gives 4,400,000 for Northern North America, 21.4 millions for Mexico, and 57 millions in all. He is in good company, yet admits that he is arbitrary. Since he occupies the middle of the spectrum of guesses, we may allow ourselves to think hypothetically in his terms.

There may be, however, more than a problem of selecting among estimates. Figures that vary so greatly overall and in the case of so many tribes and nations compel us to suspect some mysterious large force at work at some unknown time. We learn that many tribes of the 1400's and 1500's had once been more populous. They were, when first encountered by Europeans, depressed, underpeopled, recovering in numbers, occupying places too large for them, and so on - indications of a disastrous loss of population.

Two theories offer themselves, neither of which has so far been investigated systematically.

One is external natural catastrophe.
The other is plague.
Warfare, poverty, occasional droughts, infertility -
these appear to be impossible explanations.

Phoenix, Arizona, owes its final name to its proclaimed revival upon the ruins of prior settlements, like the ancient Egyptian bird rose from the ashes of its own kind. Spanish and Mexican settlements stood there amidst a large area of desolation. Archaeological excavations of 1887-8 sent three railroad boxcars loaded with Indian cultural material to the Peabody Museum (now affiliated with Harvard University), where, for half a century, they remained unexamined.

This Cibola area, as it was called, had once held a population estimated at 200,000 persons. They lived in seven cities and numerous villages. They maintained an extensive irrigation system. One Cibola study proposes that some type of exoterrestrial meteoroid stone, fire, or gas explosion caused the destruction. Many other Indian centers disappeared in the 1400's The Hohokam culture vanished around 1425. Chaco and Mesa Verde fell in ruins. Cahokia on the Mississippi River banks suddenly emptied and lay ruined. The Mississippi Valley generally was depopulated in the 1300's and 1400's. Migrations of peoples occurred frequently. Cruder life styles came about.

Most historians adhere to the estimates, large or small, from one to four millions, in the area of the USA today, and declare that a rapid decline in this number followed the intrusion of European diseases and the breaking up by force of the traditional societies. To this writer the preferable hypothesis is that in the pre-Columbian 1300's and 1400's, plagues were introduced by European Asian, and African fishermen, castaways, adventurers and persons in flight from enemies or plague.

Very recent scientific theory allows the possibility that patches or clouds of meteoroid-transported vermin, viruses, and microbial nutrient gases encountered Earth's atmosphere and descended here, there, or everywhere, infecting hosts of people. A new compilation of medieval reports from China and Europe reveals that exoterrestrial origins of the great plagues may be considered, backed up in some instances by statements of witnesses. It is scarcely conceivable that plagues originating in China or Siberia, as appears to have been the case in the fourteenth century, would move West but not East.

If the University of California (Berkeley) scholars who first advanced the estimates of eighteen millions Indians are correct in declaring that the environment was ample to support, indeed had to support, all these people in their typical life style, then some instrument for the prompt devastation of this huge number and its innumerable cultural appurtenances must be sought for.

USA Indians lived usually in small encampments and settlements, hamlets. These were as often permanent as temporary. The Pueblo constellation maintained permanent dwellings carved into rock cliffs, the Southeast peoples built plastered houses roofed with thatch or bark and fortified their towns.

Many tribes designed strong yet mobile structures. Long Houses, that served Northeast and other Indians as semi-permanent installations, could be regarded as semi-fixed trailer camps, collapsible and transportable. (Perhaps 20 times as many as all Indians, 45 million Americans, dwelt in trailers in 1998.) The wigwam and tepee, of course, are rightfully world-famous: mobile, durable, snug, permissive of privacy and a cuisine, and aesthetically pleasing, admired by several generations of romantic American and European boys and girls.

On special occasions, when large policies had to be set, of war, of peace, of moving, of territorial clan boundaries, and especially of astronomical holidays such as the solstitial and harvest Thanksgiving (whence came the Pilgrim and, since the Civil War, great American holiday), a tribal multitude would assemble, rather like the car rallies, county fairs, or more literally the Chautauqua conventions of their Caucasian successors. Gerontocratic pow-wows, like the "Appalachian Conference of Mafia Godfathers", were more frequent, and looked upon by their later foreign neighbors with similar trepidation.

Typically, as with the Iroquois, various tribal leaders would get together, program a festival for certain days, designate individuals to go around collecting contributions from people, and then proclaim the occasion. Orators would open the festivities. Music and dancing, often of an interpretative character would follow. There would be games and fortune-tellers. Religious and fraternal clubs would hold special gatherings, some closed, some open to the public.

Government among the Indians, including foreign relations, was basically comprehensible to the educated European, unless he were devoid of sociological awareness and encapsulated in parochialism. There would be a head, an executive committee, an assembly, citizenry, age groups, sex groups, artisans, a welfare clientele, specialists in natural and human phenomena (crops, the hunt, the weather), priests (specialists in ceremonies and divine communications), medical men, and the war party. Nothing that came to the clan's attention could remain foreign; it was to be explained; so there had to be priests, elders, and tribal philosophers to interpret all things according to the metaphysics of the tribe. The foundations of governance have been similar around the world.

Offices were arranged in different ways for the accomplishment of tasks. The chieftain or head was typically both hereditary and elective (not unfairly analogized with the modern practice of giving the descendants of well-known politicians - such as the Kennedy's - preference at the polls).

Approval of a new head was supposed to come through designation by the retiring chief (as in current politics very often), but if his choice of successor fell upon a delinquent or an incompetent son, the assembly of warriors or clans had the right constitutionally to reject the proffered candidate and compel a more satisfactory choice.

The head man might reserve to himself certain honors, privileges, and access to goods, hardly enough to create large distinctions of social class, but adequate to put a symbolically satisfying garnish upon the exercise of power. Inasmuch as the group that he headed was small, typically between a hundred and a thousand, his social distance and therefore his despotic potential was less than in a large national grouping, such as the Spanish and English emerged from.

Rash acts were common; the Indians were highly individualistic, rating near to their fatal American and European counterparts in this regard. Systematic tyranny, the massacre of dissidents, the persecution of minorities, the degradation of a class of people (even if slaves) were beyond tribal capacities, though these were practices familiar to the European arrivals. Torture was known everywhere, applied to an adolescent to test presumed virtues of courage and hardihood, applied to enemies to test them as well, satisfy sadistic impulses.

Warfare was as common as squash pie. Perhaps only ten per cent of the 500 tribes would pass through any political generation - 33 years - without experiencing a war. These ten per cent were mostly the same notoriously peaceful tribes. The successful individual warrior was everywhere highly prestiged, as has been true of America to this day.

Wars of annihilation and heavy casualties were rare; not that Indians disbelieved in genocide as a matter of principle, no more than the most ancient Jews and Romans, but their forces were too decentralized, their logistics too

constrained, their mental tenacity for such conduct
unavailing. Physical and psychological unity was an
impossibility for Indians long before they
encountered Europeans in considerable numbers.
Common practices in battle included looting,
burning, and taking captives for indefinite periods of
slavery and concubinage.
Mutually useful exchange of prisoners was common.

Practically all of the tribes, even if sedentary, possessed tribal
hunting grounds, with the hunts observing the
equivalent of state boundaries in important respects -
an intrusion being a *casus belli*.
Every Indian thus had a homeland.
Exile was a severe punishment.
In this regard, the civil state of Indians excelled that of the
people who would be soon descending upon them,
the English and Scots-Irish especially, whose
men, women, and children had been as a rule evicted
from their ancestral places and undergone mean
experiences of being driven from place to place, of being
jailed, whipped, and seized for transportation to the colonies
- civilly persecuted, that is - were they so much as to pause
at a hostile village or trespass upon private lands, never mind
poaching or snatching up a bit of food. The Indian would lose her home
only when her tribe's identity deceased.

Families quarreled as they will everywhere, and when
mediation would fail, and arbitration was not firmly
prescribed by tribal law, and when violence ensued, exile was
a common punishment, decreed by the tribal council more
often than by the chief, akin to the practice among the
Vikings, and notable, too, among the ancient and
highly civilized Greeks.

Typical serious crimes would be cowardice in battle, treason
or betrayal of the group, physical assault, and theft; sexually
motivated crimes such as adultery were not so gravely
regarded as these were among the ancients and their Puritan
emulators. The power of the chief usually extended

partway into serious crimes, but more into civil disputes over property rights, and precedence and procedure in political, social and economic affairs. Too, the chief was principal agent of the nation in foreign affairs.

The position of women among Indian peoples varied more than among European nations. The reason possibly lay, during the 1400's and 1500's, with the uniformity of relationships between sexes that the Roman Catholic Church had brought about for centuries among the peoples of Western and Central Europe. Catholic doctrine was not generally challenged, and only lately then - not by Anglicans or Lutherans so much as by radical Protestant groups, who went directly to the Bible, elected their own priests, and let their reasoning on religious issues dwell upon "original" sources. Even then, the position of women gained because of its practicality, not out of philosophy; radical Protestants were poor, oppressed politically and socially, and needed the consolation and cooperation of women, who were more fully developed as humans.

It is said repeatedly that Caucasian women who found themselves prisoners of the Indians were treated well. Polygyny was usually authorized, but rarely extended beyond two wives. The division of labor varied considerably from one tribe to another, more than among Europeans, but, lacking the social estates and class system of Europe, there was a much greater equality of function among "higher" and "lower" orders of women.

Sometimes women monopolized agriculture, while at other locations the men performed extensive farming tasks. Even when only men might hunt or trap large game, women might manufacture snares and trap small game. Let us put the situation thus: a farm woman in Alsace (arguably the European heartland) would experience as many difficulties adapting to the life of a Greek farmer's wife as would a Pequot woman adapting to Shawnee life. The tools -

grinding, cooking, serving, cleaning , etc. - of a Pueblo women were no less well-adapted to her style of life than were those of a Stratford English housewife, and from the perspective of domestic science as good or better.

The idea of a "tool kit" of a culture is useful in anthropology meaning, in the case of Indian and European alike, varieties of knives, pots, fire sticks, furs, moccasins, and many another household and workaday object.
It is more restricted than the notion of a culture complex, which takes in larger "items" like habitations, energy sources, medicinal and dietetic supplies, ecology (knowledge of the environment), and bits of all the sciences - very much as the ordinary American has them as scratches on the mind - astronomy, hydrology, geology, handicrafts, anthropology (regarding social psychology and especially related and unrelated tribes), sex practices, hunting techniques, cuisine, religious beliefs and practices, etc.

Some knowledge of agriculture was universal.
While Europeans corrupted Indians with alcohol, Indians plied them in turn with deadly attractive tobacco.
Bow and arrow, lance and spear, club, fish nets and hooks, weaving sticks, tanning hides, sewing needles, embroidery, and pottery were found everywhere.
Too, a variety of herbal and fungal medicines, often combined in potions of an efficacy largely unknown to the outside world then and now.

Most knowledge was destroyed with the peoples themselves. Some that survived is being reworked after centuries of neglect. The Osage Orange tree, named for the Osage Indians of Arkansas and Missouri, produces a beautiful fruit and a latex of numerous uses. The Ozark mountains were named as a corruption of the French word given the tree for the hardwood used in making tomahawks and bows, *bois d'arc*. Two outposts became Bowdark and Bodark.

The hard orange balls repel roaches and other insects. Too, Indians derived painkillers from willows, poplars, and aspens, all of which contain salicia. Wild fruit and spruce drinks were popular. Sassafras was taken for fevers and colic. Hernando De Soto's expedition came upon "Hot Springs, Arkansas", in 1541, where he learned that the Indians had been employing its therapeutic faculties since time immemorial. Many other drugs and cures might be cited; it is not at all sure that the Indian health-delivery system was inferior to the European of the times.

Likely in this total view of the culture complex, especially when related to the ecology, Indians were well ahead of and better coordinated than the first several biological and political generations of Europeans with whom they came into contact. The main advantages held by European culture, thought the Indians, were propelled explosive charges (gun and cannon), strong alcohol, and immunity from certain diseases, to which had to be added the unseen presence of an unassailable reinforcement and supply depot over the seas. Against these they could sing a litany of many virtues and goods that composed the especial worth of their people.

For most Indian tribes, religion consisted of a vague but highly sensed feeling of a supreme deity, to whom a number of supernatural familiars paid court, and who was vaguely like the Hebrew or Puritan Yahweh (Jehovah) in personality. He was rather an animation of the Universe. But he could also be unfavorable and hence punitive, if a line of conduct displeased him. Spirits and ghosts of modest, if erratic, behavior were also common.

Planets, so plainly worshiped in the Euro-Asian tradition, occur largely in the rich fund of legends told to each succeeding generation. Occasionally, as in the Pawnee human sacrifice to Venus, connections between sky bodies and religion become manifest. As Michael Coe says, "Venus was enormously important in Meso-American religion and mythology", and by inference among the Northern peoples influenced by Mexico.

Generally, Indian cultures were more gratifying personally and richer than those of the individuals and groups who came rudely upon their primordial scene. These arrived for the most part with little baggage to speak of, and with a culture that, if it were not too specialized to be useful, was inapplicable. Because history is told from the perspective of the ruling elite (to which historians adhere), it is made to appear that this arriving elite and its gangs knew a great deal more than the Indian. It is really a matter of specialization and mode of operation: the new leaders might be tragic blunderers, but they had the power of the gun and they could call on help from afar, which, rather later than sooner, would probably arrive. When they win their way, force and domination, no matter how blind, convey the impression of "intelligence".

In 1914 pioneer anthropologist Clark Wissler set forth nine major American Indian culture-areas and described their salient traits. Granted that he was working on materials that were in part current and different from ancestral ones, still he might be relied upon to sketch for us the basic paths that Indian cultures took during the century before the major European incursions began.

Where to start? It would appear that the Indians of Canada, even those of the Atlantic region, were first of the South, and later moved North (possibly with the withdrawal of the ice and the warming of the region). It seems, too, that the central Canadian Indians are but the Northern elements of the American Plains hunters. It is believed as well that the Northwest Indians of the USA and British Columbia came late to their area, possibly from the South, too. And the Inuit in their dauntless bands were late arrivals in Alaska and Canada, conquering this vast natural reserve out of Greenland or Siberia. The early Americans of the Southwest were fairly well settled peripherals of the great Mexican civilization. Upon them more aggressive tribes from East and North transgressed in time.

Following Wissler, adding one more, we may say a few words about ten major Indian cultures mainly, as they were operative in the fifteenth century. Our order of mention will be the order in which they suffered European incursions.

Puerto Rico passed a full four centuries under Spanish rule. The Island was strongly fortified and beat off assaults from various pirates and several famous English buccaneers: Francis Drake in 1595; G. Clifford in 1598; B. Hendrick in 1625; and Abercromby in 1797. It admitted the American fleet in 1898 without resistance.

Puerto Rico's inhabitants were originally some 100,000 to 400,000 Tainos of Arawak (or Aruak) Indian ancestry, well settled in and practicing agriculture. One of three large linguistic and cultural groups that contested for supremacy in the huge Amazon Basin for a long time - the others being the Carib and Tupi - the Arawak had used their river canoes to cross the thousand miles of intervening ocean to settle in the Antilles. They colonized Florida and Central America in part, too. The Caribs, a more aggressive and often cannibalistic people, settled other islands of the Antilles.

Columbus landed in Puerto Rico on November 9 of 1493 and called it San Juan Battista, but a few years later, in 1504, Ponce de Leon debarked and called it Puerto Rico, because of its richness. An unsuccessful revolt in 1511 reduced pitifully the Indian population. Then Spanish traders brought in Africans as slaves to replenish the declining population. Interbreeding among the three groups was common, with or without benefit of matrimony, as indeed occurred later on the continent and all around the Caribbean Basin.

Beginning almost at once, there came into being a large number of Black-Indian-Spaniards, in numerous genetic combinations, more Caucasian than anything else, to whom the name Hispanic, meaning of Spanish-American-African cultural heritage, can be applied. The term, properly used, could be substituted for Latinos or Latin-American. (It is larger than Chicano, the term for Mexican-Americans of recent coming.) Racially, it is totally inclusive, any ethnicity being admissible. When Puerto Ricans were asked lately to identify their race, 80% termed themselves Caucasian, 20% African.

The Arawak language family is gone from Puerto Rico and the islands, but exists in small areas of Central and South America and, in rare and isolated cases, is spoken in Florida. Castilian Spanish came to prevail in offices and elite, while Boricua, a natively developed Hispanic dialect, and a synonym for Puerto Rico itself, pervaded all social classes, after the American language was introduced, and English taught in the schools. Boricuan brought in many American terms directly, and within a century was making more progress toward an American street language than was accomplished by the English-language schools. Indian and African cultural traits and customs were carried down, and contributed heavily to the later new American civilization.

Southwestern U.S. cultures numbered some 100,000 to 400,000 persons and consisted of the more ancient and settled Pueblo peoples - of which the Hopi, Zuni, and Rio Grande were regional types that contained numbers of villages - and the nomadic tribes such as the Navaho and Apaches, these having many Pueblo traits but also having picked up significant elements of their culture from the Plains, Plateau, and even the Meccans Indians. The Navaho especially took up important traits from Europeans as time went on.

A considerable proportion of the Southwestern Indians lived in pueblo villages, a distinctive form of settlement some examples of which persist today. The individual contiguous houses are made of adobe or stone plastered with adobe, have flat roofs, are rectangular in shape, and built upon terraces in the side of hills, sometimes steep and made difficult of access for purposes of defense. The houses can be built several deep on top of one another and extend backward to allow a terrace in front. Villages of the cliff or plain would number from a hundred to a couple of thousand inhabitants. Their farms and some of their livestock would be located below. Despite similarities of life-style, several distinct languages were to be found among pueblo peoples.

Generally these Americans relied mainly upon maize and other cultivated foods, with men doing the cultivating instead of the women. Men also worked at weaving cotton with loom and spindle. They were adept at masonry, and the manufacture of well-decorated pottery. They raised turkeys, and otherwise supplemented vegetable diets by hunting buffalo, deer, antelope and rabbits, employing sometimes a type of boomerang like that of the ten-thousand-mile-distant Australians. A thousand years before Columbus, at the least, the Hohokam people dug irrigation canals running from the Gila and Salt Rivers; mats of brush were positioned to block or direct the flow of waters onto individual fields of corn.

Anomalous practices are to be found. Chaco Canyon contains some 200 miles of engineered roads lined at intervals and culminating in astronomical observation points and stone monuments. In numerous locations of the Southwest are found art work in stone and in drawings. These seem to have been the work of more advanced technologies than those of 1500, and one must consider the possibility of natural and/or human catastrophes in the preceding century.

Early in the sixteenth century the region was crisscrossed by Spanish expeditions, conveying new traits, a new authority, and the early combination of soldiers and priests that began the process of racial amalgamation and Christianization a century before the French and English arrived in the New World. Their descendants are identifiable still in New Mexico, Arizona, and California, often in isolated nooks, like those of some early Scots-Irish still to be located in the Appalachian mountains.

Across the continent and in the Southeast, extending from the East bank of the Mississippi to Florida, dwelled tribes containing in all a population of from 250,000 to one million. This region was invaded and traversed in several harrowing expeditions by Spaniards early in the sixteenth century, and numerous, usually futile, efforts occurred to settle the coastal country.

Here lived richly developed peoples exhibiting many distinctive tools and traits. Typical cultures were the Muskogean, Yuchi, and Cherokee. Of all Indian cultures, the Cherokee took the largest steps over three centuries to adapt its culture to the European culture, which was moving in upon it from all sides.

Caribbean influences were noticeable, especially to the south. Some tribes lived in circular houses, the Florida Seminole for example. Settlements were well-fortified by wooden palisades. Dug-out canoes could traverse the myriad waterways of the region. Probably the template cultures enjoyed a wealth of foods and household goods. Bread was baked of root flour or persimmon; much fish was consumed. Agriculture was intensive, with corn, tobacco, pumpkin and watermelon prominent as crops. Their only domestic animal was the small dog, which, like the pig of later British inhabitants, was both pet and food. Large mammals were hunted in the western areas, more of the small animals and fowl in the Southeast. Cannibalism was common.

Nations of the Eastern Woodlands provided a third area, to be heavily stereotyped by Northeastern Euro-American publishers and schoolteachers. Along with horse-warrior Plains Indians, they afforded practically the full imagery of the American populace about Indians. Here were the Indians who were to be written about by James Fenimore Cooper in books such as *"The Last of the Mohicans"*, printed in the early nineteenth century.

The main elements were the Iroquois and Algonquin peoples, divided into important tribes, and in all numbering between 250,000 and a million people. Since they extended along the Atlantic coastline from Manhattan to Labrador, and all along the great St. Lawrence and Hudson River waterways and into the near Midwest, they probably had many more brief contacts with the European world than are credited to them, and one writer at least has claimed that there are Scandinavian admixtures in parts of the population, while another has claimed that he could detect Gaelic physiognomy.

Throughout the sixteenth century, before the Massachusetts and Virginia settlements, there were known contacts, and maps were drawn and books written about the area. The Northern section of this regional complex ran from the Arctic North to the Great Lakes in the South and was typed by the Ojibway tribes. Culturally they were related to the Algonquin. These were hunters and gatherers, who would pen up caribou, drag toboggans, and paddle birch canoes.

The main population lived Southwards and Eastwards: the Central Algonquin, and East of them the Iroquois, then the Eastern Algonquin who were the tribes of New England and included the Delaware tribes, and Micmac and Abnaki groups of tribes. The Iroquois, of which something has already been told, occupied with perhaps 75,000 to 350,000 people an area of 4.4 million square kilometers; they included the Five Nations, so-called, and the famous Huron, Wyandot, Erie, and Susquehanna, connecting on the South with the Cherokee and others, and probably came up themselves from the South in the not distant past.

The Iroquois were competent and extensive farmers. Their villages were composed of extended family rectangular longhouses and were often well-fortified. They carved excellent wooden masks, and executed fine bone work. They employed the blowgun - found in Asia, Africa, and South America - as well as the ordinary arms.

Women, we might remind ourselves, were more influential here than in any other tribes of the Americas; the family system was matriarchal; descent passed through the mother as well; women participated in the government. They were in charge of important holy exercises; they held property; they arranged marriages; their names were carried down.

Since the Eastern Algonquin were heavily influenced by Southern practices, the feathered cloak, for instance, and Iroquois customs and artifacts, the Central Algonquin of today's Midwest are regarded as a purer cultural type of Eastern Woodland Indians. Better known are the Southern Ojibway, Menomini, Sauk and Fox, and Winnebago. Less documented are the Illinois, Peoria, Miami, Shawnee, Kickapoo, and Ottawa.

They grew corn, beans, and squashes... A good quantity of wild rice was gathered. Fishing (especially for the lake sturgeon), hunting (for deer, bear, buffalo, wild fowl), were major occupations. Small game was trapped and snared. A dome-shaped bark and mat-covered lodge for winter, and a rectangular bark house for summer helped adapt to the extreme seasons.

Copper had in some earlier period been mined, traded and used in the Michigan area, but for some reason the industry was discontinued. There are several of such discontinuities: sunken pyramids at the bottom of today's Rock Lake, Wisconsin; inscribed rocks and stone tablets; hundreds of large-scale mounds that served for burial, but possibly, too, as refuges in the case of flooding, or for astronomical observation of the horizons and religious observances (one Ohio mound takes the form of a gigantic snake whose open jaws are about to swallow an egg, or globe).

Eastern Indians derived about one-half of their food supply from hunting and gathering, the balance from agriculture. The corresponding figure for all American Indians would have been about one-third from hunting and gathering. Cultivation was probably not vital for the Eastern Indians. It was enjoyed, especially by the women and children, one suspects, since they moved about less than the men, who were continually fussing over hunting.

They were indifferent farmers, but knew some practices that the newcomers to America could learn from them; the Pilgrims were taught to use fish for fertilizer, for example. Hunting skills - stalking, tracking, trapping of game - of which the European newcomers, typically peasants forbidden to hunt, were bereft, were passed along. About one per cent of the cultivable land in the East was given over to agriculture by the Indians, anthropologist Kroeber estimated.

The Meccans culture area, with perhaps 150,000 to 400,000 people, dominated the interior of present-day Western and Central Canada down into the Northern United States. In the East were the Algonquins, possibly coming from the South, and in the West the Dene tribes, three groups of them, an Eastern group with the Yellow Knives and others; the Northwestern group with the Kutchin and others; and the Southwestern group with the Sekani. They trapped and snared small game, drove and penned caribou, ate tubers, berries, and fish. Lacking pottery, they cooked in bark vessels, and used wood, bark, and skins for practically all artifacts. Twisted bark, for instance, was made into thongs and braid. They lived in a kind of double lean-to.

The California coastal cultural area, a fifth major culture, with from 100,000 to 400,000 persons, has been divided into four sub-areas, indicating its internal diversity. The Santa Barbara tribe was characteristic. The central sub-area would appear to have been the simplest Indian culture of the continent, an odd fact, given its richness and luxury today. Basketry of coil and twine was the most impressive achievement. Of pottery, canoes, and substantial housing there was none. Acorns were the largest dietary item, supplemented by seeds, roots, and berries, along with small game and fish, where possible. Shellfish was popular. But farther South and to the North, extensive borrowing from the neighboring cultures allowed a considerable expansion of the culture tool kit.

Northern neighbors, the North Pacific Coast Culture Area, extended from today's Oregon to the Alaskan peninsula, with some 150,000 to 600,000 persons. Its numerous highly varied tribes were nevertheless divisible into three types, from South to North, the Chinook, the Kwakiutl and the Tlingit. There was a general reliance upon sea food, a large use of berries, and some hunting. Dried fish and clams were staples. All in all a diet superior to that which most Americans enjoy today. Large planked houses were typical. Impressive totem poles and posts were erected. Large sea-going canoes were constructed, sometimes with sails. Woodworking was highly developed, including carving techniques. The Southern Tlingit shared culture complexes with California culture, obtaining, for example, an acorn cuisine.

The Kwakiutl engaged in the pot-latch, a form of economic competition that involved careful and diligent saving by individuals culminating in a great giving-away party; the

most extravagant donor (or waster), the man in the
community who was able to dispose of material of the
highest value, achieved great prestige and influence.
A pot-latch resembled the great balls and banquets of France, Spain,
Italy and England of the time, where the magnates of the
realm competed in display and waste, and of the later USA
cultures of the plantation South, but especially of the
business North at the end of the 1800's.

Northwest Coast music was the most complex to be found,
especially in rhythmic structure. While it is practically true
that the whole of the region North of the Rio Grande lacked
polyphony, its rudiments might be found here too. It
employed frequent pulses and vocal tension, with dynamic
contrasts and sudden accents. Antiphony was employed as
were forms of response. Major thirds and minor seconds were
commonly employed, the melodic range was narrow,
singing had a recitative quality, whereas the percussion wove its
own designs behind the melody.

String instruments were unknown, a puzzling lack,
inasmuch as a bow string hums when twanged.
Drums, rattles, flutes, whistles, and human voices
provided the instruments. With profound cultural destruction and
depopulation went practically all compositions and
techniques, so that we cannot tell
whether Amer-Indian music approached, say,
the exceedingly rich Hindu flute and drum music,

The Plains Area contained from 150,000 to 600,000 persons
organized into at least 31 tribes, among them the Arapaho,
Blackfoot, Crow, Cheyenne, and Comanche. Nomadism,
buffalo-hunting, their mobile dwelling - the tepee -, the dog,
an artistry in animal skin tailoring and beadwork: such were
their prominent cultural traits. Related tribes to the East -
the Iowa, Kansa, Pawnee, Sioux, and Dakota -
engaged in some agriculture and weaving as well as hunting

and alternated the tepee with permanent dwellings of earth and bark.

The Plateau cultural area, eighth of our categories, connected with the Plains area on the West. It is less uniform because it is largely desert on the South whereas the North is moist and fertile. Its population of some 25,000 to 100,000 was divided into a number of tribes whose history had all but disappeared before systematic observations came to be made. The Nez Perce and the Shoshone were major elements, but intermingled with the Plains Culture to a marked degree. The Interior Salish Tribe, despite its over sixteen dialectical divisions, was more typical, with its semi-subterranean pit houses and movable summer homes of mats, sticks, and lean-to style. Deerskins were the favorite material for bedding, clothing, and caps. Dug-out canoes and bark canoes were manufactured. Pulverized dried salmon and tubers were stored against the lean seasons.

The Eskimo, or, more properly, Inuits, numbering from some 90,000 to 200,000 persons, occupied, as they do today, an Arctic space reaching from the American Alaskan Aleutians to Eastern Greenland. They and the Indians of the Northwest suffered gravely from Russian depredation and murder in the eighteenth and nineteenth centuries. They are deemed not to be Indians of race, but *sui generis* though Mongolian, a distinct sub-race.

Wherever they originated, their cultural development has paralleled all known cultures, admirably so in some regards, and lately have been given back the fourth largest stretch of land in the world as their autonomous domain, by the Canadian government. The United States has made no move to return any part of Alaska to them, and in fact has made living conditions difficult for some of them by turning a large area over to great corporations for petroleum exploration and extraction. Meanwhile, the US has

subsidized every Eskimo, every Alaskan even, by
thousands of dollars per capita annually
in every excusable way.

Inuits compounded one of the richest bodies of folklore in
the world; that they were illiterate and consigned to months
of total darkness only helped in this regard. Their techniques
of group hunting and distribution and consumption of
animals such as the whale were and are ingenious. Little of
the ancient has been found respecting the Inuits, so they
may have been later arrivals than most into the Northern
regions, perhaps as recently as two thousand years ago. Their
use of dog-sleds is proverbial, as are their winter dwellings,
igloos. Distinctive and clever as well are their several
kinds of knives; special tools and boats for women; snow
goggles; harpoons; floats; and carved implements and bowls
of wood and bone.

A multi-disciplinary, socio-economic, demographic history of
the Indians occupying America has yet to be written.
Considering them in their group context but especially as
individual persons, how did the Amer-Indians compare
culturally and in pursuit of happiness with the Europeans
who landed upon these shores? The story ought to focus also
upon relations among the Indian nations and their relations
with the many varieties of Europeans. The end product
might serve the growing science of regional histories. Once
the observer begins to operate with the universal language
and method of science, especially social science, the actors,
plots, and denouements become startlingly alike.

The ghost of pre-European America is not simply a haunting spirit of
tragedy and vengeance; it is an archetypical ancestor, who, as
we shall see, has left his and her imprint upon
the landscape, the psychic state, the conduct of the present
nation. Every day millions of cars drive down paths, now
highways, that were discovered, marked out, and worn down

by Indian explorers, travelers and migrations before the
Genoese navigator hoisted anchor in Spain. They
are paths that take us from Bangor to San Diego, Seattle to
Miami, and points North, West and South by land,
and, unmarked but remembered in navigation lore,
by sea, lake and river besides.

Every day, too, habits peculiar to Americans
of today hark back to the First Americans. The terrorist leader,
Osama Bin Laden, was slain in Pakistan by a military unit of United States special forces,
in an operation the code name of which was "Geronimo,"
the name of the Apache Chief who fought both Mexican and
U.S. Army detachments with remarkable success for some years before surrendering.

A noisy public quarrel broke out upon the operation's code name.
Indian spokespersons and Americans in and out of politics
(the products of a generation educated against ethnic slurs),
and an astonishing number of foreigners
people who knew little of American "Wild West" culture felt
that this was a racist epithet that Indians should resent,
that it equated the Muslim terrorist and the Apache chief,
the victory over a foreign rogue with the victory over the
American Natives; yet also, it brought over Bin Laden a glow
of history and heroism that was could appear most unfortunate, given the circumstances,
and that Muslims the world over will, in due time, perceive.
Embarrassing slur to the ones, embarrassing honor to the other,
one perfect fiasco.

It was probably a sociologically ignorant choice
of a code name that could also be heartily shouted (as we boys did when
we played at "Cowboys and Indians" - Geronimo!!).
in the event the soldiers had to rally against a gang of Al Quaeda's.
The person who chose the war cry was no doubt prideful, and
May have been a fan of the Apache chief.
We hear that the operation has been renamed, *a posteriori,* somewhat sadly,
"Neptune Spear."

───────────────

Modern day replica of John Cabot's ship, 1497

Part Two

EUROPEAN INVASIONS

Can one doubt that gun powder against the Infidels is incense for the Lord?
Gonzalo Fernandez de Oviedo: *General and Natural History of the Indies* (1526)

The Turks forced Europe to "discover" America and much of the world besides. After blocking ever more of the Near and Middle East and North Africa, and strangling trade and communications with the Far Orient, they crowned their conquests with the capture of Constantinople in 1453. Hopeless with regard to the East, Europeans turned to the West.
Not deliberately, of course - as by some summit conference of nations - but fumbling and tumbling and muddling for outlets.

Inasmuch as the Americas and their many peoples had long existed, the
Europeans could hardly claim to have discovered them,
except from their admittedly limited perspective.
The usage is permanently fixed, barring world revolution
(comparable to using the abbreviations B.C.
and A.D., that may be pleasing to devout Christians,
but a nuisance to most others). It is perhaps best to introduce
novel words from time to time to engender other perspectives;
we could talk of rediscovery, penetrations, encounters, intrusions,
ventures, aggressions, incursions, arrivals, landings,
immigration, settlements, expropriations, and
invasions. Columbus' landings quickly changed from
reconnaissance and encounter into aggressive invasion.
Certain Spanish scholars, Vitoria most prominently,
within a political generation of the landing of Columbus,
were trying to set up the American Indian peoples
as equal players in the games of international law.
At the very same time, Machiavelli,
himself an honest, even noble, person,
was pointing out the inability, indeed the idiocy, of any
government behaving according to noble principles,
unless these happened to benefit the narrow good of the realm, and
unless the government was armed against internal and foreign enemies.
That Machiavellism won out in America,
as it almost always has in history,
added to the anguish of the Spanish theologians,
historians, and legists, who were publicizing the often
fiendish injustice dealt out to the Americans.
Like the "whistle-blowers" of this day,
they were contemned and castigated as disloyal informants.

Not that the Indians were angels. I doubt that it can be shown that
they were better or worse on the average than Europeans.
Europeans were often absolute in two and now recently
three demands that, unless fulfilled, would bring absolute
censure upon the Indians.
First, Indians should be Christians to be tolerable
(and often a certain kind of Protestant or Catholic Christian).
Second, they must not cannibalize,

an absolute requirement that pertained to a minority, but
an important minority, of American cultures.
(The Catholics and Anglicans who ingested the body and blood of
Christ in Holy Communion were permissible exceptions to the rule.)
That any people practicing cannibalism had to be
destroyed or cured by conversion was affirmed
by men who were aghast at the large number of people
regularly killed and eaten by the civilized
Aztecs under governmental and priestly guidance.

The third "virtue" demanded by the Europeans was obedience
to the will of a remote sovereign ruler and state,
a mind-set that the Europeans themselves had acquired
only recently, and which many, the Italians and Germans,
for example, were reluctant to adopt for themselves.

But this virtue, too, had numerous contradictions,
inasmuch as many of the invaders turned against their own
sovereign when they felt that they could get away with it,
obeying the Pope instead of the King, for example, or
fleeing to the New World to practice a forbidden religion,
or ultimately rebelling against the ruler in order
to install a government of their own, as in the American Revolution
and all the subsequent ones of the West Indies and
South of the Rio Grande.

As for comparing one set of invaders with another,
we are hard pressed to distinguish the more from the less virtuous,
except in individual cases. But one must try.
A historian practically commits himself to do this
every time he fills out the answer to the question:
"Who is it that is doing what to whom with what effect?"
Historical objectivity rests in the depth of understanding of
the actors and the consequences of their actions,
not in the beating of drums for one's favorites.

Think here, too, of what was happening in Africa, Europe

and Asia. Africa South of the Sahara was a congeries of kingdoms,
prone to quarrels, the rulers of which were invariably ready
to sell enemies or dissidents to slave traders,
who would march them to coastal points occupied by Portuguese,
where, armed with exclusive commissions from the Spanish King,
Dutch captains would purchase and convey
their human cargoes to America.

Or, in conspiracy with Muslim raiders and vendors of North Africa or
the Near East, the same rulers would behave in the same way.
An estimated 4.4 million souls were forcibly removed
from their homelands and brought into Islamic countries as slaves
in the period 650 to 1900 A.D.

Up to sixteen (16) million persons were forcibly removed,
mostly from western Africa, and despatched to the Americas
(1451-1870),
an average of over 38,000 per year.
In the year 1787, over 100,000 slaves were
taken and transported, mostly in American, English, French, and
Portuguese boats, with Dutch and Danish ships carrying smallish
numbers.

(In this same year, the Americans who were gathered to
amend one constitution, but proceeded to write a new Constitution,
inserted in the new document guarantees for property in slaves and a
clause to close down the U.S. slave trade
in twenty years.)

The sixteenth century in Europe witnessed many confused wars,
foreign and civil. In one happening, Rome was thoroughly looted
amidst wholesale murder and rape by a French army and its allies. On
August 24, 1572, the French Catholic governing party massacred
many thousands of Protestant Huguenots. In the first half of the next
century the continuing wars of religion, ethnicity and dynasty
would ruin much of central Europe;
Germany's varied peoples would be starving, along with others,
when they were not being slaughtered.

During the 16th century the Russian Empire expanded East,
conquering vast stretches of Central Asia and Siberia.
Between 1552 and 1556 Kazan and Astrakan were conquered,
giving the Russians control of the full Volga River basin,
opening routes to invasion of the East.
In 1581-83 Russian traders settled East of the Urals, and with
Cossack pioneers began the conquest of Siberia.
They reached the Pacific Ocean in 1637.
By the eighteenth century they had posted themselves
from Alaska down to San Francisco.
Treatment of the conquered peoples was everywhere abominable.

Meanwhile, in 1526, Babar, descendent of Genghis Khan and
Tamerlane, led his Mogul army into India,
sweeping through that profoundly civilized sub-continent
from Punjab to Bengal in a couple of years.
In the seventeenth century, after an earlier invasion of China,
Mongols invested Manchuria and, as the Manchus,
came down upon China to overthrow the venerable Ming Dynasty.

One might conclude that much of the world was suffering
the fate of American Indians in these long periods.
It was in the early years of the European invasions
of the Americas that Machiavelli sat himself down
in a fury to write *The Prince,* which became the classic text
of modern political science, but was also a diatribe against
the foreign nations that periodically swept into Italy,
destroying, killing, and looting. His pleas for the small
Italian nations to unite might as well have been
directed to the Indian tribes of North America.

Universalis Cosmographia, the 1507 map created by the German cartographer sMartin Waldseemuller and Matthias Ringmann, which gave America its name and which shows it for the first time as a continent separate from Asia.

Chapter Four

Renaissance and Reformation

Shock at discovering that a hemisphere of the world
had been missing was hardly profound. The Renaissance mind
could comprehend the new three-dimensional space and an
enlarged globe, even when it was stretched out on a flat map.
A modern scholar has written of the receivers of the message of the
New World that *".. trained by Renaissance humanism,*
they were especially well suited to deal with the cultural consequences
of overseas discovery". Marsilio Ficino, in the 1470's, wrote,
"Man wants to be everywhere. He is not content with any frontier".
Still, it took a generation for Europe
to be sold on the idea.

The Italian Renaissance did more than provide a representative figure to discover the New World, and another to provide it with a name. It was the Renaissance that sent Columbus to America and that dealt with what he brought back. The Renaissance provided the mentality for the Age of Discovery, did its research, gave it its tools, its back-up, interpreted it, kept the fires moving from one nation to the next, until they inflamed in each nation a permanent interest group whose client was the New World.

Columbus was a "field commander", first, last, and always - like many another; greater he was, because, resolute, with a rightfully directed *idée fixe* and a pigeon-like sense of direction, he could ultimately move men and ships into a strange world. However, upon his return he had to prove his conquests, what it was that he had gained. It was up to the Spanish court, the other navigators coming and going, the scholars, the churchmen, to weigh and judge his achievement. His main effort was to get ready for the next expedition.

All fields of learning were immediately alerted for what his adventure had meant and how it might affect them. The political elite and intelligentsia began to engorge his materials and to communicate with other courts and centers of learning and religion throughout Europe - the Italian states, the Vatican, France, the Low Countries, the German States, even with England, which was not yet cut off from Catholicism.

Columbus provided a report, which was released. A new route to the Indies had been found. His position on the subject, although he did not write much, and published tardily, was the single greatest obstacle to the recognition of America as a New World. Both he and the Spanish government insisted upon referring to it as "the Other World" or "the Indies".

The Vatican cooperated. Pope Alexander VI on May 4, 1493
issued a Bull, law to all Catholics and
hopefully a warning to the rest of the world. It declared that
God owned the World and the Vicar of God, to wit,
the Pope at Rome, might dispense
all that was not already in the hands of Christians,
and that, of this non-Christian land with its false titles,
Spain was to own all that was to be found beyond a line
drawn 100 leagues or more West of the Azores and
Cape Verde Islands. If the Bull appeared to be pro-Spanish,
it may have been because the Pope was himself Spanish.

A year later Portuguese and Spaniards signed a Treaty of
Tordesillas, which moved the Pope's line of demarcation
270 leagues further west.
Portugal was to have all the lands East of the new line,
Spain all lands West of it. The Treaty hardly made sense unless the
Portuguese had already touched upon the hump of Brazil, which
would now become their domain.

Columbus held but a hypothesis, and within the next political
generation, his hypothesis would be rejected. It would be nullified
because ships of five countries would set out to duplicate his
discovery, not once but twice or several times, depending upon the
resources brought to bear. There would be scores of ships skirting the
shores of the New World and landing there.
(Often wrecking upon its shores, or at sea coming and going:
a rule of thumb would assign one-third of the ships and
their human and material cargoes for the first generation
to "Davy Jones' Locker", roughly the percentage of
Europeans lost to bubonic plagues of the fourteenth century, of
Germans lost to the Thirty Years' War, of the percentage of Irish lost to
Potato Famines of the 1840's to come.) What they found was far
different from the fabled lands of Cathay and India.

Scholars everywhere hastened to their shelves to do library research.
Ancient books were brought out and reread, even back to Aristotle,
nay, the Bible, to see whether something had been missed and

whether what was reported was in line with what had been said in the past. The zoological claims were questioned. Where were the elephants of the Indies? Not there. But gorgeous parrots would be proffered, just as one would expect.

Sketches were made of the landfalls, of coastlines dimly seen, of people by their huts... Protocols were taken of interviews of natives, of their responses to interrogations by drawings, by gesture, by a few words hastily learned, of the interrogation of informants brought back as exhibits and to be interrogated *ad infinitum.*
There would be exhibitions of New World collections. From the museum of Charles V, ruler of Spain and much more of the world, on whose empire, a German poet would declaim, "the sun never set", the same expression that British subjects bruited about three centuries later - an exhibition toured the realm.

Germanic art genius Albrecht Dürer saw it in Alsace and the treasures of Montezuma astonished him. *"I saw among them wonderful works of art and marveled at the subtle ingenuity of people in strange lands. I do not know how to express all that I experienced there".* His *"Ideal City"* of 1527 seems to have been influenced by the City Plan of Tenochitlan, which was shown there.

Theologians must ruminate, argue: Were the Indians true humans, with souls to be saved? Did their conditions of life prove the blessed situation of Christendom? Which of their mess of customs had to be disposed of to qualify them for baptism and the holy communion? There was a rush of fine talent to go to America as missionaries.

Investors offered themselves, with and without capital. The departure of the Jews, many of their assets dissipated and in effect seized, interfered with capitalization of enterprise in America. Gentiles then, as now, often believed that money came, went, and accrued without benefit of astute management. When stolen American gold and silver began to flow into Spanish coffers, expulsion of the Jews seemed no longer to matter.

The cross would inform, the sword seize,
and the Court spend.

Voices of the crew and officers added a new dimension
to the knowledge and awareness of the Age.
If scores of boats returned from the New World within the
first political generation, some thousands of
mariners and soldiers would have been released upon Spain and
Europe. If 8,000 men told one or more stories to only two persons
per month for twenty years, nearly 4,000,000 persons
would have heard eye-witness accounts of the New World.
If these four millions had told what they had heard
to someone else, which they would, not once, but twice or more,
and to several others besides, over the same period of time,
the total population of Europe, estimated at 70 millions
in 1500, would have heard several accounts. Since this was
an age still of personal transmission of news and opinions, there is
no doubt that, whatever the duplication in the figures just cast out,
only a rare person in all of Europe would not have a store of
facts and fancies about the New World, and
many would know considerably more.

It happened that the Renaissance achieved one of its triumphs
with the invention and perfection of movable type,
paper-making and printing of books, leaflets, manifestos,
proclamations, bulletins, and picture-collections.
Gutenberg's famous press, itself burgeoning from a set of inventions,
began printing nearly a half-century before the voyage of
Columbus. Two years after Columbus landed, Aldo
Manuzio started the Aldine Press in Venice
in order to print true editions of books.

Within a socio-political generation, printing presses and
books were found throughout advanced countries of Europe.
Although Latin was still the universal
European language and hastened the distribution of
New World news, the dissemination of news

written in the popular languages accelerated greatly
with the printing and publishing industry.
The industry was ready for the big news-break.
Soon a brisk trade in Americana was carried on at the
annual Frankfurt Book Fair, then as today.

In 1507 in an Alsatian town called St. Dié,
a printer and a geographer gave the New World its name:
"America".
Why-so was perhaps better understood at the time than later on,
but today one can see in it a classic case of the
Free Press vs. Government.
Unlike Columbus, Amerigo Vespucci, Florentine navigator,
had cultivated a wide range of acquaintances, and had
written vivid and humane accounts of the New World.
He claimed to have been on several voyages to the so-called Indies,
had descended the whole of the North Atlantic Coast,
had circled the Bahamas, and had sailed down to explore the
Southern Atlantic coast, first for Spain,
then for Portugal, between1499 and 1501.
In 1499 he participated in the Spanish
expedition of Alomod and Hejida.

At least one of these expeditions may have been imagined,
nor was he captain on these voyages.
There is little question as to his navigating abilities, and
he might well have been a consistently effective leader;
probably the captaincy went to an investor and managerial type,
while Amerigo, more of a scientist and scholar,
acted as navigator.

His attitude towards New World inhabitants was modern;
for a month on one occasion he went to live among an
Indian group as a member of the community,
a participant observer, writing an account of it afterwards.
He described the mainland of America,
implying that he had seen it before Columbus,

who had never seen it, or before anybody else,
which was not true. He declared that he had not gone to
the New World to make a profit, but to
observe and learn.

He argued that a truly new continent had been shown to exist,
this by himself and others. Whatever he did and said
carried a substantial validity if only because
Europe expected miracles of art and science to emit from
contemporary Florence. No matter that the letters of Columbus were
published immediately upon the presses of
Barcelona, Rome, Basel, Paris, and Strasbourg.
A German version appeared in 1497.

In 1504 Peter Martyr's *Libretto* about
three voyages of Columbus appeared. A number of
Portuguese voyages were described in publications
appearing at the same time as Vespucci's.
His little book, based on an account sent to
Lorenzo the Magnificent in Florence, was called
Novus Mundus and came out in 1540.
The book was an instant success and was promptly translated
into several languages.

When news of his discoveries had reached Florence,
for three days palazzi torchlights burned in celebration.
Machiavelli pondered risks and glory, and commented ruefully that
"it has always been no less dangerous to discover new methods and
institutions than to explore unknown oceans and lands"...
(Though innocent, he had been imprisoned and tortured for
conspiring against the rulers of Florence.)

Vespucci was obviously not a creature of the Spanish Crown or
any Emperor; as a Florentine in correspondence with the famous
de' Medicis, he would be more *simpatico* to the intelligentsia,
especially those from the autonomous towns of the Upper Rhine in
Germany, Switzerland and Alsace. Geographer Martin Waldseemuller
was preparing a map of the New World; it appeared in the
book, *Cosmographiae Introductio*, labeled *America*.

Intellectual snobbery, perhaps, which to us seems to be
magnificent presumption: that these gentlemen of the press could
take it upon themselves to give a republican name, a
working author and navigator's name, to great new lands,
instead of calling them Carolusia for the Emperor Charles V,
or by some other noble name.
This was the famous Renaissance bravado. The world accepted it.
In England, the word "America" appeared for the first time in a
work by John Rastell in 1519, seven years after
the death of Americus (feminine = America) Vespucius.

The literature of the period did not reveal a concern for
American explorations and problems more profuse than
the literature dealing with the Turkish threat, religious disputes,
abuses and uses of political power, and popular science and medicine.
News from the Near and Far East competed
less seriously, because it became evident that the
human story would be coming from America;
people were soon sailing to and from
those shores in large numbers.

During these two centuries: 1500 to 1700,
Europe had to contend with the aggressive and culturally voracious
Turkish Islamic Empire, now moved deeply into Europe.
The effects on Venice and Austria were paralyzing.
Did New World diversions finally determine that Turkey
would remain dominant in Southeast Europe and the Near East, and
that Islam would retain North Africa?
The price of the New World should then be revised to include
the cost of the incapacity of Christian Europe to
contain and repel the Ottoman Empire.
If Spain, with the West's most formidable armies and vast fleets,
consistently had turned its might to help Venice and
Hungary in their war against Turkey,
after winning the great sea battle at Lepanto,
and had driven the Ottoman Turks from Europe,
would the value of retaining for the West for several centuries

the cultures of Bulgarians, Serbs, Greeks, Romanians, and
possibly North Africa, be greater than the value
to the world of the European conquest of the Americas?

It is legitimate, if futile, to ask such a question, because such
conjectures lead to better-trained and
at least fairer judgements. By the same token,
one may ask whether the exploitation of
the Americas was worth the experience with syphilis
that the mariners of the Pinta and Niña brought back to Europe.
The distribution and digestion of New World information,
in all of its real and fanciful forms, hardly
kept ahead of the fast-spreading disease.

From time to time it has been alleged that syphilis came
not from America but had been anciently present in the Old World.
Was it a new disease? Did not one of the groups that happened
upon America much earlier, the Norsemen, for example,
contract and spread syphilis?
Various studies have refuted this hypothesis.
Examination of 30,000 ancient Egyptian skeletons
revealed no trace of it. Occasionally a skeleton will be found
here or there from pre-Colombian times outside America
that has signs of the disease, but not at all conclusively.
Almost surely syphilis was the unwitting revenge of the
natives of San Salvador for the cruelties and deprivations
visited upon them by Spanish and later exploiters.
The disease was transmitted by sexual contact,
erupted in sores, would subside, erupt again, and again,
in muscular and nervous disorders, until in its final stages,
five to thirty years after catching it,
one would often go blind, mad and die.

Just as they had been avid for the Arawak women,
crews and soldiers were eager for their own wives and women.
They moved around Spain, then Europe. They invaded the Low
Countries. They joined the Spanish Army on its way to fight the
Neapolitans, and infected the population of Naples. A French Army

came to the assistance of the Neapolitans and, when the Spaniards had
been driven out, enjoyed the fruits of victory. The French then
returned to France, bearing the Neapolitan Disease,
while the Italians called it, quite as unjustifiably,
the French Disease.

An Italian physician, Dr. Fracastor, analyzed it
in a long dramatic poem about a shepherd called Siphilus,
struck with the illness by Apollo (God of Medicine) for a
fancied insult: thus the name. Soon it was everywhere,
moving with the velocity of stories about the New World.
If not all Europeans came down with syphilis,
it was because the number of virgins of both sexes,
and of monogamous females and males, increased out of dread.
Perhaps Luther, who suffered from the suspiciously similar ailment,
gout, demanded the purity of monogamic marriage,
in contrast to weak-kneed celibacy,
out of fear of the disease.

Possibly the violent hatred against the Catholic Church, Luther's
"Whore of Rome", came in relation to the plague that would devastate
Europe for over 150 years, and
of course would go back and forth from America,
unleashing severe symptoms, with never a sure cure,
and then coming under a sort of easement and relief through
sulphur and other ointments until the advent of
penicillin in the 1940's.
It was calculated, at the end of the nineteenth century,
that a quarter of French males had contracted the illness
by the time they had finished lycée.

Still, today, syphilis is rampant, and, if the estimated 3,000,000
cases in the United States are not apparent, and lower figures are
otherwise cited, it is because syphilis today is often cured in
its early stages unnoticed, by means of an antibiotic
administered for a feverish flu or a stomach germ or
accidental wound. (Even so, 297,707 cases,
contracted after induction, caught American
servicemen during World War II, about

the same number, 291,557, as were killed in the War.)

Charles V himself, 1500-1558,
the magnificent Majesty of the world's greatest empire,
contracted syphilis. So did Francis I, King of France
during this period of our interest, and most likely
Henry VIII, father of Elizabeth, Queen of England,
who had grave trouble siring an infant who would live.

The disease arrived in Bristol from Bordeaux in 1498.
With Vasco da Gama's crew, it sailed to India in 1498,
and from there went to China in 1505.
Probably it was from this original Portuguese source that the
first cases arrived in Japan by 1512 and
spread out wildly.

A former Surgeon General of the United States wrote -
there was every indication - that Columbus was afflicted:
on the voyage of 1494 he was ill;
in 1498 he had a seizure of what was called "gout",
which mimics some of the symptoms (and vice versa);
he had delusions that he was the Ambassador of God;
rebellious officers bound him in chains and sent him back to Spain;
recovering somewhat, he was dignified with a fourth expedition, and
upon arrival in the "Otro Mondo" had to be carried ashore.
He seemed, writes Dr. Parran, to have had all the symptoms
of syphilis in its final stages; he died in 1506.

The search for cures was on immediately, to little avail,
until the disease became "tired", less virulent, and then mercury,
a dangerous cure, came to be administered with good effects.
The curative barks and herbs that had been rushed from the New World
appeared to be futile. Apparently Indians had been resting with the disease
more or less comfortably. On the other hand, it should be recalled
that Indians were incredibly sensitive to diseases brought from Europe and
could not evolve immunity to disastrous plagues,
even after three centuries.

America brought other returns, more benign, although when one
thinks of tobacco and coca, one is not so sure.

However, there were truly excellent new plants for eating,
ornamental display, and medicines and drugs.
If the Age of Discovery had been confined to America,
greater enthusiasm and interest would have been given the New World
and its products, but once again it is well to remind oneself of the
preoccupations with the Ottoman Empire, and the
triumphs of exploration and trade in Africa, the South Pacific and
the Far East. Neither could our flattered new
Indian pharmaceuticals match the immense Chinese
pharmacopeia.

The terrible wars of the age, regularly called religious, but
incorporating every human motive in its worst aspects,
did not exclude anti-semitic persecutions, though
these had been occurring in nearly every generation
in one or more European countries more or less severely.
One of the worst occurred in Spain, at the very moment
that Columbus was set to sail for the Indies, for
then it was that the Jews were cast out of Spain, and shortly
afterwards out of Sicily, which had fallen to the Spanish Crown, and
out of Portugal as soon as it was joined by royal marriage to Spain.
Remarkably, almost all of the Jews survived,
dispersing to here, there, and everywhere, including the Americas;
many felt compelled to convert to Christianity.

Inspiration of ideas of utopias and natural living
came from the New World - ideas about
life without Christianity or Islam.
Simplistic conceptions of liberty, as an absence of all
restraints, not realizing the abundance of constraints under which
Indians labored. Thought many Europeans:
"Oh, to live like a simple, noble savage!"
Romances of America began quickly to flip from
the presses, which, then as now, made their
big money from violence, sex, political subsidy,
payoff, and scandal.
Finally the great historians of the Renaissance,

Italian or Italian-trained, would, under the very windows of the
already committed Church and the Crown of Spain and Portugal,
and whether they had been to the New World to
conduct field researches or had assimilated
all the data from the field - would announce
in volume after volume the massive evidence designating
the discovered lands to be truly a New World,
materially, naturally, humanly, culturally
rich and varied, capable of Europeanizing
(as would not be the true Indies and Cathay)
but also forever substantially unique.

As early as 1530 there could have been a conference
of all concerned with western conquests, to decide
whether this was a New World, and what it was like, and
what to do with it.
Perhaps the occasion could have been the appointment of
Orviedo as official Spanish Chronicler of the Indies.
Would this group have emerged with divided opinions,
a consensus? It would not have followed the Spanish line.
Nor the Vatican line which followed that of Spain.
It was a New World and generally called *America*.

Thus, the old generation must die for a new paradigm.
Renaissance and Reformation finally defined
what Columbus had brought to their attention.
Now the history of the Americas would be played in
harmony or cacophony with their themes, as well as with
those of natural history and of the Indian peoples.
Although many romantic European males would dream
of it wistfully, including famous philosophers and theologians,
the American scenario would never be
*"Brave virginal hero from Europe
meets virgin American Indian queen,
object marriage"*.

Ferdinand Magellan, leader of the first circumnavigationr of the globe
(1586 portrait in a French book of 'Illustrious Men')

Chapter Five

Portuguese and Dutch

In the Thirteenth century, which, from an old idea of the
Catholic Church, was greatest of centuries -
the century of Dante Alighieri and St. Thomas Aquinas,
of the Gothic cathedrals, of the transfer of the principle of

representative government from religious orders to
political orders in England, Spain and Sicily,
of the founding of great universities, and a
unified Catholic Church from Ireland to Poland
(but with criminal Crusades to Palestine and
frightful massacres of heretics in Southern France) -
Portuguese ships were already fishing the Newfoundland Banks
for the prolific cod. They called Newfoundland the
Terra do bacalao (Codfishland).

In 1270 they were probing the West Coast of
Africa for fishing grounds and plunder. They would sometimes
seize Moors driven from Spain, enslave them, and
deal with their families to exchange them for Black Africans.
In 1291, two Genoese commissioned to sail
West in a search for a sea route to India.
They were never heard from again. By 1340,
the Canaries were invaded by Portuguese Captain Malocello,
but assigned by the Pope to Seville, which was ultimately to be united
with the rest of Spain. In the early 1400's
the humanist Gianozzo Manetti was remarking at the high
intellectual powers that were involved in the Portuguese
explorations of the central Atlantic Ocean.

When Prince Henry "the Navigator" (1394-1460)
became King, the Portuguese ranged
even farther in all directions.
He worked with Italian merchant-traders, who had settled in
Portugal and were already providing expertise and connections.
His interests were also missionary; he even forbade the slave trade
in the latter part of his regime, four centuries ahead of his time.
(There was always Catholic opinion that frowned upon slavery.
As the splendid power of the Church itself was a
historical contradiction of its primitive poverty,
so was Christian slavery, for the roots of popular support
for early Christianity lay with serfs and slaves.)

The Madeiras were taken up beginning in 1418.

The Azores were occupied over a period of four years,
1427 to 1431, by Diogo de Tieve (Seville) and Pedro Vasquez;
in one storm they were blown North from the mid-Atlantic and
may have skirted Newfoundland.
(The population of the Azores grew afterwards, but
did not much emigrate to America for over
400 years, then supplied a
quarter of a million people to the USA.)

Alvise da Cadamosto, a Venetian captain of Henry,
explored the Senegal and Gambia Rivers far down the Coast.
He landed upon the Cape Verde Islands in 1455-7.
(These, too, would much later send their contingents
to New England.)

Sometime in the years 1472-6, a
joint Danish-Portuguese expedition is
believed by many to have sailed Westward.
Joao Vaz Córte-Real was the Portuguese partner
working with Dederik Pining, Hans Pothurst, and the
Polish Pilot Johannes Scolvus.
Probably they explored the coast of Labrador, and
Newfoundland, but failed to locate a Northwest Passage to China.

In 1488, Bartolomeo Dias
rounded the Cape of Good Hope (his name for it).
Open seas to the East beckoned the navigators;
surely the Indies lay beyond, with their spices.
They did.
Vasco da Gama, sailing with four ships in 1497
reached Calicut (Malibar), India, on May 22, 1498.

The price of spices in Western Europe dropped:
by 1503 you paid in Lisbon only one-fifth as much for
pepper as in Venice. In 1509, the narrow
Southern end of the Red Sea, at the Straits of Tears,
was blocked by a Portuguese fort and boats.
Thus Venice could thank other Christians
for helping the Turks to deny it access to the Orient.

The Portuguese were firmly grounded in India, Indonesia and
China. Profits from trade were immense. Profits from the
slave trade were large, too, but, for this,
the source was Africa, the market, America.
The Portuguese sent known expeditions to the
New World in 1499 (Jóao Fernandes),
1500 (Gaspar Córte-Real),
1501 (Amerigo Vespucci) and 1502 (Miguel Córte-Real):
The procession of boats headed West begins to read like
the old trans-Atlantic ship schedules.

Credit for the "discovery" of Brazil is accorded
Pedro Alvares Cabral. He was a substitute for
Vasco da Gama, who was too exhausted to go again forth,
once returned from his epoch-making trip to India.
Cabral went to sea with thirteen ships, and sailed first to the
Canaries, then Cape Verde Islands, whereupon he fell into
the Doldrums. Drawn across the South Atlantic, he
finally sighted land, and ordered boats ashore at Porto Seguro
on April 22, 1500.
After some days he hoisted sail.
On May 1, 1500, Pero Vaz de Caminha,
in an address to the King, described landfall in Brazil
for the first time.

By 1520, sugar in large quantities was being shipped
out of the Port of Pernambuco. The sugar-producing
potential of Brazil was realized quickly, but exploitation
took a generation. Portugal already had, in Madeira especially,
a major source of sugar for Europe, the others being
Sicily, Spain, and the Near East. Puerto Rico joined
in the production of sugar in the 1500's, and in
the next century sugar was introduced to the New Orleans area.
In 1689 came the first sugar cane refinery,
this in New York. (Not until 1789
was sucrose extracted from beets, this in Germany)

Without knowing the extent or characteristics of Brazil, the Portuguese had a problem in organizing its economy. It had developed two methods of exploiting newly possessed land. One was the Italian pattern, the other the Plantation pattern. The first had come out of the common Mediterranean practice of the Middle Ages: given a richly organized land whose people could not be readily subjected, a post was set up at an appropriate point, where trading, processing, and shipping were possible. A troop was stationed to defend the installation, and ships at sea used to protect approaches to the area. Such was employed by the Portuguese in India, which was more likely to envelop the Portuguese than the obverse.

A plantation system would work best where large areas were to be taken over, its people absent or dispossessed, and there tracts of land cut out and turned over to favored concessionaires, who would bring in gangs of compatriot workers or slaves. Some of the plantations of ancient Rome were acquired and worked in this way. So were plantations granted to seignorial lords by the king, as and when the Portuguese were pushing the Moors out of the country. On the islands, particularly Madeira, plantations could be founded.

The system was tried in West Africa, but the African kingdoms could not be conquered and depopulated so readily, that the African Coast was organized by the Portuguese according to the Italian model. Forts were positioned and built at strategic locations for trading and guarding. Other nations followed suit. It was these forts that, in addition to their other functions, carried on a trade in slaves.

Indian-Brazilians could be dispossessed and pushed aside and killed off. Great stretches of vacant land could be allotted, and workers, at first some of the Indians, later Black slaves, could be organized into continuous work teams. Practically the first to understand and develop the resource were a few Jews of Portugal, under intense pressure

to leave that country, as they had already left Spain.
A party of Jews was licensed to sail to Brazil,
and within several years had cleared and set up plantations and
created an export market in sugar of large proportions. The
striking contrast between this instant wealth and flourishing in
Brazil and the slow, pinched development of the Puritans of
Massachusetts a century later needs be marked.

Soon slaves were brought in from Africa and sold to the settlers. A
plantation system began, but, unlike the slave culture that
would come later to the U.S. South, here the same people were
owning and trading; up North the plantation class and trading class
were distinct. For some years the Portuguese attempted
both models of exploiting foreign lands, but
finally settled upon the plantation system.

The Portuguese authorities took an early opportunity again
to expel the Jews, and they scattered - some to Peru,
some to the West Indies (whence in the next century
a number journeyed to New York and other towns
of the continent, but especially to Rhode Island, which had
acquired fame for its large religious and racial tolerance),
and others moved to Holland. With the stupidity usually
characterizing political leadership, the Portuguese government
used Brazil as a place to send convicts and unwanted
persons. And even then wondered whether it was not letting
too many people out of the homeland, a concern that was voiced
as well in Spain and much later in England.

Development of this rich and immense country was slow,
despite its winning independence in 1822, and
was almost entirely due to the labor of slaves.
In the second half of the 1600's, slaves broke free
and set up a federation of new African villages, the
Kingdom of Palmares. Its expansion was halted
and it was finally destroyed by a Portuguese and
Indian army. Slavery was finally abolished
late in the nineteenth century, at which time large numbers of
immigrants began to arrive from Spain and Italy.

The population in 1600, Indians excepted (because uncountable), was about 100,000, of whom 30,000 were genetically and culturally European and 70,000 were Black and in many cases combinations of Red, White and Black. A century later the population of non-Indians had risen to a mere 300,000, in the same proportions. In later times, the population rose hugely.

Portuguese and Dutch, two small peoples
devoted to the sea and trade, bear comparison.
By 1530, Portugal, with its one-and-a-half million inhabitants,
had accomplished a great deal.
The Dutch came later by a century, were really a congeries of small
states, but they too moved overseas spectacularly.

With determination, newly developed skills and impetuosity, the Dutch, practically afloat on their marshes at home and beleaguered by larger enemies - English when not Spanish - tackled the immense job of establishing a worldwide network of forts, trading posts, and ships, with the naval forces to secure these. Whereas the fate of the Portuguese was tied into that of Spain, Dutch destiny was bound up first with Spain and then with England.

In explaining the course of Dutch imperialism, a connection ought be made between expulsion of Jews from Brazil, and throughout the Spanish-Portuguese world, and their settlement profusely in the Netherlands. (There were always networks of Jews communicating from the many points of their Diaspora.) In several places the Dutch succeeded, usually by violence, in replacing the Portuguese. The Dutch went to Brazil, even, but were eventually forced out there.

Settled originally by Batavians and other Teutons, the low countries descended through Charlemagne as fiefs of various petty dukes, and then were accumulated by the Dukes of Burgundy through a century of noble intermarriages until they ended up in one marriage too many, this with the daughter of Ferdinand and Isabella, thence to the Spanish throne in direct line. In 1556 Philip II of Spain inherited them as the Seventeen Provinces, the Northern part already Calvinist Protestant, the Southern portion Catholic. From 1568 for nearly a century, until 1648, revolts of nobility and populace erupted, were stifled, and once more broke out, until, in the end, there stood an independent Republic of the United Provinces in the North, based upon a Union of Utrecht of 1579.

A Protestant, commercial, and seafaring nation, it warred intermittently with Spain, England, France, Denmark and Portugal. The House of Orange changed from a republican institution, the Stadtholdership, a kind of fascist Duce, to a hereditary line, subsisting up to this day, always limited in power by councils or parliaments. Even while struggling against Spain in the 1500's and 1600's the Dutch managed their own Renaissance of the arts, again a century behind Portugal.

The Dutch East India Company was founded in 1602 as the major arm of Dutch imperialism in the East. Its forces took Ceylon and Malacca from the Portuguese, then the Cape of Good Hope, to which many Dutch and French Huguenots repaired, and Sumatra. With its multi-nationalism, agrarian-mining-industrial development, civil wars and racist disturbances, over a period of 400 years, until the formal acquisition of a democratic government by plebiscite in 1994, South Africa would afford some meaningful analogies with the United States.

In 1619, it had been a Dutch ship that appeared off Jamestown, Virginia, as if smelling a new market from afar, there to sell twenty African slaves, the first such cargo to be delivered to the English colonies of the mainland. (Recall that Indians had been enslaved all over America by the Europeans, and that the Spanish had brought African slaves into Florida long before now.)

In 1621 the Dutch West India Company was founded and given jurisdiction over American and African affairs. Its agents became active in Pernambuco and Brazil; they settled several islands of the

West Indies. They operated plantations and were active traders on their own account and for others.

The big bargain was Nieuw Amsterdam. The United East India Company had sent Henry Hudson, an Englishman, to search for a Northwest Passage to the Orient, and it was he who in 1609 toured the East Coast and came upon the Hudson River. A New Netherlands Company was formed then; so with three companies and Dutch officialdom involved, a round of quarrels began over territorial jurisdictions.

Meanwhile a company of Swedes, in a brief fit of aggrandizement under King Gustav Adolphus, settled in Delaware, only to be turned out by the Dutch later on. (After standing off for 250 years, hundreds of thousands of Swedes would return to settle in the upper Midwest.) The Dutch spread also into New Jersey, across the Hudson River. There were hundreds of coastal miles in the total setting invaded by the Dutch.

A village was founded on Manhattan Island and soon acquired a cosmopolitan touch with the arrival of twenty Portuguese Jews who had been expelled from Brazil. The Dutch by then were Calvinist; some Lutherans showed up and were tolerated, but the Governor, Pieter Stuyvesant, would have liked to send the Jews on their way, on grounds that they were bound to be blasphemous, usurious and deceitful in trading. His Dutch superiors at the home office were in partnership with Jews, and anyhow were not as much interested in setting up a new Holy Land as they were in the "bottom line". The Jews stayed, rather longer than did Pieter.

In 1664 an English expedition captured Nieuw Amsterdam and renamed it New York, claiming it on tenuous grounds for their own. Although the Dutch returned to take it a few years later, it was promptly given back to England when peace came in 1674. The local government changed from one Governor to another, no one of them popular with either the Dutch or English residents.

Dutch settlement, quite apart from later immigration singly and in groups, to locales such as Michigan, and notwithstanding its brief tenure on the Atlantic seaboard, marked indelibly the elite to come of New York and New Jersey, and lent to these areas a style, various customs, a technology, even folklore to merge into the American pot-pourri. Grave social problems were presented, too, however, in connection with the huge land holdings granted by the company to a few families, the patroons so-called, up the Hudson River Valley. The Van Rensselear family acquired a million acres. Immigrants were sought, advertisements sent out - deceptive, speaking not of the severe climate or perils of crossing but about fat turkey cocks, *"six weeks sayle from Holland"*, and *"the best clymate in the whole world"*, like Barbados, it was said.

The patroons not only exacted rents, but set up services of supply - milling, sawing, and so on, that their tenants had to patronize. The patroon system was attacked by populists and democrats for being feudal, which it was, treating the large lower class roughly and poorly. It was subjected, in consequence, to riots and rebellions by the poor, the landless, and the oppressed tenantry. But it persisted in some regards indefinitely, serving as the basis of many American fortunes of this day.

For the monumental impact of the first centuries upon America, however, one turns to the Spaniards.

Christopher Columbus, the Genoese who brought Spaniards
the Giant Empire of the World

Chapter Six

Spaniards

Landfall was expected. Birds and weeds were being spotted.
At 10 o'clock of the evening of October 11, 1491,
Roderigo de Triana, mariner, from his watch

aboard the caravel *Pinta,* sighted an uncertain
light dead ahead. At 2 o'clock, white cliffs loomed out of the
darkness. Their estimated distance was two leagues.
When a party went ashore, it came upon Indians,
who were friendly. But they were surprisingly uncouth and
under-supplied with the gorgeous stuff of the Indies.
Still, "Indians" they were to Columbus, and
no one was inclined to argue with him just yet.

Columbus was a typical Renaissance man in some ways.
He was self-taught, eager to learn, highly skilled,
self-confident, ready to fight for his ideas.
He was born in Genoa into a family in modest
circumstances; at least they possessed a small stone house that still
stands, to believe one's eyes and the Genovese authorities.
At the age of 12 he went to sea.
He worked at many jobs in 37 years of sailing,
yet remained full of ambition and cunning.
He was stubborn, an obsessive type.

That he should ever have believed that the Earth was flat is an absurd slander.
Eratosthenes had calculated in the 3rd century B.C. the circumference of the
terrestrial globe with fair accuracy, but these measurements had come down to him
via the retranscription by an Arab scholar, Alfraganus, who had used the
Arab mile in measuring the distance spanned by one degree of longitude,
while Columbus surmised he was using the shorter Roman mile.
He also erred in regard to the girth of the Earth, and thus landed ahead of
himself. Seemingly he had done all research possible. He was an
excellent navigator; that wasn't the problem. He had in mind the
estimation by Ptolemy, the ancient Alexandrian astronomer,
of Asia extending over 180°
of the globe's circumference, instead of 130. He had Marco Polo's
opinion, based upon travels across Asia over 200 years earlier, that
Asia was long across, too long, it appears.

There were no contradictory theories. No authoritative versions of an
extra ocean and a great body of land. So far as one knows,
neither Norse not Celtic sagas,
chanting of the great western forested country, had reached his ears
on his visits to Iceland and Ireland. (He had also sailed to Madeira,

West Africa, England, Flanders, and Tunis. He had been
shipwrecked in the English Channel.)

Whatever input had come his way had not signaled the presence of a
land of great mass, prolific peoples, riches and sophistication.
Columbus was commanded by wishful thinking, yet he made a special
trip to recalculate a minute of arc. He calculated and recalculated with
the incorrect data, always coming up with the wrong answer: 7000
nautical miles were missing. As computerites say:
"garbage in, garbage out".

That lands to the West existed was fairly certain; the Azores, the
Canaries were there, and probably the rest of it if one could sail far
enough and had the courage to persist against all obstacles, especially
the psychological ones. Gossip filled the waterfront cafés, year after
year, of fishermen and mariners returning from strange sightings -
lands, people, plants, animals, monsters of the sea; something might
be made of them. Columbus acted on the evidence.

He chose the right Royal Court, especially since the Portuguese had
rejected him. One cannot imagine that he would have gotten far in
Venice, Naples, London, Paris, or Amsterdam. The Spanish were all
wound up to go. The eviction of the Jews could relieve religious and
middle-class pressures for economic opportunity by providing many
estates and business openings. Still, something had to be done to get
rid of lower class energies also; luckily the Jews were expelled before
being put at the mercies of gangs of demobilized soldiers, together
with the tough chaplains who had been trying to save their souls.

(One respected writer has argued that Columbus himself was of Jewish
origin and converted to Christianity; his chief pilot was, too;
others say, wasn't it anti-semitic to beg support from the
very people who were leading this ruinous religious purging?
But a man obsessed will waive all other considerations.)
Three small ships were a start in the right direction.

The Kingdoms of Castile and Aragon were in a frenzy of nationalism
and unification in 1492. The Moors, who had given Spain some of its

intricate and rich culture by merging Romanic-Catholic culture and the high Arabic Muslim culture of the Middle Ages, were now wretchedly departing for Africa. The Cross supplanted the Crescent (and the Star of David) everywhere on the Peninsula. Hand in glove with the State, the Catholic Church was triumphant. Italy and Germany were mostly geographical areas, with multitudinous ethnic subdivisions. France and England suffered from internal dissension, with respect to feudal barons and counter-claiming monarchs, and, like Germany, were trending toward frightful religious struggles within the coming century. In Spain, as will be seen, religion was a united, supportive, and propelling force on behalf of the Crown.

No swifter, larger and more definitive expansion
has ever happened before or since: the newly
united Spaniards, within a single memorial generation,
from 1492 to 1550,
brought under their flags the peoples of nearly half the globe,
major nations of Europe, and sundry lands
like the Philippines elsewhere. They ruled
most of this empire for over three hundred years.
They explored most of the United States and
established the first settlements in its ultimate bounds -
in Puerto Rico straightaway, in the Southwest a little later,
and in Florida, within the living memory of
people who welcomed Columbus on his return
from his first voyage. How did they do it?
What was it like when it happened?

Like Portugal even earlier, the Spanish began by taking territories within the limits of a familiar world. The Canary Islands were hardly a discovery, for they had long been known to sailors. Still, there suddenly seemed a reason to contend with the French and Portuguese, and the Spaniards finally acquired them, annihilating, with the help of their aforesaid rivals, the autochthonous Guanche people, who were inoffensive except for being in the way of absolute foreign mastery of the Islands.

Once unleashed upon the *Otro Mondo*, Spain's expeditions followed one upon another, then in multiples at the same time. A score of prominent mariners by sea were operative, while the parties of approximately one hundred conquistadors scouted, pillaged, mapped and organized the islands and interiors. This amounts to an incredibly small force for such a large task.

However, their fantasies and greed were boundless, and their energy and capabilities were most extraordinary.

A year after Columbus set sail on his second voyage to America, Amerigo Vespucci sailed in the expedition of Alonso de Hajeda, which sighted the Atlantic Coast, explored it to the South and turned Northward to return to Spain via the Bahamas. Ponce de Leon, Alvarez de Pineda, Francisco de Gordillo, Esteban Gomez, and Pedro de Quexos explored and mapped the coastal areas from West Florida up to Nova Scotia between 1513 and 1525. Across the North American continent, Francisco de Ulloa, Hernando de Alarcon, Juan Rodriguez Cabrillo, and Bartolome Ferrelo sailed the length of the North Pacific Coast from Mexico to Oregon, including the Bay of California. Sebastian Vizcaino followed in 1596, firming up the Spanish claims. In 1527, not long after the return of Magellan's expedition, A. de Saavedra sailed from Mexico to Manila, opening up communications around the world for the Spanish Empire.

On the land, we confine ourselves to expeditions striking upon territory later to be incorporated by the United States. Following upon the seizure and consolidation of Spanish rule in Puerto Rico, Ponce de Leon began to explore the coasts of the mainland and in April of 1513 landed below present-day Daytona Beach. It was Easter Sunday, the holiday of the Feast of the Flowers, Pascua Florida, that, together with hosts of magnolias in bloom, suggested he name the region Florida.

He journeyed North and fell upon the marvelous Gulf Stream. This would soon then become the regular route of Spanish vessels upon voyaging back from Spain. The Stream came to benefit ships of all flags.

Motivated in part by reports of springs affording eternal life
to those who drank deeply of them, Ponce again set out for
Florida from Cuba with 200 men in 1521 and
landed near today's Charlotte Harbor. He was wounded in a
fight with a Seminole tribe and died; his men returned
without carrying out the idea of a settlement.

On the Atlantic side of the continent, Vasquez de Ayllon
touched upon Cape Fear (now in North Carolina);
the year was 1521. Then, seven years later, he returned,
possessed of a royal commission to found a colony
and claim all lands for the Crown, but explicitly and
primarily to instruct the inhabitants in religion and to
convert them to Catholic Christianity. He was ordered to
take along priests, and so he did, one of them being
Antonio Montesanos, who inspired the great Las Casas
in the latter's life-long struggle against the
mistreatment and enslavement of Indian nations. They
settled near the later Jamestown on Chesapeake Bay,
but after several trying years, 150 survivors
of the original 600 returned to Hispaniola.
Fourteen years later, De Soto found
rosaries at their settlement site.

However, in 1528 a group of 500
would-be colonists appeared at Tampa Bay,
led by Panfilo de Narvaez. These roamed as far as
Tallahassee looking for gold, found none, and
set sail for Mexico, but were shipwrecked.
A survivor, Cabeza de Vaca, worked his way westward to the
Gulf of California, arriving finally at Mexico City,
eight years later, bringing a full account
of the peoples he met en route,
of how he was at one time slave,
at another time a healer and fakir,
then nearly cannibalized, while
often hearing tales of fantastic cities of gold.

Hernando de Soto, Governor of Cuba,

himself led an expedition of 600
soldiers to West Florida in 1539.
They went up the Savannah River and explored
the Blue Ridge Mountains, and cut down to the Gulf
where Mobile stands today. The next year they marched
North to near present-day Memphis where they crossed the
Mississippi and headed westward through the Ozark Mountains
into present-day Oklahoma where they wintered.
Returned to the Mississippi, Hernando took sick and died.

Led by Luis Moscoso de Alvarado, the
company hiked West to the upper Brazos River and
wintered near the juncture of the Mississippi
and Arkansas Rivers. The following summer they built boats to
sail down the Mississippi River, thus returning to base.
A strong Spanish claim was established to what came
later to be the Louisiana Territory and West Florida.

The Florida territory was not neglected, but offered
disasters to all who would come. A 1513
expedition failed. After 1550
there were several that languished, beset by Indians,
plague, hurricanes, and the swamps. Missionaries were killed, a
settlement at Pensacola Bay died, and an
approach that reached Cape Hatteras (N.Ca.) by sea
failed to land a permanent party.

After a Huguenot group from France built a
colony near Fort Caroline in Florida,
the Spanish built one farther South, at St. Augustine,
with 1500 settlers, in 1565.
By September 8, Pedro Mendenez de Aviles,
its leader, was able to proclaim the founding there of the
first permanent European Settlement in the continental United States.
The at-first-friendly Seloy Tribe of the Timucuan Nation
burned the place down within a year,
another was built, which was destroyed in a mutiny, and
finally a new settlement was built nearby.

In the next couple of years, the French and Spanish exchanged

massacres, the French retired after a naval defeat in 1580, and the
Spaniards established military and missionary posts
as far up as Chesapeake Bay, losing in
several encounters with the Indians but at other times winning.
In 1586 Francis Drake of England happened by
and destroyed St. Augustine, which was rebuilt by the turn of the
century. Priests under Friar Juan de Silva were able to
convert hundreds of Indians, but the Gualeans finally
forced the cessation of proselytizing.

A Dutch-Spanish map of Florida was published in
1625, displaying the names of many
Indian towns networked throughout the region,
resting mainly on rivers, and not only
St. Augustine but numerous other Spanish
points of settlement and exploration, including
Cape Canaveral (Punta del Cannaveral).

The De Soto and Coronado expeditions could have met,
as they had planned to do, if they had some means of communicating.
Francisco Vasquez de Coronado set out from
Mexico for the North in 1539, and
seized a large Zuni pueblo at Hawikuh that had been
chanced upon the year before by a Franciscan missionary friar,
Marcos de Niza. He proceeded to present-day
Albuquerque, wintered there, and journeyed
to Kansas before turning back in 1541.

Meanwhile there were two spin-offs from the Hawikuh pueblo, with
one party reaching Grand Canyon, another the Texas Panhandle. A
supporting group sailed from Acapulco (Mexico)
up the Gulf of California, into the Colorado River
(today a mere puddle at this point)
which it pursued by boat and afoot to the Gila River.

A great trek was accomplished in 1598
up the Rio Grande into the heart of the Pueblo country.
The Onate expedition of hundreds of men, with

scores of wagons, herds of horses and thousands of cattle,
marched seven hundred miles beyond the
Santa Barbara mines of Northern Mexico.
Upon arrival in the designated area, it built villages,
established churches and missionary centers, and seized land for
Spanish settlers. The New Spain cultural system,
by this time well-developed, emplaced itself directly
on top of the Pueblo and nomadic systems.

In 1609 the town of Santa Fe was founded in New Mexico.
It, and all other towns, were laid out according to
specifications contained in 38 chapters of the
Royal Ordinances called "The Law of the Indies".
Only one village today remains manifestly faithful
to the Code, Chimayo, in the Santa Cruz Valley,
North of Santa Fe, a walled village surrounded by
small settlements using irrigation systems
for farming the land around.

The Code required a central rectangular plaza, with ecclesiastical
buildings at one end and governmental buildings at the other.
A grid of streets crossing at right angles worked out from the plaza.
An arcade of shops and houses surrounded the place and
marched outward to the town walls. These all were to be
built in a uniform style "for the sake of the beauty of the town".
Beyond these came common pastures and woodlots, and
fields to be assigned to each family.
Finally came the open range and Indian country.

Indian relations were, off and on, comfortable.
In the later 1600's, a radical
independence movement was organized by Indians of several
tribes under the leadership of the charismatic leader,
Hope', who sought to extirpate Christianity in the Southwest.
He succeeded in breaking the control of Mexico for a time.
In 1696 a second revolt broke out,
but was also suppressed. Still, some
tribal elements of the Zuni and the Moqui of Arizona

maintained their freedom in the mountainous region
for a long time afterwards.

The Southwest region was too dry to support heavy European
settlement without extensive irrigation projects. About
fifty thousand Indians, a few thousand Hispanic
settlers, and a number of missionary priests managed to carry on
a tidy society there for some 200 years,
until in the goodness of time - or was it "the badness?" -
Eastern American farmers and stockherders arrived.
These tried to exploit the area like a humid zone and
suffered a great many failures before devising
by hit and miss an accommodation with nature. The
sinking of deep wells awaited our century of
keen bits and high power.

At the start, the campaigns against the Moors had given Spain myriad
seasoned warriors who were all too ready to cause trouble or,
knowing little else, to go to war again. It became absurdly easy to find
competent soldiers, both officers and men, who were ready to take a
50-50 chance on surviving an ocean voyage, combat, and disease
while struggling with the aborigines of America.

Promise of immediate riches was implicit in every undertaking; an
assurance of old age pensions was unnecessary.
Loot, rape, enslavement and slaughter;
travel through new and exotic lands;
quick promotions and honorary titles;
land free for the bloody taking;
sinecures; camaraderie.
What more could a Renaissance soldier ask for, or
most soldiers, most times, most places, in history?

Equally strong was the motive of the priest and monk:
conversion of a world of people who had never before
heard the name of Jesus Christ, the Virgin Mary, or
the saints, not to mention Good God Himself.

And the priest could be sure of the wholehearted support of
his King, country and Church, whatever the means required.
Actually, the priests did form a self-confident and
striking contrast to the soldiers of New Spain.

The two groups had long worked out a division of labor.
When fear overcame the soldier - in a storm, in battle, sick to death -
he could count upon a rush of religious solace.
When the priest was beleaguered by hostile Indians,
he could dart behind the sword.
Martyrdom could be provoked at will.
(Thus, as Secretary of the Florentine Republic
during some of these years and as an isolated political scientist
at other times, Niccoló Machiavelli could not
discern in Spain or in the Americas what he wished
every principality to have:
a citizenry who were devoted to civic obligations, and
who were trained soldiers at the same time.)

Motives of the rest of the newcomers - and
they were soon in a majority - were as clear
in their main outlines. Traders of few scruples and
offspring of merchants were quick to follow.
Some of the loot was diverted to them.
Several plants and crops soon came quickly to their
attention as exportable. They could trade in slaves as well,
both Indian and African. For a few years every ship
brought what it needed; then with materials from home and
the wrecks of old boats and the wonderful woods and ropes
that nature could provide, local industries were set up.

There came peasants, artisans, land-ridden sailors, veterans, women of
ill-fame and some of good repute, Jewish-Christian *conversos*
(also called *marranos*, pig-eaters, when suspected of remaining
secretly Jewish) and plain Jews, along with others who were political
dissidents as well as religiously in disfavor. One writer guesses, with
reason, that the emigration to New Spain of the seven brothers of St.
Teresa of Avila was connected with prejudice against the family for
being of *converso* origin. Conditions were rarely comfortable for the
majority of Spaniards, nor for the majority of people anywhere in

Europe, so that one may even wonder why so few made their way
to the New World. One answer is fear - fear of
even more disease than rampaged in Europe.
Fear of the sea, of Indians, of unjust officials.
Justifiable fears.

The answer is hardly exhaustive, no more so than the answer to the
question of why people emigrated from all other countries of the
world, some of whose subjects and citizens at one time or another
over the next four centuries would end up in the Americas.
The motives are usually simple as to the first cause and
then require intensive sociology,
ending up in psychoanalysis,
to bring forth the full complex of causes.
Each person had his unique story.

Only the reason of the slave was clear, *force majeure*.
Perhaps slaves should be honored for their lack of motivation.
They did not want to come in the first place:
let others contend for higher ranking motives of immigration.
Please do recall that the basic, behavioral necessity -
an unspoken part of the bargain, a motive in effect -
was to disperse and exploit the invaded societies.

The vast majority of Spanish emigrants were despatched from
Andalusia, especially from Seville, for the first century. The Crown of
Castile was the formal title-holder to New Spain, though
Aragonese and others were allowed to emigrate. Of a group of about
2,000 emigrants of the years 1595 to 1598,
one-third was female; their proportion had been increasing slowly.
Women were only one in twenty between 1509 and 1539.

Of the men, about 6% carried the title of "Don", a gentleman's
appellation. About half of the males were listed as servants, causing
the enumerator, Peter Bowd-Bowman, to believe that many young
men who were relatives or dependents of other passengers were so
listed. There were 43 craftsmen, 27 merchants, eight royal officials,
four notaries, two pharmacists, one physician and one bookseller.
Titles of Bachelor of Arts were noted for eight, ten were licentiates,
and two held the degree of doctor. Of the 2000, only three

were headed for Puerto Rico, ten for Florida.
About 300,000 Spaniards (with some foreigners among them) emigrated to New Spain in the first century. In the 1600's, about 450,000 went West. That would be 750,000 from a total Spanish population that over the two centuries averaged eight millions, not far from 4,000 per year, a negligible proportion.

The ships in which they came were not much larger than those of the Phoenicians two thousand years earlier. In the period 1506-1540, the average of 178 boats that crossed to New Spain per year was one hundred tons, with a crew of 30 and 15 passengers, plus some goods. The size and capacity of the boats increased steadily. In the period 1626 to 1650, the average of the 136 boats per year making the crossing was 300 *toneladas*, triple the size, and carrying 80 crew members and 40 passengers.

They came in convoys after 1543, and until 1748, a system that the Spanish invented to protect their ships from attacks by pirates and enemy forces. Hawkins, Drake, and other buccaneering patriots of the English Crown had their times of glory and rich plunder, but the development of the galleon, a formidable battleship and carrier, along with the convoy system, eventually put their kind out of work. Over the whole period, and casting a glance at the Pacific convoys as well, which worked in and out of the Philippines, it is clear that the two together practically closed down costly assaults upon shipping. Small settlements along the vastly extended coastlines of New Spain were more vulnerable to pirates and privateers than were their boats on the open sea.

Women attained the New World increasingly. Everyone needed a permit to go there. A royal decree in 1604 warned (when it was too late to do anything about it) that more than 600 women had found berths

on the prior sailing of the fleet for America, whereas
the number of licenses issued to females numbered under 50.
The scarcity of Spanish women, especially in the early years,
nor were they ever more than a fifth of the total of
fully European males in Spanish America
for at least a century, invited miscegenation.

Spaniards, while they might be fiercely nationalist and Catholic, and
often were determinedly brutal, were only vaguely racist, and, from the
common soldier to the most successful of conquistadors, sexual
commingling and in some cases marriage with Indians were common.
This helped Spanish culture and Christian baptism
rapidly to spread over New Spain, from Chile to Texas. But more
important to this end were the organization, the expertness, and
dedication of the Catholic priesthood, largely Jesuit,
operating without immediate familial entanglements.

Most of the Indian cultures were destroyed as entities,
although there still remain to this day many more
authentic ones in Latin America than the USA.
Tribal identity deteriorated while a general Hispanic
culture came into being. Mestizos of the sixteenth century
mingled with the families of the parents, most often the mother.
By virtue of their rapidly growing number, they developed
into a rather distinct social order in the next century.

An unexpected result is that today the population of Hispanic origin of
the United States, consisting of about 13% of the total American
population and rapidly growing, is already third in absolute numbers
of descent after those claiming all or in part Germanic and English
origins, and is more Indian genetically than the recognized Indian
tribal population of the United States, who, while striving to protect
their specific culture traits, are themselves largely interbred with
White and Black strains. The largest Caucasian immigration into
Hispanic and Latin America as a whole would come
in the latter part of the nineteenth century, when finally
(with some representation from several other European
countries, including Germany and Great Britain)
large numbers of Italians and Spanish arrived.

Soon after the opening up of the Indies, the people were being
driven into slavery everywhere. Stricken by infectious diseases,
disoriented by the newcomers, frustrated by the superior weaponry of
the Europeans, the Indians of the Bahamas were transported to
Hispaniola (present-day Santo Domingo and Haiti), their
cultures in smithereens. The pacific Arawaks held hopes
for foreign help against the combative Caribs,
but the foreigners smashed them both.

Here first, and from sympathizers of the slaves,
one heard the theory, possibly well-founded, that
Indians were too delicate constitutionally
to withstand the rigors of slavery, and could not or
would not work cooperatively and under direction.
In any event they retreated into the wilderness,
or dwindled and died on the plantations.
Blacks were sought in ever larger numbers.

By 1619, when the first slaves entered Anglo-America,
a million Blacks had been abducted from Africa and forcibly enrolled
as slaves in the Portuguese and Spanish colonies.
Almost all of them were to be located in the tropical and
sub-tropical regions, few in the temperate regions or
in the mountains, which would also be the case
in the United States later on.

The elimination of professing Jews in Spain and Portugal deprived the
Iberian Peninsula of its most vigorous economic and cultural element,
those who had much of the know-how for modernizing the culture -
researchers, cartographers, economists, instrument-makers,
information specialists (that is, people who managed an informal but
effective system of international political, economic, and military
intelligence). Expectedly, Jewish interests had served Moors as well as
Catholics over the centuries, so that eliminating Jews
along with Muslim seemed to many Spaniards both logical and just.

One should not underestimate the havoc.
It was as would be a sudden expulsion of American Jews today,
with their analogous business holdings and eminent roles
in the professions, education, medicine, sciences,
the media, philanthropy and government.
With 250,000 out of a population of four millions at the
end of the 1400's, Jews constituted double the
percentage of Spaniards that American Jews do of Americans,
6+% *versus* about 3%.

Maybe the Spanish Catholic elite thought that Jews
would choose to convert to Catholicism rather than
leave the country where they had led productive lives
for centuries. If so, they were mistaken.
Pride, religious conviction, and a well-founded suspicion that
as *conversos* they would be discriminated against,
determined most Jews to leave.

Perhaps the Spaniards had dreams of developing this great cultural
complex now by themselves, or by calling in Italians,
emulating the birth of enterprise and mercantile
capitalism in late medieval Italian cities.
Idiocy, one might say, but governments are
prone to such. The Spaniards and Portuguese,
backed by the Vatican, were deluded.

Spain and Portugal would hardly have been able to exploit the
discoveries of their explorers, were there not found an
alternative solution to Italian and Jewish capitalism and
business management, one more adapted to the Spanish character.
Such was the theocratic solution,
offered by Ignatius Loyola and his Jesuit order,
48 years after the critical landfall.

Here the other side of Italy showed itself:
the Papacy, gravely upset by the surge of Protestantism in Europe,
reached out for reformers, not capitalists

who would then secularize society, but devoted Christians,
who would carry reforms into the Church while
fighting its Protestant enemies.

The Jesuits were a major event in world history.
They gave a new direction to Spain,
externally directed, fanatic, bureaucratic.
Aristotle, St. Thomas, St. Gregory, St. Benedict, and
now the Saint in the making, Ignatius Loyola.
Although this line of ideology and action produced instant
resounding results, it ultimately led Spain into dormancy,
while Northwestern Europe and the USA, fallen under
Protestant domination and Northwestern European practices,
including the Jewish contributions, sprang forward -
however huge the misery and anomie -
into empiricism, the industrial revolution and
technological supremacy over the Catholic world.
Casualties of capitalism were high, but the system would appear
to be determining the world's future at mid-twentieth century.

Within the Spanish governing order, the Jesuits,
as an on-the-spot organization, greatly extended the
conciliar and interruptive emergency role always
played by the Catholic Church in the affairs of state.
The Spanish governed New Spain by a relatively simple system,
originating in the Roman Empire and Roman Law,
passing through the great monastic orders of the middle ages, and
carrying into the familial patronage business
surrounding the Throne.

A sub-division into provinces would be followed by the appointment
of governors, upon whom would be conferred a regular and special set of
powers by the Crown, and who would be advised and to a degree
controlled by a Council, appointive and then elective, and inspector-
generals roving about in search of deficiencies and hearing complaints.
Offices were filled by a combination of merit and patronage.
There was much alike, when it came down to structure and
operations, between colonial administrations of
Spanish, Portuguese, French, and English. If one asks:
what of the principle of "consent of the governed?"

one would have to be informed that there was more of this among the small Indian tribes and clans than in the provinces of the Viceroys of the Crown.

Uniquely, however, arose this parallel non-formal *de facto* governmental set-up in the form of the Company of Jesus, that had the ability to penetrate all levels of government up to the Crown itself.
The future St. Ignatius Loyola was a Basque (as was the famous Jesuit of India, St. Francis Xavier), noteworthy because of the small number of Basques to be found in Old and New Spain, and for explaining the extraordinary character of the Jesuit idea.

On September 27, 1540, a papal bull, *Regimini Militantis*, founded the Order, whose vows were "poverty, chastity, obedience". Members of the Order were to be militants of the Pope in the struggle against Protestant Reformation and various national "particularisms" in the Church.

The Order recruited thousands of devoted priests and sent them forth to the Americas, on the heels of the Franciscans and parish priests in many places. They became masters at organizing and bringing administrative order into the frequent chaos of settlements and expeditions. They became the sharpest critics of divine right of kings, whether Catholic or Protestant, and fought continuously against the archaic world order.

A psychiatrist would call "obsessive-compulsive" the amazing set of self-disciplinary and organizing rules that Loyola brought to play upon his followers and to a degree upon all the military, officials, and civilians, whether Spanish, Indian, Africans or Mixed Ethnics with whom they dealt.

Jesuits came under unremitting attack as soon as

the weightiness of the Order was recognized,
by Protestants and Catholics alike, and
of course from humanists and secularists.
What they effectively accomplished in the Americas
over 250 years was to pump lifeblood
into a statal organism that was moribund to begin with and
hardly suited to governing half the world.

As with all authentic, successful movements, their
members were to be found at the centers of policy and at the
farthest reaches, where, as in California,
they set to work building missions,
for teaching, moral guidance, protection, and technical counsel
of the inhabitants, old and new. In the two centuries of
American history, beginning in the mid-sixteenth century,
they helped immensely the Indian population,
even while pushing for conversion,
and in counseling and consoling incoming Europeans.

One can judge a person by the character of his enemies.
The Order was banned at one time or another in a
dozen nations, for example Portugal in 1759,
France in 1764, 1830, and 1880,
in Spain itself in 1767 and on three more occasions,
in Germany, in Brazil, in Italy in 1870, in Russia in 1828.
Allegations against the Jesuits usually
had to do with accusations of secret conspiracy against
the government, evading the rules and routes of the established
Catholic Church, using unfair tactics against Protestants,
supporting revolutions, blocking revolutions -
altogether too many reasons for being
penalized to let one judge the Order
absolutely or offhandedly in generalities.
Over time the Jesuits seemed to be as much the enemy of
cozy arrangements between State and Church in
Catholic countries as of Protestant movements.

Yet they also worked hand-in-glove with
anti-secular and anti-scientific movements,
not without some reason, to be sure, but

on the whole weighing against scientific
creativity and freedom of expression.

That they came to constitute a major factor in the
determination of present-day America is beyond question.

In the broadest vision of their role, they are seen to have engaged in a great Southwestern arc around the United States, matched to the North by a Canadian, Great Lakes and Midwest sweep, as we shall see, and with early penetrations in Maryland and a later massive occupation of the major centers of the country proceeding with the great Catholic immigrations beginning in mid-nineteenth century.

Before the Jesuits came to the "USA", a record of cultural creativity and criticism had already been established. Printing came early to the New World. By 1540 books were being published in Mexico. Religious and legal works were preferred, then "useful" books -
almanacs and the like.

The same would happen in the French and English colonies on the North Atlantic a century later. The first print shop was opened in the English colonies in 1638 at Cambridge, Mass., and was operated by the widow of its founder, a non-conformist minister.

In the seventeenth century, 1,228 titles
were published in Mexico City. Some of these were probably the
first American printed works to circulate in
what would become the United States - in Puerto Rico,
New Mexico, Arizona, Texas, California and Florida.

Eleven years after printing was introduced, the
National University of Mexico opened its doors, and
in the same year of 1540 a University was opened
in Lima, Peru. Colombia soon followed suit.
In the next century, universities were founded in
Argentina (1613), Bolivia (1621),
then Harvard College in Massachusetts in 1636,
Guatemala (1676), and

St. John's College in Maryland in 1696.
The curricula of all the schools were similar,
stressing theology and law, and the medieval trivium -
grammar, rhetoric, and logic - with Latin and Greek.
One can, of course, become better and better at these subjects,
but basic reforms in the direction of empirical natural and social
science, including history, had to wait for
two centuries, when they would strike
the New World first in North America.

Leaders of Early American Thought

Although hardly affecting instruction in the universities of
South or North America for a time,
there was a "new history" of the Age of Discovery,
an outstanding feature of Spain's
Renaissance in its New World manifestations.
Once more the line of descent goes back to Italy and
its "New History", with names like Guicciardini.
Early historians of the New World were also Italian,
Peter Martyr and Pigafetta especially.
Martyr, who never traveled to the New World,
nevertheless culled the reports and wrote a total history,
attending to nature and to anthropology,
a total reality instead of the history of kings.
Pigafetta voyaged around the world with Magellan, and
began to collect the vocabularies and grammars of the
American languages.
The most influential of Spanish cultural heroes was Oviedo, who
was thoroughly impregnated with the Italian Renaissance by
studies, residence, and service in Italian courts.
Born in 1478, he became Chronicler of the
Indies at the Spanish Court of Charles V in 1630.
Again, his history was total, from cannons to butter,
a biology, a zoology, the plants of the future
like rubber and cocoa, scribbled in many notebooks,
published in several volumes during his
lifetime and posthumously.

Desiderius Erasmus, the Humanist of Rotterdam,

was highly regarded in Spain; he called himself
a citizen of the world and a pacifist.

Juan Luis Vives (1492-1540)
in turn demanded that all wars be prohibited, and
called for an education fit for the New World,
its peoples united in a community of nations.

Bartolemeu de las Casas (1474-1566)
began as a clerk on an American plantation.
Seized by the Gospel, he renounced the life of commerce and
took up a scholarly and religious dedication to the true
story of the Indies and protection of the welfare of the Indians.
His book, *Destruccion de las Indias* denounced the miseries heaped
upon the inhabitants of New Spain, creating a stir at home but also
providing an indelible indictment of Spanish culture and rule in the
New World, all too readily exploited by France, the Netherlands,
England, all in short who opposed Spain, including the
United States to come. Yet and as a result, he became
Procurator General for the Indians, in Spain under Charles V.

Francisco de Vitoria was one more grand critic of Spanish colonial policy. He was, with Grotius of the Netherlands, founder of the discipline of International Law. Advocate of the rule of natural law, he argued that no right to conquest existed. Further, the use of violence to convert unbelievers and heathens was unlawful and impermissible. He advocated radical doctrines in the sixteenth century: the right to free trade, of emigration, and of freedom of the seas.

Suarez, of the same school of thought, declared, *"The governments of pagans are as legitimate as those of Christians"*. Too, Domingo de Soto argued likewise and appealed for a new and genuine collaboration between Spain and the Indians, and with all different faiths and nations. There also grew, among the Jesuits of the period, the theory of political science which defended the "right to resist tyranny".

The scholars and humanists of Spain put in a great performance, but their words and deeds were overwhelmed in the clangor of armor and

declamations of *raison d'état*. The story would be repeated again and
again in American history. The forces of humanism and reconciliation
would always, it seemed, arrive too few and too late,
as here in the Age of Discovery.

The Spanish would build an immense partly-new civilization, with
many fine cities recalling the best of the Old World, with idyllic
pastoral scenes of the multi-faceted, grand familial hacienda.
By 1600, Mexico City was a nicely-sized town of
25,000 inhabitants, built upon
a neat plan, with fine architecture. It published hundreds of book
annually. It held a university. It also endured an Inquisition that saw
to it that no one studied subjects "wrongly". As with other towns,
it educated a considerable Indian artisan class,
whose artwork and constructions were up to the European
level of the Baroque Period.

But there did not appear to be a New Human Being,
a Person multiplied a millionfold, who could do here
what his brothers had not done in the Old World.
And, in the balance, the Non-New Man dragged
the level of the Indians down a little - here down a great deal,
there perhaps up - merging them, to be sure,
in a way that would not be matched farther North -
or was this because there were simply too enormous a
population and set of cultures in Central and South
America to be destroyed willy-nilly?

There are many questions to be asked.
Was New Spain in general a success,
more so than the great republic and autonomous nation
of the North to come, the United States and Canada?
Or did New Spain, even after all of the revolutions against
Old Spain ended in independence,
possess less constitutionalism,
less democracy, less science, less technology,
less of the ordinary goods of life and less of
social mobility and freedom of opportunity?

And, if so, was the explanation of Spanish monolithic religion to be
found in the over-burden of Roman history,
in having been ruled by the Moors for a time, or what?
Suppose that the great Spanish cultural heroes had been
supported by a Catholic Britain, while the
Huguenots and the rest remained within the Church to fight. Are we
saying "Would the Americas have been better off
had Henry VIII been allowed his divorce?"

The Spanish experience on American soil was coeval with the
Portuguese, and prompted English and French into sending out
exploratory probes. But these latter and the Dutch would be delayed a
century in setting sail in earnest. And after five centuries passed,
Latinic culture prevailed over three-quarters of the hemisphere. The
Hispanic territories that were lost to the United States in the
nineteenth century - Southwestern America and Florida - even
appear to be recapturing their earlier Hispanic cast.

As present demographic trends are projected, the
United States itself may within a century
enjoy a plurality of citizens of Hispanic descent,
speaking the American language, with an enhanced number of
Spanish usages, adding slants of character, and a heavy fraction of
Indian genes, with definable elements of at least some
Indian cultures. Here may be found, oddly, the major
future influence of Indians on Americans.

The example of enormously successful Spanish lands of the
South affected but few Americans, yet including
Cotton Mather and Samuel Sewell of Boston,
both of whom learned Spanish to reform the Catholics.
Sewell wished to engage in propaganda
"bombing" and said *"I rather think that
Americana Mexicana will be the New Jerusalem"*.
Fantasy aside, Hispanophobia was endemic in the
Protestant root cultures, following the
first great successes of the Spanish
at the end of the fifteenth century.
Begun in envy and hate, whether of Catholicism or

of the riches and power going to Spain in
consequence of Columbus' discovery,
fostered by confessional works of the Spanish themselves,
fed by tales of buccaneering exploits against Spanish forts and ships,
kindled by war after war in Europe and the Americas,
inflamed by easy American victories over weak
Hispanic governments in the Southwest and Southeast and
against a moribund empire as the nineteenth century closed:
the collection of ethnic sentiments issuing from this historical
experience posed more targets of ethnic hostility to the
heterogeneous U.S. populace.

The racial miscegenation that underlay much of the
Hispanic population antagonized and inflamed many
Nord-Americanos who conceived themselves to be of a
purer race of some kind. In all of this,
the failure to appreciate what happened in Spain and the Hispanic
world of the Americas from 1492 onwards
was practically total. Schoolbooks, popular culture,
politics, and religious propaganda in the United States
were continuously hispanophobic. Only after
1960 might a significant change be detected.

Pàre Marquette - North and West USA - The Jesuits

Chapter Seven

The French

The French elite could have made most of North America a
Francophone culture had they put their minds to it. But they were
usually embroiled in prestigious Continental bickering. Besides, they
had less pressing needs than the Spanish and English for a
New World - dietetically, climatically, economically, and socially.
As for sugar, this could come from a couple of
Caribbean islands. And their fish were brought up
from fishing grounds all the way to offshore America,
the rights to which they never gave up.
The seagoing men of Bretagne and Normandie had
long possessed traditions of great lands
on the other side of the Newfoundland Banks.

Still, the French had their share of Renaissance psyche.
In 1524, a little late, King Francis I

authorized an exploration of routes to the true Indies,
it being now acknowledged we were treating
with an intervening set of continents.
Sites for expediting exploitation of nature -
furs, fish, oils, and timber - were a priority,
and possibly the settlement of colonists to back up pioneer
traders and fisherfolk.

Leader of the King's expedition was another Italian navigator,
Giovanni da Verrazzano, the last of the "Big Four" -
Columbus, Cabot, Vespucci, and now himself -
to hoist anchor for America.
Departing in 1524, he explored the
Atlantic Coast from Cape Fear in the Carolinas
to Newfoundland. He ventured into New York Bay and
up the River that came to be named a hundred years later for a later
explorer of the region, Henry Hudson. He made a second voyage.
Verrazzano was an enlightened man, friendly and concerned for the
Indians, whose life was cut short by a misunderstanding. Having gone
ashore in a dingy one day to palaver with some men
whom he had sighted, he was seized, butchered, and
eaten by them before the horrified eyes of his crew,
watching from a safe distance aboard ship.

It is not known whether the Indians were quite hungry, or
whether they took him for one of the bad guys
who had already brought miseries to their kin, or whether
this was standard practice in respect to foreigners.
One source says that he was roasted before eating.
(On the importance of this distinction, one may consult
Claude Levi-Straus, *The Raw and the Cooked*.)
At that, his finale might be considered more sacrificial and
worthy than that of Henry Hudson, last seen alive
set adrift by his own mutinous crew.

Ten years later, Jacques Cartier set off on the first of several voyages
that brought him into the region of coastal Canada
(St. Lawrence Bay, Newfoundland, Labrador, Nova Scotia, and Maine, and
laid claim to these areas by the usual "International Law of
Acquisition by Conquest". He was not perilously contested by the

Indians, who had no "international" law, so far as the Europeans could tell. He was a better explorer than assayer of minerals, for on one trip he brought home a cargo of iron pyrite ("fools' gold") which he thought to be gold, and one of quartz which he thought to be diamonds. He did not, at least, take out his frustrations, as did Columbus and the early West Indies Spaniards, on hapless Indians for not disgorging precious metals.

In 1562, Florida received the French settlement referred to earlier, recklessly, for it was distinctly claimed by Spain, which had the boats to enforce its pretensions; it was wiped out by the Spanish, a massacre five years later reciprocated by the French. But the Spaniards managed the last massacre.

The French made an incursion at Rio de Janeiro in 1555 and were rebuffed, and a party of French Jesuits proselytizing in the Amazon were ousted. The French, however, were never without a few delightful islands in the Caribbean, where plantations were rich, slaves plentiful, and life for the *colons* easy, until the French Revolution of 1789 and the first abolition of slavery by the French National Convention in 1794, amidst country-wide celebrations, at the height of the reign of Terror, an advance unfortunately to be reverted by Napoleon, ever mindful of the interests of the wealthy.

French activity in America picked up with the extensive Northern explorations of Samuel de Champlain that began in 1598, by which time, we noted, the Spanish had created a vast New Spain complete with

cities, cathedrals, universities, slaves and Inquisition.
In 1604, with Pierre du Gua de Monts,
Champlain set up a colony of 80 persons on St. Croix,
located on what is today the boundary between Maine and
New Brunswick (Canada), of whom 36 died over
the first winter. Survivors moved across the Bay of Fundy to
establish Port Royal in today's Nova Scotia.
It was descendants of these people of French
Nova Scotia who, for refusing allegiance
to England, were exiled in 1755
by the English to Louisiana (then French).
There they founded the *'Cajun'* culture.

Upon traversing Northeastern Indian America,
Champlain founded Quebec in 1608.
Thereafter French explorers, with furs, religion, and
national honor in mind, busily investigated the giant region
quartered by the Alleghenies to the East, the Great Lakes
on the North, the Mississippi on the West and the Gulf of Mexico on
the South. Illustrious leaders of the exploratory parties,
who gave names to places later prominent, were
Jean Nicolet (in the Great Lakes region),
Father Jacques Marquette and Trader Louis Joliet (who
moved farther West still and descended the
Mississippi to the Arkansas River), and
Robert de La Salle.

La Salle had two prominent co-leaders, Hennepin and Tonti.
He reached the mouth of the Mississippi by land in
1683. Two years later he returned by sea,
but could not find the River's mouth again and
sailed West to Texas. Turning back, and still looking,
he was killed by his own men, who, reasonably,
were tired of proceeding up one bayou after another.
But their own colony in turn was destroyed by Indians.
Meanwhile Tonti, an Italian conquistidorial type
with an artificial arm of iron, made his way
down the Father of Waters toward a rendezvous with
La Salle, which, of course, failed to occur.

Still, within ten years, Frenchmen had firmly established
themselves in a huge region generally called Louisiana,
with strategic settlements at Biloxi and St. Louis.
Jesuit explorer-missionaries went practically everywhere,
building mission houses, converting a few Indians, and
writing many volumes of early anthropology.
In 1701 Cadillac founded Detroit, "the Straits"
between Lake Erie and Lake Huron.
In 1718, New Orleans was founded.

Cadillac became Governor of Louisiana,
despite a reputation for being a troublemaker
among the Indian nations and a bootlegger of liquor at
"elephantesque" prices to the natives, according to
Quebec Governor Frontenac. Its exploitation
was turned over to a corporation, in this regard
following the English pattern,
the Compagnie des Indes Orientales.

For various reasons,
such as superior economic conditions in the
home country and the cold climate of Canada
(though not in the territory of Southern Louisiana),
French settlement proceeded at a slower pace
than the English - after an earlier start.
Their settlements were well-organized; their desertion rate was
less than of the English colonies; the sobriety of the
Franco-Canadienne culture under Catholic tutelage
could have been a model for the Puritans down South,
had the latter not hated them so.

The supply of immigrants was never satisfactory.
(Nor is it hardly ever to a colonial elite.)
There were numbers of beached sailors and fishermen,
friars and acolytes, and the usual consignments of convicts,
destitutes and orphans, vagrants, and persons deemed a
nuisance for prostitution or pimping.
(The heroine of the important
French novel, *Manon Lescaut*,
later the opera *Manon*, was of this ilk,

transported to New Orleans.) Many poor came as indentured
servants. About 80% of the emigrants went to
the Antilles, 20% to Canada, in the years
1640 to 1715, perhaps
45,000 in all. Louisiana, a little later,
came in for a small share of the emigrants. Since France held
twenty million inhabitants in this period,
most populous of European nations,
the overall rate appears pathetic, only six hundred a year,
most from the Northwest of France.
At the end of the sixteenth century Henri IV
assured his people of *"la poule au pot tous les dimanches"*,
echoed in America only centuries later as a
Republican slogan of prosperity, *"a chicken in every pot"*.
Across Canada and the upper United States of today
scurried the *coureurs de bois*, the forest runners in their
moccasins and snow-shoes, assimilating with Indians often,
and sometimes intermarrying, trading illegally for furs,
which were supposed to be the preserve of government trappers,
and which, during most of the seventeenth century,
were garbing the ladies of Paris .

Matters went fairly well for New France.
A bad of it was: too few people.
A good of it was: they were well-counted.
Between 1666 and 1760,
thirty-six censuses of the Canadian population were taken.
Ecclesiastical baptismal, marriage, and death records were
carefully maintained. Essentially from the fifty thousand
came the millions of *Québécois* of today,
plus two million United Statesians in
Northern New England, Louisiana and elsewhere.

Whatever their overall domineering and occasional
gruesome episodes, the French earned better relations with the
Indians than Portuguese, Spaniards or Englishmen,
these being more intent upon conquest, exploitation and
extirpation than accommodation.
The mollifying, even anthropological, attitudes of the
French Jesuits toward the Indians helped greatly.

Not that the French were free of gross errors.
Indeed Champlain himself could be held initially
responsible for a system of tri-cornered hostilities that
lasted a century and a half. He inexcusably shot and
killed an Iroquois chief. The Iroquois Federation
thenceforth sided with the English.

At all times, it was ordinary for the French and
English to incite Indians against the other,
and to ally themselves when convenient with the tribes.
All manner of diplomatic tactics and nasty tricks
were pursued. Money, liquor, goods, and propaganda
plied the Indians; notwithstanding, the Indians had
already for centuries found enough cause to nourish traditional
enmities, such as between the Algonquin Tribes of the
North and West and the Iroquois of the Hudson Valley region.
(The powerful Mohawk tribe of the Iroquois Confederation
commanded the vital great fault of the Hudson Valley that
divided the Adirondack Mountains from the
Green Mountains of Vermont.)

Agreements were made and broken all around.
Indian allies decamped when they felt like it.
Not that the English colonials set them a proud example:
Colonial militias were the bane of the English regular troop
commanders; they were undisciplined, casual, erratically dedicated,
and prone to quit for home. The Indians had not read
Machiavelli's "Prince", but they knew and practiced
all of the tactics that he described; also, true to form,
as I mentioned earlier, they were no more capable than
the Italian states, the most sophisticated in the world, or
the German states that were chopped to pieces in the
Thirty Years' War of 1608-48,
to consolidate and throw out the intruders.

More destructive to France-in-America than any contrary
Indian alliance that could be formed by the English was the
course of French experience and therefore policy in Europe

during the eighteenth century. This was what wrecked all
that had been so well-founded in North America:
a great set of opening gates in the St. Lawrence region,
a vast area between the Alleghenies and Mississippi,
down to West Florida and New Orleans, and the
huge unmarked stretches of the West as far as the Pacific,
where Spanish claims ended,
English claims were weak, and
Russians had hardly begun to arrive after the
long journey down the Pacific Coast from the Bering Straits.
England and France fought the War of the League of Augsburg, and
this was called King William's War by the colonists.
The Iroquois supported the English, the Algonquin the French.
When it was over, the *status quo ante* was largely re-affirmed.

There followed from 1702 to 1713 the
War of the Spanish Succession, that English colonists termed
Queen Anne's War. Its end in the Treaty of Utrecht
re-sorted various claims, and gave to England monopoly
of the slave trade to Spanish possessions. (Since English
slavers were becoming the cheapest and most efficient as well,
there was little opposition on the part of
Spanish slave-buyers.)

Speaking still of true wars involving the nations and
not of the continual and deadly skirmishing of the frontier, the
next war to occur was the War of the Austrian Succession
(1743-1748), familiarly
known by the colonials as King George's War.
Back and forth raged the contestants in Europe and
on the seas, but then a kind of truce
prevailed and ended the fray in America.
Meanwhile, despite all warfare, irregular Virginia and
Pennsylvania traders had reached the
Indian villages along the Mississippi River.

In the 1750's the French put up a determined effort
to defend the Ohio Valley from English colonial encroachments.

Hot bloods like young George Washington,
who was a land surveyor by occupation, and
had a speculator's interest in land acquisition,
found the French activity distasteful, and were
quite ready to fight to stretch the boundaries of Virginia
westward. He was commissioned in the Virginia militia,
built a small Fort Necessity, and had to surrender his
detachment and the fort when attacked by the French.
The true crisis of North American colonial history came with the
Seven Years' War, in America called the French-Indian War.
Although Quebec was captured by the British in a famous struggle,
on the whole the French and Indian alliance had
conducted itself rather well,
achieving its share of scalps and burnt villages,
minor victories and even several larger ones.
Still, its results were disastrous for French state
interests in the development of North America.
For, in Europe, the French alliance was doing poorly.
And when it was "over, over there", French diplomats
dipped deeply into their American pockets and
turned all of Canada and all of the territory
South of Canada, West of the Alleghenies and
East of the Mississippi over to the English.
Exception was made in the case of New Orleans.
Even Florida was conceded to Britain by Spain.

There would later on occur another chance to be clever,
but the French government failed this time as well,
with Napoleon Bonaparte as fool instead of some King Louis,
because the Louisiana territory West of the
Mississippi which France would soon acquire from Spain
(1801) would be sold treacherously for a trifling sum
(that some say was never paid over anyhow).
The French people, as such, could hardly be said
to have suffered a perceptible diminution of
their living conditions, nor, for that matter, the English an
improvement, with the Treaty of 1763.

Still, because of the imbecility of most wars,
the French-Indian War has reason to be declared important,

and it is well that West of the Atlantic syncline
schoolchildren are taught about it, even prejudicially,
to make them feel that the ancestors of some of them had not been
sold like trinkets over a velvet table abroad, but,
rather, had heroically smashed the French and Indians.
Indeed, such was the imbecillity, that
the victorious English were required by the costs of their victory
to impose burdens on their colonists to the extent of firing up the
movement toward revolt and independence. In this sense, children,
France could be deemed to have won the French-Indian War.

French emigration to America continued, so that French
lineage is traceable in some 5% of Americans.
Catholics trekked over the border from French Canada into
the practically indistinguishable topography of New England.
French Huguenots, exiled or out of resentment at the
treatment accorded them in France, emigrated to
various points up and down the Atlantic coastline.
The Catholic Louisiana contingent maintained a
Francophone character, while merging into the
Southern Plantation culture and its aftermath.
French America, like Spanish, Portuguese, and British America,
would find itself in the relationship of
client to American America.

Apart from demography, political relations
between France and America usually prospered.
A revolutionary alliance, a twin ideological revolution, and
alliances in great wars outweighed
occasional inimical encounters.
Gradually, American presence and culture swelled in
bulk and attraction until they would fashion
more French attitudes, decisions, and customs
than *vice versa*, in war and in peace.
But this would follow the world wars.

Treaty between Plymouth Clony and Chief Massasoit

Chapter Eight

English

Without counting Irish and Scots, who were directly under the English heel, we should consider miserable over a period of, say, 1400 to 1850, most of the English people themselves. Plague, famine, warfare, misrule, technological backwardness, overpopulation, and other processes continuously and contrapunctally composed a

concerted oppressiveness. The new Norman elite
of 1066 took centuries to acquire a taste for
the populace, mostly stubbornly Saxon by culture.
Parliament, a nest of indifferent lords and
bishops in one House, plus another
nest of servitors of the landed and town rich
in the other House, abetted the
afflictions of the common people.

The English elite was not ready for the Age of Discovery.
Bubonic plague had killed a third of the people and
the population was only 2.5 million for England and Wales
as the 1400's began. Death scythed
new crops from time to time until the plague -
this plague, not smallpox and others -
ceased with the Plague Year of 1665.
We are talking about four million people
when we speak of England and Wales in the 1600's,
about the same as the Netherlands or Portugal in number, and
catching up with their higher culture and technology.
At the same time, Scots numbered less than a million,
the Irish 1.25 millions.
Europe all told held 100 millions.

The English were disillusioned over their
One Hundred Years' War with their French cousins.
They would not be able to hold onto a French domain.
Having, with the help of the Church,
burned Joan of Arc at the stake,
they had pocketed their history of victories
and defeats and retired.
So had gone much of the 1300's and 1400's.

The Catholic Church came to own one-third of the land, but,
unlike the feudal lords, was loath to use the
lash and the sword upon its dependent peasants.
The tiny secular elite held title to much of the rest
of the land, and even more when King Henry VIII
disowned the Roman Catholic Church. The monasteries were

dissolved and large-scale evictions of long-time tenants
took place. There were created in abundance vagabonds,
beggars, prostitutes, criminals, and paupers, who would provide
one solution to problems of manning growing fleets and
settling foreign parts of the world. Hanging was still
preferred as a way of coping with disorderly conduct,
such that in the reign of Henry VIII,
a long political generation,
2% of the English people, who then numbered in
all 2.8 millions, were so despatched.

The Crown had been consolidating an inner empire
that consisted of Wales, Scotland, Ireland, and the islands about.
In the process, not at all completed when America was discovered,
it had been gaining experience with difficult populations.
In the early 1600's the Crown thought it might punish
Irish independence fighters by transferring bodily
a hundred thousand hungry Scots to the North of
Ireland, creating the Ulster enclave of the Scots-Irish,
a fateful move, both for Britain and America, as we
shall see. From time to time, well-connected families and destitute
colonists also settled themselves upon the hapless Irish indigenes. Irish
insurrectionists massacred 15,000 of the newcomers in 1641, but
revenge fell upon them with the savage depredations of
Dictator Oliver Cromwell's republican army.

Waves of consolidation of lands into
pastures for sheep surged over the peasantry and village folk.
Each century saw more of them.
Greed and misanthropy were the commonest motives:
sheep were more profitable than people.
(Continental demand for wool was steadily increasing.)
A larger-scale agriculture was continually developing as well.
Probably British cottage industry would have lasted much longer
had the peoples' cottages not been burned, and the industrial
revolution turned in another direction, a better one possibly, that

would reconcile high technology with decentralized production and life.

As America came into the news, King Henry VII, the first by the name of Tudor, was occupied with insurrections in Cornwall and Scotland, working his way toward despotism. When explorers returned practically empty-handed from the West, he could see little to gain from lands without gold or spices; he owned such wretched properties next door. Englishmen of 1516 could, however, read a future classic work, Sir Thomas More's *Utopia*, that purported to describe a country well-governed and prosperous under a set of institutions and with customs that he of course imagined might work; its people were ethically reasonable, economically communist, and politically in a state of liberty.

The narrator of the book is supposed to have sailed on three of Amerigo's voyages. The model was surely drawn from Amerigo's writings and the general European dream of a happy state of nature. A considerable literature familiarized Anglo literati with America. Toward the end of the century, one would recognize in William Shakespeare's drama, *The Tempest,* a wacky setting inspired by stories of the New World.

England was technologically under-developed in 1500, not as progressive as France and Spain: ideas, science, materials, and personnel of the Italian Renaissance had not been crossing the Channel in abundance. These would have included technical innovations, methods of ship construction, accounting and trade practices, improved firearms, and cartography. The exploratory attitude of derring-do was only moderately excited. Nevertheless there were those among the elite who thought something must be done about the open West.

So the ever-present Italian navigator came to the fore,
Giovanni Cabotto, a much traveled merchant prince
who had settled in Bristol in the 1490's.
After fruitless despatches of other men to the far West in
search of tropical products, himself he captained an
expedition that cruised the Northeast Atlantic Coast

before returning. He set out again, 1498,
this time with his brother Sebastian, and
retraced the route, reaching farther to the South,
probably to Delaware Bay. Exaggerated claims in the
Crown's name were filed away for later use.

John stayed back, but Sebastian adventured once more,
this time to explore the Rio de la Plata for merchants of Seville.
Ultimately the brothers disappeared elsewhere
than into history books with the
Anglicized names of John and Sebastian Cabot,
sending, some say, descendants to New England.
The 1500's brought Englishmen to America to seek a
Northwest Passage, which would have been a marvelous discovery,
unless permanent ice overlay it; but,
failing, they drafted maps to be useful later on.
Meanwhile buccaneers ventured upon the Southern seas -
John Hawkins, Francis Drake, and Thomas Cavendish, to name three
of the most famous. Drake and Cavendish rendered the world a
service by duplicating Magellan's circumglobal trip, collecting
treasures from unlucky Spanish boats en route.
Drake also landed at San Francisco,
claiming the region as New Albion, notwithstanding that the
Spanish had been exploring the area for some time
now and had long ago put in their claim.

Voyages to the East Coast of North America
ensued to small effect, but an urge toward faraway lands arose.
One of its propellants was an anthology of accounts of
English voyages everywhere, the publication of a traveler and
scholar named Hakluyt. The volumes of Hakluyt amounted to
consciousness-raising and morale-building for the
still second-rate power.

Other events helped even more, as the century closed.
The Spanish, betting against the mischievous weather,
sent a huge armada to land upon and
conquer the country, and lost. Nor could all the precious
jewels and ores of the Indies buy back the huge
fleet and army that scattered before the furious storm
and was set upon by English craft.

On North Carolina's coast, in the late sixteenth century,
happened the worst drought in 800 years,
measurable now on the tree rings of bald cypresses.
Spanish colonists debarked in the region,
but their survivors had to sail off shortly.
An English group was deposited on Roanoke Island
by Walter Raleigh, but left after a bad year.
They were replaced by another group in 1587
that disappeared before the return of their supply vessel.

In May of 1607, 127 Englishmen and 3 Germans
waded ashore at what was to be Jamestown, Virginia,
and the beginnings of a profitable and glorious future.
Captain John Smith became their undisputed leader
for a time, not without incredible trouble from the ill-assorted and
incompetent group, including the "damned Dutch" as the
Captain called them. He saved some of them from dying at the
hands of the Indians, or by starvation, or by disease
during the first winter. He kept with him always his
copy of Machiavelli's *Art of War*. Like General
Eisenhower and other commanders, the Captain wrote a
memoir of the experience, an incomparably more valuable historical
(and literary) document than most such, including "Ike's".

All might have gone for naught, but for outside help:
Indians taught the squatters to grow potatoes and corn.
Large reinforcements of settlers arrived. Tobacco was
discovered and shipped to the Old Country,

which took to the weed with great pleasure;
and so began endemic lung cancer.

Better, the first lot of African slaves arrived,
transhipped by a helpful Dutch packet. Since it came from
the West Indies, it must have been anticipated.
Who needed hi-tech machines now?
For over two centuries to come, the South would be able to
get along largely with manpower and horsepower,
at a cost to compete in world markets; never mind the
new-fangled contraptions of the industrial revolution.

The first charter of Virginia, granted to enterprising favorites
by King James in 1606, was fantastic.
It gave them exclusive title and total rule over a
hundred-mile-wide belt of land running from the
Hudson River to South Carolina; it prohibited any group
from settling behind them without their permission, and
they were given full governmental powers,
including the right to a private army and navy,
and were invited to repel any trespassers by force.
All natural resources were theirs. They were tax-exempt.

In the year 1619, the Virginians set up
a kind of representative assembly, the first in
America, to which each plantation, a small village
in effect, could elect and send two delegates.
Like practically all colonial institutional devices,
it copied an English practice, giving it a special twist,
a single chamber; there were no lords for a House of
Lords. It is notable that this score -
a Governor, Council of State, and Assembly of Burgesses -
was orchestrated by the board of directors of a
corporation for profit, the London Company.

King James I - he of the Divine Right of Kings and
pronounced to be the Senior Direct Descendent of
the first man, Adam - was furious with his own Parliament just then,

and aborted the Virginia embryo in 1624.
He made Virginia a royal colony and imposed upon it
his Governor and his Council of State.

But the thoughtful corporate headquarters also rounded up
a load of "marriageable" women and 100 London
slum children and shipped them to the aid of the men of the colony.
The women brought about 120 pounds of tobacco each, when
sold on the dock. This was in the fateful year of 1619, and in
1627 additional shipments of about 1500
kids were taken into custody or kidnaped and the survivors
sold to settlers upon arrival. The word "kidnapper"
(kid-nabbing) originated in the 1670's to denote
one who snatched up children to be transported to the
American plantations.

With some frequency, various lots of males were transported,
some of whom were free to sell their services -
the deluded and the hornswoggled among them.
Convicts came early to serve out their sentences,
lightened by allowances for the miseries of the voyage,
through which half survived. Some 20,000 of these
arrived in the latter 1600's in Virginia alone,
about the same number as then arrived in Massachusetts.
Even a hundred years later, Benjamin Franklin could
complain to the authorities of the practice of settling convicted
criminals in America - it gave the place a bad name -
but it took a Revolution to conclude the practice,
and turn the flow to Australia.

Still the temptation erupted continuously. One colony,
later one state, would dump its convicts upon another,
even one county upon another, and one town upon another.
(In the 1970's Dictator Fidel Castro
of Cuba opened his jails to let his convicts take refuge

in Florida. In the 1990's Albanian jails were opened
by the bankrupt communist government and the
convicts let to escape into Italy and Greece.)

Then there were sailors enticed from their frightful hulls,
wanderers or escapees from the West Indies, and petty clerks who
struck a bit of luck and never made it back to Old Blighty. This would
be a common pattern for the settlement of most colonies.

In the main, the arrivals were impoverished persons
under contracts of indentured service, severely enforced.
A man did not know his master until he landed
in most instances, and went into the keep of whoever
bought his contract on arrival, much as it was with slaves.
Masters came to prefer slaves, for various reasons,
among them that slaves on the average were more docile
and performed more work.

When their contracts were done, the men were hired on the
plantations, or settled outside the plantations in villages, or they
picked up promised packets of land, or moved West to squat upon
vacant or Indian land, or joined a crew to return to England.
They were an unruly lot, and not a minority in the colony.
Many deserted before their time was up,
though they would be whipped and jailed if caught.
In a memoir of the year 1676,
Governor Sir William Berkeley wrote,
"*How miserable that man is that Governs a People when six
parts of seven at least are Poor Indebted Discontented and
Armed*". (Correct spelling was not a qualification for governor or
most other personages until the nineteenth century.)

They kept coming, more and more of them from Northern Ireland, the
Scots-Irish. They were already settling in the hills and would pervade
the Appalachian Mountains, where their descendants would remain,
sending out workers into the mines and factories, farther and farther
West, too, but rooting here until the war mobilization of the
1940's, whereupon they exited in a great flood.

Yet never had a motley crowd shaped so fast an aristocracy.
Partly this occurred with the corporate opportunists;
they came and got stuck; or they promoted themselves into big fish
when they might have stayed small fry at home;
there were those of the families of Anglican priests
who could breed and climb the economic ladder;
there were also Puritans and Huguenots among them,
self-disciplined and print-oriented;
there were purchasers of large lands with little cash, too.
There were also, out of the many bums and wastrels and
war veterans, who called themselves Cavaliers
and had been thrown out of England by the victorious Cromwellians,
some clever and worthy characters,
even a few who escaped with modest material means.

Within three political generations a few families came to own and control most of Virginia. They lived rudely, but began to buy avidly whatever was offered from abroad. They appeared to have been there forever, with their slaves, liquor, tobacco, and plantation complexes. Far from being devout, they took their Anglican rites cavalierly.
By the third biological generation they were
rewriting their genealogy and history.

Perhaps one should stress the inadequacies of the Anglican clergy, having mentioned earlier how helpless were the Spanish priests in the face of massive greed and brutal force. The English Church was morally and organizationally depressed when de-Catholicized. At a time when the Jesuits were proselytizing the world, the English Court's anglicized clergy, land profiteers, royal favorites, and younger sons were still splitting the swag from Henry VIII's divestiture of Roman Catholicism, and seeking preference.

Ill-managed multi-national companies, little more than several cronies of the Crown and Court, made deals with the most unreliable elements - cavaliers, marginal religious sects, soldiers of fortune - to go forth and find gold, collect furs, cut timber, set up fishing stations, grow silk, rob foreigners - and do whatever else came to mind.

The situation in the North in what became New England was
markedly different from the South and Middle Colonies.
The Pilgrims, too, had a corporate patent to settle
on lands claimed by the Crown of England,
but, with corporate reorganizations and altering boundaries,
no one quite knew where they were and
whether they had any kind of right to be there,
quite aside from claims of the Spanish, French and Indians.
Their license was *"to plant the first colonie in the
Northerne parts of Virginia"*. They were not the best of navigators,
the officers of the *Mayflower* of 1620.

They were an unprepossessing lot overall:
crew and passengers came to over a hundred.
Two matters worked well for them:
Most of them believed that God was their co-pilot. The
leaders among these divines had the foresight to get
the men to sign a contract, the famous Pilgrim Compact,
that they would behave properly and accept authority upon landing:
this was to keep the party from quarreling and
sundering into vanishing fragments.
It worked.

The second advantage in their situation was
that they had women among them.
These kept the men from quarreling violently,
bucked up the frightened souls,
reduced the incidence of drunkenness,
took care of details,
made the Indians whom they met feel less threatened.
They could be blamed when things went wrong,
provided the men with home-cooking, and
managed other bodily comfort over the cold months.
Tied to their skirts, men were less likely to desert.

Doubtless almost no women would have been so foolish
as to venture into the New World were they not

in the permanent condition of indentured servants,
brainwashed by Old Testament admonitions
on the role of womankind.

The Pilgrims stood offshore by Cape Cod.
After a month of casting about, they landed and
settled down far to the North near
what is called Plymouth Rock today;
the day was December 21, shortest
day of the year, hardly the time to plant -
not that they knew what to plant.
They would have starved to death had not the proverbial angel
for all subsequent immigrants, an English-speaking native,
appeared like Bugs Bunny out of the dunes brush.
Squanto he was called, and he explained the lay of the land, and
introduced them to Massasoit, the local Chief,
who saw to it that they could last out the winter.

The culture shock was too much, however, and
they never did learn to be comfortable around Indians.
They thought all good luck came from Divine Providence
and fantasized that they were an honest-to-God
replay of the Children of Israel in the Wilderness.

Most of the Mayflower party were not along
out of religious motive, and certainly not from
religious conviction alone, which should surprise no one
who has studied the history and sociology of religion.
The core group had, of course, angered many and
suffered much in England - where, as a breakaway
sect from the Dissenters, who had themselves renounced the
Anglican ministry, they were regarded as dangerous radicals.

Holland gave them surcease from religious persecution, but
they were still a caste apart. What they heard there of
America made them think in Utopian (read Exodus) terms, and
when they returned to England they were able to muster the
requisite funds and personnel for the journey. Probably a
third of the little party were continuously in a state of

religious exaltation. Then there were the crew, the
dutiful wives (not all devout), children,
indentured servants, a few Francophone Flemings,
even a Danziger, and security guards, with
Captain Miles Standish in charge.

The most decisive European disembarkations in the
"USA" were those of the 15,000 or so
Puritans of the years 1630 to 1645
who landed in Massachusetts.
They came to avoid persecution (leaving most of their
brethren behind to destroy monarchy and behead the King)
and to run a polity in their own way. Or because their
family made them emigrate. Indentured servants were
numerous. (One of these "White serfs" was a Samuel Lincoln,
possibly grandparent of Abraham Lincoln, six times removed.
If so, America was hardly the land of opportunity
for the Lincolns. It would be no more accurate to say,
"From Log Cabin to White House in one generation", than
"From indenture to the presidency in seven generations".
And perhaps less meaningful.)

On the whole the Northerners' qualifications for survival were
superior to those of people who hopped ashore in the
Southern colonies. It can be pointed out,
as it often is, that 140 of this large number were
college-educated (which meant a certain social
cohesion and presumptuous leadership more than
high technical, intellectual or material qualities).
Ninety were theologically trained, which allowed them
a valid basis for a theocracy, if they could
figure out a proper way of covenanting
among themselves - which they did.

Governor Winthrop had a ship of 60 tons
built by July 1631, and a sawmill was
built at Portsmouth (N.H.) in 1635;
the rivers and streams flowing toward the Atlantic Ocean would

provide many sources of water power,
from Maine to Georgia.

An invidious comparison is invited with the unfortunates who had gone and continued to go to the Chesapeake Bay area. So many died in Virginia or returned home. One remains aghast at the awful poverty or compulsion that let them face a likelihood of death by drowning, disease, hunger, or hostilities with Indians, or maltreatment and a wretched subservience to an unknown master for half a dozen years or until maturity, and a prolonged or absolute separation from the joys of domesticity, such as family, mate, or children afforded.

But, then, too, possibly the lucky, beloved, strong, skilled, or quick might survive, with a spread of land in fee simple, a tract stolen from dispossessed Indians, a possible escape into the forests, rumored gold mines, envisioned settlements free from the abominations of harsh authority. Better than suffering in England, begging, starving, wandering, prison, whipping, sexual exploitation for woman or boy, a grudging reception wherever given precarious employment, arbitrary imprisonment, forced service in a barbarous army, impressment into a buggering navy, or a life at sea.

Over half the immigrant arrivals in America from Britain in colonial times were indentured servants or convicts. Historians, try as they might for three centuries to prettify the picture of the early settlers, have come around to granting it authenticity. It is well, because you cannot write a prescription for a country's problems without a true case history; observing symptoms is not enough, especially when obscured by a false history.

In the years from 1630 to 1700, an estimated 100,000 persons entered the English mainland colonies, the large majority from England, with some French, German, Scots, Welsh and Scots-Irish. About three-quarters of them would be considered of the underclass, as the term has

come to be applied today to some 20% of Americans.
With descendants and some 30,000 Blacks and 200,000 Indians,
they constituted a population of about 500,000.
Comparably, the English-controlled Caribbean Islands
contained 50,000 Europeans and 150,000 Africans.

The wretched conditions of travel and living often killed
en route and upon arrival as many as half of those
who had begun the journey, that is, a 50% mortality rate
(the Spanish death rate seems to have been much lower.)
The outflow from England amounted to about 10,000 a
year from a population pool of perhaps 5 millions,
a higher rate than that of other nations
sending people to the Americas. This may be a
measure of the excitement for adventure, or of greed, but it more
likely is correlated with higher degrees of poverty and
social disorder within the English inner empire.

There were Englishmen who expressed alarm at the outward flow, but the elite was glad to be rid of practically all of them. The Kings and Bishops had a strong distaste for Dissenters; the local authorities Couldn't get rid of the poor and criminal elements fast enough. Even when the Dissenters turned out the monarchy for two decades, they were pleased not only to see cavaliers take to the sea but also the Puritans and Levellers who were pressing for too radical a republic.

Sir Josiah Child, a vastly successful London businessman, large landholder, and despotic Governor of the East India Company, invented various schemes for putting the poor to work in England, but when it came to the discharge of people to America, he waxed eloquent at the opportunity this had been affording for getting rid of the dregs of the population, people, he said, who would have had to be supported all their lives, or crowded into jails. This was 1688.

History begs conversion into irony. Would the French and Spaniards, with their better organized, more rational schemes of settlement, have been capable of denying ingress to English boats had not the English lower middle class turned partly into a class of religious fanatics and had not the lower classes been miserable and brutalized and banished? Does America owe much of its character even today to England's insane criminal laws, the casting out of the poor, and the enclosure movement?

Was it not of this same large class, perhaps one-fourth of the population, the underclass, without hope in life, that England also bludgeoned together the crews of its rapidly growing navy in the 1600's and 1700's? How could the navy sail the seven seas with this tortured humanity? Slave-driving officers with powers of life and death over them, for one answer. As High Lord of the Admiralty frustrated by his admirals, Winston Churchill once jested: "Traditions of the Royal Navy, bah! Rum, prayers, sodomy and the lash!"

It is neither exaggerated nor partial to say that, for a person to go to America as an indentured servant meant that hope for a decent existence had been abandoned. He and she were the bottom of the very large base of the English, Welsh, Irish Catholic, Scots-Irish, Cornish, Manx, and Scottish peoples of Greater Britain.

A gluttonous, selfish, inconscient, stupid and quarrelsome ruling class, stinking of nepotism, continuously engaged in war or civil strife or feuds, or about to so engage, could not attend to the direst needs of its people. Yet such was the helplessness of the people, and the character of their exploitation, that they could not escape, nor help themselves, nor revolt except to risk horrible retaliation.

The idea that America was spared the religious strife of Europe is common but delusive. By the time that Americans became "reasonably" (never fully) tolerant, Europe, in fact and in law, had already arrived at the same stage. Every colony had its prejudices and all the colonies were intent upon destroying the religion of the Indians: is it not religious warfare to kidnap, bribe, dispossess, and kill a people whenever possible, all the while proclaiming their inferiority, wickedness, and savagery and blaming it upon their religious beliefs? With major precedents in the Florida region under Spanish control and the Spanish missionary pushes into the great Southwest of the

USA-to-be, and with the French priests hard at work alongside
gunslingers and traders in Canada and the Midwest,
Puritan onslaughts in New England,
coordinated with assaults along the line moving Southwards,
can be regarded as part of a three-pronged attack
against Indian religion and culture.

Amongst themselves, the Europeans were equally uncharitable.
We have mentioned near exceptions - in Rhode Island and
Pennsylvania - in persecution of differing Christians.
Catholics and Jews had to be on the *qui vive* everywhere.
the Presbyterian Ulster Irish were unwelcome in most places;
Anglicans in New England.
It truly never ceased, from the center to the outermost
reaches of Empire - to the Philippines, to Hawaii,
to Samoa, to Alaska:
Christians, it seems, at least of the Americanized type, could
never let another cult rest in peace. Nor could they
let the non-religious alone.

Beyond New England were cool acquaintances in the colonies of New York, New Jersey, Pennsylvania, and points South. The New Yorkers, I have already indicated, were Dutch and then English and a variety of others in the more tolerant ports of New York City and Newark. It had rulers from London for most of the time, no one of note for the good. One Governor, not content with the usual bribes, let his wife confiscate the clothing of any ladies dressed to her taste and himself was a transvestite who walked the ramparts of the town in the evening dressed in women's clothing. The peasants under the patrons and the English land-grabbers grew more and more restless, at one point taking up arms under a German named Jacob Leisler, to no avail.

Pennsylvania, to modern tastes, would be the best of the lot of colonies. Founded by William Penn, a radical and Quaker (a sect contemned by English Church and Court alike

even more than the Puritans) managed to get permissions
from the Crown for land and a free constitution.

Penn journeyed to America, took charge of affairs,
founded the "City of Brotherly Love",
made fair treaties with the Indians,
drafted democratic constitutions and laws right and left,
and let his weight be felt in affairs of Jersey and Delaware.
For a century the Quakers, from a highly
effective government, ran the colony. By admitting on a
not-quite-equal footing practically all Christians,
even Jews and Catholics, and non-Anglophones as well,
they were able to generate a first-class democracy
with a well-functioning assembly.

New Jersey began as a typical racket, 1664 variety.
The Duke of York obtained a Crown grant to a
huge section of the coastal region (including
Dutch holdings); he gave what is now New Jersey to
two cronies; these expected large profits from land sales.
However, following a politically correct trend,
they set up a representative assembly and promised
religious tolerance. Squabbling over boundaries, possessions, and
jurisdictions took up most of the century.

The area of now-Maryland attracted Lord Baltimore and a band of
Catholics, the first legitimately to settle in English possessions.
They ran Maryland until outnumbered and displaced by Protestants in
a coup d'état, and underwent a mild persecution thereafter.
Delaware came into William Penn's hands.
With slaves and Virginians, Maryland, and for a time Delaware,
both situated on Chesapeake Bay, fell within
the orbit of Virginian plantation culture.

Charles II, in 1663, called back to the Stuart throne upon the death of

Cromwell, granted eight noblemen who had survived the Cromwell republican dictatorship the whole region from Virginia to Spanish Florida, and from the Atlantic to the Pacific Ocean to own and rule. Shortly they hired the best political consultant they could find, the philosopher John Locke, to draw up a constitution for the Carolinas. This turned out to be, contrary to Locke's progressive reputation, a prescription for a noble house, a popular house with limited suffrage, and a governor appointed from England. It did not work well; it read insanely in light of settlement conditions.

To the South of Wilmington and other settlements of (now) North Carolina, in 1670, a group of West Indian planters from British Barbados squatted at the mouth of the largest river system of now South Carolina, there founding Charlestown, where, before long, they were joined by sundry French Huguenots, Scots, and Germans. The Huguenot role, in the North (the Hudson Valley and Boston) as well as the South (New Bern, N.C., and Charleston, S.C.) was large relative to numbers, as was the Jewish part, only 3500, by the time of the Revolution, in Newport, R.I., Philadelphia, in the North and in Charleston and Savannah in the South.

(Charleston's was a culturally superior mixture from the start and the town developed into the outstanding cultural center of the ante-bellum [Civil War] South, perhaps sharing honors with New Orleans, which fell into the Union a century and a half later with the Louisiana Purchase, and overlaid the slave culture with a Spanish-French coloration.)

The colony of Georgia had its piquant story, too, but it was delayed until the early 1700's. Here, once it appeared that the Spaniards would not insist upon destroying any settlement, the initiative was taken by a group of English philanthropists, led by James Edward Oglethorpe. A first party of settlers was landed at the mouth of the now Savannah River in 1733, 126 years after the first Virginia settlement. The same year these were reinforced by

40 Jews whose ship happened in and
who were granted permission to settle. The trustees of the
foundation for Georgia, for that was its form of organization,
promised to defend the territory and Empire
against the Spanish to the South, if needs be.
Their colonists were to be restricted to penniless and homeless
Londoners of promising character. Thus the persistent problem
of the impoverished English underclass was to be solved.

As to what they would do upon arrival,
they were to grow silkworms on mulberry trees
and send the silk back to Britain where it would
command a fortune upon sale there and abroad.
The town of the settlers was planned in every regard,
with the command post, or one could hopefully say,
the civic center, in the middle of the rectangular set of blocks.
An allotment of land would go to each settler as he earned it,
the system of inheritance was to be closely regulated.
No alcohol was to be permitted within Georgia,
there were to be no slaves, and
no religious fanatics were to be permitted entry.

What a noble scheme!
Everything went wrong.
Only some timber, pitch, and plants went out.
The mulberry trees proved to be of wrong species.
An Italian silk expert who was sent in tried his hand at
production and processing, then disappeared into the wilds.
A set of designs of equipment and processes
for silk-making that an Englishman had stolen
in Venice could not be materialized. The men often refused to
work. Many deserted long before their time was up.
Alcohol was soon appearing out of home-made distilleries.
Slaves were sneaked in from South Carolina.

Year after year, more that was novel was abandoned,
the settlements fell into a state of disrepair, and
neared abandonment. The trustees gave back all their rights
to the Crown, having spent more than they

felt they could afford out of pocket, and a new regime, with the
typical vices of the age, came into being.

Early Georgia was a tragedy.
What was not? - one inclines to say.
Not only there, but in most of America,
a great many Americans were in today's parlance
"engaged in the drug trade:" as drug producers,
drug distributors, drug dealers, and drug users.
We can hardly guess at the incidence of trade and use,
as there were no restrictions on the carriage of drugs
like cocaine and opium into the country,
or the hallucinogenic drugs. People were trying
everything that the natives and travelers said might cure
what ailed them or contribute to the meager pleasures of life.
The country was not excited about the problem,
as it is today, but accepted the burden of needed controls
on an individual basis.

The major drugs
(and the largest causes of death unto this day)
Were alcohol and tobacco. Tied in with these was sugar, used to make vast
amounts of rum, and also employed in the highest degree possible by
every sort of person and culture. Corn whiskey was invented early by
a man named Thorpe, and before long the Southern wilderness was
studded in a thousand places by personal stills.
Coffee, known for the first time,
was soon heavily traded and consumed.

In fact, if one were to journey down the coast
from Maine to Florida, ranging into the western hills,
one would find that half the population
was living from and on drugs: alcohol and tobacco, and
in the occupations concerned with these:
dealing, transporting, slave-trading, slave-holding,
piracy and smuggling, Indian hunting, and all other

criminal activities that could be added to the picture
of a huge social system on the make.

It is a forbidding lesson: between
1607 and 1700, roughly,
starting from a broad spectrum of desires -
the whole of human values one could say -
stretched over nearly two thousand miles and hundreds of
miles in depth, there occurred a consolidation of societies into
oligarchies. The colonies had each its own type of madmen and
fanatics, idealists, who wished and worked for a new world,
but it was all settled into oligarchies
by the end of the century and would
become more so until the Revolution,
which, in one way, was an attempt
to return to the restless womb of the 1600's.

The colony of Georgia was last of the string of experiments in
colonization to be credited to the English.
The seventeenth century was an anthropological
renaissance in North America. Running down
from the St. Lawrence French, the Algonquin, the Iroquois, the
Puritans, the Rhode Island and Connecticut Dissenters, the New York
Anglo-Dutch, the Pennsylvania Quakers, the Virginians, the
Carolinians North and South, the Cherokee, the Seminoles,
ending with the Florida Spaniards: there was a
fifteen-hundred mile series of novel, busy,
crazy, interlocked, interrelated,
but autonomous ventures.

Never again would this happen.
With the passage of the 1600's into the 1700's,
cultural uniformity and crystallization would set in.
Cultural differences between early eighteenth century
America and post-Revolution America were,

in important regards, less than those between
seventeenth and eighteenth century America.
For those who like the new and exciting,
injustices on a grand scale and
opportunities to match, changes galore, the
seventeenth would be their preferred century.

It may not be coincidence that the culture
of eighteenth century England, too, was duller
and more conventional than the culture
of the preceding century.
One exceptional force began in the second half
of the eighteenth century to play upon the scene,
however, an elite movement, "the Enlightenment",
more in America than in England.

The mind of Englishmen,
no more than any other mind,
could hardly revolutionize itself in the face
of the New World's challenge. The cry to be different
from the old is the most agonized of the age.
Yet ordinary men knew not then, any more than
now, how to be different except by becoming wilder.
Many of the customs, practices and ideas of the settlers
from North to South were medieval, not late medieval,
but early medieval for that matter.
Still virtues of Americans in the 1600's
were the considerable virtues proceeding from the
miserable and mad, the raging peasantry, the
holier-than-thou, the misfits.

Ms Lazarus' inscription carved
upon the Statue of Liberty
in New York Harbor, erected in 1886,
inviting in the wretched, yearning, huddled masses,
suits the earliest immigrants better, much better,
than it does the immigrants
of the late nineteenth century,
when Bartholdi the Alsatian,
using his mother as a model,

was sculpting it. What it does not say
about all of them is more important.
Indeed, it would be well to erase the inscription and
let the Statue speak for herself.

Improbable Survival

Chapter Nine

Africans

Slavery was big business, and,
four hundred years ago, as now,
Africans were under-represented in top management.
Worse: they were the product itself.
It all had to do with other end-of-the-line products.
Sugar, rice, tobacco, became crops with

world markets in the 1600's, cotton and
coffee later. Their life cycle began with
large cheap tracts of land; money for seed;
labor for breaking ground and following through on the
several stages of production prior to
shipment abroad.

Capital came from Genoa, Amsterdam, and London,
where bankers had learned all about techniques of
extending credit, bills of exchange, limited
partnerships, joint-stock enterprises,
marine insurance, and double-entry bookkeeping.
(Economists who demand free enterprise in
all walks of life must logically see in the
slave trade a practically perfect model of
free enterprise, taking human beings as the
commodity instead of silver, corn, or pork bellies.
Would they interfere in this trade, and, if so,
how would they object to interference in
any trade that societies disapproved of?
The labor of children, for example.)

The English colonists were not good at figures,
but could learn from a century of Spanish, Portuguese,
French, and Dutch experience.
Intensive labor, working in gangs, under overseers, was
required for the New World agro industries.
The Atlantic slave trade was 200 years old
before it could find a customer in Virginia.
Several colonies established thereafter did not like the idea.
Rhode Island passed a law in 1652 that
limited to ten years the term of any forced labor.
(Fifty years later it began a career of slave-trading, and
did not free its slaves until 1784;
the slave trade tempted many Puritans
beyond endurance.)

The plantation economy, under capitalism or socialized enterprise,
coveted a large supply of underpaid workers.
The earliest American exploiters of such economic possibilities,
the planters, brought in the underclass of Britain.
Not enough of these could be forced or induced to come,
and they were troublesome. The colonists dragooned the Indians.
The Indians melted away: they resisted, they caught
fatal diseases, they retreated into the wilderness.
The invasion of America might have come to a halt
if no source of slave gangs were found. Wrote the Governor of
Maryland to Lord Baltimore in 1664,
*"Wee are naturally inclin'd to
love neigros if our purses would endure it"*...
The Carters and Byrds and Harrisons, who got in early
and big in Virginia, were beseeching traders in the West Indies
to ship them more fine healthy slaves.

Often, it was the newly acquired slave, with an
oral tradition stemming from long generations of the
trade as experienced in Africa, and familiar with the
more "advanced" slave cultures of the Islands,
who taught the inept master some aspects of the
"proper" relations between them.

The English and their colonists took some time to settle upon a
word and spelling for black or brown persons of
African origin who had traits described by physical
anthropology as Negroid. The time taken here to
explain related words evoking such burdensome
prejudices will be, I pray, forgiven.

The Portuguese and Spanish, exemplars for the English in these
matters, used the word "Negro" meaning Black, while the
French used "noir", also meaning Black and then
"nègre" that seems to be derived from "Negro" and
acquired a negative connotation. Englishmen used

the word "Negro" and an early citation of the negatively
connoted "nigger" is to be found in a work of Charles Lamb
of the late 1770's.

A law of 1654 of the colony of Rhode Island,
already referred to, used the term "neger" in
forbidding involuntary servitude for more than ten years,
whether of White, Black, Indian or interbred.
This seems to originate from the French word
"nègre" and to be the source of the term "nigger",
which therefore may have come from New Orleans and/or
slave-trading circles into common Southern usage.
To the Anglophone, the two words would sound alike.

The term came to be universally used in America,
except among a small group of sensitive intellectuals, but
is now generally avoided for being impolite and indecent;
it is also likely to cause fights. In the late
1900's the term "African-American" came forward,
coursing ahead of "Black", far ahead of "Negro",
which some Blacks, especially the younger,
claimed should be abandoned.

The term "*mulatto*" to denote a half-African or
partly African began with the Spanish,
meaning simply "the mule". The term "*mulat*" was
used in 1604 in French, but competed with
"*mestice*",(Portuguese), "*métis*" (French), and "*mestizo*" (Spanish),
from the cloth that mixes two different fabrics, "*mestiz*".
An early English spelling of mulatto occurred in
Francis Drake's *Voyages* as "*mulatow*".
The term is improper; it meant "mulelike" in Spanish,
which is not only unkind but incorrect;
no one described Africans of mixed race or
Afro-Europeans, *au contraire*.
Spanish and Southwest Americans, Floridians, and
Puerto Ricans used *mestizo* to mean of
mixed race, but generally the term came to be
applied to Indian-Caucasian mixtures.

The French word *métis* is better,
for it means simply a combination of races.

The term "race" itself offers problems.
Questionably, the races are often divided by physical
anthropologists into Black, White, and Yellow, with
Red being attached to the Yellow, and these are given
terms like Negroid, Caucasoid and Mongoloid, the
"oid" meaning "like". Some separate the
Red and Yellow, some separate
Polynesians and Melanesians of the Pacific.
Some separate East from West Africans
The Caucasian itself is divided into several races or
sub-races, heavily intermingled:
East Indian, Mediterranean, Alpine and Nordic,
with East Indians increasing as rapidly as all the
rest, and Nordics rapidly disappearing.

Others add the Celts to the other three, but
these are so intermingled, with traits so generalized,
looking something like Mediterraneans at
one moment and like Nordics the next,
that there is little to pin a name to,
except their speaking originally a kind of Gaelic and
sharing a long-ago basic culture that is still vaguely operative.
Finns, Hungarians, Basques, Guanches, and Gypsies
pose hard problems of classification.
But so it goes with Reds and Blacks, too.

Returning to persons of mixed African and European ancestry,
refined terms have been used,
quadroons (fourth-Black), octoroons (eighth-Black) and so on.
These terms have historical importance;
Adolf Hitler did not invent racism.
Some parts of the human species, and all,
at some point or another, have been racist.
The Hebrew Bible is colored by racism, and

has for 3500 years, more or less, been
an ever-present source and danger of racism,
a phenomenon that relatively more Jews than
Christians have been ready to recognize.

To be constructive today, one would refer to
Americans of mixed European and African ancestry
as Eur-African Americans, when the designation is
good and proper; then one would have Eur-Asian
Americans, Eur-Indian Americans, and Euro-Americans.
Skin color is a cosmetic factor, and should be named separately -
possibly as white, pale, pink, ruddy,
tan, olive, dusky, brown, and black -
all of these present by the millions in America.
Some anthropologists have maintained not only that
there is an original admixture of races in Black Africans,
but also that most have acquired Caucasian elements
in the course of time. At one point, the
almost neutral and even favorable word
"colored" was employed widely in the North, where
well-disposed adults and well-behaved children
used "colored" as a preferred word.

Inasmuch as no one in the world is un-colored except
rare white-skinned albinos - who incidentally occur
indiscriminately among Africans - and, moreover,
the color of people's skins - including Caucasian or
so-called white skins - runs along a rich palette,
from deathly pallid to tubercular blush -
it would seem to have been a logical way to
ease into a system of referring to a given person by
one's individual skin color regardless of race.
Early on, Indians called Europeans "Palefaces",
an appellation no more precise than "Blacks".

A microscopic specimen of any organism will
afford a DNA determination of

relationship among organisms. Surprises
abound, amidst myriad discoveries.
People who thought they were by accident
named "Cohen" found that they shared a particular gene
with other "Cohens", "probably going back
on a line of Hebrew priests to Biblical Aaron.
South African Lembas (Bantuphone) also
tested positive for the Cohen gene, authenticating
their age-old Hebrew practices and tradition that
they were led out of Judea by a priest named Buba.
Almost certainly there are "cohens" among
their American descendants.

However, the distinction of color is in the end
subordinate to manifold distinctions of wealth,
education, respect, freedom and power
that separate White and Black.
The war front of invidious discrimination is long, and
American history is a history of this war, too,
where salients and thrusts penetrate the resistance,
now here and now there, and not all engagements are
victories for the forces of all colors.

The slave as product was grown and cultivated in a
thousand villages of coastal and central Africa,
snatched by hostile or greedy raiders and chiefs,
sold to traders, brought to stations along the African
Atlantic Coast, sold again to ship captains,
carried to seaports of the New World,
sold under contract or by auction and
turned over to its purchaser, the planter.

Inasmuch as most of the enslaved were prisoners of
war, hunters, kidnaped children and poor workers, or the
enemies of ruling families, and in all cases
had to have some physical qualities to recommend
them to potential purchasers, the relative social
status and individual qualities of the transported

Africans would have been rather above the average
level of the Whites coming in from England, Scotland, and
Ireland at the corresponding time.

Most were bought at fortified trading stations,
set up at first by the Portuguese and then by the
several other trading nations at a dozen points
around the West African hump, the Guinea Region, into
Nigeria, gradually reaching down to the mouth of the
Congo River and then much farther to Angola.
Others were purchased at recognized points along the shore
where boats from the ship would beach to
deal with the slavers.

About a fourth of all American mainland Africans
came from the Windward Coast and the Gold Coast,
another fourth each from the Bight of Biafra and Angola,
and the balance from several minor locations, or
from the West Indies unidentified as to
where they or their folks had originated.

Of those whose cultural origins were known among
the 91,591 Africans
entering South Carolina from 1700 to 1808,
Bantus from Angola and Zaire were the most numerous.
The Mande culture of Senegal also was represented by
large numbers of people. Many came from Ghana,
Liberia, and Nigeria. A few hundreds came from
as far away as Mozambique.

Bantu culture has persisted most strongly in the Sea Islands,
coastal Virginia and greater New Orleans.
The Mande of Senegal are believed to have exercised
the largest effect on Caucasian culture,
while the Bantu have had the largest share of
maintaining African culture *per se*.

African rulers of the places of exchange made
considerable profits from the trade.

They suffered the boats to come, and the stations
to be built, and kept order outside the forts.
They let slaving parties pass coming and going, and
themselves provided such parties on many occasions.
When the Ashanti went to war, for example,
which they did with increasing frequency,
they would bring back as many prisoners as possible
to sell as slaves. If they had been Mexican Aztecs,
they would have sacrificed and eaten them.

Instead, they got manioc and maize from the foreigners, and
these New World products became their staple food ever after.
Black crew members of slave ships were not rarities.
Let no one argue that all Africans were buddies,
who wept at the misfortunes befalling their race.

Other items were traded at these African stations:
Europeans brought in guns and gunpowder,
rum, textiles, knives, metal ware, and ornaments,
seeking in return - besides slaves - gold,
hardwood, ivory and wax.
Between 1650 and 1700, the price
of a slave at the African source, "at the wellhead",
was between 3 and 4 pounds sterling. The price
rose to 17 pounds in 1740 and
fluctuated around that level for some years.
A low price, indeed, for lifetime services
and the services of descendants forever after!
But, as the world should know, it
was a bargain with the Devil.

The business of the slave trade was not without severe risk -
to the product, and for other less important reasons.
Perhaps over the whole period only half of those
persons who were removed from their village lived long
enough to be unshackled at their new destination.
Crowding, disease, brutal treatment, exhaustion,
a killing sun, starvation and thirst, a ship

foundering in the storm, gunfire and sinking by hostile boats:
these factors culled the dreadful immigration.
When the prisoners were able to revolt,
casualties were high, often total.

Strangely, the proportion of slaves dying on the sea did not
exceed greatly the death-rate of Europeans -
immigrants, convicts, soldiers -
coming from the Old World to the New.
Even freemen went to sea under incredibly
bad conditions in the centuries of the slave trade;
still, they usually had a captain or chaplain to
pray for them when their situation deteriorated.
(Europeans then and later would not conceive of the
Africans as having a religion - just a lot of
superstitions and mumbo-jumbo.) Perhaps it was
because slaves were physically select. Still,
remarkable and unexplained is the similarity of
proportions between European and African
death rates at sea.

Some clue may be given by what happened in the last period of the
slave trade. With better boats, and several laws regulating the
trade for the better preservation of the cargo,
death rates declined greatly in the European,
but considerably less in the African boats.
How did this happen?
A psychiatric hypothesis is called for:
given the profound despair of people torn from their roots,
many deaths from "broken-hearts", abysmal terror, and
suicide would have occurred.
This would have happened also to many of the earlier
million who had been tossed into the wave.
Ten percent was a common rate of death
in transit toward the end of the 1700's and
carried well into the next century.

Once in North America, African infant death and
mortality rates did not significantly differ

from the White rates or, for that matter, in England.
Life expectancy in the Chesapeake Bay region in the
seventeenth century was 25 years, in
New England 38 years.
Colonial medicine was sporadically superior to
African medical practice in pediatrics and
occasionally in most other fields. The Southern climate and its
accompanying environmental conditions were
unfriendly to longevity.
The rice-growing regions of South Carolina were especially deadly.
Drinking and eating habits of Southerners (but not their slaves) were
probably no better or worse than the Puritan-inspired diets of the
Northerners, but probably inferior to the more
international cuisine of Middle States residents.

A recent estimate gives 11,345,000 souls
as the enslaved arrivals in the New World
between 1501 and 1870, and
adds another 5,000,000 who died en route.
(A figure of 18 millions in all is also used.)
Here is an enormous wrong extended over centuries,
to be placed in the museums of history alongside the German
Nazi holocaust, which seized, transported, and murdered some
4,000,000 Jews in the five years,
1941-45,
not to mention millions of gentile civilians of Europe.

Moreover, the Arab African slave trade,
beginning much earlier and continuing much later,
took an estimated 14.4 million persons to
Islamic states of the Mediterranean region and Middle East
between 650 and 1900 A.D.:
loss of life en route was less.

Brazil received 4,190,000 slaves; Spanish America 1,687,000; the
British Caribbean 2,443,000; the French Caribbean 1,655,000; the
Dutch Caribbean 500,000; the Danish Caribbean 50,000; the Atlantic
Islands (Cape Verde Islands, etc.) 297,000; and, finally, the British

North Americans 523,000. (Another source gives a figure of 651,000 for these North Americans, with 50,000 in the 1600's, 451,000 in the 1700's, and 150,000 in the nineteenth century.)

The Portuguese, profiting from the papal bull that gave their government all Christian rights against infidels of the Old World, plus an opening to the West, were the earliest slave traders, building a monopoly for a century and a half until the Dutch broke it and did their own brisk business for some years. The Spanish did little, because of the aforesaid papal bull, which gave them most of the New World, but called Africa off-bounds to Spain.

In the later seventeenth century, French and English began to muscle in on the trade, and in the eighteenth century, when it was at its greatest extent, carried half of it. Liverpool in England and Nantes in France achieved their peaks of wealth from the slave trade at this time. (School books suppressed these facts until very recently, even more than in the United States, where Northern schoolteachers liked to scold the South.)

North American colonists and United Statesians were involved from the earliest times, yet did not trade vigorously until the latter part of the 1700's, but then kept up the practice until long after the United States prohibited the Slave trade in 1807. (Banned in the Louisiana Territory in 1803).

Only 3% of total slave imports landed in the 1500's. About 14% arrived in the 1600's. Then 60% came in the 1700's up to 1810. Still, 23% were brought over illegally in the period from 1810 to 1870. Most of the 6% that the United States received before and after Independence came in during the 1700's, but it is

noteworthy that the U.S. slave trade speeded up
just before it was halted in 1807, and then
flourished as a criminal activity until the
defeat of the Southern Confederacy.

In the 1600's the Caribbean Rim was economically
the most developed region of the New World.
Tidewater Virginia and Maryland were a Northern extension
of the rim. It was a Black region already and
would long remain so. In 1700 the number
of Africans in the continental colonies, 27,000,
totaled only one-sixth of those in the British Caribbean.
Perhaps some 15,000 of these were original immigrants.
The total number then surged in both areas.

There is reason to regard the Caribbean Region as the
first culturally creative and mature part of the New World,
given the nearly total destruction of the principal Indian cultures,
the total shock accompanying the seizure of the Africans,
the poverty of new features in Spanish and Portuguese possessions,
and the almost total absence of any redeeming
cultural activity in the English continental colonies.

Bahia, in Northeastern Brazil, peopled by Yoruba slaves,
carries today the melodious speech and arts, and
community practices of their African homeland.
This wholesale transfer of culture could occur where the
slaves themselves were of the same locale, and then were
prevented from assimilating to the larger society -
unlike the transient "ghettos" of the USA-to-be.

New music, dance, medical and psychic therapy,
herbal remedies, poetry, stories, and a
new cuisine burgeoned with the Africans - some
but not all of which can be adduced in pages to come.

The new African Caribbean culture was
almost entirely underground. In most places,

plantation existence disrupted completely the sense of
time and place that marked the people from the different
African nations. The often flourishing African
cultural models carried in the heads of the kidnaped
people were broken into fragments. Slaves of
the same plantation spoke languages as different as Russian and
English. There were no tools, no artifacts,
no furnishings of their own.
They were forcibly compressed of soul and spirit,
of living room and possessions.

Their African skills, that in the 1600's were producing
universal artistic treasures in Benin and elsewhere,
were practically lost; a few practices that could be
accommodated to the new conditions, like the technique
of husking rice, were seized upon by the masters.
Their diet shrank into unrecognizable substances;
their etiquette disappeared;
their religion became one of a dozen of the surrounding
African rites threatened by something called Christianity.

An imperial culture, itself barren and bottom-level,
claimed all values as its own and for itself;
provided to the slaves was the minimum for survival,
whereas extracted from them was maximum productive toil.
Out at dawn, sick or well, a dip of molasses, a pancake,
a trudge to the fields and work until, in midsummer,
there might be a pause out of the scorching sun;
work until darkness fell;
a struggle back to the camp of shacks,
a soup, a mash, a tuber, a smoke, talk, imprecations and
prayer, talk in the dark, songs, sleep.

Of course, never underestimate the cleverness
of forced and involuntary workers at finding a moment of relief,
a chance to lay back, a way of distilling liquor in the woods,
a time to make love.

The too sick and too old were put to lighter tasks,
with smaller rations, and finally set aside in quarters to die.
Slaves learned Spanish or Portuguese, or French or English
rapidly. Before a generation had come ashore,
variations of Indo-European tongues had become
common linguistic currency.
Some African forms, one from the Congo, one from the
Guinea Coast, and so on, would persist and
African accents coalesced, until over large regions,
general dialects of English could be detected.
Among them were several dialects developed in the
mainland English possessions, though basically probably
Caribbean-derived, for slaves were transported
from the islands to the mainland in large numbers.
The language of the lowlands South not only received gifts of
syntax and words, but also the famous Deep South
accent itself, in large part from African-Americans.

Excellence forced its way upwards - the glib, the musical, the
medically adept, the nurse, the "responsible", the handyman, the
storyteller, the literate, the bearer of sturdy, healthy babies.
Also prospered the informant, the rate-buster, the concubine
(male or female), the manager, the
sadist who could whip on his fellows, the
cross-racial ones whose legal status was sometimes
partially or totally free.

Psychic destruction among the Africans coming to the
New World was pandemic. They were socially destroyed,
uprooted in practically every sense of the term.
They were one and all wounded souls that had
to lose their very cultural support even on the
brink of the most terrible of voyages.
While the Puritans could pray under their pastors
when the seas became rough, the Africans could barely move,
much less foregather. Moreover, they would ordinarily not
understand the speech either of the crew or of their fellows.
It has been shown how in many slave systems of
history, the slave suffers the mutilation of his
social self. Rarely has it occurred so cruelly as

under the doubly accentuated conditions
of the American slave.

It all begins, of course, at the dawn of human kind, but
becomes highly pertinent to us in these pages with
Christopher Colon and the Spaniards and all the
others who followed to the Americas. They were
pleased, especially where they could not find
gold and spices, to discover that they could overcome by
force the Indian peoples and make slaves of them.
The slaves might mine for metals and minerals,
construct churches for the new God, till the soil,
be sexually exploited, and act as domestic servants -
in brief, do all sorts of work in exchange for
merest subsistence.

The natives fought and died, or fell ill with European
diseases and died, wherever the invader established himself.
No less a heroic humanitarian than De Las Casas
opined that, given the incapacity of Indians as slaves,
it would be necessary, to avoid their extinction,
to bring in Africans. He said this after the fact.
In 1501 African slavery was introduced
into Santo Domingo, where Columbus had implanted a
garrison on his first voyage, and where the Indians were
diminishing from half a million (a high estimate) to
a few thousands in a couple of decades.
It was genocide and disease that did it.

Columbus was not so vicious as he has been recently pictured;
that is, he did at first comment admiringly on
the good-natured, generous, and open - not to say naked -
qualities of the Indians whom he first met. He would have set
a better precedent in Indian relations had he not been
obsessed with the notion that there had to be lots of gold
around somewhere, and infected others with his lucubrations,
including the King and Queen.

❖ ❖ ❖

It must be remembered that Columbus shared most ruling
opinions of the age, that people like Moors, Jews, heretics,
anybody in fact, could readily be forced to confess
many "evil" thoughts and actions. Furthermore that
force was legitimate and rational. Too, he was a
representative normal scoundrel of the age, in that,
trying to figure a way of using people -
"what are they worth?" -
he thought also that Indians could be enslaved.

Spanish lawyers were familiar with slavery from Roman Law,
which countenanced slavery but also gave the slave a
variety of rights, none of them, of course,
sufficiently potent to make you want to be a slave,
but better than nothing.
Spain had lost people to slavery, too,
under Muslim rule, and had, like all European
countries, some experience with slavery at the hands of
pirates, Vikings, and other marauders. Notably,
Roman Law was color-blind; a slave
could be of any ethnic or racial aggregate.

The situation was not the same where England was
involved, because the English had as much
common law as Roman Law in their system,
and were naive in the handling of new issues of slavery.
When the first Blacks came to Virginia,
a critical conflict of American history arose, and
the good guys lost: should the slaves be treated as
indentured servants and let go after a while,
welcomed into the society, and
given whatever privileges poor people had?
The answer was a tortured "No".

Tortured, because, for perhaps two political
generations it seemed as if the American slave

would become something basically different than
the slave under Roman law, that one
might be treated as a servant, that one
might become a Christian,
that one might be freed after a time,
that one's offspring would be naturally free,
that one might marry whom one pleased,
that one might hold property, and so forth - in
short, that one might be treated as a human being
instead of a commodity and piece of property.

That, in the end, a resounding negative came forth -
conditions of slavery worse than typically to be discovered
in the Spanish or Portuguese or French or Dutch colonies -
has to do with the large presence, in the earliest
Anglophone colonies where Africans appeared,
of the people who would always henceforth be their chief
enemy, the mass of highly deprived Whites.

It is a common error of people, scholars or laymen,
who are rationalists for lack of anthropological or
sociological training, to believe that downtrodden people,
the poor and miserable, must be sympathetic to
other humans in similar or worse situations.
One could follow the contradictions to this notion
throughout history, but can begin here and now with the
poor and downtrodden Whites of the colonies,
especially the Southern places, where the
slaves entered in large numbers.

As might be glimpsed in More's *Utopia* or
Shakespeare's *Tempest,* the aborigine was not
perceived as an inferior or outcast creature.
Shakespeare's *Othello* might show a "Black" Moor
complaining of discrimination, but his fine Venetian wife,
his power and social status and his luxurious life style
tend to move his problems rather into the

realm of psychiatry. Turning to the colonies,
discrimination on grounds of race was far less than
discrimination against different religious groups.
You could live more nicely Black than Catholic in Boston.
Even much later, Herman Melville's crew
aboard the *Pequod* exhibited a concatenation
of ethnic variations.

The negative connotations of a black or brown skin and the
other secondary features of Negro race among
American colonial Whites originated with the
underclass of Whites, meaning, alas, the large majority of
unfortunates dumped upon the shores of the New World.
Any device of psychology or economics that could
be used to create a class even worse-off,
a pariah class of untouchables, would
augment their self-esteem and give them areas of
life and liberty in which they might take pride.
It was to their interest that Blacks remain
fully Black, heathen, and prisoners,
even though they owned hardly anything themselves,
were debt-ridden or bound to a master's work gang
or mistress' kitchen, and lacked all political and most civil liberty.

In the 1600's instances can be shown when
Blacks and Whites united against the White oligarchy that
was establishing itself. Such instances were not to be
found later on. If anything, the Blacks had to rely upon
the planter class of Whites for their basic protection,
the right to exist. The racial detestation
cultivated among deprived Whites played directly
into the hands of the ruling class, since,
however stringent the rules applied to slaves,
including those of the crucial areas of
manumission of slaves and inheritance of the slave bond,
the White underclass would approve of them as
enhancing, relatively speaking, their own status.

Even the Christianization of slaves, which one would
expect to find a popular White cause,

divided the Whites into a minority who thought it to be
a blessing that would bring a better treatment of slaves and a
fulfillment of the Divine Will, and those who felt
it would threaten to bring about a rise in the status of slaves.
Christianizing could only proceed when
legislation and practice decreed it must not
interfere with the hereditary bond of slavery.

In the beginning, too, Tidewater slaves were
not punished severely for engaging in sex relations
with White women or vice versa. Nor were
White men penalized for intercourse with Black women.
There was about a 3% incidence of
births of mixed race in the first two generations of slavery.
This is surprisingly high, given the cultural and
linguistic differences between the races, but
surprisingly low, considering the intense need
felt among White males unprovided with
females of their own ilk.

However, most poor Whites soon backed
severe measures against miscegenation, and
in this case were supported
by planters and religious ministers.
In consequence, the children of inter-racial unions
were not freed from the slave bond, and, if of a free
Black and White, were legally categorized and
psychically perceived as Blacks.

There was to be no subtlety, no shades of difference,
once the full logic of racial discrimination got going
in the American South towards
the end of the first century of slavery.
To possess the slightest African descent was to become
totally subject to laws governing Blacks;
this, too, was an attempt to prevent any close approach of a
Black to the most deprived "pure" White.
The experience of mainland Blacks
veered away from that of the Caribbean islands Blacks,

because on the islands, the Blacks would compose over 80% of the population while on the mainland at first they composed less than 20% and rarely more than 40% in Southern areas. The poor White class, which was always large and increasingly aggressive politically in the mainland colonies and thereafter in the states, rarely constituted a large and aggressive element on the islands.

Camaraderie between the sexes and flexible sexual associations were characteristic of slave society from the beginning, going back to the original African societies. Indo-European and Semitic societies for thousands of years were patriarchal and female-suppressing. This was not so in Africa where Negro Race prevailed. A deep cultural difference could be found between the two races, that, we know, was not genetic, because, since the liberation of the slaves in North America, there has been a fairly successful attempt, principally by means of organized religion, to re-sculpture nuclear relations in the form of the "traditional American family". False more often than not, when applied to the White family, it was doubly false when applied to the Afro-American family. The typical and normal family condition in all of the regions from which the African-Americans came was matrilinear and rather matriarchal, much different from the European Catholic or Protestant family, which was tightly organized in law and religion, and to a large degree in practice, around the male head of household. Males and females were separated for various purposes in African cultures, but the sexes were fairly equal. Female Africans were co-operatively engaged and even dominantly involved with males in important extra-household areas such as agriculture. The males stood low in the households;

they could possess, though not be the boss in, several
households. In West Africa,
and to this day, male relatives of the
mother tend to wield greater authority over the
children than their father.

In the African interior slave trade,
women brought higher prices than men,
whereas in the Atlantic slave trade
the prices were about equal.
In one deal, of May 20, 1790,
between a trader from Nantes and King Pepel of the
Niger Delta, a nubile female was bought of the
King for two bolts of cloth, three guns,
20 knives, hats, chains, a bowl and
other items. Perhaps the demand for female slaves was
greater in the more highly developed Arab countries,
raising the price of women.
Certainly they would have less need for field hands.
Also, American planters, duped by their European attitudes
toward women and the employment of women,
may have believed they were being choosey
when in fact they were being deceived.

Fewer women were shipped to America, often in
ratio of one-to-two, or even one-to-three.
Yet in America they were more valuable than men,
also, for they did much the same work as
men and had valuable skills off the field.
Furthermore they could bear children, a matter of
great moment to the master, who had to think
whether paying the small charge for several years of
infancy would be preferable to paying for an older child
or adult male at the slave auctions.

The double independence of Black women in America came about
because the master was not bound by law to keep a slave family
together, even when they were bound in Christian marriage.
(He could prevent the marriage in the first place.)

Therefore, the African-American female slave would be effectively head of household even where there was a known and partially responsible father. Any master or mistress-supplied child welfare assistance went through the mother, and therefore strengthened the role, power, and economic position of the mother.

All of this prevented the African-American father from assuming a legal and actual role as *pater familias* comparable to the position of the White father and head of household. It contributed in some degree to the inferiority-feelings of the Black male. Although he could be a giant at work and gang management, in the sphere of the family, he could be made to appear largely useless save as a progenitor and mother's helper. If the White man's imagery and conceptions were ignored, as they often were, the role of the male in this environment could be conceived of as having its own rewards. (Something will have to be said later on, however, about how this has worked out on the recent American scene, with the drastically changing situation of the various types of American families.)

———————

Benjamin Franklin in Paris with his grandsons (popular illustration)

PART THREE

EIGHTEENTH CENTURY CULTURES

> In matters of style, swim with the current;
> In matters of principle, stand like a rock.
> *Thomas Jefferson*

If you could have flown three centuries ago in the mid-1600's,
from Montreal (French Canada) to St. Augustine (Spanish Florida),
via Boston (Puritan English), Nieuw Amsterdam (Dutch),
Fort Christina (Swedish Delaware at Wilmington), and Jamestown (Virginia English),
you would have passed over about the same number of
important Indian nations as you would states of the
United States today.

The Indian nations began the 1700's,
five memorial generations ago, as a majority of the
inhabitants of the first thirteen States-to-be, and
ended the century in a distinct minority, even
counting all Indians West to the Mississippi River.

If one did not know that the beachheads of the several
infiltrating nations and the hundreds of Indian tribes
were distinct and autonomous units,
the full North American drama would appear to be grandly
coordinated, with the Indians surrounded on all sides by
continuously reinforced Europeans, including even
Russians coming down from Alaska: a "World War" of
Native America versus an Imperial Alliance of Europe.

As England's settlements and Canadian conquests of 1763
solidified, the policy of the Home government would
seem to be clear enough, even logical,
even rational. And the view would be shared by
responsible and respectable public opinion
in the American Empire:

*

Introduce law and order up and down
the Atlantic Coast.
*

Draw a line of settlement North to South, that
would provide as much land for colonial immigration and
export crops as the Homeland might require.
*

Keep peace with the Indians as a whole and among the nations.
*

Direct as much of the fur trade as possible to England.
*

Hold Spain and France at bay.

*
Maintain a Caribbean balance.
*

Remember that the Orient holds the richest prizes, and
one cannot let the search for a Northwest Passage
deter trade with the Old World.
*

Each of several areas of British North America
might do its part in this scheme:
from Canada fish and furs;
from New England fish, timber, and boats;
from the Middle colonies, cereals, timber and boats;
from the South, sugar, rice, tobacco, indigo.
The British navy gained sailors and bases, and
also boats, timber, pitch, and rigging.
(The Sea ruled - and now, who would rule the Sea?
An infant Virginia Colony died because its
relief boat of 1590 had been held back
on the threat of the Spanish Armada.)

The United Kingdom was already a congeries of ethnicities
by the end of the 1600's, what with an original base of
Iberian-Ligurian, Celtic, Roman,
Angle, Saxon, Dane and Norman,
that hadn't fully amalgamated, and the
Cornish, Scottish, Irish, and Welsh peoples
that had more recently been attached, and were being
drawn upon for the military and marine,
and for a chaotic enlargement of cities.

The traces of these peoples were by no means
obliterated. They persisted: Gaelic from Catholic Ireland
was long spoken in Newfoundland, Welsh in
upper New England, the Scottish dialects in sundry enclaves.
Non-British centers of ethnic and sectarian concentration were
set up in America and also persisted -
Germanic, Hispanic, Dutch, Swedish, and French.

The intense civic education given American children for
centuries would be fixated upon Pilgrim myth,
an engrossment of primitive facts,
discounting not only other settling and developing
elements that were of English origin and influential,
such as the Quaker and the Southern Cavalier,
but also denying credit for Americanizing
America to Spanish, French, Dutch, Africans, and Germanics.
It was not imperial Germany of the Kaiser and Bismarck,
but a hundred autonomous Germanic baronies and sects that
sent their myriads to the New World until
the latter Nineteenth Century. Germanics -
Americans were forced to believe -
brought over little and gave it up quickly.
From the early Eighteenth Century to this day,
whatever was needed was coined as fiction and "spin"
to repress reportage of the industrial, scientific, educational,
administrative, cultural eminence of Germany
over two centuries.

Even in the Heartland of Germanics in America, like Chicago,
the single-minded Anglo myth was spoon-fed to
kindergartners (although the very word for
advancing the education of post-toddlers was German.)
And, indeed, social myth believed becomes fact.

Overwhelming these failed competitors -
and in time assimilating them -
were several large cultures, distinctive,
one from the other, in ways that bore small
resemblance to England. By the mid-1600's
no large part of the Colonies could be said to be
"a chip off the old block".
In the large, England, having suppressed most of its democratic
propensities, headed into a century of firm oligarchy.

By contrast, the American colonials had been pre-selected
as several alienated, ungovernable, and dissenting types
who were unreconcilable when

it came down to suppressing themselves.
(Upcoming were four centuries of such "negative liberty".)
Later on, we will gather together what we can of
traits that came to characterize all Americans.

Given their diversity at the source, Americans began
right away to perform complicated exercises of role-playing and
assumption of multiple selves at a given time and
all through life. A continuous and anxious-making stress
thus accompanied them. High physical mobility and
technological strain interacted heavily with a widespread
yearning to become "the typical American".

Every group that came to exist in America divided itself
into ethnics and assimilationists. (Indeed, what were
Tories and Patriots if not ethnics and assimilationists?)
Thus groups were to be "utopians" in this sense,
and all were to fail in being sufficient unto themselves.
All have tried to push and pull "the American" toward
their own group character. All changed in
this regard, too. Each was different from another.

In the past century, populous southern-type hill groups,
whether black or white, have found assimilation to
more national attitudes and behavior difficult. By contrast with
these and, too, with groups such as the Poles or Puerto Ricans,
part of the success of Jews after arrival in the United States
can be attributed to many centuries of watching
non-Judaic cultures and emulating them when needs be,
especially their ruling and educated classes.

Americans have always desired to some greater or lesser degree
to render themselves indistinguishable among the
general population (or to what they believe are the
traits and behavior of the Americans whom they consider they
should be like, their model). This tendency has
been an ineradicable part of, and also
producer of, a most typical American character:
to be what one has not before been, a type, not new,

else not recognizable, but inevitably new anyhow,
viewed objectively. Playing at being an Indian has been
a child's and often an adult game for 400 years, for instance.

Playing at being a planter, a trader, a scout,
a rancher, a respectable wife and mother, a pioneer,
a rebel soldier of the Revolution or Civil War,
a "queen of society", "an "ordinary guy", and many another role -
all the while fumbling toward a common identity -
the hypothetical common man of egalitarian
aspect and conduct: such impulse has driven Americans
continuously through one generation after another.
But we note the following, too, that some persons and
some groups do better at "being themselves",
while "being the others", whereas some people
have more trouble in going to and fro, or
adapting as fully to the one as the other.

So now we are to focus upon four indigenous American
sub-cultures, developing and taking geographical form.
We may call them the New England Yankees, the Pluralist
Middle Colonies, the Southern Slave Culture, and the Frontier.
They overlaid the European antecedent cultures and
replaced largely the Indian cultures over large
swaths of territory.

They were able, by the time of the Revolutionary War,
to impress themselves upon people newly arriving.
Immigrants acquired mental, moral, religious, political,
behavioral, technological, customary and even to a degree
physiognomic attributes that belonged to the culture.
(By physiognomic is meant posture, vocalizing,
gesturing, body weight and height, and locomotion.)

Indeed, before migrating, often many years before,
these cultures were fashioned mentally among those who would come.
Prospects were trained in many cases by returnees,
veterans of the cultures. Recruiters were sometimes chased

out of towns by authorities and parents. The frontier culture became so familiar to the European general public that the sprite lurked in those who finally boarded ship.

The hey-day of these culture-complexes would be the period from 1700 to 1850. Their period of decline would be the period of 1850 to 1940, and from 1940 to the present they must be regarded as largely defunct, replaced by a national urbanized industrial culture. We must remember, however, that the past never quite dies. It rests in layer upon layer beneath the soil of the present, like archaeological layers, and stubbornly dominates troglodytic niches. State and local elites persist who believe themselves to be, and are believed often to be, with whatever reason, of the unchanging "good old" cultures.

With the flourishing and the decline came a period, roughly between 1780 and 1900, when the United States, as it grew, followed the lines of, and could be divided into, regions that reflected one or another of the four elemental cultures. The early cultures, that is, moved North, South and West, duplicating themselves to a considerable extent as they pushed along, contentiously. Much more will be spoken of this process.

Furthermore, America developed readily new centers that, if not fully idiosyncratic cultures, became as distinctive as the rest. Such were the New York Metropolitan Region, the Sun Belt, the Pacific Coast, the Iron Age Region, the New England Educational Industrial Area, the Mid-Atlantic Service Sector, and several others sometimes nominated. Practically all of these were urban and nationalized; anybody with a Social Security number could move in and out of them, paying scant attention to their historical pretensions. Every nation of the European Community has

kept its historical sub-cultures more intact than America.
It is probably just as well:
not one of the four larger original cultures
had in itself something so grand as to glorify the future.

The Yankees would have to get rid of pure puritanism,
the pluralists of unmiscible greed,
the frontiersmen of savagery, the South of slavery -
all this just for starters!

What means the word "pluralism?"
Pluralism, in the sense of culture, pertains to a
defined area that holds groups of different cultures
or a culture of differently acculturated individuals
or a culture tolerant of conflicting religious,
economic, and social interests,
or any combination of these. In general,
American culture has been pluralist from its
Indian beginnings, with major exceptions, and it is
today pluralist, in all three of these criteria.
Early Yankee and New England culture I consider
to be too narrow in origins and too uncomfortable with
diverse ethnic and religious groups to be
called a pluralist society.

The pluralist culture of colonial times was present in
New York, Pennsylvania, New Jersey,
Maryland, and Delaware, in most places,
and most of the time, and includes the Indian nations of the
region. The region had no formal structure.
Each named element was de facto and de jure
under the direct rule of the English government, with the
exception of the Indian nations, whose sovereignty was generally
acknowledged, but not often respected

Should we not also explain the word "ethnic",
often a primary dimension of pluralism.
Its usefulness in discussions of American history

will have been, I hope, apparent in this work.
Our usages and their significance is as follows.

An American is anyone who has resided in the United States or its earlier confines for some years, and considers himself now or considered himself then an American. Americans before July 4, 1776 ought, when convenient, to be called "colonial Americans" or "American colonists". A hyphen (*- American) designates an American whose national or cultural origins, whether his own or of his ancestors, include all or part of the nationality replacing the *, thus: Anglo-American, Afro-or African-American, Polish-American, German-American, Franco-American, Italo-American, Lithuanian-German-Irish American, even Shawnee-American, too, Jewish-American.

All Americans can be called hyphenated Americans, correctly, although some use the term "hyphenated American" to refer disparagingly to Americans suspected of putting another ethnic loyalty before their American loyalty. The prefix is most properly used, however, only when it contributes significantly to the understanding of its context. A distinction is made, where possible, when international relations are meant; the full adjective is carried, thus, British-American consultations, French-American *rapprochement*, German-American peace efforts, and Polish-American loan arrangements.

The term "Anglo-Saxon" is not a proper referent and is not to be used here. The British and English are neither Angles nor Saxons, any more than the French are Romans. The English lived longer as Celts, longer, even, under Roman rule, and then after 1066 under French of Scandinavian origin. Certainly then, Americans are in no way "Anglo-Saxons". The inclusive term for the two

Anglophone or English-speaking peoples is just that: "Anglophone", although Winston Churchill (himself half American) once jested that they were *"two peoples separated by a common language"*. Indeed, the American language was also distinct, in all its dialectical parts, and might better be called the American Language, as did Webster and Mencken, but more aptly, as did ordinary people, putting additional pressure on the newly arrived or native-born to master the tongue. Socio-psychologically, and linguistically, "English" is a foreign language to most Americans, to wit: *"Why do I have to learn English to be 100% American?"*

America, United Kingdom and "Anglo-Saxons"

The name of the United Kingdom of Great Britain was adopted after 1800 when official juncture with Ireland occurred, union with Scotland under a single crown having been declared in 1707, these two places being honored with separate attachment to Great Britain in the United Kingdom. In 1876, Emperor of India became part of the name of the Crown. After World War II, Empire became Commonwealth, the term British Empire was no longer used. Nowadays, the names U.K., Great Britain, England, even Britain, are responded to with some indifference as signifying the whole, realizing that only Scotland and Ulster in Northern Ireland remained effectively under the Crown of the United Kingdom after 1921.

The term "Anglo-Saxon" is little used in the United Kingdom (or UK) nowadays, but gained currency in the imperial hey-day of Great Britain. We find the term being used to distinguish Anglo-Americans from scornfully treated Mexicans in the 1820's,

ominous prelude to the Texan revolt and Mexican War.
Some inferiority-stricken, anti-Celt,
anti-Norman nostalgists joined with some
Teutonic racists of the type of Houston Chamberlain and his
wife, daughter of the German composer Richard Wagner,
to somehow make up a race of people to whom the
world might be turned over.

Some German-Americans and Anglo-Americans
used the myth to cozy up. Historians began to
weave fables about American democracy
as being the reincarnation of a largely mythical
primitive democracy of the Teutonic tribes.
(The same people had little use for a similar
democracy of the Indian tribes.)

New England racists, conveniently evading the large pre-Saxon
Celtic element in their makeup, ignoring the considerable
Welsh-American and Scots population,
claimed that the newly arriving Irishmen were
racially different, ascribing to the absolutely deprived and
humiliated newcomers simian features of character and
appearance. It ought be said now, to be retold later, that
these racists produced the school-books of the
next century and a half in the United States.

By well-known mechanisms of psychopathology,
the inferiors adopted their own abasement when allowed.
Putting aside the English-American melange, and the
German-Americans, who hardly knew what was going on,
but did not mind their incorporation, the
majority of Europeans who were the Scottish,
Scots-Irish, Irish, Welsh and French protestants,
were often co-opted as Anglo-Saxons as soon as
they cleaned up their cabin, went to church or
owned a slave.

For a long time, invidiously discriminating Americans
(like Madison Grant, a witless popular writer

late in the century) joined the party, particularly as this would enable them to attack a number of ethnic and religious groups that were moving into America at the time.

(The term lingers at home among French and Italian journalists and politicians, rarely German, significantly, who use it especially when suspecting some connivance to their disadvantage among Anglophone nations. So one reads items like *"The Anglo-Saxons are trying to reduce France's nuclear capability"*.)

The acronym W.A.S.P. or WASP, standing for "White Anglo-Saxon Protestant", also goes unused here, because it is an ethnic slur (though, like others, it is often not resented), and also because the term "Anglo-Saxon" is improperly used, as was just explained, especially when applied to Celts such as the Scots, Welsh, and Irish, while various other Protestants who are of Germanic or another origin are mistakenly caught in the net. Furthermore, many so categorized are not Protestants at all, but rather are foremost secularist free-thinkers and non-Christians.

Also, the term is used almost always deliberately to refer to persons of wealth and pretensions of high social standing, whereas a great body of White "Anglo-Saxon" Protestants consists of poor people, especially the poor of the South. These latter Americans are often referred to as "hill-billies, "red-necks", "crackers", and other pejorative terms that are to be avoided for being invidiously discriminative, even, again, when they are lightly dismissed by those to whom applied.

Probably the reader has already noticed that

I use the term Scots-Irish in preference to Scotch-Irish, following the desire today of the Scottish inhabitants of Great Britain at least, also Scots for the Scots of Scotland. The Scots-Irish were and are (as the Ulster Irish) the descendants of Scottish Protestants transplanted to Northern Ireland, in one of various attempts to reduce native Irish resistance. Anglo-Irish is used for those English and their descendants who got placed - corruptly, violently, and unjustly - in Ireland with the same motive in mind, and generally to obliterate authentic Gaelic culture. "Irish Catholics" are just that, but, when referring to Irish-Americans, the religious designation is taken for granted, and "Irish" alone is the popular name.

The term "Jew" and "Jewish" is used in context to refer to someone whose cultural origins, if not his religious beliefs, are in the social context of the Judaic religion. "Hebrews" is closer to a religious designation. A reasonable usage has been proposed that keeps "Hebrew" for the language, and for those who were of the Hebrew religion and the Tribes of Israel before the Exodus from Egypt (perhaps around 1450 B.C., perhaps by latest guess, 700 years later), using "Jews" for the same people thereafter. Israel is used for the nation of Israel and "Israeli" for its citizens, in recent history.

I do not refer to Indians as "Native Americans", for the usage confuses; all but 10% of Americans are native Americans. Furthermore, it is an endeavor to award the continent to the present generation of Indian descendants and take it away from the others, and as such is pathetic. Besides, most Indians are not of Indian descent alone, and I doubt that most of the Indians of the year 1492 were of a single racial descent; some of them may have come to America in fairly recent history, too.
I have discussed earlier the terms employed in

referring to African-Americans. Often, Americans,
speaking together, will refer to themselves or other
Americans simply by the country of origin, thus,
"This is a Slovak neighborhood, but used to be Italian".
This is not invidious usage; Americans
typically have two meanings for every ethnic name:
one referring to the American, a second to the foreigner.
Thus, Mexican may refer to a person from Mexico,
or to an American whose ancestors moved into
modern U.S. territory four centuries ago;
a "Milwaukee German" will go back perhaps eight
biological generations; (interestingly, a
person of however long a German ancestry
who comes from elsewhere to live in Milwaukee, or in
Eastern Pennsylvania, for that matter, is
not a Milwaukee German or Pennsylvania Dutch).
With lots of paper and ink, we can spell out the
full designations when we need to use them.

And when an American asks another American
about his ancestry, which he may not do ordinarily
unless an acquaintanceship is being developed,
a nice form is *"What countries did your folks
(or family, or ancestors) come from?"*
This is a preferred manner of asking, because,
for instance, if you asked *"What nationality are you?"*
you may be wrongly presuming a person to be foreign
from his name or appearance or conduct, or because,
if you ask *"What kind of name is Batmann?"*
you are already too abrupt;
most names have been changed in one way or another,
a name usually does not contain the complete roster
of a person's origins, women carry their spouses' name
often , and, further, the intonation of the question may
inadvertently seem unfriendly.

But plumbing the etymology of onomastic etiquette,
must not delay our straight tracing of the
several larger cultures of America.

The 1634-1638 war with the Puritans almost exterminated the powerful tribe of the Pequot, who had already lost 80% of their population in a small-pox epidemic in 1633. In the picture, the Pequot are shown as ruthless aggressors.

Chapter Ten

Indian Recessions

The bubonic plague that killed one out of three in Europe
arrived by the ancient silk route at Kaffa in the Crimea
in 1347. From there, rats, fleas, and men
carrying the germs of *pasteurella pestis*
set out on their Grand Tour of Europe:

Constantinople, Greece and the Balkans, Italy,
France, the Iberian Peninsula - broad
successive waves carrying them up through the
British Isles, Scandinavia, and Eastern Europe,
by the year 1353.

It is not known whether the plague reached the Americas.
Probably it did, be it from Asia or Europe.
Evidence that a terrible plague has struck will disappear
almost completely unless a written record is preserved.
There is some slight indication of such a plague in
the hundreds of untended large mounds,
the size of football stadiums, that dot the
vast Ohio-Mississippi drainage basin.
Used for religious rites and burials, their mysterious
builders might have been practically extinct by plague.
No one could remember when the mounds were built and
last employed, though some seemed recent.

I noted, in the second chapter above, the many
possible intruders upon the Americas. Some of these,
if they landed, would have handed over their germs to the
Americans whom they encountered. So depopulation
could have begun then and there, before Columbus.

Additionally we hinted at another possibility.
Claims were made in the worst of plague times,
the 1300's, that rare atmospheric and
celestial disturbances were occurring, and that vermin falling
from inner or outer space (*sic*) produced plague on Earth.
If so, the Americas might not have been spared the infestations.
Nor would infectious mammals be needed as carriers.

Whether again, or for the first time: poxes and influenzas struck
America devastatingly in the century of "discovery". They
accompanied not only the voyages of Columbus, but also the many
landings before and after him, up and down the coasts of the
continents and around the Caribbean Sea. The susceptibility of
Indians to European disease was the greatest ally that the
Europeans possessed when it came to seizing and

occupying North America. Even the most peaceable
European group engaged perforce in biological warfare.

So quickly had pox and fevers spread to the farthest
reaches of the land that the earliest expeditions
following upon the very first contacts
found their path cleared by death. When
Hernando de Soto's company arrived at the Mississippi
River early in the sixteenth century, they came upon the
Indian city of Cahokia, near the present city of
St. Louis. Cahokia had numbered 40,000
persons sometime before, as large, therefore, as
London and Paris. But it had been greatly reduced by
plague and it could afford no opposition to strangers
coming and going on its territory.

Jacques Cartier in his voyages up the St. Lawrence River
in the 1530's had visited several large towns,
including Stadacona and Hochelaga.
By the next account, rendered in 1603,
they had disappeared.

Pilgrims of 1620 came upon a land of empty huts,
and upon cleared but vacant fields. Many of the Wampanoag,
Massachusetts, and Pequot peoples had died of disease.

The Iroquois related that before the Christians came
their population had been ten times as great as it was afterwards.
Their number was estimated at 75,000 in the
mid-1600's. Therefore, they would have
once numbered 750,000.

The widespread Cherokee nation, with original territory of
100,000 square miles, would figure prominently in
history well into the 1800's. But it would be gravely
injured by smallpox. Earlier plagues had reduced
its numbers greatly. Then six successive

plagues in the 1830's reduced its population
from 30,000 to 10,000, just as its
relations with the State and National Governments
reached a crisis. The last plague came with a
slave-carrying boat that also held trade goods
thereafter exchanged with the Indians.

One of the Indian survivors, reputed the most handsome
warrior of his tribe, fell sick, recovered, but was so
disfigured that he swore undying enmity to the Whites;
they had, he felt, tried to destroy him, and he did
in fact lead his people into futile battle. (There were
known instances of English plotting, if not using,
biological warfare against the Indians, notably
in 1763 the case of Lord Jeffery Amherst,
whose idea was pox-laden gift blankets;
in his honor Amherst College was named.)

Had their numbers not been so severely diminished,
there would have been little chance of successful settlements
except upon terms acceptable to the Indians.
This is deducible from the difficulty which French and English
had in pushing back the Iroquois and Algonquin nations,
not to mention the resistance offered by the non-affiliated
independent tribes along the whole of the Coast. It took almost six
political generations (10 biological generations)
to cast out the Indians East of the Appalachians or
bring them into subjection. It took only
one political generation to move them almost
entirely to West of the Mississippi.
It took only one more political generation to reduce
all remaining nations "within" United States territory to
White government rule.

Historians have been reticent lately, possibly to placate
Indian pressure groups, about the continual warfare
among the Indians themselves as a factor in their general decline.
Despite all the troubles inflicted upon them by

the Europeans, the tribes were all too ready to join
with Europeans against another Indian nation.
Not only tribes, but individuals and gangs:
the typical European-American stuck to
his tribe more than the typical Indian. Furthermore, as
Indian morale generally fell, and Indian
social bonds became weaker with diminished numbers
individuals could be bribed or persuaded into treason.
Moreover, the decentralized tribes of the North did not
ordinarily recognize and in fact unconsciously denied that the
defeat of one tribe meant the defeat of the other.

Nor was the fighting between Indians any less ferocious than
struggles between White and Red. Indeed the Indians'
methods of fighting among themselves were generalized into the
methods of frontier warfare followed by all parties in the
vast areas of North America that could contain it.

Glancing over at the conduct of warfare in Europe as the
1600's moved into the 1700's, one can
perceive a lessening of butchery and massacre, including of
women and children, proceeding down the years.
The usual remark at this fact is,
"The Enlightenment! That's the reason".
At any rate, in the colonial struggles, participants
behaved rather like the Serbs, Croats and Bosnians in their
civil wars of the 1990's.

Scalping was only one of the gruesomeries of battle.
Many tribes practiced cutting off a large hair-bearing
portion of the headskin of a downed enemy;
this would be exhibited to all and sundry who had not
the good fortune to witness the battle. Eastern
Woodlands Indians would appear to be stuck with the infamous
invention, which, however, diffused successfully to their
European opponents, who evidently exulted in collecting such
trophies as much as did their ruddy enemies.
During a century or more, cash bounties were paid
in certain settlements for Indian scalps.

Consider the rapidity of Spanish conquests of heavily
populated and well-organized nations of
Central and South America:
why would this not have been the case with the
invaders of New England and Virginia?
The Spanish conquistadors and their companies were
state-of-the-art fighting machines,
capable of devastating blitzkriegs.
Pilgrims, Puritans and Virginians were amateurs at battle,
save for the few mercenaries and Cavaliers among them.
Some would have liked to hunt for gold and did,
but the main effort went into taking up and
consuming the resources of the earth, while acting only as
nasty toward the Indians as might be required
to get what one wanted.

Could it be that something else, also intangible,
lay behind the quickness with which the Spanish and, also,
the French, came to lasting terms with Indian nations?
Could it have been a factor, call it the racist factor, or
perhaps the rigidity factor, which is not far
removed in psychogenesis from racism, that brought about
this contrasting set of results?

Quite possibly. Under the circumstances,
Indians as well as Anglo-colonials became more racist.
There were cooperative and pluralist elements in both populations,
but generally and increasingly the dominant attitude on
both sides became, *"It's them or us"*.
Gradually, for the Indians of all the tribes, a sickening
despair arose with the thought,
"It will be us!".

The Indians would not bend; the English and Scots-Irish and the
continental sects would not bend; Presbyterians do not bend,

Protestants in general do not bend culturally.
This has to do, of course, with miscegenation,
as well as flexibility in all kinds of interrelations;
the French home government even promulgated a policy
favoring intermixture of the French and Indians. And the
Spanish policy was evident in the large mixed racial groups that
flourished everywhere in the presence of priests, and -
who will say no? - with their cooperation.

Protestantism overall did not pretend to the
universal membership that Catholicism claimed.
This allowed Protestants, more than Catholics,
to believe that whoever was not of their sect was strictly foreign.
There was a tightness and newness in feeling Protestant,
a sharpness of distinction between those who gave evidence of
being saved and those who were without hope of salvation.

Catholics were long habituated to dwelling among passive
believers and skeptics. The Jesuits went to live
among the Indians from the Arctic down to Patagonia.
Protestant ministers and missionaries living
among the heathen in the English colonies were rare.

Moreover, English Protestantism was tied into a
pronounced enhancement of nationalism. The destruction of the
Spanish Armada after a century of fear and envy
sent the patriotic spirit soaring.
England joined France, Portugal and Spain as a
modern nationalist state. This could only bode ill for
other peoples and races. England moved, as
historian Benjamin Nelson once labeled the process,
"from universal brotherhood to universal otherhood".

The lower social orders were most affected by the transition.
They were afforded a new self-respect,
simply by being permitted, even encouraged, to
define themselves as part of an aggregate that

included the King and Queen and their ilk;
and they could consign to the nether regions,
figuratively and literally, all those
who might be "otherhood".
This process, often ignored by historians, should be well-marked.

Every low-brow immigrant aggregate that was to land
upon our shores from 1565 onward was
infected by its own nationalism; the
universality of the middle ages had passed.
So, in reacting to their own frustrations upon coming ashore,
each and every immigrant group,
whether from the slums of Belfast or of Naples,
had its vocal element who claimed to incarnate
in themselves the glories of the Old Country and would
demand recognition as representatives of the Old Country.

There was no turning to the disunited Protestant
churches, or relying upon the Church for protection against
secular misrule, as might be the case in the
larger part of the Americas that were under
French and Spanish rule. Oviedo and De Las Casas and
the rest: where were their counterparts in the English colonies,
or even in the new American states?
Puritan and other Protestant types felt alienated from the
State often, but then it was their peculiar version of the
Divine that became their Mentor; and He would not truck
with Indians on any but rigorous terms.

The Quakers once more are exceptional, and their influence in
Pennsylvania and elsewhere and into the future was
phenomenal, especially in consideration of their sparseness.
They may be justly accused of resigning from politics
in order to make more money (although the excuse was
usually their aversion to force and domination in human affairs).
Even Ben Franklin, friend of the Indians,
by virtue of exhorting ever more European immigration,
and by promoting huge land sales such as the Vandalia scheme
that would have his syndicate owning much of the
hither Midwest, helped push the Indians

out of their ancestral grounds faster.

Because of the exceedingly decentralized manner of
extending the colonies' decatriapodal tentacles,
and because of the innumerable different boatloads and tribes
involved, we should be describing the recession of the Indians
in statistical terms over time. But the data are not to be had yet;
the job remains to be done. What is left is
a series of generalizations illustrated by incidents,
compiled by darting in, here and there, and
plucking them out.

Very well. The Europeans came ashore all along the line from
Nova Scotia to Key West, in dribs and drabs,
sometimes heavily armed and aggressive, at other times
so peaceful as to invite martyrdom from the
not necessarily benign natives. In all cases there were
Indians around, and contact was made, usually in a
curious and apprehensive spirit on both sides.

Then the Whites would have to subsist, so they traded with the
Indians for necessities and got information from
them as to how to survive in an indifferent natural setting.
Trading pepped up as the months and years passed, and a
number of conflicts had to be settled. Since neither
knew what standards of legitimate action the other practiced,
each assumed that its own rules would be the rules of the game.
Also, since Indians had everything and Europeans nothing,
save a few axes, beads and misfiring muskets, Europeans were
the more determined about trading and acquiring.

How Europeans Appropriated Land

This was especially true of land. I have heard of few incidents when a
conflict came about because Europeans fished where the Indians
fished; so generous were the Indians. Nor did Whites fall into a fury
when an Indian decided to take something back, like a buckskin shirt,

that the White man thought he had been given, but the Indian evidently
believed was part of himself that could only be lent out considerately
until a feeling of wanting it back arose. Thus, "Indian-giving", the term
of reproach of the Whites for Indians and children who haven't had
rigorous discipline in the theory of conveyance of property
according to the Roman or common law.

But when it came to land-grabbing,
settlers went into a veritable feeding frenzy,
such as can only come to men who have been booted off
somebody's land in the Old Country too many times to mention.
In the non-slave areas, there was little else
worth buying and selling except for timber and furs that
Indians began to bring in. There was to be no concession to
"Indian-givers" here, not for at least two hundred years.

The foreigners misunderstood what territoriality
meant to Indians, a sense of collective sovereignty
over a stretch of land, never with papers,
until Whites introduced documentation
(often false and in any event non-binding when it suited them),
to replace oral agreement or mutual shoving
until a settlement was arrived at. Yet, early
maps of America dutifully drew in the boundaries of
Indian nations, as if the Whites did regard
Indian country as having a legal foreign status.

Can we distinguish the several guises in which land was
transferred from the Indian to the White, here, there and
everywhere for three hundred years? Possibly.

First, the "Virginia sale". It is doubtful that Virginians
paid anything, although some small objects were handed over as
gifts or payment. The Pilgrims cannily chose a spot that
looked as if it were vacant. Again a few
exchanges would suffice, to their way of thinking.
The Manhattan sale had the Dutch Director, Peter Minuet,
paying the famous 24 *thalers (Dutch dollars)*
worth of *tchotchkes* (Dutch for trinkets) to
certain naive Indians, who,

for all we know, may have been impostors.
Too, if they had entrusted the sum to a reliable bank
at 6% interest compounded annually (more fantastic
than the true story) they would be able to
buy back Manhattan today.

William Penn, who managed to be both a Quaker
and *persona grata* at the Royal Court, obtained an
enormous tract of land that was named then perchance
"Pennsylvania" and acquired fairly strong claims to the
plains and marshes going down to the sea that were to be
called New Jersey. Even so, Penn paid the Indians
what they considered a fair price, and did not
chase them off afterwards, and did many a deed that
makes him an outstanding candidate for the greatest and best of
American colonial leaders, alongside
John Winthrop and Benjamin Franklin.

By present standards of what constitutes legal title,
no legal title to U.S. land goes back for more than
several political generations without becoming shaky, and
no Indian land title was vested in an individual,
so that all sales to be legal had to be made by duly
constituted tribe officials. Title to all the land in the
United States of America is based on the practical fiction that
there was once a title, and the premise that we must not go
beyond a certain point backwards in time, this date
to be set by the prejudiced fiat of the
contemporary law-making body.

The stupendously large lands sold by the Indians for
practically nothing would incline an American court
today to void such sales on grounds that the vendor was
ipso facto and *prima facie* legally insane,
or drunk at the time of sale,
or selling what did not belong to him in the first place,
or had been bribed,

or had scratched his "x" on a document under
duress or fraudulent deception.
The colonial gangsters from Europe knew all this well.
Examples of these good deals in the 1700's were the
one million eight hundred thousand acres
Southeast of the Ohio River bought from the Iroquois,
another treaty with them giving away most of
western New York State along with a region between
Ohio and Tennessee, and an agreement with the Creek Indians to
move their South Carolina border West and South.
By this time, all of the aforesaid land had been
claimed several times, beginning with the cruise of
Giovanni Cabotto, and going through companies and
individuals and societies and governmental units.
Ultimately it was the jurisdiction that commanded force and
claimed legitimacy in the region of the sale
whose title was effectively conveyed.

(In the Europe of these times, governments sold and swapped
territories and peoples as well, and everywhere world-wide,
and today, too; however, the title being exchanged there
included the exercise of general rights and the powers of a
government over territory, not rights to the real property of its people.
Still, often such transactions enabled the new
government to dispossess whoever it did not like
in the newly acquired lands.)

Some American sales were so fantastic that
they must be true: Daniel Boone, famous hunter and fighter,
whose sons were killed by Indians but who was a forgiving man,
joined with a drinking buddy and, who knows, possibly
some alcoholic Indians, to purchase for a negligible sum
the territory now encompassing Kentucky and Ohio.
A deal so droll as this one quickly got out of hand, and
could be used mainly as one more implausible
argument for removing Indians from their lands
in the years to come:
"Any group so irresponsible as to sell its land
for so little should not be allowed
to have land in the first place."

A great deal of land could be identified as occupied by squatters.
They might be detected by
their suspiciousness at any sign of
Indians returning to claim the land,
or an inquiring officer of the Crown or colony,
by the rough timbered shacks they threw together,
by the smoke arising as they burnt forests to make way for corn,
and by the rooting snorting pigs.
There would be a family scattered about, a mule, and
perhaps a horse. There would be no deed,
no purchase price, never, until a man rather resembling a
lawyer would come by one day and offer to register a
title to the land for a small sum and a jug of whiskey.
Chasing away any defenseless Indians often worked to
clear the *de facto* title, and where that did not serve,
killing off any resisters -
what would be termed in the jargon of international lawyers
just coming into being in the universities of Europe as
"acquisition by conquest".

Thence occurred more formal ways of taking Indian lands:

They could be seized upon the declaration of a state of war
by one or more of the colonies.

They could be occupied following an official
formal declaration by one of the numerous colonial and later
State and Federal governments that would ban
Indian occupancy of an area after a certain date
(such a ban assuming that the land did not belong to the
Indians in the first place but to some public or
private owners, so designated, in vaguely defined
earlier actions or non-actions, which were usable as
precedents, once they were dressed in suitable
mumbo-jumbo legalese.)

There might be a fine treaty drawn up, employing
flowery terms and phrases -
*"Great White Father who always Thinks
of the Interests of His Deare Children…"* -
such as the White Americans thought to be the proper way of
speaking to savage Americans (reminiscent of the
famous banquet scene in the film *"Some Like it Hot"*,
in which the mafia don's suave and complimentary
speech is followed by the execution of its subjects).
Some money would be passed to the Indians
and many rights would be "guaranteed" to them by
negotiators, who had neither the power nor the will
to fulfill the guarantees.

Too, a legislature would on occasion pass a law to
govern the Indians, although the Indians rarely gave their consent
to be governed by the intruding tribes of Whites, and
many precedents acceded to by the White Americans
assumed that sovereignty had originally rested in and
continued to be vested in the Indian tribes.

A French jurist, Jean Bodin, had not too long before
[1576] written an influential treatise,
one highly popular, also, among rulers,
"demonstrating" that absolute final decision
over the affairs of a domain rested in the head of state
usually a King. Enthusiastic White lawyers
and politicians could readily see in this doctrine,
not a new dogma pointing to the vigorous future of the
centralized national state, but an acknowledgment of a
pre-existing reality, that is, that
"The Great White Father owns it all,
so stand out of the way!"

There were many cases where Indians let Whites
co-occupy their land and form a neighborhood
where both sets would persuade away or fight off
intervenors whatever their coloration, and
otherwise engage in mutual aid. Notable
instances of this occurred with Quakers, the Society of Friends,

who may have quaked and trembled in the presence of their God,
but were open and amiable with Indians,
much to the disgust of aggressive gentiles who,
because they were so fearful of the Indians,
became embroiled in mutual massacre.
These people forced their way into Indian territory,
outnumbered and took power from the Quaker oligarchy that
ran the state, and ended up ruining much of the
promise of Pennsylvania.

There were frequent incidents, each fascinating, of Whites going over to the Indians and a few, mostly male, Indians going over to the Whites, but one hears almost nothing of Whites, male or female, bringing tracts of land into their White community as a result of marriage or consanguinity. Even when an Indian "Princess" would enter the White world, her dowry would be meager personal possessions and some tobacco and useful family connections, such as
lots of bear meat on the table.

Several methods could coalesce to create large holdings. Robert Livingston, a Scots immigrant, paid Indians a trifling sum for 2,000 acres on the Hudson River in the 1680's, and had the Governor give him a patent on the property. He did the same for another tract bordering on Massachusetts, and the Governor, Thomas Dungan, then gave him the connecting land, over 100,000 acres, for a quit-rent of 28 shillings. Much of this was Indian land, but the Indians were not consulted, to our knowledge.
Nor was the amount of the bribe paid to the Governor made public; a couple of thousand pounds sterling would suffice.

Governors had to live off their bribes, considering how little fees amounted to, and how stingy the legislatures were,
and how pretentious was their life-style…
Only a century later did the Crown give governors
a fairly reliable source of income, from customs duties. A usual bribe to a governor was a half or third share in the property being conveyed illegally. Sir William Johnson, who was appointed by the Crown to defend the rights of Indians in upstate New York, and indeed did take up the Indians' cause in some important cases where they were being

threatened with fraud or expulsion, accepted from them, the very Indians, a gift of 100,000 acres of Mohawk land; on this he paid the government a quit-rent of two beaver skins and received an official title. Practices in other colonies were on the average not quite so stinking and extravagantly corrupt as in New York.

Women were elevated in status, in many Indian societies, if one can believe the new anthropological history. This is of course hard to measure. I have mentioned their participation in elections. Women could become Chiefs in some Eastern tribes, *sunksquas* or *women sachems*. Women might also hold property, it was learned when property came to be recorded on deeds. Colonial Anglo-American women who had experienced Indian captivity or enjoyed Indian husbands reported no significant difference in the esteem accorded them, in work allocations, in personal possessions, and in liberty of local movement, by comparison with their colonial European conditions of life.

Of all the stories of Indian collaboration in the English colonies, it could be Squanto's that would win the prize, not Pocohontas, Indian princess veritably, who married John Rolfe, he an early Virginian, in a dynastic marriage to keep the peace, and went off to England, there to catch her death of cold. Squanto, we recall, was the internationally traveled Indian who turned up to greet the Pilgrims after they finally made up their minds to stay ashore.

Squanto was a Patuxet. In 1615 there were an estimated 20,000 to 25,000 Patuxet dwelling in villages (that with their sprawling wigwams looked like a later-day suburbia, if a drawing by an artist of the Cartier expedition can be trusted) in the general area of "Plymouth Bay". In 1616, a plague - the English curse - struck the Patuxet people. English visitors were immune, but 75% to 90% of the Patuxet fell sick and died.

Bartholomew Gosnold had sailed in with a 1602 expedition seeking sassafras and fish, but it could not have been his fault. It would have been the later vagabonds, sailors and fishermen who jumped ship, men from boats anchoring off-shore for fishing and trading. It could have been French traders who were active all along the North Atlantic Coast: furs were already a hot item, often traded for corn among the Indians, but also traded for export abroad (as recorded by Captain John Smith, who was sailing in those waters in 1614.)

Again, it might have been sick Europeans, marooned by their comrades in the solicitous and gentle manner of the age.

By 1610 kidnaping Indians and conveying them to Europe for display was typical English conduct. Thomas Hunt, prior to returning with a load of fish, seized 27 Indians, among them Squanto, and sold or abandoned him in Malaga, Spain (of all places). According to Smith and to Sir Ferdinando Gorges, a prominent Puritan leader, it was this incident that turned Indians into Anglophobes.

In 1619 Squanto got back to Plymouth Bay, in time to welcome the Pilgrims. He became their economic and diplomatic consultant, losing some friends in the Indian communities thereabouts as a result, and rising in influence to the point where he was taking an important part in the decisions affecting the Puritan colony. Some say he had ambitions to high office. A typically slippery treaty was concluded between the Pilgrims and the Pokanoket, who then took Squanto prisoner and released him only after the
Pilgrims paid them a ransom.

The next year, 1622, while conducting an English delegation to treat with a Monomoy Indian village, he contracted a fever and died. It is said that, on his deathbed, after distributing his few possessions among his English friends, he expressed a hope of joining their God in Heaven, forsaking, for the nonce at least, his old God Hobbamock, who, like Yahweh, appeared better known for the harm he caused man than the good he did.

The conclusion of New England Indian supremacy came with King Philip's War in 1675-6; "Philip" was actually Metacomet, son of Massasoit, the primal benefactor of the Pilgrims.
Destruction and casualties made the little war proportionately worst of American wars.
After several victories and massacres on both sides,

combined colonial forces captured Metacomet through a betrayal, killed him, and enslaved his family.

It is universally believed, and has been from the beginning, that Americans are amateurs at diplomacy and statecraft, a statement which, if assented to, is followed by the explanation: they are a new country, without experience. That this has always been nonsense should long ago have become obvious to the thousands of scholars who have assumed it as fact and taught it to others.

Whatever the many mistakes of American diplomacy - which have probably been typical of professional and non-professional diplomats everywhere - they commonly occurred from causes other than inexperience. Few nations exist whose people have had the continual experience of Americans with independent Indian tribes, autonomous colonies and states, and bordering empires, colonies, and republics. This is not to say that Americans lack peculiar and characteristic behavioral flaws in the field of foreign relations as well as in all other fields; nor for that matter, that we can hope for better in the future.

The Indians, who had achieved a satisfactory social equilibrium in generally analphabetic circumstances, were continually being pushed by the White Americans to agree to wordy documents and sign them. Like proverbial Levantines, the Indians got along well enough, it would seem, by pow-wowing on a subject in a collective encounter, arriving at an apparent consensus, and, if so, adjourning with pledges of peace and performance.

There would be some admirable oratory, at which some Indians, like Homer's ancient warriors, were champions - Conasatego of the Onondaga Iroquois might be set up as the Demosthenes of America, the precursor of Daniel Webster - and which same evocative skill, along with revivalist preaching, may well have been the basis for American Western bombast and orating style.

There would be story-telling in the course of negotiations, again a form of conference behavior more familiar to American management behavior than to anywhere else in the modern world. Behind the scenes (like the lobbies to come) there might be an exchange of promises for the private good of the diplomats of either side, bribes, in short. It was not uncommon for Indians to turn against their leader who had agreed to a deal, whether because of allegations of dishonesty, or of not being cut in on the deal, or because the Indians lacked a full idea of representation: that we are stuck for better or worse with the decisions of our delegates.

Indian customs might have suited some medieval European warriors, also illiterate usually, or some types that would grow up on the frontier in the belief that a handshake would be sufficiently binding to sustain promises. It did not suit the growing legal, bureaucratic, and merchant classes; it particularly did not suit the lower classes who had just learned to read and write, and were full of Bible-like covenants, and who felt that they might lose their social standing if they did not put things down on paper.

International relations could be complicated. After Miantonomo succeeded his uncle as Chief of the Narragansett nation in 1636, he allied with the colonists of Massachusetts and Connecticut against the Pequots the following year, and signed a treaty of perpetual peace with the white settlers and the Mohegan nation. Five years later he broke the treaty but was defeated and captured by the Mohegans under Uncas, and handed over to a tribunal of white Boston clergymen for judgement. They decreed execution and he was duly killed by Uncas.

Many agreements only promoted further conflicts, and led to typical resolution of issues by violence - personal fights, irregular clashes, guerrilla skirmishing begun by one side or the other or by newcomers both on the Indian and on the European side, who would ignore or scorn the jurisdictional competence of the accord. Considering the strong court system that developed later in America and even took upon itself the status of a third branch of government, one might wonder why the courts could not be used much earlier to settled the thousand trials that should have been carried into judicial, if not an arbitration or mediation, process.

The easy answer is that the jurisprudence to justify such a solution had yet to develop. Besides, rare were those who would obey the courts and hence, if they focused upon problems of Red and White, whatever general prestige courts did possess would be attrited.

Certain of the larger statements just made can be illustrated by the story of the French and Indian Wars that took place between 1689 and 1763, the several parts of which were given their European and American names here above. In all of these, fighting took place along the seaboard and the rivers, as well as in the frontier regions. Generally the Algonquin Indian tribes sided with the French and French-colonials, the Iroquois with the British and the Anglo-colonials.

A multitude of skirmishes, burnings, killings, and movements back and forth typified the wars. American legend has it that the British encountered disaster in attempting to capture Fort Duquesne in 1755 despite the diligent effort of George Washington's Virginia militia to rescue the regular troops and their General Edward Braddock from the folly of their rigid tactics, and that another British army under General John Burgoyne had to surrender in 1777 near Saratoga because of disdain and ignorance of colonial and Indian unconventional tactics.

Still, when it came down to it, and granting that their forces badly outnumbered the French, British regulars did well enough in several critical engagements at Louisbourg (1758, where a fort guarded the approaches to the St. Lawrence River), Fort Wayne (1760, where the French had maintained an old Indian town as a fortified post for a hundred years), and Quebec (1759).

The Americans irritated their English overlords no end by avoiding their share of the costs of the wars; nor were the numbers of American volunteers impressive, although it was the Americans, particularly those along the frontier, who aggravated the Indians and caused the French to set up strong forts that were painful to capture.

One such effort to obtain American support occurred in 1755 when a congress at Albany was called by the Boss of the Colonies, the British

Board of Trade, a notoriously bungling and corrupt office of the Crown most of the time, but here struck by the intelligent idea of having the assembled representatives of the colonies draw up plans for their concerted and consistent management of Indian relations. The delegates instead drafted a scheme to have the elected colonial assemblies elect in their turn a grand council, presided over by an executive who would be named by the Crown. (A plan on this order had been originally presented to the Board in England in 1697 by William Penn, in vain.)

The Albany Plan, proposed by Benjamin Franklin with amendments by Thomas Hutchinson of Massachusetts, failed to win assent either in America or England. Franklin tried to shame the colonial delegates into a union by citing the remarkable success of the Iroquois Confederation "savages" (his word): to no avail. It would have been an excellent way to handle the land problem and Indian relations in general. Instead, a Northern and a Southern commissioner were appointed to take over Indian relations, North and South.

English policy early on took an opposite tack to the American way. The most intense wish of most colonists was to clear the Indian out of their future, push him West or into oblivion. (Ancient Egyptians had the idea that the soul of the dead went West; Americans thought West was the place to escape a poor life, but also said of a dead person that "he's gone West".) The Massachusetts legislature on November 3, 1755 proclaimed the Brobscot Indians enemies and traitors; a bounty of forty pounds was offered for every adult male scalp and half that for a female scalp or the scalp of a boy under twelve years.

Colonial politicians, businessmen and traders, settlers, and even scholars painted increasingly unfavorable and pessimistic pictures of the Indians, their style of life and their conduct, their recalcitrance, their unassimilability. They wanted Britain to supply the armed force needed to destroy Indian resistance. But English officials, even the military commanders, generally saw the Indians as victims of aggression by the colonists.

They could cite the bloody Cherokee War, the larger support that

Indians gave to the French in the French-Indian Wars, and then a
three-year war (1763-6) in which Chief Pontiac of the Ottawa Indians
mobilized many tribes in a climactic effort to push back the British
colonists from the Ohio Valley and Great Lakes region: all of these
were outcomes of the maddening pressure of Whites
upon Indian nations and their lands.

Pontiac, after several victories, was deserted by some of his tribal
allies and defeated in 1764; some time later he signed a treaty of peace
with the English commander, Sir William Johnson at Oswego, but,
although he steadfastly maintained proper relations under the Treaty,
he was assassinated three years afterwards by an Indian said to be
paid by an Englishman engaged in illegal trade.

Court opinion was represented in the Royal Proclamation of 1763,
following the astonishing, for the America-centered person,
Treaty of Paris of 1763, which gave all of New France to England,
save for several rich tiny islands
(actually more productive and comfortable than Canada
and the Near Middle West at this time).
Afterwards the English commander demanded oaths
of allegiance from the Canadiens of Acadia, now become Nova Scotia,
and dispersed into the Southern colonies the six thousand souls
who refused the oath; naturally he was making
potential rebels against Britain.

The Royal Proclamation declared that Indians must be protected in
the peaceful possession of their lands, and that boundaries would be
drawn to ensure that no settlement would occur on their lands;
furthermore it was ordered that persons settling upon lands
not legally ceded by the Indians should be removed.

A Southern North-South boundary line already existed, and
in 1768 a Northern connection was made.
The Western boundary between practically all
Indian and colonial settlement would now run from the
Eastern edge of Lake Ontario straight South to the boundary of West
Florida on the Gulf of Mexico. Some of the colonies

formally acceded to this line; more than a score of
Indian nations also subscribed to it.

Still, the settlers who were already trespassing were not forced out.
The British colonial administration had no money to enforce the law,
and no central colonial administration for Indian affairs. The colonies
were supposed to supervise its observance. Within several years an
estimated 60,000 people had moved into the region between
Pittsburgh and the mouth of the Ohio River.
Indian protests went for naught.

White South Carolinians warred with the Cherokees from 1759-61.
With both sides heavily damaged, peace was made and an open
boundary area set up that soon was occupied by White settlers.
In 1776 fighting broke out and the
Cherokees, now heavily outnumbered owing to remorseless
demographic trends, lost more territory and freedom of action.
Struggles continued, with Georgia involved as well;
more territory was given up in 1791.
The situation of the Indians only worsened.
A scum of White society, gangsters, no less, were attracted
from everywhere to the approaching destruction of the Indians.
Cherokees, Creeks, and other nations of Southeast
North America had not long to live. The Cherokee,
one of the most progressive of the American nations,
had only two more political generations in which to
carry on its old life in its old territory.

The Indians were not without friends. After all,
it was an independent Congress of the United States of America,
operating under the Articles of Confederation,
that passed in 1787 the famed Northwest Ordinance
for the governance of the territories to the Mississippi River.
Among other highly important provisions, the Ordinance pledged the
"utmost good faith towards the Indians;
their land and property shall never be taken from them
without their consent"...

If laws were to be passed that would affect them, these would be only
*"for preventing wrongs being done to them and
for preserving peace and friendship with them"*.
A truly enlightened policy.

Yet fifteen years later, a prospective President of the United States, renowned for his distinguished relatives and his learning, declared to a meeting of the Sons of the Pilgrims that the
"law of nature" gave the Indians only a domain
sufficient for their subsistence. For
*."what is the right of the huntsman to the forest of a thousand miles
over which he has accidentally ranged in quest of prey?"*

(The orator was definitely not implying that a serendipitous Colombus conveyed no rights by his discoveries, nor the Cabots, the Cartiers, the Hudsons, the de La Salles, *et al.*)

And when John Quincy Adams went on to argue
*"Shall the liberal bounties of Providence to the race of man
be monopolized by one of ten thousand for whom they were created"*,
surely he would not be
intending to impugn the great wealth amassed by a few Pilgrims of his own society, he among them? By 1802, each of this elite possessed on the average the wealth of 10,000 Indians, and of
10,000 of the general population.

The Shawnee Tribe, with about 600 warriors, was sold 6,000 gallons of whiskey annually by criminal traders. Its Chief Tecumseh, son of a Chief killed in battle against the whites, was inspired by his white lady friend's reading him of the life of Alexander the Great. Laulewasika, a drunk and brother of the esteemed Tecumseh, found God at a Shaker revival meeting in 1805. He preached abstinence, and, urged on by Tecumseh, found in his trances communing with the "Master of Life", a message to return Indians to their old ways, to unite them, and exterminate the White man. (Conversions with dismaying frequency fly off the handle.)

His new name was Teuskibatawa.

At Greenville, Ohio, where they had signed a treaty with "Mad Anthony" Wayne, whose troops had defeated them, the brothers set up a center for agitation, propaganda, and organization, occupying a large meeting house and many cabins for converts. Tecumseh then traveled all the way to Lake Superior and down to the Gulf of Mexico. His message to the individual tribes brought some refusals, but also many pledges of support.

However, while he was gone, Governor William Henry Harrison, with bribery and alcohol, enticed a group of chiefs into trading him three million acres of land for a few thousand dollars. Tecumseh, returning, denounced the sale as fraudulent, and resumed rallying of the Indian nations for war.

This time, while he was gone a-rallying, Harrison collected militiamen, some regulars, and allied Indians, and marched upon a large assemblage of Indians near Tippecanoe. Fearing an attack, Tecumseh's followers fell upon Harrison's forces. Although the battle could be termed an Indian victory for the casualties inflicted, the Whites were left in charge of the field, whereas the Indians withdrew, and therefore the victory was assigned to Harrison, who became President later on, with Tyler as Vice-President, under the corny catchy slogan, "Tippecanoe and Tyler, too".

When Tecumseh returned and the War of 1812 was on in earnest, the British-Canadian force retreated into Canada, finally stood its ground for a moment, rallying under Tecumseh's stern counsel, then fled again, leaving Tecumseh and his warriors to die like the Spartans at Thermopylae.

The Creek Indian Nation went to war, too, on the side of the British. A large Indian force conquered Fort Sims

(near Mobile, Alabama) in August of 1813,
massacring some 500 White men, women and children,
taking a few Blacks and mestizos as prisoners. At the battle
of Horseshoe Bend, next year, General Andrew Jackson,
aided by Cherokee warriors, destroyed a
Creek army of 1,000 men, and by 1824,
various treaties had been signed giving Whites
three-fourths of Alabama and Florida, one-third of Tennessee,
one-fifth of Georgia and Mississippi,
parts of Kentucky and North Carolina - besides the
seizures and purchases of earlier years. Jackson's
role in these times, save as a war leader, was ignoble,
yet served to enhance his popularity among
common people.

With a scarcely credible hypocrisy and the rhetorical madness
typical of the times, President Jackson was soon
commiserating with civilization, saying that a
*"country covered with forests and ranged by
a few thousand savages"*
should be not be compared with the art, industry, cities
and prosperous farms of a country of
*"more than twelve million happy people, and
filled with all the blessings of liberty, civilization and religion".*

And so, when the Indians refused to sell more land,
wanting to keep a modest portion for themselves,
Georgia declared that they must bow to the will of the sovereign State.
The Cherokee Nation sued the State,
and Chief Justice Marshall declared for the Indians,
that the law of Georgia was a nullity.
Georgia ignored the Supreme Court; President
Jackson ignored Georgia; the Indians lost their land and more.
They were moved by the President under the Removal Act of 1830
all the way West across the Mississippi River,
where we shall be meeting them again later on.

It was a "death march", this march of the winter of 1838-39.
With a U.S. armed military escort and the Indians pre-figuring the
roles of the Japanese guards and the beaten U.S. Army prisoners

of the "Death March of Bataan" 105 years later,
a fourth of the Indians perished on the way -
men, women, and children. A few Cherokees
escaped the roundup, and survived in their
mountain fastnesses of the East to this day.

There was something proto-nazi about early Americans.
When one of the chief architects and organizers of the
Third Reich (Albert Speer) came to his memoirs, he wrote,
*"Hitler often cited the fate of the Indians in the United States
as an entirely feasible method of territorial occupation".*
Hitler was speaking of Poland, Russia, the Ukraine, Byelorussia -
Slavs in general - on such occasions, for he had in mind
to subordinate at forced labor and decimate these peoples,
meanwhile removing them beyond the Ural Mountains
to make way for Germans.

How did the Indians change under the continual bleeding of their
rights to the country?
Recall that they did not know this to be the case.
They thought part of the time that they were only being scratched, that
the Europeans were not so numerous and that their lands were far too
great to be taken up by even the most greedy of White tribes. When
the Europeans came ashore, the Indians did not panic nor charge down
upon them. They accepted the newcomers with little more ruction than
would attend three centuries later the gradual advent of a
new ethnic group into an urban neighborhood.

Rather soon, however, their life style began to change.
The clothing of the newcomers was hardly attractive;
Indian clothing was more enhancing and functional.
The moccasin passed over permanently to Europeans.
The metal axe and the firearm came, iron knives and hoes.
Brass kettles supplanted earthen pots. The pig came to replace
the fattened bears and dogs. The cuisine was not so different; Pilgrims
and Indians partook of the same first Thanksgiving dinner
more or less together. Turkey was not served.

Alcohol made a stunning impression. Indians could not cope with it.
They still cannot do so. Puritans, Virginians, Americans in
general, could not handle it. It was and is the preferred drug and poison
of a considerable part of the population. Perhaps for the early Indians,
it was connected with mourning and depression over the continual
plagues that took the joy out of life. The colonists as well had
much to forget, many sorrows to drown.

Drunken orgies became common among the Indians,
these serving as well to accelerate rates of sexual promiscuity,
rape, sadistic acts, and fatal quarrels as described in
numerous reports of missionaries and colonial authorities
and in the occasional recorded sad words of Indian leaders.
No one would or could stop the ever-increasing alcoholism
among Reds or Whites. Only the Blacks were partially protected,
ironically, because it was in the interest of their owners to
prevent them from thus abusing themselves.
(There were of course many illegal whiskey stills,
possessed and operated at hideaways by African-Americans.)

Some of the Indians had known other less potent drugs,
the peyotl cactus root of the Southwest, for instance.
In 1620, the Inquisition banned its use because it was
"an act of superstition" and
"the devil was the real author of this vice".
The coca plant was widely used in South America
but not exported to the North. Heavy tobacco chewing
and smoke inhaling were used to induce disordered visions
and to inspire stories.

The joy of the newcomers in hunting, fishing, and trapping was
rendered ecstatic by the memory of how suppressed
were these activities in the Old Country.
A man who once was jailed and whipped for snaring a rabbit
on manorial ground, or whose vision of nature was
of London rats, might now bring down deer for his own table
with prayers of praise to the Almighty and a rifle.
It is so hard not to sympathize with this man,
and his wife, when and if ever she would arrive,

for his devouring of this new life, forgiving him in turn his
trespasses against the silent removed native and
his greed and cruelty to Nature.

The Indians minded, but not so much as to destroy it,
the fresh elation of the deprived newcomers from over the sea.
They felt until the very last that they had only
to remove themselves a mile more from the direct scene
of the settler's orgy to restore their primordial equilibrium.
For that was the state of North America when Europeans
came upon it. Equilibrium may not be the proper word
for their condition. Probably there were many and great
demographic movements and advances and recessions of tribes
in the centuries before the European coming.

Within one mnemonic generation of the first landings,
there could be heard Indian voices complaining about
the sundering of their social fabric by the White man.
Yet, on the whole, the Indian civilizations seemed
to have been in balance, and the Indians themselves spoke
continually of their previous social equanimity,
and of the contrast between their own normal state of mind
and that of the frenetic British.

One would hardly find in the whole length and breadth of the
USA-to-be what could be recognized as the *angst,
anomie, angoisse,* dissociation, adolescent rebellion,
and other conceptualized basic societal diseases.
The Indian nations were not straining to go somewhere.
In the light of history, from a functional, anthropological perspective,
this condition could not be termed tragic,
nor deplored as going nowhere.

Some of the Indian's nostalgia became a fixture of the
larger American mind. Two centuries later,
in 1908, a great movement known as the
Boy Scouts was formed by a homosexual Englishman,

Baron R.S.S. Baden-Powell. (In 1998,
a federal court stopped the American Boy Scouts from
discriminating against homosexuals. Apropos,
the modern [1896] Olympic Games were
first organized and promoted by a French homosexual,
Baron Pierre de Coubertin.) In America the
Boy Scouts were driven toward and effectively modeled on the
life of the Indians, with small improvements from two
centuries of scientific and industrial progress.
If the life of the Boy Scouts failed to satisfy youth's
adulthood, it was more the fault of the crowded industrial
urban or agro-industrial society,
which brought the disappearance of the birds,
fish, deer, bears, camping sites,
wilderness trails, and starry clear nights that were
part of the fantasy and ordinary being of the Indian.

But of course the Boy Scouts could appreciate only rarely and generally little of the total Indian life, its torturing rites of passage from boy to man, its frequent wars against neighboring tribes, and the mutual cruelties and savagery of combat. Nor could the Boy Scouts be quite confident that tribal knowledge of medicines and therapy would be up to modern standards. And they might be sure that, however satisfying the frequently fine weaving and *compositions vivantes* of Indian art, the wonders of the written word and the wide panorama of European culture might be lost to himself.

The Boy Scouts and Girl Scouts were hardly ahead of the public in having their attention called to the destruction of the environment. Not before World War II was played out would they address analytic questions to concerns that they did note personally and regret when they were tramping about town and country a generation earlier. The environment had much deteriorated.

The Indians, too, ignored effects which they or the newcomers would have on the environment. If the Indians had been more numerous and used up fossil energy on an industrial scale, they would have presented the European newcomers with a partially devastated environment.

A case has been increasingly built up to consider Indians as
nature-lovers *par excellence,* adorers and
conservators of Mother Earth and
all her creatures and forms of life, great and small.
Undoubtedly, many Indians, introduced to the bizarre life
of American towns, could not wait to get back home.
And in no case did a functioning Indian settlement go modern,
redesigning itself voluntarily -
unless it would be the Cherokees and Creeks,
who won the ambiguous appellation "civilized"
early in the nineteenth century.
Nor did any Indian culture take on the totality or even a
major fraction of any European culture.

Terrific rates of erosion in pre-Columbian agriculture
in Central Mexico have recently been measured.
Crude slash and burn farming was a typical technique
among Indian tribes everywhere; too much
was burned, often, and erosion was invited. It was
common to farm sunny slopes and lose the soil
to draining rains in a few years.

The so-called primeval forests that New England and colonial
reporters and poets admired were second growth, owing to
Indian de-population; the earlier forests had been cut or burned to
make way for Indian farming.

Another theory, vastly exaggerated, ascribes the loss of numerous
species of large mammals of the post-Ice Age period to Indian hunting
methods that killed far more animals than could be skinned and eaten.
The tactic of cornering more than a small herd and driving it
over a cliff was logistically non-rational, if clever and
necessary under the circumstances.

More rational and a lesson even for today,
notable in Wisconsin, Michigan and Mayan locales,
was the practice of raising terraces between water ditches
for better drainage in wet weather and hand-watering

from the ditches in drought. Too, in the semi-arid Southwest, sophisticated irrigation systems were employed.

Spaniards and Indians built a road from St. Augustine, Florida, to Fort Carolina, seventy kilometers distant. Indian trails guided this and the network of roads built by the Spanish in the same and next century in the Southwest. One road reached St. Augustine from Natchez (in today's Mississippi). St. Augustine also acquired the first street, made of seashell concrete around 1680. In 1632, a Virginia statute had set forth the means of laying down roads.

The first manufactured road was constructed by the French in 1721 between Montreal and Quebec, on an old Indian route. The way to the Ohio River was Indian; surveyed by George Washington, it was cleared for wagons in part, and afforded the setting for the destruction of General Braddock's British army by Indian ambush in the French and Indian War. (Benjamin Franklin mass-produced 150 Conestoga wagons for Braddock's expedition; Daniel Boone drove one of them.)

The route from Philadelphia to Pittsburgh used three Indian trails for its basic alignment. So it went everywhere. The West was won along Indian trails. Most accounts of explorers and pioneers slight the aid given by Indians and their roads. Yet they proceeded usually by approaching knowledgeable Indians and asking them to point out and guide them along the proper routes to their imagined destination.

It has often been asserted that no single great good ever came to any tribe of Indians from the invaders. Or should we consider the horse? The Spanish brought the horse first to the desert nomads of the Southwest, the Navaho and Comanche. The Plains Indians Culture became the quintessence of the horse culture.

All is not as myth would have it. The Hollywood horsemen were the Western Sioux, the Teton-Dakotas. They were not indigenous to the great prairies. Domino-like, resembling the Germanic tribes that invaded the Roman Empire, they were first of all far to the East and were pushed to move West by aggressive tribes who were being pressed by Europeans. It was the

1700's. The Sioux then ousted one after another
the tribes that stood between them and the rich buffalo lands
of North and South Nebraska, Wyoming and Montana
(all of this being already under French and Spanish claims
as recognized by "international law").

Before then, the hunting peoples of the Great Plains did nearly
everything the same as later, except that the horse was missing until
the sixteenth century. They were pedestrian and used dogs and pulled
skids carrying their portable skin lodges. The Spanish, without
knowing it, offered the fully assimilable new element to the culture.
The horse went wild and was broken and employed so
quickly by the Indians that the first Europeans coming in
reported that the culture was characteristically mounted.

Yet the evils that came ashore were more numerous -
alcohol, slaughter of beaver, bear, otter,
and other species for the fur trade, destructive lumbering,
firearms, oral cultural illiteracy, disappearance of useful arts
like canoe-building, mental dislocation, appropriation and
conversion of waterways and fishways and
animal breeding grounds into sewers and mass traps,
plus the general build-up of an alternative civilization of
machines and industry that came down with crushing force upon
Indian and European-Americans alike.

There were few signs that the Indians comprehended
intellectually that they were in a love match with Nature.
They made a living, they had their good times and
bad times, they were proud of themselves,
they did not need the European, his religion, his metal pots,
his guns, his horses, nor practically anything else.
The advent and posturings of Whites presented a long-running comedy
for Indian adults and children, but one faraway day
they would be moaning with il Pagliaccio,
"*La commedia e finita!*"

In concluding this chapter, it may be well to recapitulate the factors contributing to the fatal decline of the Indian nations of the United States. Almost all have to do with demography. This is natural; the end of a group comes with its disappearance and fading from memory.

1. I note first the *motive-force and tenacity of the invaders* of the New World. Tremendous forces were driving Europeans of first one ethnic group and then another. These can even be pin-pointed: the Castillians, not the Catalonians; the Breton, not the Savoyards; the English, not the Irish Catholic; the Moravians, not the Prussians. No sooner did one culture group descend upon America than another was seized by the notion that it must go to America. This process has been going on now for four centuries.

2. *Disease*, whether it struck before or after Columbus, invaded in wave after wave in forms for which Indians lacked immunity: smallpox, measles, whooping cough, chicken pox, bubonic plague, typhus, malaria, influenza, intestinal worms, amoebic dysentery, and diphtheria. Yellow fever may have been indigenous. The Indians had known encephalitis, poliomyelitis, hepatitis, and syphilis.

3. *Warfare*. In the "USA" the Indian nations had lost the overall war to contain the Europeans at trading stations and fishing places by 1700, at which point in time their numbers were equal at the "war front" to those of the Europeans, who numbered 110,000 in the "USA", 45,000 in New France, 5,000 Mexicans and Spaniards in the South and West (heavily outnumbered by the surrounding Indians), and contingents of professional soldiery from the Old World. Then in less than 2 political generations (4 biological generations), European immigration and birthing had arrived at three times the number of Indians East of the Alleghenies; they counted over a million in all.

Europeans were already members of larger societies and cultures. This had an most important effect on the conduct of warfare. Like the technological system of interchangeable parts invented over a century later (and it happened in gun-making), the "invention" of a society of larger loyalties and more general affiliation permitted soldiers (whether

civilian or professional) to be fed into battles and wars
that were not necessarily parochial.

From the earliest moments, Euro-American military formations could employ various ethnic types shoulder-to-shoulder: Welsh, Irish, German, Bohemian, French, even Indians, in a "British" or New York unit. The Indians were incapable of this except on rare (and effective) occasion; the Whites were hardly capable of it at first. But the difference was significant, increasing, and permanent.

Failing to emulate the organization and logistics of the Europeans, Indians could use small weapons effectively, but could not readily obtain, maintain and use artillery or even wagon trains. Indian discipline was poor (as was the colonial), and military units disappeared overnight upon the whim, or in panic, or in disgust, or in victory.

4. *Forced labor and deliberate or neglectful starvation and malnutrition* caused many Indian deaths and again de-population. Mass transportation of Indians to suit the settlement or war plans of the imperial authorities resulted in severe losses.

5. *The inability to unite tribes for war or peaceful dealings* was damaging. So was inter-tribal warfare, and aiding European armies to fight one another. An impressive united front to discourage potential enemies was impossible. The colonists could count on this weakness.

6. *The diminution in size of tribes reduced the potential marriage pools*, and customs of endogamous marriage forbade reaching out to intermarry.

7. The heavy use of the worst kinds of *alcohol* - "firewater" truly - unhinged the minds, maimed, defertilized, and killed its many thousands. Many stories were told of tribes gone out of control because of the social behavior resulting from alcohol abuse.

8. A *decline of morale* of substantial proportions developed, reflecting the effects of these prior happenings. Suicide, whether actual or psychic, was common.

A loss of the will to reproduce or to
care for infants occurred. The will to rebuild
damaged tribal social and physical fabrics lessened.

All causal factors interacted with other factors.
In the end, the decline in their numbers of warriors and
the inability to mobilize their resources
would appear to have been decisive for the defeat of the
Indian nations. Ironically, through the seventeenth and
eighteenth centuries, the popular pictorial image persisted of America
as an Indian Queen, then later a Prince.

Americans generally believed, as they do now, that there could have
been no accommodation between European and Indian cultures.
This conviction may be unjustified.
Policies of gradual occupation and mutual adjustment
were rarely and weakly employed, and
overwhelmed by conflicts.

An outlook upon nature and wilderness, foodstuffs, plants, animals,
medications, construction techniques, canoes and rafts, clothing,
common terms, shared facilities such as roads, rivers, and fishing
places, inter-racial friendships - all of these and many
more cultural traits, processes, and transactions between
Indians and Whites were notable.
Conscientiously advanced and promoted,
they might have resulted in a civilization superior to the one
that came to prevail in America overall from the seventeenth
to the nineteenth centuries. But to begin to contemplate
what form an accommodating civilization would have taken
requires that a person feel strongly in the first place
that the oppression and near-extermination of the
five hundred Old American nations of the country was
a grave and reprehensible set of events.
The New Americans did not feel so.

Chapter Eleven

Dependency and Development

The British government hardly gave a damn for its North American colonists. Its elite was interested in gobbling up valuables if such were to be found, but you would be hard put to discover altruistic or sympathetic statements or policies relating to the colonists. So harsh and neglectful toward its own people at home, it
could hardly be kinder to its colonists:
out of sight, out of mind.

The Board of Trade managed the colonies after 1696;

there were no ministries of culture, social welfare, or education. (There was the Anglican Church that dabbled in these matters, and voluntary religious and social groups were starting up.) Economic development was the dream of the English elite: the well-behaved colony governed by royal appointees and engaging in well-regulated activities and trade for the good of the home government. However, everything done to tie the colonies to imperial policy ended up in one way or another by strengthening the colonies and making their posture *vis a vis* the empire more aggressive and frankly selfish.

Today we look at Singapore and Hongkong on the map, lying next to Indonesia and China, and find it hard to imagine their high productivity relative to such large and heavily populated states. Similarly, viewing the great expanse of continental Anglo-America in the seventeenth and eighteenth centuries, and especially given its very high productivity today, we cannot easily imagine the time when it depended upon tiny islands like Bermuda, St.Kitts and Nevis, Barbados, and Jamaica for skilled personnel, lessons from experience, methods of agriculture and shipping, raw and processed material, and survival itself. In the first years of Virginia, foodstuffs from Bermuda may have preserved the colony from extinction.

The British mainland colonies could develop in relative independence from England by dealing with the West Indies. There would be less supervision, fewer bribes to give and take, and less snobbery and arrogance. The Islands were the heaviest purchasers of timber products. One could put together more complicated and profitable schemes, such as the notorious Afro-American triangle, in which major ingredients were slaves, molasses, and rum, with tobacco, indigo, rice, junk jewelry and several other commodities. European trade was rather more complicated, with imports that made the difference between civilization and barbarism - fashions, books, pamphlets, furnishings, tools, machines, visitors - needing small space aboard ship.

What could be said of the British islands could to a lesser degree, except in times of Colonial-Homeland conflict, be said of the island possessions of Holland, France, Denmark and Spain. It was a cozy trade, yet often a violent or at least fiercely competitive game played among the Caribbean Islands and between these and the mainland colonies. Patriotism was only a weak rule of the game. Smuggling was rampant.

Actually the very poverty of much of the mainland, its difficult climate (cold and hot in turn, moist, marshy, insect-infested, contrasting with the superior climate of Western Europe, even, all things considered, of the British Isles), its inaccessibility, its seemingly unconquerable native inhabitants, and its useless mountain ranges - this discouraging poverty invited a crowd of individualistic Caucasians for whom few need feel responsible or accountable, and in time they came to be a bustling and hustling society of vast spatial proportions, who, not content simply with territorial space, took to the seas for fish, whale oil, slaving, and transport of traded goods. The islands, with their slaves and almost no truly independent Whites, could not become true nations.

Suffering did not produce love at home or abroad. Even later, the English elite were not especially fond of their brave colonists who were enriching their coffers. For these became more and more troublesome. By 1763 the cornucopia of India was guaranteed to the English. France bowed out with a tiny enclave; the Portuguese and Dutch had been defeated earlier and held only minor positions on the sub-continent. India provided wealth beyond comparison with British America. It had brought riches even much earlier.

The enormous fortunes, which turned around the English aristocracy and enriched it with new title holders, were earned in Continental trade, the Orient and elsewhere than in America. To the English elite

America appeared as nests of troublesome subjects
who as often as not did not play by the rules
(one of which was that the Home elite could break rules).
It took a canny Scot named Adam Smith,
unbefuddled by royal prerogative, to realize,
before most others did, how an individualistic people could
create a wealthy nation while pursuing their personal interests.
The American colonies were getting richer by saltations.
They were populating, too, at a great rate.

At the brink of the Revolutionary War, the wealth of the colonists is estimated to have been 110,000,000 pounds sterling; of this total, 88 millions were in land (60), livestock (10), other producers' goods (9), and consumer goods (9). About 22 million pounds were invested in human slaves and bound servants. In dollars of 1978 value, the total wealth of the thirteen colonies of 110 million pounds translated into about $6.5 billion. Not included in such figures is public property, which, however was not a significant factor, except for great tracts of land; it included inexpensive public structures, arms and ammunition in small amounts, forts and stockades. Churches held land and buildings also.

All such figures are questionable: setting a value on the land of the colonies borders on fantasy. Probably no more than one in a hundred acres was cultivated or grazed. Much belonged to governments and foreigners. Much was under disputed title. Land prices changed with dazzling rapidity.

Since the Industrial Revolution had hardly begun in America, the production goods were mostly inventories of goods and boats. There were grist and flour mills, iron works, and quarries. Life for a majority of people was from, by, or on the sea. Most communications and letters were conveyed by boat. Sea routes were better and safer and quicker than land routes. By 1770, the thirteen colonies and West Florida (temporarily in English rather than Spanish hands) possessed 118 topsails and 283 sloops and schooners, for a total of 20,620 tons.

Livestock could be evaluated properly and meant nearly what it means today. Humans are another matter. The valuation of slaves is derived from prices at the auction markets, but the slaves as human beings varied greatly from the average market price of 34 pounds ($1845 in 1978 dollars); moreover the question arises: since the free worker is deemed to own and dispose of his body, should this not be considered capital, too, and valued at the average lifetime earnings? And since the adult White free worker disposed of the work of his wife and children, too, should not the value of all this be entered into the national accounts system?

The wealth of nations is always difficult to measure and is always figured relative to the interests of the calculator. On paper, the per capita wealth of the colonies seemed to be nearly equal to that of England and Europe and above that of undeveloped countries of today. Moreover, the trend was rapidly upward so that one could feel certain that in the foreseeable future, per capita wealth and then total "gross national product" would exceed that of England.

An observant economist might perceive that the colonists might not yet have become inventive, but that they were adept thieves of other people's inventions, and that England, though it may have been behind by a century in the Renaissance, was a century ahead in its Industrial Revolution.

Having adapted the Renaissance, evicted the Roman Catholic Church, tamed an enterprising lot of radical Protestants, cleared the grazing lands of people, gotten rid of large numbers of undesirables, having gained dominion over its Isles around (hence tax receipts), having opened up grand markets in the true Orient, England's alliance of aristocracy and expanded middle class were enjoying creature

comforts and the leisure to invent. Beginning in the late 1600's and moving through the 1700's, Englishmen invented and applied to the realm a panoply of inventions. The Americans, clever and ambitious copy-cats, would profit enormously thereby.
At that point in time, it might become advisable to transfer the Capital of the British Empire from London to America: so said Adam Smith. Smith was well-informed by Americans such as Franklin, and they by him. For a political generation, leaders and Framers discussed and cited him.

I set forth earlier the several wars in which Britain engaged during the period of American colonization until the Revolution, and described how each affected Indian relations and was in fact given an American name to denote this facet of the wars. Each of them resulted *de facto* or *de jure* in an extension of the western domain. Although this frontier factor is most popular among historians, the seaboard and marine factors were probably more important, for the colonists used each and every one of the European wars to strengthen their fleets, extend their trade, become state-of-the-art with all the piratical, buccaneering, and smuggling tactics then practiced, broaden their political and international horizons, and learn to behave as belligerents.

Exhorted to apprentice themselves on behalf of the mother country, they signed up and mastered many arts. The merchant and artisans of the long coastal region lifted themselves at least to the lower and middle levels of the English, Dutch, Spanish, and French diplomats, international lawyers, traders, and sea captains.

During the times of which we speak in this chapter, the population of the British colonies grew rapidly, from 275,000 in 1700 to 2,205,000 in 1770, or 800%. England and Wales numbered about 8 millions in 1770 but with Scotland and Ireland about 13 million. Boston, Philadelphia, and New York City at this time held between 5,000 and 13,000 inhabitants. New Orleans was larger than any of these by the end of the century. The Pacific Coast, Florida, the Midwest, and the West contained many Indian tribes and a few thousand French and

Spanish with a growing number of English. Father Junipero Serra was founding settlements in California, beginning with San Diego de Alcala in 1769.

The death rate was high. Women were still in short supply at the beginning of the century. They led hard lives throughout the century, having few legal rights even if born to riches, often performing a great variety of kitchen and barnyard tasks, including the processing of foods and the making of clothes. Their death rate was higher than the rate among men, despite their much more frequent abstention from tobacco and alcohol. For the latter half of the century, they gave birth at the high net rate of 3% per annum.

Immigrants came increasingly, from England, and, too, from several other European countries; there were Germans, Scots-Irish, Highland as well as Lowland Scots (two fairly diverse cultural types), Welsh, Dutch, Swiss, Sephardic Jews, and French, plus miscellaneous entrants unlabeled.

Dour and tough, bred to poverty, with an agrarian crisis and a depression in the linen trade to propel them, the Scots-Irish came in large numbers, most of them as indentured servants. Their effect on the country was continuously heavy, but most historians and therefore the public have tended to mention them too briefly, as if they lacked ethnicity, whereas, as we shall see, their peculiar ethnicity has been the closest shadow of general American ethnicity.

Over all the colonies, they entered to the number of 250,000 in the half-century before the American Revolution. The Lord Primate of Ireland estimated that less than one in ten had money to pay for the passage to America. In New England the Scots-Irish were hardly welcomed. A public figure referred to them as *"the blockish Presbyterians from a barbarous nook of Ireland"*. Mobs gathered in Boston intending to prevent boats that were carrying Scots-Irish from landing.

The same had happened with African slaves earlier and would now be happening with every new wave of immigration; whoever got there

earlier would resent making room for newcomers.
Irish Catholics were barred ingress to South Carolina,
in the same statutory clause that forbade
various criminal types to enter.

Scotland itself was shaking off its children. The Lowlanders had been
coming for some time, many of them making their way along the
English roads to the seaports. Now the Highlanders came, fleeing
poverty, cattle blights, higher rents for their poor tenancies, and
evictions so that their masters, as often English as Scottish, might
make ready sheep runs. England could sell wool now in
vast quantity to the Continent.

Many villages were torn down or abandoned. The land
passed into few hands, first the lairds, then
absentee Englishmen, and in late twentieth century,
buyers equally bizarre from all quarters.
The people never returned. The year 2000 saw
half of Scotland held by 350 persons,
80% of the country in 1,500 estates.

The peak of departure was 1763,
when it seemed as if the Highlanders filled the roads to the sea.
They differed sharply from other Britishers,
and in the New World appeared as bizarre as Indians, with their
pronounced Scottish dialect, special social customs and dress. (A
British cartoonist of the times, called upon to imagine the ancient
Scots and Picts, drew them in Indian dress.) A large number settled the
Cape Fear Valley of South Carolina, particularly after
their revolt of 1745 against the English failed.

Speaking Gaelic, they had everyone else in the Valley speaking
Gaelic, Blacks included. "Assimilation"
(a loose yet useful word) of these new folk,
Americans thought, would be difficult; it was not -
except in one vital regard: they would for the most part
be Loyalists when the Revolution came.
Then, from being Tories, they became

Federalists of the party of Washington and Hamilton.

Wherever mining was to be done, the Welsh were
called upon. They were employed to dig copper
in New Jersey in the 1700's, but their works were
closed, and they to the number of 160
were deemed Loyalist, herded out by American troops,
after the Battle of Princeton in 1777, and exchanged for American
prisoners of the British.

German-speaking immigrants from several countries appeared on the scene in the 1700's. Many had a religious motive; they were early Protestant sects, well-disposed toward Calvinism but in certain cases more chiliastic. Prominent among them was the Moravian sect, from, it happens, Moravia, caught among a lot of Catholic neighbors. They moved solidly into Pennsylvania, welcomed by Quakers, behind a screen of highly mobile Scots-Irish. They showed other Americans how to farm properly. They respected the land more. They were more patient. They saved more and wasted less. They were less vindictive and punitive toward Indians, although they shared in the trespasses upon Indian lands and suffered Indian counter-attacks.

They soon began to print newspapers and books in German,
they held religious services in German;
they conducted schools in German.
Musicians and singers came in with them.
There was some wonderment about whether they might not
grow too numerous, then abstain from the motley culture
about them, and would not use the English language.

Like all other immigrant groups, they tended to divide into two large categories, a readily assimilated portion that disappeared both ethnically and geographically into the larger population, and a defensively ethnic part. Even two hundred years later, at the time of World War II, it was not impossible to find people in small-town and rural Pennsylvania who could speak "Pennsylvania Dutch" (for "Deutsche", meaning German). Even at so late a date, too, a significant pro-German and anti-English attitude in foreign affairs

could be unearthed among the districts of Pennsylvania and
Ohio where persons of old German origin were numerous.
As the twentieth century came to a close,
Germanophones were still among them.

Germans, like the rest, were often fooled into emigrating by promoters
of American immigration, boat captains, land agents, the King himself.
They had to endure the thieves and gangsters who abounded
everywhere. We find early in the century a pitiable petition to the King
carried by representatives of the much reduced group of 4000
Palatinians (Pf´a¨ltzer), who were first invited to settle in England and
work at processing raw materials for the English military. Badly cared
for there, they were not too concerned when they were forcibly
persuaded to take transportation to the New World, upper New York
State specifically, where they were to settle in and again
work for the British armed forces.

A great many died at sea or soon after landing from hunger and disease.
The remaining two thousands were dropped off in the
wilderness; no one took responsibility for them.
They lacked most means for survival and,
despite numerous pleas to the Governor, to colony officials,
to everyone around, they went hungry and wretched,
without tools, and without a cent of the money promised them. They
were put to work making pitch and tar for the Navy.

When war with the French and Indians came, they were issued
weapons, marched off, and when they returned had their weapons
taken away. They found that the land on which they had settled was
claimed both by Indians and by land speculators. They were ordered
off, but enough force could not be mustered to throw them off. They
persisted, spread out, and ultimately made places for themselves.

Germans from Philadelphia tried to bring the law
to bear against fiendish ship-captains who would, for instance,
get people to sign up to become indentured servants or
redemptioners in return for their fares,
and then inveigle them into taking on the debts of relatives

who might die on the way to America.

In vain their calls for help, because the authorities were in cahoots with the captains. The reports of deaths at sea were suppressed. One boat carrying 400 German immigrants in the year 1745 arrived with only 50 left alive. Emigrant vessels sailing from Holland packed their passengers in a space of two feet by six feet. Rations were little and foul. The passage was especially hard on small children, most of whom seem to have died en route to the Promised Land.

As happened first and always in America, some of the worst exploiters of the immigrants were their fellow countrymen. Newcomers would be promised non-existent jobs, sold false land titles, duped out of their meager belongings, and literally led astray. Henry Muhlenberg, arriving in 1742 to take charge of pastoral activities among the Lutherans of Pennsylvania, discovered self-appointed, greedy, and scoundrelly "Lutheran" ministers wherever he turned; one Pastor Valentine Kraft had set up a widespread hierarchy of preachers, numerous "worthless, drunken schoolmasters, who wander about the country as preachers and make money with the Lord's Supper, baptism, and weddings".

Indians nearly everywhere were showing increasing signs of social disorganization as the 1700's proceeded - what with their disbandment - from the new ailment of social dissociation, as well as from poverty, disease, unsettlement, and alcoholic excesses; yet they were relatively stable in their tribal configurations compared to much of the White population. Given then the slaves and the character of the larger British immigration, experiencing their first or second generation in America, it would scarcely be possible to calculate the depressed and oppressed until well into the 1700's at less than 90% of the population.

The figure is horrific, but then one has to recognize that the British people during all of this long period was in a bad state, with far more than two millions on the edge of destitution or worse. Their American counterparts had more hope - justified or not - of betterment, and could scent whiffs of free air in the turbulent drafts of social disorder.

Still, far from being the noble state of natural society that
European salons and later historians claimed it to be, the
New World substantiated the state of man in natural society,
as portrayed by the English physician and political scientist,
Thomas Hobbes, in his mid-sixteenth-century work, *Leviathan*:
"mean, nasty, brutish, and short".

A favorite portrayal of early colonists has them at prayer.
Rather than ridicule this as nonsense, one had better
consult the sociology of religion:
whenever conditions are desperate and sad, people pray,
out of fear or lack of other recourse,
driven to it by their authorities,
out of force of habit, and
to commemorate their sick and dead.
The abundance of such motives indeed would make the
prayer scene typical. Of course, it was also a cliché
going back to early Christian art, the prayerful Christians
of the Roman Circus as the lions came slavering in.

Religious development proceeded apace among the Protestant sects.
Some 62% of the churches in 1790 were Calvinist in orientation.
Defining these as sects upholding the Five Points, they would include
the Puritan Congregationalist Churches, Congregationalists generally,
Presbyterians, Baptists, Dutch Reformed, German Reformed, French
Reformed (Huguenots), Calvinist Anglicans (Dissenters). (Notably,
then, not Lutherans, Quakers, Catholics, Moravians, Unitarians,
Methodists, or Anglicans - who would become Episcopalians - and,
for that matter, not Jews (whether Orthodox or non-sectarian), African
Christians, African Spiritualists, Freemasons, or Free Thinkers, or
other minor-sized groups, with very many to come. In New England,
except in Rhode Island, Puritanism was established by law.
Virginia and South Carolina were strongly Anglican, which,
it happens, was established by law as the
official church of the colony.

In Maryland, immigrants of at least five different Protestant sects came
in to outnumber, then to dispossess, then to allow the return of the
Catholic Church. (Naturally the Catholics did not disappear; they went
underground and played at being primitive Christians.)

The best estimate has the average church congregation in America numbering 75 members in 1776. There were, it is known today, some 3228 congregations. The total of church membership would then amount to 242,100 adults. Factoring in children produced a national religious adherence rate of 17%, excluding Indians. Blacks were discouraged from setting up churches. By the time of the Revolution only the smallest fraction belonged to a recognizable church congregation. The first African-American church was organized in North Carolina before the Revolution, as a Baptist congregation. The second was established after the Revolution, in 1787, in Philadelphia, in resentment at treatment in a hitherto interracial church, by Richard Allen, and here started the extensive and influential African Methodist Episcopal Church.

Dividing the country into three regions, and confining the figures only to Europeans, we find that the New England, Middle Colonies, and Southern Colonies afford respective regional church adherence rates of roughly 20%, 19% and 17%. One might argue that children do not count as serious church members, but I believe that children are an active and fast-learning part of the population, with "allotted places in heaven" like the adults; therefore the method of factoring them into the figures is justified.

Most Americans of past times have been deluded as to the overall reality of church membership in people's lives in colonial times. The figures do not bespeak a people enthralled by religiosity. With one out of six persons (including all people) encountered being church members, the role of churches in the developing country is brought into question, especially since these estimates pertain to a point in time when the momentous revivalist movement known as "The Great Awakening" was happening.

One may correctly declare that most powerful and wealthy Americans were church members, and that the clergy, being more or less professionalized at its tasks - that is, earning a meager living at pushing their version of Christianity upon society - was a moderately strong force in shaping standards of opinion, conduct and public policy. Since the actual behavior of the sects was shaped largely by their leading laymen, who supported them, and since both sects and their churches multiplied like rabbits, there could be about as large differences among churches in such standards as could be found in the population as a whole.

A person could find a church or parson to suit his needs as he or she (most church members were women) defined them, or start up one's own congregation, or even become a minister without portfolio, so that in the end the American system of religion gave a person as much leeway in confession, repentance, penitence and absolution, as the severely criticized, "relaxed or loose or highly varied" procedures that the centralized and authoritarian Catholic Church had given him once upon a time.

In Reformed and Presbyterian churches of the Middle Colonies in the 1720's, there arose a demand for heightened religious devoutness. It assumed larger and larger proportions and spread from one church to another, one sect to another, one colony to another, ultimately sweeping through New England and down South through Georgia, sinking finally in the wake of the American Revolution.

Membership in a particular sect and cult was de-emphasized in favor of the brotherhood of Christians. Preaching and worship were changed into highly agitational forms of seeking and giving response to the religious message. People were besought to adopt Christ and Christian symbolism emotionally, not so soberly and ritually and catechistically as they had in the past. The personal commitment, profound, heartfelt, became more important than formal pledges and adherence.

Preachers like George Whitefield, an Anglican revivalist of England, roamed the colonies drawing enormous crowds - his final convocation, at Boston in 1740, drew about 30,000 hearers to the Commons, 50% more than the total population of the City! Great numbers of people dissolved in tears at the thought of his leaving

them. He implored them, in his own words,
*"steadily to imitate the piety of their forefathers;
so that I might hear, that with one heart and mind,
they were striving together for the faith of the Gospel".*

One member of his Philadelphia audiences was Dr. B. Franklin, who, characteristically skeptical and scientific, measured the distance at which Whitefield could be heard by the vast crowd, estimated the crowd's size, evaluated his delivery and style, and, by hearing him often, was able to distinguish the new from the old sermons by the excellence that practice had brought to the older ones, concluding that itinerant speakers have an advantage: stationary ones cannot well improve their delivery by so many rehearsals.

The most important American figure of The Great Awakening was Jonathan Edwards, a Calvinist theologian, who wrote the best contemporary psychic analysis and defense of revivalism - "true" revivalism, of course, there being revivalists, like James Davenport, who brought disrepute to the Awakening among the upper class on account of his emotional "excesses".

The Great Awakening as a satisfying religious experience
in a thrilling crowd was one thing;
as reformer of the moral attitudes and conduct of men and women it was something else; as a typical instance of chiliastic crowd behavior
still another; as a contributor to a more sympathetic relationship
among the widely separate constituencies of America again another;
and as an episodic American phenomenon was one more thing.
We shall be reading of other revivals of the nineteenth and
twentieth centuries, some local, some particular to a certain sect, some
regional, some national, even international.

Perhaps what harm and good they may have done is capable of
generalization. Pragmatically and a priori, the Great Awakening made
masses of people feel alive and dedicated to lofty abstractions;
it lifted them up from miserable and insignificant concerns
(or maybe took their minds off their miseries and
important problems needing material solution).
It made the individualistic American feel more sympathetic
to his fellows in Christ

(but outside Christ? and would not the cure for excessive individualism better be in exercising practical projects of social reform and social life?) So it went into history, The Great Awakening, and
we would ask one more question of it.
Did it condition people to collective emotionalism such as would be required for bringing on and waging a Revolution? If so, could one offer this opinion: The Great Awakening was one of the causes of the American Revolution, which erupted as the Great Awakening movement was ending.

Fantasies and promises abounded, notwithstanding disastrous expeditions and forays inland and on the sea. Or, one wonders, was the formula that goes "desperate need - great risk - copious self-delusion" operating? For the seeds of hope spring best from muck. Prominent among those of the colonists
who were atypical of the social norms of England
but in the colonies could circulate widely,
were religious turncoats, cultists and prophets, disbelievers, blasphemers, traitors, men on the run, disgraced women, troublemakers, and psychotics.
Penniless losers fled their causes, Puritans, Quakers, Cavaliers, Huguenots, Pietists, Levelers, Moravians, Scottish rebels, Palatinians, Jews, apostate Irish Catholics - begging, borrowing, pledging as they went, sometimes dragging along a family.

Even the worse convicts may have been improved by transportation to America; there were, in the years 1718-75, 66,000 of these, 50,000 out of English courts,
16,000 from Ireland; and who knows how many others came who had escaped dungeons in other countries by expulsion or flight: certainly here was a "born again" experience. (Naturally one could expect the rare realist - there were such - a convict who begged to be hanged rather than be transported to America.)

A small number of men of seemingly better qualifications made the crossing and some of these stayed: university students, desperately poor clergy, and the employees of the several corporations entitled to take all they could find and divide it amongst corporate sponsors, the

King and themselves: to search for valuable minerals and export crops, to mark off land holdings, evict squatters, and sell in part huge tracts of land, to organize and supervise the slaves and bondsmen in the establishment and working of plantations. Officials, too, were sent over to collect taxes and impose generally a semblance of order. All the land of the thirteen colonies had been distributed to less than a hundred companies and proprietors, and it was from these that individuals pried loose pieces large and small for their own accounts.

It takes only a few men to own and manage a legal oligarchy, which is what the colonies, all of them, were set up to be; the system sometimes seemed to be getting out of hand: that is, there were more than a few around willing and capable of cutting themselves into the action. But for the vast majority, conditions were not just tough, such as a man or woman could stand, but rotten.

Luckily, Americans were already afflicted with that phenomenal quality so helpful to top dogs; they were individualistic to a fault. Lacking a sense of community, a neighbor's death or departure could often be perceived as a chance to better one's circumstances; an injustice was a chance to escape.

Hope sprang eternally. And out of hope came the proverbial optimistic individualist American. Typical then as now. Anything could happen in America, and did.

Going back to 1600 and counting up to 1770, about a million persons from Europe and Africa survived the trip to jostle the Indians (perhaps no more than a quarter of a million in the Atlantic regions now) in creating the new nation. Probably half the total had set out from an English port.

As was to be true for every war that the "United States" engaged in, the population increased tidily during the French and Indian War, and the Revolutionary War. Elapsed social time for the 160 years since first settlement would have been 2.4 mnemonic generations of 65 years, 4.8 politico-historical or Jeffersonian generations of 33 years, and 8 procreative generations of 20 years.

In comparison, Francophones of Canada numbered only 65,000; the reasons included not only the severe climate, but the higher quality of life for the lower classes of France relative to Britain.

The English government was implicated in the slave trade. The Americans were but earnest imitators, and late starters. When the Virginia legislature in 1723 passed a law forbidding importation of slaves, its masters at the Board of Trade in London objected for various reasons. They were pressing slaves upon the colonies because they wanted more plantations under cultivation to provide more supplies for the Royal Navy. The London trader interest wanted to obligate the planters as much as possible also, to the extent that plantation society as a whole would be in debt to London usurers.

We speak now of American participation in the slave trade, aside from the purchasing and use of slaves. American colonial slave traders conveyed 425,000 Africans to the Americas in the years 1620-1807. This would be about 10% of all persons abducted by Europeans for the American trade. Rhode Islanders provided the largest number of boats, manning them with scummy crews from everywhere.

Forgiving one's ancestors comes easy to most people; one strains to understand or ignore, if not to sympathize, with people of one's own stripe. Yet, to defend the wrong side in history is wrong today. The slave trade, especially, is so revolting that it must call into question the worth of every facet of the trading society. A people's economy reflects the people's character; how a person makes a living suffuses one's whole life. Any attempt to divorce the two introduces hypocrisy in large measure.

In 1770 the colonies exported, in order of their total value, the following articles: tobacco (0.906 million pounds sterling); flour (0.504 m) ; fish (0.405m); rice (0.341m); wood in various forms (0.155m); furs and skins (0.149m); indigo (0.132m); wheat (0.131m) plus much cereal and flaxseed (to Ireland); whale oil and products (0.104m); a score of additional less extensive exports including rum: all of these totaling 3.438m pounds sterling. Shipping earnings for the year brought 0.615m pounds. They bought and supported the credit needed to buy amply abroad from or through England.

The Northern colonies had a harder time mustering the exports required, if they were to import the goods they needed. Since they had to import through England, the English authorities encouraged them to trade with Africa and the West Indies, in other words to get into the slave traffic and into the rum business. The market value of imported slaves amounted to 0.108m pounds in 1770, a low year, the average for the surrounding years running about twice the value. It is well to note that the slave trade was less profitable than most others, returning on the average less than 10% on invested capital. It was considered a high risk, with a chance of rich returns.

Alcohol was a way of life for a great many Americans; they spent much of their lives making it and as much of their time drinking it.
Molasses used in making the rum and for other purposes made up a considerable import item, and a lesser amount of its exports. Rum was supplemented by corn, barley, rye, and wheat whiskey, distilled products, beer, homemade wines and the alcohol from any fruit that would lend itself to the process of potable fermentation.
So goes the ballad of 1630:

For we can make liquor to sweeten our lips,
Of pumpkins, and parsnips, and walnut-tree chips.

About four million gallons of rum were disposable in the colonies, of which about 300,000 gallons only were exported, almost all to Africa, to buy slaves. (A tiny portion of the rum went in a potion with sugar and opium to quiet infant cries and tantrums.) Americans were distilling and drinking a great deal of whiskey at the same time, probably twice as much as the rum they consumed.

Calculating from the potential number of male adult drinkers in the population, something like 16 gallons of alcohol per annum would have been their average annual consumption; that is, the average American male drank over a quart of booze per week, plus whatever beer and wine came to hand. Women are excluded in the argument, for convenience; actually they probably constituted one-fourth of the alcoholics.

Alcoholism was a grave problem in America to begin with. Now, if today, alcohol abuse costs the nation about $100 billions annually, and is implicated in two-thirds of all homicides and half of all vehicle accidents, and involved in from 25 to 40% of all general hospital cases, the costs to early American society must have been at least proportional. Nor are the human costs of alcoholic work-accidents, wife-beatings, and child abuse included. For the amount of liquor consumed per capita then was more than it is today. New England alone had hundreds of licensed dispensers of alcohol, and a common criminal complaint had to do with unlicensed vendors. Operating a tavern was the chief non-domestic occupation for women in those days: widows, that is.

The alcohol problem transported itself directly from England, where, it has been computed, in 1750 and 1751 more than 11 million gallons of hard liquor were drunk. This would not be quite up to American norms, but it was enough for a Bishop Benson to write,
"There is not only no safety in living in this town [of London],
but scarcely any in the country now,
robbery and murder are grown so frequent.
Our people are becoming what they never before were,
cruel and inhuman. Those accursed spirituous liquors..will..destroy
the very race of people themselves".
Suppressive legislation followed shortly thereafter, and presumably is what saved the English race. At least a noticeable decline occurred in the rate of dropsy. Gin was blamed more than anything else; it had come in with the Hanoverian dynasty

from Germany; a compensating merit might not be easy to find.

A quantitative sort of mind was developing with the progress of science in Europe and America. One detects the beginnings in the thought processes of persons such as Governor John Winthrop of Massachusetts, for instance in his economic lucubrations and social planning, who deserves, for this and other reasons, a place alongside his contemporary, Isaac Newton.

But I would refer in the context of alcoholism here to the calculations of a London magazine article of 1789 who estimates the habitues of London "tea-gardens" to number 200,000, spending at least half a crown each, totaling £25,000 in the course of the day. Returning home, these tipplers can be divided as follow: sober, 50,000; in high glee, 90,000; drunkish, 30,000; staggering tipsy, 10,000; muzzy, 15,000; and dead drunk, 5,000.

As I indicated earlier, this was soon to become the Age of the Enlightenment in England as in France, and the Age of the American Revolution and Enlightenment both. Better than either of these for the English working classes was the advent and rapid progress in England and Wales, and right away thereafter, in America, under the inspired tutelage of the Wesley brothers, of Methodism. Not only did John Wesley preach at home and in America the needed message that *"Cleanliness is next to Godliness"*, but he weaned scores of thousands from the bottle.

This was not the "Social Gospel", so-called, but it was the next best thing to it. What the Methodists thought of the Anglican establishment is predictably near to the unprintable: *"We would fain draw a veil over them, if the truth of history would permit it..."*, wrote the first Methodist Bishop in America, Thomas Coke, in 1793; *"they were, with a few exceptions to the contrary, as bad a set of men as perhaps ever disgraced the Church of God..."*

In 1999, people think that they know what crime is all about and believe there has never been more of it than now.

They could not be more wrong.

Corruption and criminality were part and parcel of the settlement and development of America. The process began early and has continued to this day with scarcely a let-up. A persuasive case can be made that America has never been more law-observant than it is today, and, if this seems to be absurd, the fault lies with the records, the definitions, and the historians: In comparison with the countries from which they came, Americans - regardless of race, color, or national origin - have consistently ranked low in the various indicators of justice for all, and high in disobedience to just, or just ordinary laws.

To define corruption and crime to include only what has been explicitly demanded or forbidden by legal promulgation, and court judgements on its violation, prejudices the historical search for crime rates. That is, crime rates are misleading, even where statistics on the number of convictions are available or even the number of crimes reported. Beating up people had always been a crime at the common law, but personal violence commenced and prospered in America as in no other country on earth. Witch-hunting was not a crime in seventeenth century Massachusetts. Kidnaping and selling humans into slavery was not forbidden in most American jurisdictions; even after the slave trade was legally prohibited, it went on at a considerable pace until the Civil War broke out in 1860.

The crime of trespass, punished so severely in England for centuries, was common behavior in America, often in the enduring form of squatting; the punishment, unless it ended in deadly quarrels, was rarely more than mere eviction. Ridding Indian country of squatters was even less possible and attempted only half-heartedly by regular British troops, the militia of the colonies being ridiculous toward this end.

Crimes against "public morality" were vastly numerous. Fornication, often a crime, was universally indulged. Prostitution as well. Adultery was universally forbidden, with dire penalties threatened, but often the "best people in society" enjoyed affairs, while the frontier and the seven seas beckoned the family deserter and left the folks back home to philander.

The scandal of Merry Mount in early Puritan Massachusetts is irrepressible. It was America's first indigenous utopia - certainly therefore worthy of mention for a nation that has seen thousands of utopian communities born and buried. An errant Cavalier named Morton founded the commune on the principle of hedonism and to it flocked hippies - English, French, and even Indian. (He asserted that the Indians descended from Homer's ancient Trojans.) They gathered to eat, drink, and be merry, perchance to work, but minimally. They brewed a good beer. They erected a 90-foot-tall Maypole with buck's antlers atop it, for dancing around on Mayday, which ancient custom called for. But the Puritan authorities despatched a troop to the scene, under the redoubtable mercenary, Captain Miles Standish. The colony was dispersed and Mr. Morton was shipped back to England in bonds, there to write a spoof of his experiences.

Personal fighting, family feuds, vendettas, and gangsterism were not usually taken up as matters of public concern. Mayhem and disabling injury were part of many thousands of personal quarrels annually; commonly, the combatants aimed at gouging out an eye of the opponent. Calling a man disdainfully a "Scotchman" was enough to incite a dangerous no-holds-barred fight in the back country of the Middle and Southern colonies and States. Public opinion was not sufficiently civil or strong to oppose such conduct.

Nor was there an opinion sufficiently strong to stop intimidation and gangsterism in the conduct of elections generally. The climax of election violence would be reached later on at the peak periods of Jacksonian democracy, the Ku Klux Klan of the 1870's and later, and the political machine bosses of many cities and counties all through history until after 1965.

The British officials out of England exhibited profuse corruption, and their example indelibly marked the colonials. The Virginia House of Burgesses in one case forgave the enormous peculations of John Robinson, Speaker and Treasurer, one of their own, unhappily now deceased, who, it developed, had lent out to legislators and members of leading families over 100,000 pounds of public money, about $10 million in current exchange.

Several Royal Governors, during the French and Indian War, sold flags of truce to American ship captains enabling them to do business in the West Indies on the pretext of coming in to exchange prisoners. The flags were hardly needed, so flagrant and common was the smuggling carried on with islands of all nationalities.

In times of peace, American merchants normally avoided the bans on direct trade with countries other than Britain. They procured false papers clearing their cargoes as bound for England but they would carry them to Holland or elsewhere, be it furs or tobacco. St. Eustatius, which belonged to the Netherlands, was a grand assembly and trans-shipping point for illegal goods; it was no accident that when the colonies declared themselves the independent United States, St. Eustatius was the first foreign station to salute with cannon the entrance to port of a ship flying the American ensign.

Trading with the enemy was widespread in every war that involved the colonies, or even the States in revolt, or for that matter in the crises of the Embargo period and War of 1812 later on. The French-Indian War, which American historians cherish for its building of a sense of union, should also be celebrated for having helped to build the American merchant marine and enrich the coastal cities through smuggling, buccaneering, and profiteering. American boats were in and out of non-British and Caribbean Island ports continually. The British Royal Navy could not stem the traffic. "A lawless set of smugglers", Lord Loudoun called the Rhode Island merchants who were briskly trading with the French.

An English customs officer in Boston, who was paid 100 pounds annually, could count on picking up 6000 Spanish dollars in a year. Several years' service in America would provide a custom official with enough money to purchase a seat in the House of Commons from one of the numerous "rotten boroughs", districts whose population had been evicted, or gone to America, or departed for other reasons and or other places.

Franklin, with his careful mind, gauged the average market price of such a seat at 4000 pounds sterling. He probably exaggerated for effect when he claimed that the whole British government could be bought by the expeditious expenditure of two million pounds. Franklin was one of many Americans who blamed the American penchant for corruption on the examples afforded by their English rulers. But why did it then continue forever after?

We should not worry, however, to hear that America was born in sin and corruption. In the first place, nothing can be done to correct history. In fact, we should be pleased to learn of it, inasmuch as we have gained so little in virtue by imagining our ancestors to have conducted themselves better than in truth. We should also put such matters in perspective. Human government, wrote the German-Jewish political scientist Oppenheimer and many another, began with conquests. Slavery began with the winners and losers of the first struggles. Noah got unabashedly drunk from the first grape pressings after the Deluge, relates the Bible.

What began in colonial times has not ended to this day: the tug-o-war between admiration and scorn of European culture, which the English had too little of, and also a contempt for, was reinforced with their extensive emigration to America.

Poets appear to have been rare (a volume of them is available but is generously inclusive) in the colonies, although from time to time poetasters' clubs appeared. Early seventeenth century New England had Ann Bradsheet rewriting her daily prayers in doggerel, while in Mexico Sister Juana Inez de la Cruz was composing plays, lyrics and delicate spirituals, a poet's poet. Possibly - we may never know - there were Indian and African counterparts but hardly among the Nord Americanos.
No indigenous original music, except for the Afro-Americans and Indians, could be heard, and these were persecuted, suppressed, ignored, contemned. Many of their liturgical and historical chants would have qualified for an anthology, but few have been preserved.

No painting, sculpture or other fine arts, of intrinsic value, struck the eye until after the Revolution. We have to speak as archaeologists:

The first family portrait by an American artist that is extant is Feke's "Royall Family", dated at 1741; that seems incredibly recent, four memorial generations ago, while Mexican painting had long been in flower.

There are earlier individual portraits. The pre-eminent portraitist was John Singleton Copley, who painted sweet pictures for the Boston elite, crowding the ambiance with objects unaffordable by his clients; but he (and his work) became depressed as the Revolution approached, so he exiled himself to England.

The first professional theatrical troupe came from England to play at Williamsburg, Virginia, in 1752. It does startle: that a century and a half would pass before an American could buy a ticket to a play.

Education was mainly in the basics of reading, writing, and arithmetic, early prescribed in Massachusetts for every township to dispense, not commonly elsewhere, or provided by tutors, with a few private schools to which a poor child might rarely aspire. Colleges had been founded in all colonies by the time of the Revolution; they did not equal the universities found in every one of the 42 European countries then existent, including Ireland or Scotland, without exception, nor did they yet outshine the Universities of Central and South America, even after 200 years of settlement.

A few men had gone to Oxford or Cambridge, and were observed to be superior beings. A few artists had studied in Italy, and were *ipso facto* unquestionably *comme il faut*. (Benjamin Rush, best of the lot, tarried thereafter in London for the rest of his life.) The persistence of Bible studies and of Greek and Latin in the curriculum, plus a modicum of astronomy and physics, to the exclusion of pragmatic education, so badly needed, shows us how desperate were the elite colonists to emulate the homeland.

A good sign was the penetration of Harvard and Yale College libraries by works in German on philosophy and science, and translations of a number of European classics. That Wolfgang Goethe was alive and well was appreciated by a great many German-readers around America, but the great man, his pal Schiller, who fervidly supported the American Revolution, and for that matter Voltaire of France, had only decimal followings. Obviously a great set of educational tasks awaited the future.

There were indications of achievements in science to come. At least there were men who were touted as the greatest in the world, a sure sign - this attitude - of the early acquisition of boastfulness by the American Character.

One of these was Benjamin Franklin, whose general experimental frame of mind was useful in all spheres of life, whose largest scientific achievement was the demonstration of the identity of the electrical "fluid" in both lightning and ground electricity. He originated the Franklin Stove, a useful refashioning of the old. His famous Almanac was a bright example of the European species. He was also the first media mogul, investor in a chain of newspapers, in this case the frail budding newspapers that the German immigrants fell to printing as soon as they settled a place. His diplomatic genius in England and France over a vital stretch of years was even then legendary. But he was most clever in every way, at whatever he looked into, Maestro Benjamin, Dr. Franklin.

He introduced pornography to America with his "Advice to a Young Man on Choosing a Mistress", (1745). Around the same time, his manuscript, "A Letter to the Royal Academy at Brussels", was circulating, purporting to contain a scientific way of deodorizing farts. He imported the first copy of *Fanny Hill* into the colonies; these colorless "Memories of a Woman of Pleasure", in an American printing of 1810, had to be destroyed, and endured many silly escapades with American authorities well into the twentieth century.

Franklin invented a sturdy stove. Unfortunately, what was cooked on the stove or in the clumsy large fireplaces was a poor version of the at best mediocre cuisine of the British. The better fares of the Germans, French, Spanish, and Dutch were a joy to their settlements and to travelers. Caribbean Blacks and Whites were doing some good in this regard as they were transshipped to the continent. The Cajun bastion of Louisiana was just developing its defensible peculiar cuisine. "Plain and hearty" might be said of the American cuisine wherever the modified British prevailed, when in good supply, and certainly more of the population had adequate food than had the British. The situation has prevailed to this day among their descendants.

Chunks of meat and potatoes (an Indian contribution) were the ideal. Pork offal was both affordable and popular to half the people, so also corn and bread puddings. The peculiar American fruit, nut, and squash pies, such as apple, pecan, and pumpkin (Indian) pie, resembling many others in Europe, nevertheless had and have a commendable quality of their own.

A second genius of the 1700's was David Rittenhouse, an autodidact, who made his living from clocks and instruments, and therefore built telescopes and studied the heavens and arranged a great convocation of amateurs to watch the transit of Venus on June 3, 1769, at which moment, exhausted from his efforts, he fainted beneath his telescope. He was a most successful propagandist of scientific activity.

A third would be Thomas Paine who wrote books on political science that compare favorably with any similar works until the 1920's. Paine justified the American position against England and provided a philosophy of direct radical democracy in *Common Sense* and the *Age of Reason*. But he did not arrive in America from England until 1774, when he was 35 years old, and, after delivering America from the enemy, went back to fight the good cause in England, whence he had to flee to France, where he fought for his direct democracy again and ended up in a French Revolutionary prison, where most of the great French revolutionaries also landed, - there and on the guillotine, which he mercifully escaped. George Washington spat an obscenity at his name, but granted his book on independence was worth a regiment. More, I think.

The practical arts were modestly innovative. The Pennsylvania or Kentucky Rifle, so-called, was a weapon that had been improved by Swiss-Germans of Pennsylvania. So was the Conestoga Wagon that became the standard vehicle for transporting people to the western territories. In 1789 Samuel Slater immigrated, carrying plans for various cotton mill machinery in his head; he had been an apprentice to the best of English inventors since childhood and had been reached by American advertisements for machines. He was hired, his memory pumped, and the British machines reconstructed by the syndicate of Moses Brown in Rhode Island.

Eli Whitney patented his cotton gin to comb out cotton seeds mechanically in 1793; it enabled an exponential growth in the amount of cotton that could be processed, and with an economy of labor, all slave. It guaranteed the South would take a hard position against the abolition of slavery. Soon cotton became king and hundreds, then thousands and tens of thousands of spindles were put to work spinning cotton.

Whitney also was an inventor of the system of interchangeable parts, on the basis of which he obtained military contracts to provide muskets. This fundamentally simple idea was, in his words, *"to substitute correct and effective operations of machinery for that skill of the artist which is only acquired after long practice and experience; a species of skill which is not possessed in this country to a considerable extent"*. Precursors of the system had occurred in France and England, and in America Simeon North had worked out a similar method for the manufacture of pistols.
Here was another clear example of military requirements stimulating inventiveness, which the Greek philosopher Heraclitus had noted 2500 years earlier and which would characterize much of the most recent innovative development of American industry - in aeronautics, condensed foods, nuclear energy, computers, tele-communications, acoustics, and so on. Necessity is the mother of invention, but necessity is acutely defined by those who command violence; that is, warfare is a prolific father of invention.

In the more artistic sphere, shadowed from the sun by the sails of the clipper ship, itself partly developed by American mariners, was the wood-whittler. Whittling proffered some cute variations. It could be pure "free-standing" sculpture or applied for interior design. The art was particularly suited to the seafarer, at home and on the seas.

It is surprising to discover so few major novelties before the turn of the century into the 1800's. Hispanic architecture in the Southwest was beginning and would one day offer an original look here and there in California, Arizona and New Mexico. Settlers built slightly modified adobe cottages that descended the centuries till now.

Habitations on the East Coast were copies of the Old Country houses, simple frame, swollen in size in New England when one's wealth allowed, ornamented and columned like some of the classical imitations found in England, Georgian mansions transported. The log cabin had its European antecedents, Finnish it is claimed.
The wigwam and long house of the Indians had their imitators.

If we turn our attention to the methods of agriculture in America, we are bound to be disappointed in them. There were not enough Germans to go around, or perhaps, when scattered, they succumbed docilely to bad company. Inventiveness was lacking; only incremental adaptations of tools, notably in the axe and gun, were made. Farm structures were poorly assembled, despite the plenitude of cheap wood. The Christmas-card paintings and drawings of the habitat of the early Americans were and are hokum.

The people who descended upon the New World seemed to be singularly innocent of the major occupation of the Old, farming.
"..the aim of the farmers of this country, if they can be called farmers".. wrote George Washington near the end of the 1700's, has been to get the most out of the land with the least labor because labor is expensive while the land is cheap. Some years earlier a Swedish botanist, Peter Kalm, had written that *"the grain fields, the meadows, the forests, the cattle, etc. are treated with equal carelessness".*

Then, in words that should bring the contemporary environmentalist back to our beginnings, *"..their eyes are fixed upon the present gain, and they are blind to the future".* Blindness to the future: this was to be generally true, not only of the environment, but of other areas:

slavery, property rights, industrial growth, crime and corruption, city development, the legislative process and passage of laws, human welfare and many another.

Labor-saving, which can be another word for laziness, is logically achieved when people squander resources to avoid tending to them, and confine their attention only to the present. It would be silly to deny that this trait has not been widespread in America: an ignorance, denial, and contempt of foresight.

The fact that this image of Americans is denied will only introduce that element in the national character called "hypocrisy". Hypocrisy consists of assuming a false appearance of virtue or goodness, the Oxford Dictionary tells us (as we all too well know). Hypocrisy can be conscious and unconscious: for instance, any number of defenses of bad farming practices can be made, like a poor plow or lack of help, but if the unspoken reason is personal laziness and unkemptness, we have a case of hypocrisy. If the lazy farmer truly believes himself a hard worker cursed by bad land, then he is a sincere hypocrite. And if he says in the same breath that "This country has a great future", he is more clearly hypocritical. But, too, most likely a sincere hypocrite.

The question is resolving into "When did the trait that most peoples of the world ascribe to Americans - hypocrisy - develop, and how?" The trait is usually raised in connection with the contradiction between the virtues a person ascribes to oneself and those that one possesses and evidences by his conduct. Thus, scientists of the history of religion note the correlation between peace-preaching and blood-spilling, and remark that the claim to love peace when accompanied by aggressive behavior is hypocritical. Further, the more intense the demands made by a religious dogma upon a person, the more likely that a hypocritical evasion of the demands.

In the reformed Protestantism that dominated churches, schools, laws, and public opinion in early America, hypocrisy was rife, and as the century that culminated in the Enlightenment passed, more and more people threw off religious dogma and rituals, but these same people could not be expected to reach down into their souls and perform something that today the most sanguine psychiatrist will tell you is most difficult to bring about, the consistent and total reconciliation of what one believes with how one behaves.

Indeed, not until modern social psychology and psychiatry, infiltrating the social sciences and even reformed religion, came about, and developed a large audience for introspecting and clarifying personal motives, did there appear to be any lessening of the American penchant for hypocrisy. The composition of the American population from the beginning was so mixed, undistinguished and deprived, that there were myriad opportunities and every wish to assume a hypocritical past and identity.

England had probably already acquired something of a reputation for raising an unusual quota of frauds and swindlers - the preacher Samuel Purchas wrote as the 1600's began, of those who were *"exceedingly subtill, hypocritical and double-dealing"*, a significant concatenation of epithets. Many times, writers, including this one, have indicated the large role of the promoter, advertiser, and booster in America from the earliest solicitors of passengers for the New World to the latest shenanigans of the securities and exchange industry.

Foreigners wondered at the eager friendliness of Americans despite a known penchant for violence, racism, a moral code justifying self-serving, and aggressiveness generally. In Europe an ordinary person's character was more likely to be read as suspicious, sour, open or indifferent upon first contact. But Americans for centuries have been trained to "be nice to people". The plethora of people's backgrounds demanded this trait. As a result, hostile tendencies have not been apparent, until, surprisingly, they are exercised.

It is notable that until the end of the 1700's the printing of books, even including bibles and law books, waxed with exceeding slowness; meanwhile, however, the newspaper, pamphlet, and handbill prospered. There was exhilaration in the immediate, and the extravagant from one end of the colonies to the others. If a person today were to sample the nation's weekly press and many of the daily newspapers from the smaller cities, she would discover a remarkable parallelism with the newspapers of Franklin's day. Very early, one could observe that distribution facilities determined ownership, profits, and control, just as it does today in the mass media.

The earliest entrepreneurs of the printing shops discovered that they could best survive in business if they started up newspapers. Americans also had a haste about them, already known to the world at large, and they were more interested in the ephemeral and newsworthy than in the Great Books. Authors of the better books often published their own works, and printers, by virtue of their facilities, often became authors of a sort.

By 1691 hundreds of papers had appeared and thousands flourished and expired before the seventeenth century was out. Printers interested themselves in the postal services to obtain a prompt delivery of their product, and often a town printer would be publisher of newspapers, advertisements, notices, legal proclamations and books, and carry on also the functions of postmaster. Benjamin Franklin was prototypical of all of this.

There was much censorship, but it was personal, arbitrary, and spottily effective; controlling the press, as this has to be called, was no more possible than the controlling of alcohol abuse. The case of Peter Zenger in the 1730's was exceptional, though it became the standard-bearer for all future legions defending the freedom of the press. He was a "hired gun" of colonial leaders, who financed his newspaper because they were hostile to the quarrelsome and tough royal Governor Cosby of New York. Zenger was arrested and tried for publishing a criminal libel, but freed when the jury was swayed by barrister Andrew Hamilton's plea that publishing the truth was not a libel.

The newspapers of those days were not at all better than those of today, but were not worse either. Contents?: the weather, elections, crimes, economic conditions, sales of all kinds, comings and going of notables, proclamations of laws and court trials, editorials, sailing technique, medical nostrums, and deaths. The wealthy and powerful, and therefore healthier and knowledgeable class of people, read the newspapers, the number growing speedily with increased literacy.

It is usually to these thousands of readers, one in ten perhaps, on the average, that historians have referred, producing a highly colored image of an optimistic, sturdy civilization, assigning offensive behavior mostly to English officials on temporary duty in the colonies and to bad Indians. Pictorial documentation, whether sketched or painted then or depicted "in the light of history", is skewed toward the minute upper-middle and rich classes and, among these, in their romantic impressions of an ideal life-style.

Studies of the belongings left by the deceased, as contained in probate court records, are illuminating. (Only a minor proportion of the population were represented in the records, because the Afro-American population, 20% of the total in the latter part of the 1700's, could legally leave no property; and the Indians, another 15% of the colonials perhaps, could not either; nor did the poor Whites leave wills.)
Still, we can examine five cases, briefly, to glimpse what people might have and did have in the way of personal property. Notable in all cases is the awful care with which the trivial remnants of a life were detailed, evidence of the universal poverty in material goods. Buckets, spoons, chamber pots and "chairs of necessity" (*chaises de nécessité*), mosquito nets, and pillows were carefully registered. A riding horse was fairly common, a carriage rare.

A highly privileged case:
Thomas Gerry of Marblehead, Massachusetts died at 72. He was a very rich merchant. His physical wealth totaled 5,741 pounds. His real estate was in a warehouse, adjoining land, five houses, two schooners and two small boats. He had much Jamaica fish, sugar, beef pork, 100 casks of whiskey, rum, raisins, Malaga wine, molasses, many kinds of clothing and notions. He had a slave, unusual for Massachusetts, Canto, ticketed at 37 pounds. He had silk gloves, gold buttons, velvet suits, pewter ware, brass ware, much silverware, books, ten cords of

wood in the cellar, along with a goodly amount of liquor.

A decent case:
A widow, Sarah Brown of Queen Anne's County in Maryland, had died aged 45 or more, leaving much less: 2 pounds worth of apparel, "1 old Negro man named Durham", valued at 7.5 pounds, a 16-year old black mare appraised at 2.2 pds, and a small colt worth 3.6. She left a feather bed, a walnut table, a spinning wheel, several silver spoons, an old pine chest, crockery, a half dozen glass bottles, pails and tubs, etc. Her net worth came to 14 lbs. She had no real estate, crops, or financial assets.

A barely decent case:
John Nickerson, a mariner of 45 years, died leaving 7 lbs from his last voyage at sea, and 7 lbs worth of property, composed of a bed, articles of apparel, a looking glass, miscellaneous household items, 5 old razors, various jugs and bottles, and 26 gallons of molasses.

A barely decent case:
Thomas Ring, a laborer of Medway, Mass., died at 21, leaving a horse and saddle, a hog, a dapper wardrobe, 2 sheets and bedstead, a few kitchen items and a candlestick. Could he have sung "Yankee Doodle Dandy"? No, that came later.

A fairly privileged case:
Hugh James, a farmer of Charlotte County, Virginia, aged between 26 and 44, left land estimated at 99 lbs and physical wealth of 206 lbs. He had four Negroes, valued at 83 lbs, 1 horse worth 4 lbs, 14 hogs, some leather, some feathers, and some corn. He owned a gun, pewter, a punch bowl, 2 beds, an assortment of modest furnishings, a bell, and a hogshead of tobacco.

All in all, about 5% of the adult population held assets of over 1000 pounds in personalty and 1000 pounds in land. This amounted to half the wealth of the whole country, plus one-seventh of the whole population as slaves. Probably 90% of the American population in the period before the Revolution owned less that the average college student today brings with her to school come September.

Personal property, however, does not define and measure all that we understand by the good life. Wealth, influence, and welfare, we recall, are the basic components of well-being for the individuals of a society. So we must cast a judgement upon eighteenth century American society over the span of all components, and do so in regard to the proportions that would be deemed miserable, decently provided for, and privileged. In this case we emerge with the following estimates for the three centuries that have occupied us until now.

	1492	1600	1700	1800
Population in millions	1.5 = 100%	0.7 = 100%	1.2 = 100%	4.2 = 100%
% Miserable	31	36	85.5	75.5
% Decent	67	62	14	24
% Privileged	2	2	0.5	0.5

The table offers a set of guesses, framed in quantitative form. If it contains surprises and is perplexing, this may be because one is habituated to a historical myth of a fully White middle-class America. We think that the Indian nations in the year 1492, who composed 100% of the population, suffered some unknown sum of misery from disease and the ordinary miseries of life.

The beginning of the next century, 1600, was still fully Indian in the "USA"., but suffering from diseases carried in from all sides by occasional intruders. The year 1700 saw them still suffering heavy losses from disease, and they were being deprived of power over their lands and undergoing humiliation in wars. In 1800 we find the Indian population, the Afro-Americans, and the White population all severely deprived by disease, hunger, warfare, and oppression.

The situation improves considerably for parts of the White population by the time the new century begins in 1800, but, one recalls, the proportion of slaves in the population was increasing greatly and the Indians were continually losing along the whole spectrum of values.

Only one in every two hundred Americans in 1800 gets a good average grade on a full set of life's values: wealth, respect, affection, knowledge, health and power. That would be some 21,000 persons in a population of 4.2 millions, practically all of them adult male Caucasians of the Eastern seaboard.

This "privileged" level and the "decent" level would, of course, be at the standard obtainable in that age. These might not be what in present-day America would satisfy even a modest person. Exceptionally, one would make the trade happily, so as to escape crowding, industrial and consumer noises, the speeded-up pace of life, and other insistent malefactors of modern existence. Or perhaps one would truly appreciate a crude and simplistic life, without social services or certain "higher" cultural pursuits - to be a Campfire Girl forever.

Councils and Courts

Chapter Twelve

Structures of Government

By the 1700's people of the continental colonies of Britain, when referring to themselves, called themselves Americans; so did some of the French and Hispanic Americans of neighboring non-English colonies. Most British called the colonists

Americans. King George III may have slipped into the practice,
but pretended that the colonies were individual entities,
and should be handled as such, refusing to treat with
any collective representations by a congress or the like.
George was born in 1738, reigned from 1760
to effectively 1811, for he became finally
too patently insane to be plausible, and was
represented by a regent until he died in 1820.

Perhaps George III's madness had some basis
in the unmanageable colonies that frustrated him at every turn.
There was more than a measure of lunacy
in their forms to begin with. The medieval
notion of the monarch as personal owner of the realm
held sway, an idea that was being eaten away by
the notion of a state as distinct from the royal person and
property, and a state that was to be
ruled by an elective assembly.

Worse, to his view, there were all manner of subjects running about
claiming sovereignty to reside in the people, whoever they were;
New Radicalism, the theory was called.
It seemed to be the old Leveller movement of Commonwealth days.

But since the colonies were foreign conquests, they came
under the monarch's dispensation, the executive branch,
we would say, and he could parcel them out as he pleased.
The chief methods were the
proprietorship, a one man-one colony system, and the corporation, an
evolving concept for imperial enterprises, that let a
group of well-connected men have the right to own, develop and
govern a colony, with the Crown holding an ultimate veto and
right to re-organize, while requiring a share of the pelf.

Laughable though it be, the Puritans were let to proceed to
America on promise of turning a profit. They ended up by
paying what could better be called taxes.
They were corporate tools. So were the Virginians,

those who came to be called such. These were even
more wrongheaded than the Pilgrims, who at least
explored the coast, and stood off for a time,
keeping the Mayflower at their beck and call
until they might be sure of surviving for a while.
(Only half of the hundred did in fact survive.)

The Virginia settlers came, and went, and disappeared,
and came and fled home, until finally one beachhead held,
and they came to stay.
They were corporate hirelings, no mistake about it,
no religious nonsense except for some early Dissenters
and other odd sorts, and Catholics.
("Papists", these were also called, to stress that the English
cultic offshoot was the real Catholicism.)
But as site selectors, planners, personnel directors,
diplomats, agronomists, militarists, campers, survivors -
they were bunglers. Still, they muddled through,
which shows how long the English have been up to this.

Carolina's proprietors hired a philosopher and
political scientist, John Locke - the wrong one;
they should have hired Thomas Hobbes, who understood
better the grim state of nature and human nature -
to write a Constitution. This broke down immediately.

So did Roger William's Rhode Island, which was taken over by the
Massachusetts Puritan gang, whose noses he had
put out of joint some years before.

So did the Georgia scheme of Oglethorpe, as I mentioned earlier.
Since it came later than all the rest, it had to hurry up to fail, and did
so within a single political generation.

The Penn family miraculously maintained its ownership of
Pennsylvania, where the Quakers not only ran and developed an
enormous territory, but even permitted people as weird as themselves
to come in, until they were pushed aside politically by
Scots-Irish, Germans, and others. (We cannot help but note that the
Quakers' success was itself a contradiction and

showed how tech'ed they were: they claimed that the way to govern
was not to govern and demonstrated this by governing the
best-run of the colonies for a long time.)

The other people of Pennsylvania were so stupid as to want to
rid themselves of the Penn family in favor of Crazy George. The
Crown did take over, but gave it back to the cleverly manipulative and
endearing Penn family after a while.

All of this experience goes to show that you
do not have to be well-equipped, well-organized,
well-planned, and sane to build a new nation.
In fact, it may help to be none of these.
Although the fact may be unpalatable,
ecclesiastical formations have throughout history
supplied the political and governmental spheres
with most of their fundamental inventions.
I have mentioned that the practices of representative
government and the doctrine of consent in politics were
devised by medieval church orders, the
Benedictines, Dominicans, *et al.*

Not only institutions and formal practices,
but attitudes and ideologies are important.
Thus, we can designate the principal sects of the
American 1600's by their attitude toward
and behavior in respect to their internal government.
Separatist Pilgrims were democratic.
Puritans and Presbyterians were oligarchic.
Congregationalists stood in-between these two political forms.
Baptists were communally-minded and democratic internally.
But they were not as consensual as the Quakers,
who might perform marvels of cooperation
while remaining basically anarchic.

The Anglicans were hierarchical and monarchical,
taking these qualities from the overall government of the Catholics.
(The Catholic Church, it must be said, could contain a

number of institutional variances, consensual orders, dictatorial orders, etc.) Most Indian religions tended to be "Presbyterian" or oligarchic in the sense that their rites were authoritatively handed down to the young by priest and elders, and efforts were made to enforce conformity. There were other religious sects operative in America of the 1600's and working their ways into politics and government. The German Lutherans might be considered similar in attitude and practices to the Congregationalists; so would be the French Huguenots. German Anabaptists were akin to the English Baptists.

By the early 1700's significant portions of the intellectual and cultural elite of Massachusetts had become in fact or sympathy Unitarians, dispensing with the Holy Trinity - Father, Son and Holy Ghost - in favor of a single-minded rational deity who was ready to extend salvation to the whole human race if only people would behave a little better. The Universalists of the same area came along a little later to voice the same sort of general appeal, addressed to a more ordinary constituency. In the 1700's more and more colonists would become Deists, believing in a God who preferred that his people on Earth pursue a rational and enlightened course, never minding about heaven and hell, or immediate divine supervision. If this sounds like persons prominently engaged in leading the politics of the country in the time of Revolution and Constitution-building, the surmise is correct.

Possibly the largest of all "sects" were the colonists who were religiously apathetic and unconcerned, except that on critical occasions or pressed for comment, declared that God did exist, and He would from time to time take a hand in personal or general human affairs. If this sounds like the average unconcerned citizen, such is true also.

The above statements would continue to be generally correct for the nineteenth and twentieth centuries. That is to say that a public opinion poll of the American people taken at the end of the twentieth century would show significant clusters of the above-mentioned religious groups centered upon the stated attitudes.

In due course, large innovations routinize or bureaucratize. The particular form that deterioration took in British North America was the replacement of pre-existing governments by a royal government, that is, the replacement of the chief executives of each colony by a governor appointed by the Crown, and an annulment of whatever powers the colonial assemblies thought they possessed that would make them little Parliaments.

The doomed governments were of three types. The charter or corporate colony was farthest from the King's control. Initially a joint-stock company, ancestor of the modern corporation, its aim was to make money for its sponsors. The company owners, granted their charter by the monarch, would proceed to lay down the conditions of rule in America. These were at their imaginative height in their very beginnings and became less and less so as the pressures from England (some would say "common sense") made them into replicas of the English parliamentary system without the aristocratic-theocratic House of Lords - that is, crown-appointed independent governor with an executive council, together with a single assembly of members from constituencies of townships or counties, chosen by an electorate of a limited number of property-owning males.

Inasmuch as a considerable independence of mind was forthcoming from the corporate inventions, they were mostly undone and superseded by royal forms of government. In 1660 five of the then seven colonies elected their governors. By the time of the Revolution only two of 13 colonies did so, Connecticut and Rhode Island.

The most extravagant original form of rule was the proprietorship.
The king simply granted a lot of land that he had claimed for himself
to one or more favorites, and they might govern it as they pleased.
Such was Georgia, we recall, which was given back right away.
Such also was Pennsylvania, that held out to the very end,
along with Delaware and Maryland. The others appeared obstreperous
to the monarch and were transformed into royal domains.

The royal colony was simple enough.
The royally appointed governor dominated an elective assembly.
He could veto displeasing actions of the assembly.
He could also promulgate laws, rules and orders
coming from London without consulting the assembly.
He was a creature from the English ruling class,
often unqualified, invariably corrupt - a bad example for
reputedly naive nature-children of the New World.

Meanwhile, the British government began to cut back
religious liberties in favor of the Anglican Church. And the
legal system was shaped to conform to the English model.
Vice Admiralty courts, operating without juries and
under Roman Civil Law, took over much of
the jurisdiction and procedures of colonial courts.

The colonial governments had not only to worry about hostile
takeovers from London, but also rebellions from below.
Southern colonial ruling groups had slave revolts
on their minds from an early time, and it seemed that
the more savagely they acted in the actual or presumed case
of a slave uprising, the more anxious they became.
On occasion, uprisings of free men, indentured
servants, bondsmen, and bound tenants, also
were experienced in every colony from Maine to Georgia.

The governments of Massachusetts, New York, Maryland, Virginia,
and North Carolina were unseated briefly or enduringly in the

course of the pre-Revolutionary period.
Riots were common everywhere.
Strikes were occasioned wherever workers were free and
sometimes where they were not.
So much for the idyll that
the colonies were calm until the Revolution came.

Local government was allowed considerable discretion,
if only because the miserable state of communications and
transportation defied controls. Whatever the form,
local political formations, widely differing with personalities and
the kinds of groups setting up territorial shop,
made most decisions that are now made by state and
federal officials and legislation.

Whether this resulted in good or bad
on the whole is debatable.

The conventional view, which commands myth, has until lately
portrayed a New England whose townships (everywhere else called
counties) were models of direct democracy, in which all people
dutifully assembled and discussed and decided public issues.
Roberto Michels' "Iron Law of Oligarchy" prevailed: the few males
who were first-arrived and richest and in harmony with religious
dogma almost always determined the course of these myriad
little New England democracies. As the power of the
center waxed and waned, the power of the
townships (and counties elsewhere) reciprocated.

We must stubbornly recall that, also reciprocally,
as the centers of power swelled and shrank,
the frontier area and people were independently expanding and
pausing. Hence, when both the central power waned
and the frontier expanded, formal structures of government were
largely meaningless over a large scope and domain.

Throughout colonial history, the right to vote was a subject of
controversy. Yet, after a century and a half, no jurisdiction gave its

whole people the vote, nor the half of them, nor the third,
although at this fraction an argument may be made that,
barring Blacks and Reds and women and the unpropertied and
unregistered and aliens and men under twenty-one, and
Jews and Catholics and another group here and there,
most men could vote, but didn't because they were uninterested
or didn't like their politics to be known (the ballot
often being *viva voce* or by a specially colored paper
provided by the candidate - leaving in all then
a not negligible minority whose ballots were counted.)

If not even a third, still there were enough of these voters,
and enough of them were independent, to permit us to say
that the several colonies were individually little republics.
That is, a considerable number of persons played a
major role in choosing the chief officers of the local and
general government, and were permitted to voice their opinions
so as to influence the conduct of the government.
Unlike an oligarchy, in a republic
constituencies were present, formal, vocal, and influential.
But another organ of popular or republican government
was the disorderly demonstration. Rowdy gangs,
mobs, and crowds played a more than occasional role in
pressuring colonial governments for or against specific policies, or
simply as expressions of intense anger at the political elite.
Individually and as a whole, the colonies displayed a
kind of government unique in the world.

Counties and townships kept records, which made them useful for
future historians on these and other matters.
Their courts kept records which are also useful. The records
not only tell us who decided what happened and when
(but not how, *cf. supra*) in the way of general legislation,
but also who bought and sold what to whom. Thus
a patient scholar could examine the signatures of 18,000 recorded
transactions in seventeenth century Virginia, and discover that "X"
was good enough as a signature in the case of over half the men
and three-quarters of the women, though signifying full illiteracy,

and these not being the Afro-Americans or Indians or,
for that matter, men who could sign their name but inscribe little else,
and most poor Whites who need never sign a document,
once they had X-ed their indenture contract.
In short, practically all Virginians were illiterate in the 1600's.
(In England the statistics were a little better, but not in the British Isles
as a whole. In a few places in Europe - Tuscany and several Swiss
cantons, for example - most people were literate.)

The good news is that by the time of the Revolution
many more Americans could read and write, and a few actually did,
among them a growing number of preachers, schoolteachers,
bookkeepers, lawyers, factors, doctors, planters
of culturally ambitious parentage.
Literati were rare, a few of the professors and journalists,
less than a hundred among several million inhabitants.

Whatever the structures of colonial government or of their local
branches, the few who were rich (or in rare cases famously devout)
dominated them. We shall zoom in soon upon the situation in the several
colonies, when their cultural peculiarities are discussed.
Since all were Protestant and no one had to take an oath of poverty -
unlike, for example, Jesuits of Canada, Florida, and Mexico,
religious authority could lead readily to political power
and wealth, in New England especially.

Like religious connections, social connections with English families
helped one get a lucrative appointment in the colonies.
Even literacy, the possession of knowledge and education,
because of its rarity, was an avenue to political power.
Personal physical durability, in a time of
generally bad health and early death,
was an asset in climbing and
holding on to the rungs of the political ladder;
from up there wealth
could be plucked from the public lands,
tax receipts, goods in custom
houses, and commissions legal, extra-legal and illegal. Most of the

activities of government officials that are considered today to be criminal were profusely enjoyed in colonial times.

The custom of bribing voters was well-developed at an early date and more extensive than it is today, at least in its obvious forms. Outright hospitality in the form of ample meats, cakes and rum, etc., was generally available to voters at the polls - but then, many had come long distances to vote and were hungry and thirsty. In Virginia they could have a ball, and bed and breakfast. Robert Livingston's agents paid about 40 shillings each to get his tenants to the polls; he was a wealthy, prominent signer of the Declaration, later a diplomat.

Stuffing the "ballot box" (where there was such a thing), intimidating the opposition, voting the unqualified, the promise of favors in return for votes: these were common practices. They were well-known from England. Continental elections, though less familiar and less frequent, were more properly conducted.

The power elite was omnipresent, as the muscle that wrought political reality out of formal structures. At no time, in any colony, up to the crisis of the Revolution, did more than fifty men (and no woman to my knowledge) make political decisions of import - large economic, religious, and legislative, as well as political, decisions. This would give us a political elite of well under a thousand for all thirteen colonies.

But, since the colonies were largely isolated and distinct entities, there would be no national elite to speak of, that is, men making decisions for the whole. There were instead perhaps a score of men who made up an "All-Colonial Leaders Team", with potential national influence and power, with names like Livingston, Washington, Winthrop, Adams, and Franklin.

All of the political, economic and social illnesses and disorders of Europe occurred in America, plus some new ones. Governments seem to have been threatened by the mob on the streets and by inflexible bureaucracies - the two extremes - almost as soon as they emerged from the womb of the Old World and emigrated to America. The widespread idea, then and now, that institutions and individuals went through a cleansing bath on the way to America, is nonsense.

"The First Thanksgiving at Plymouth"
By Jennie A. Brownscombe (1850-1936)
Painted 1914

Chapter Thirteen

Yankees

A "type" is a commonly found cluster of traits among members of a larger group. A typical member of the group may be part of a majority or a minority of the group, and may be one of several types. There are and always have been many types of Americans, and one of the ludicrous and sad strains of American history has been the frequent disposition of some one type to regard itself as the only true American type.

As an example of a New England type, we may pose a young woman of a God-stricken family of Norwich Dissenters, who receives a letter from an uncle recently arrived in Massachusetts, say 1638, who beseeches her to find a man who would marry her and further indenture himself to accompany her to New England, where they would become the indentured servants of a farmer who would be paying for their passage. Mortgaging their future services, they board a vessel that shakes them up and feeds and bunks them miserably for two months, until it docks at Boston.

Turned over to their master and allotted a shed leaning against his frame house, they go to work from dawn to dusk except on the Sabbath, when they attend church. Their life is poor, their social status low, but at least they know that, unlike in England, their services are sorely needed. They have seven children: one dies in childbirth, a second of infant colic, a third of the smallpox; one marries a boy of a nearby town and gives birth four months later; one boy goes to sea at thirteen and never returns; the oldest boy stays on and raises corn and rye on an eighty-acre farm that his father, the immigrant, had come to own. (Maybe it was his rye that spoiled, and gave such strong hallucinations to people around Salem that they acted like witches or put "witches" to death.)

"New England", wrote Sir Josiah Child in 1693", is the most prejudicial Plantation to the Kingdom of England".
This commercial magnate and economist meant that its people were alienated from the Old Country: moreover, their economic activities fitted poorly those of England. There was no love lost between the two cultures. The Puritans had been given their moniker in England to begin with as a religious slur against them; they were "purist", concerned overmuch with their souls and behavior - and those of others.

After outliving their purism, they still did not please people, and so were called Yankees, another ethnic slur. Later on, and especially by Southerners, all Northerners were called Yankees. Then the Yankees came to call themselves such, and the rest of the world began to call all Americans Yankee, including Southerners. So it became sometimes and in some places, where Americans of all sections of the USA had outworn their welcome, *"Yankee, go home!"*.

Perhaps the name came from the Indian attempt at pronouncing English, to wit, *"Yengees"*. Or from the Cherokee epithet, *"eankhes"*, meaning *"slavish coward"*, used by Virginians in referring to their New England allies. The New York Dutch may have had a derisive term for New Englanders, *"Janke"*, the diminutive of *"Jan"*, that is, *"Johnnie"*.

The word was used to describe the peculiar dialect of many New Englanders, full of special words (later conveyed vast distances by internal migration), spoken in what uncharitable linguists still call a *"nasal whine or twang"*:
"They spoke in Yankee, which I couldn't make out".
Then it was extended, *viz*,
"The coast was infested with Yankee privateers".
By 1755, it could serve as the subject of a song, *Yankee Doodle,* composed in derision of the American provincial militia by a British surgeon named Shuckburgh serving in the army of Lord Governor Amherst. (In slow tempo, the song has in it a typical sound of the musical age of the Baroque.)

The Pilgrims so-termed were leftist (that is, more democratic) precursors of the thousands of Puritans that came in the next decades to Massachusetts. When the Puritans began to arrive in numbers, in the 1630's, they confirmed what had begun to shape up, a theocracy, that is, a government by elders, reluctant to claim their legitimacy in the name of the King, just as loath to base their authority on the large body of people, but eager to speak in the name of God, which they did, at great length, with a powerful elders-directed oligarchy, enamored of laws prescribing and proscribing conduct, still with a

Governor (John Winthrop outstandingly), a council and councils in
each township that they set up, councils that in
most cases were town meetings of the
few that held the right to vote.

Winthrop, in a master stroke, arranged for the seat of the owning
corporation to be transferred to Massachusetts from London.
Thereupon the colony could be governed by the men on the spot.
This kind of government turned out to be too strong for
the King of England to extirpate. Although he might remove the
Puritan governors and appoint a royal governor -
as he would before the century was out -
he could hardly penetrate the decentralized autonomous
middle and lower ranks of governance.

The years 1629 to 1640 saw a total of perhaps 198 boats, carrying
according to original sources some 21,000, but, according to recent
indirect statistical studies, about 10,000 Puritans, across the ocean to
Massachusetts and away from intolerant and intolerable Charles I and
his Anglican Archbishop William Laud. Economic depression and
plagues were over the land, compounding political troubles.
Equal numbers, more or less, emigrated to Ireland,
the Netherlands, Germany, and the Caribbean region.

The numbers of this type of emigrant dwindled with the short-lived
triumph of the Dissenters in England; some settlers even returned
home to fight the struggle or profit from the victory of the
Parliamentary Party. The emigration was not resumed, and New
England was not a heavy receiving center for two centuries,
but for convicts and other odd batches and persons,
until the large immigration of the traditional enemies of the
Dissenters, Irish Catholics, commenced.

A majority of immigrants came from an area of sixty miles radius
around the market town of Haverhill in East England.
The balance came from a thousand parishes representing all except two
counties of England. New England fertility
became proverbial;
families of nine children were
common. Averages of seven and eight children per

household were the rule in a number of seventeenth century towns.
Three centuries later there would be ten million and more Americans
with one or more ancestors
among this single set of immigrants - 1,000 for 1.

Puritans came mostly in family groups, mature
men and women, with children under sixteen equaling them
in number. (In the Middle States, except for German sects, and
especially in the South, men outnumbered women greatly
for several generations.) Again in contrast to
other American immigrants of the time,
most of them paid their passage.

If they were to be assigned to a social class, on, say,
the six-level Warner scale one would place
them largely as lower-middle class. Two-thirds of the
adult males could at least sign their names; most were skilled
or semi-skilled. About one-quarter were farmers, a smaller number were
servants and laborers, another quarter had been in the
cloth trades, and a larger number had been in other crafts and trades.
They were urban folk, as much as a third from large towns,
with a small fraction having lived in the country.
The rural image of New Englanders, an American
nostalgic myth, developed from the American experience.

Cleverly, the Puritans settled in villages right away.
Not only was it traditional with them, but their creed
called for a communitarian life, together
under God and their ministers. A group of them would be
allotted a town site, where it would put up a meeting house in the
center, surround this with a commons where each family could
graze its animals, assigned each head of family
a lot for his house and a patch of land to till.
The farming land was extended outwards as the population grew,
to the edge of the wilderness. Within two biological
generations developed a high correlation among several conditions:
large amount of land held (100 acres or more), church membership and
leadership, and political power.

The Puritans did not like the wilderness.
It sheltered devils, incubi if not succubi,
not to mention Indians and wild animals.
They built paths and stuck to them.
They cleared the wilds in groups. The wilderness in many
places had been farmed by Indians, but most Indians had died from
disease, and a second wild growth was there to be
chopped down or burnt. The Indians around them also
believed that nature was full of spirits.
Puritans did not have the enchanted interest in
natural surroundings that the Indians possessed.
They believed, with the Bible, that
man was on earth to subdue nature and exploit it.

For housing, they erected a familiar Kent and East Anglia
form, the Salt Box. A square floor plan, two stories,
with an attic beneath peaked roof, a central or
off-side fireplace, a kitchen lean-to on one side, and
an outhouse. They built of wood, as was the custom in the East of
England. For two centuries they cut and planed oak,
hackmatack, white pine and cedar, until these
hard woods were exhausted except at impossible prices.
Thereafter softer and cheaper woods were employed.

Clearing wilds, building roads and paths,
erecting bridges, and a number of other tasks were
for the public good and every man could
be called up to work at them. The village green or
the commons often was too trampled by beasts or
drilling militia to be more than a tawny muddy mess.

The militia, a famed institution of colonists everywhere, was an
impressed body of males called up to fight against
Indians, rioters, foreign intrusions, and other militias if needs be.
The butt of ridicule by professional soldiers, and thereafter
by historians, the militia served until the Revolution
usefully, if untidily, and rarely attempted to
take over the civil government or abuse the population
as professional soldiers had a way of doing.

Militiamen were assembled more often than anyone would be
summoned for jury duty. If they were held too long,
or their rations were not forthcoming, they would begin to desert
and the show might have to be called off, whatever it was.
On the march the Massachusetts soldier was promised
a pound of pork, a pound of bread, and a
gill of rum daily.

The authorities tried vainly to keep people within a
short distance of the physical center of town, but
gradually the population's increase and the ambition to farm
ever larger farms - an individualistic itch and a
craving for privacy, too - drove men to dwell far off.
A passion for fences began early, perhaps out of
fear of the wilderness, possibly, too,
from a lower-middle-class and Protestant covertness and anxiety
over property rights. Anyway the abundant stone
needed to be cleared away for farming. Fence building
and fence mending took up as much time
as watching television today.

Puritans, we have noted, were townsfolk -
and landlubbers, one might add. Fishermen rarely
came with the Great Migration.
Where did all the fishermen then come from, who brought in the cod,
built the boats and manned them, settled the fishing villages of
New England, and ultimately sailed the Seven Seas?
We are inclined to find this population in a large casual
immigration that the records of ship lists
and organized migrations will not contain. A close study of two
villages, Gloucester and Marblehead, has afforded
rich material to contemplate.

At one and the same moment, a site at Cape Ann beckoned to a
newly formed Dorchester Company and the Pilgrims of Plymouth.
Both groups dreamed of a fishing fleet profitably operating
there and being supplied, again profitably, with

food, salt and ship supplies. The Dorchester expedition had
poor boats and for two years arrived after the
potential catch of the fishing grounds had swum off.
The Plymouth company set out in 1624 but
arrived late, too, and besides spent more time in bibulation
than with the fishing lines. They constructed a fishing stage
for drying the hoped-for catch.

But when they returned the following season,
Captain Miles Standish at their head, they found that
the Dorchester crew had seized the platform and was ready
to do battle for it. Standish decided to retire,
and brought his crew home. The Dorchester crew
failed once again, and quit.

Next Cape Ann was settled by a group from around Salem that
numbered several who had experience in fishing out of Gloucester,
England, so renamed the site by Cape Ann as Gloucester
and set to work.
They were joined by a score of Welsh families led by an English
pastor. The fishing enterprise began to work well, but the Welsh and
the English began to quarrel and divided the village into two factions,
who composed two political parties, who fought over the town
leadership and government for a decade and more. Perhaps it was the
first urban ethnic conflict of American history,
the first of thousands.

While Gloucester stabilized, and grew to 300 persons
by 1680, its neighbor to the South, Marblehead,
grew faster and obtained about 600 inhabitants,
a disorderly community, as it turned out. Its population was
mobile and diverse. It was settled by immigrants from the ports of
Wales and Ireland, English West Counties, Jersey (of the
Channel Islands, where the language and culture were French), and
Newfoundland, having usually fled from creditors or
ship masters or constables.

So, what with men calling one another
"a thievish Welsh rogue", and a *"knave, Jearse cheater, and French dog"*,
and the court docket loaded with suits for debt,

defamation, assault and battery, sexual molestation,
drunkenness, and general disorderliness, Marblehead
acquired a certain notoriety among inlanders and the
Massachusetts government.

The women of Marblehead made up in boldness,
lewd behavior and ferocity what they lacked in numbers.
When, after some distressing losses at sea and the
pirating of fishing snacks by Indians up the coast,
a boat returned to port with two Indian prisoners,
seized while attempting to capture the boat, a
gang of women flew into a frenzy at the sight of them.
Screaming like Bacchae, they beat off their menfolk
and hacked the prisoners to pieces. Bring them to
Boston, the women shouted, and they would surely be freed.
People of Marblehead hated their rulers in Boston, and the
authorities from Salem as well, whom, on one occasion,
they drove off riotously and tumultuously when these came
to requisition the town's only means of defense, two cannon.
They hated, too, the inland merchants who stripped them
of their earnings. Martial law was
imposed on the town at one point.
Nobody in town was qualified to vote for the colonial legislature.
Their selectmen, who made up the town council,
were often in trouble for graft and theft. Most men
shirked taxes and labor service for the town, and
did not attend town meetings. "Participatory democracy"
would have been cusswords to them.

Still, Marblehead was productive and growing. As a result,
proper executives and merchants were sent in by the moneyed
interests from elsewhere and the town finally had an elite of its own,
and instead of one church that could barely survive,
it had two that contested bitterly the leadership of
the town, one of the affluent, the other of *hoi polloi*.

While in many places of New England the one Puritan mind
was certainly dominant - the one that myth-making has found
convenient, the stable, godly, repressive, conscientious type -
a second, erratic, troublemaking, boisterous, defiant

mind was operative in many other places and
even underground in the same places.

North of Massachusetts was New Hampshire, and
men of Puritan stock may have gone there,
but they shed virtues on the way. They mostly
had quit the fisheries and the salt flats, or had left home to become
adventurers. They dealt in rum and furs, two quarts of rum for an otter
skin, and the Indians got drunk and the men made
more on a single trade than in a week's honest toil.

The French Jesuits had banned the trade, but the Dutch of New York
continued to sell liquor and the New Hampshire men did so as well.
Not only did French trade diminish sharply, but shifty
Indians let themselves be baptized as Dutch Reformed and
Congregationalists as part of the rum bargain.
The Jesuits had to admit to lifting the restriction.

With the proceeds, New Hampshire built its New England villages, and
when these declined from losses in the Civil War and the
destruction of the environment and the out-movement of small
enterprise, the villages were gentrified by New Yorkers and others.

The Puritans and those who dissented from them at
Plymouth, Connecticut and Rhode Island, promulgated
the religious doctrines of Jean Calvin of France and
Geneva, Switzerland, correlated with those of John Knox of Scotland,
transmitted as Presbyterianism to Northern Ireland, and
elsewhere with a dozen sections of so-called Reformed churches.
They fed theologically also upon certain German divines,
the most prominent being, naturally, Martin Luther.
A strong belief of immediate relationship to the God of Israel
and Christ demanded a much simplified ritual and liturgy,
crowned with a sermon by the one in closest relationship,
according to those who had elected him, the minister.
Several cardinal doctrines distinguished the Church
from other Christian sects, theologically speaking
and anthropology aside. The several doctrines are to be

lived, enforced, repeated at larger council
meetings, and made the basis of everyday conduct.

A person is predestined to salvation in Heaven, and, logically,
could also be sent to Hell, by an Act of God;
we do not argue with Him; He chooses us.
When we behave well, and are successful in life,
we do not earn a place in Heaven, but only
demonstrate that we are among the elect whom
God will be calling to Himself. Most people are not
so lucky: witness their lapsing conduct.

Humans are totally depraved by nature, and
the majority will never be able to atone for their sins.
As for those who do not recognize the Christ,
there can be no apology for being, no rights.
Any sympathy for the Indians resides in their
potentiality as Christians, and this was often
doubted. (One needs note the parallel with the Papal Bull that
declared non-Christians to be without territorial rights.)

By the same token, the chosen few are irresistibly graced.
Men will recognize the authority of these elect
just as they would recognize the authority of Jesus.
They shall be the legitimate elite. They are the
elders of the church. *"Democracy"* was termed
by top elder John Cotton in 1664
"the meanest and worst of all forms of government".

By the end of the 1600's the Puritan government,
which came later in American textbooks to seem
divinely inspired and democratic, got into
trouble with its own people and with the outside world,
both colonial and overseas, not to mention the Indians.
Several Puritanical features were offensive.

For one, despite its assertion that church and state should form
exclusive and separate organs, the theocracy firmly united church and

state, a medieval Catholic idea that the Dissenters of
England were even then fighting against.
Separation of church and state was to be a
basic idea of American thought, even when
contradicted hypocritically in practice.

Puritan government was paternalistic, interventionist,
a welfare state. There was no philosophical or
theological principle inclining the elite
to keep their hands off of other people's business,
personal or commercial. In this sense, their
economic theory was Old Testament.
Interfere, restrain, forbid, guide, and prescribe
whatever God seems to indicate to you is
good and proper. Generally this meant being on
the side of the rich against the poor,
for the status of men on earth reflected their
standing in the eyes of God.

The price of basic goods was fixed.
Certain luxury goods were banned.
Rates of pay for workers were determined by law,
and were as low as could be set without
prompting them to leave town. Relatives were
held responsible for the keep of the sick and penniless,
while luckless ones without caring relations
managed slightly better through the agency of the Church
than the elderly slaves of the South.

So quick to impose laws upon their people,
the Puritan oligarchs could hardly be expected to have a
tender regard for human rights. Constables were
permitted to enter homes without warrants. Indeed,
none of the esteemed rights contained in the American Federal
Constitution were deemed to have extraordinary merits
at law or in principle. The liberty of the Church,
as a corporate body, from outside religious or secular control
was the paramount liberty.

The government was quick to punish religious crimes.

Blasphemy, for instance, was punishable by death,
but could be confused with sedition, also punishable by death.
In 1631 a man was fined, whipped,
had his ears cut off and was banished for *"uttering malicious
and scandalous speeches against the government and church of Salem"*.
John Cotton, in 1636, as if rehearsing for the
Ayatollah Kohmeini *vs.* Salman Rushdie affair
three-and-a-half centuries later, defined
capital laws *"which is a cursing of God by atheism,
or the like, to be punished with death"*.
In 1639, Ambrose Martin was merely fined
and sentenced to reeducation by a minister for speaking
of the church covenant as a *"stinking carryon"*, and
arguing that God would never let preachers
take the place of Jesus. Joseph Gatchell of
Marblehead had his tongue pierced with a
hot iron in 1684 for arguing
vehemently that preachers were duping people,
telling plain folk that the Scriptures were
verbatim the words of God whereas they were
only the sayings of men.

In 1641, the Massachusetts General Court, by which name the representative assembly was known, promulgated the "Body of Liberties", a code of one hundred laws. Many of them would be considered repressive in a modern democracy, and were thought so even by fellow-Puritans of England, especially by the radical Levellers. There was to be no slavery among Puritans but only among prisoners of war and strangers who *"selle themselves or are sold to us"*. The articles portray naturally, through their theology, the oxymoron which was clearly enunciated in the twentieth century by Fascist Duce Benito Mussolini as *"compulsory voluntarism"*, to wit, that a good citizen must logically wish himself to be good and therefore welcome the government's compelling him to conduct himself properly.

Such doctrines rid the colony of some difficult characters, among them Roger Williams and Anne Hutchinson. For preaching the equality of man, tolerance of opinions and religion,

and the general brand of radical democracy excrescent in
England, Roger Williams was banished, and set up shop
at what was to be the State of Rhode Island
and Providence Plantations, not far down the road.

There Anne Hutchinson found him, when she was banished for
preaching against the Puritan party line.
Williams, in fact, laid the foundations of the Baptist Church
in America, the membership of whose several branches is second
only to the Roman Catholic Church in numbers.

Also at odds with the Puritan Elders was Samuel Gorton, who
displayed such impieties as denying the Three-Beings
Holy Trinity doctrine, decrying the payment of
ministers, asserting each man is his own priest,
casting doubt on heaven and hell, allowing
every person a chance at salvation, and of course
democracy in government.

It may have been that he was much influenced by German
theological circles of the times, that included not only
Luther but also Agricola and Johann Andreae.
Many Puritans had emigrated to Germany and were in touch with
their movement in England and America. Still, the fully
operative ideational force bringing pressure
upon the political mind of the Puritans would have been the
Levellers movement in the Commonwealth Army of Cromwell.

When questioning themselves or asked by others the source of their
authority, the Puritan leaders would reply that
God had granted them this legitimacy because of their
understanding of His word and will.
God had covenanted with them as He had
with Biblical Abraham; telling them what
they must do and compelling them to agree to do it.
Right reason would persuade anyone of this.
To their critics, naturally, right reason as the
source of legitimacy had even less of a presence
than God when you needed it.

❖❖❖

They believed in covenants, and psychologically they were thus prepared to believe in a contract between the source of legitimate authority and the subjects of the authority. The ideas of popular consent, democracy, elections and representative government were invented before the Puritans thought of coming to America, but the idea of written constitutions to which all responsible members of the community pledged their adherence owes much to the idea of men being bound by religious covenant. Magna Carta of 1215 was a contract between king and barons. The "Compact" signed aboard the *Mayflower* was a contract or covenant standing above the parties, to which all pledged loyalty.

The Connecticut contribution to benign democratic rule was larger. Thomas Hooker and his Congregationalist followers moved out of Massachusetts with the express purpose of ridding themselves of a "magisterial autocracy". They drafted and signed the set of *Fundamental Orders* that was a true constitution of state, separating church from state to a large degree, and basing authority on the free consent of the people.

The people, to them, also meant a larger body of free and voting citizens than was the case to the North. Constitution-drafting was a catching habit. Spreading from colony to colony and from one kind of group to another, it was applied to all forms of institutions in America. Nothing could be done, nothing had validity, without an initial constitution.

As the power of the first three generations of Elders waned, the People became an obvious choice as the source of authority; the People could act by themselves, or, using a legal fiction, be represented by persons acting in their name. Such persons would have to be chosen, and if chosen by the People, they would be anointed with Popular Legitimacy and Authority.

America would spend a hundred years and more arguing over just who constituted the People and how their Collective Will could enter the brain and vote

of the Legislative Representative, but in principle
there it was. The atom had been smashed;
the source of legitimate authority in modernity was to
occur in the fast-breeder of democracy.

There was reason to expect this to happen. The anarchistic
conditions of the first settlements of the country and the turbulent
contemporary history of their homelands let few
Americans believe in the King as the god-given or charismatic source
of fundamental authority. Many believed
in God as the Supreme Ruler of the Universe,
but once the Puritan ideology softened, few outside of the
Puritan congregations believed that God was specific
enough to designate the Puritan Elders as
His agents for secular official affairs.

Puritans were not at all deprived of lust by their religion.
But the authorities were meddling and officious.
Sometimes the controls they exercised over sexual conduct
were distinctive. They allowed courting couples to speak privately,
while sitting, by means of a double-belled trumpet;
the enamored could speak and hear through it, but their
elders around and about them could hear nothing.
They also allowed courting couples to bundle into
a bed together, with a board between them and
the girl wrapped from the waist down.
Wrappings and board and clever fingers and teeth....

Marriages were simple ceremonies; rings were not exchanged.
Ministers declaimed continuously against the perils of lust,
masturbation, fornication, and dating without a chaperon.
Contraception was strictly forbidden.
Adultery was a capital crime, yet often indulged.

The repressive moral code of the Puritans has long been shown to
have had a reverse. Fornication was common. Conception out of
wedlock was frequent, entailing an obligation to marry.
Prostitution was deplored but widely practiced.

Syphilis and other venereal diseases were known and feared.
A disgusting story told by Governor Winthrop
concerns a wet nurse who contracted the disease from her
mariner husband and spread it among seventeen infants
brought to nurse at her sore breasts.
Bestiality was punished by death.
Deformed piglets provoked a determined search for a human parent.

Unlike Spanish and French Catholics, Puritanical Protestants
brought with them a frequent aversion to and fear of sex among
themselves, which was projected onto the foreign races next to them,
Indian and African, and engendered sexual, personal, social and racial
disturbances. Guilt and punishment attended any overstepping of racial
boundaries in matters of affection. The contradiction of great
temptation and severe repression induced sick attitudes on
both race and sex.

Too, some of the circumstances abetted homosexuality.
Close quarters on boats, long voyages, reliance of males upon males,
the presence of helpless small boys everywhere. First Massachusetts
Governor William Bradford's *History of Plymouth Plantations*
wonders why *"sodomy and buggery (things fearful to name) have
broke forth in this land"*, and lays it to *"our corrupt natures, which
are so hardly bridled, subdued, and mortified"*.

The extraordinary Governor John Winthrop a few years later,
in his *History of New England,* remarks on a married man
with a record of sodomy in England who *"had corrupted a great
part of the youth of Guilford by masturbations"* and,
when questioned about the lawfulness of his practices,
declared himself skeptical of God; he was executed at
New Haven in 1646.
Studies of English society in this period show
widespread homosexuality. The employment of children
and the around-the-clock proximity of master and apprentices in the
economy and households are reasons that come readily to hand.

The quality of affection, one of life's basic goods,

is a priority question in seventeenth century America and
by extension in the centuries ahead. Would it be correct to say
that Americans began their collective existence with palpable
problems of affection, worse than beset the French,
Spanish, Germans, Italians, Dutch, Irish, and
English of the Age? The answer would be, yes,
with certain prominent reservations.
Beginning with the heavier German and Irish Catholic
immigration, and continuing, markedly reinforced,
with later immigrant groups, with the more frequent occurrence of
family groups and with the lesser presence of the
"Puritan shame complex", affection may have come to
be in larger supply (granted that immigrants would always be
attitudinally dominated, as in the social, economic, and
political spheres, by those who came before,
the "affectionally deprived".)

The slave culture, as we shall examine it, also wreaked
havoc upon affectional relations: letting
people develop intense relations, as they will
under oppressive conditions, and then breaking them
up frequently and traumatically. Although we are only in the
beginning of Euro-American history here
we need to recognize a condition of general
affectional deprivation and demoralization
at all ranks of society, and especially in the lower ranks
(in respect to other values), whereas often the
poor have at least been let alone to be loving.

Today American magazines carry many stories and counsels
concerning everyone's need for love and how to increase one's
affectional receipts and how to expend love upon others, including
one's children and senior citizens. But historians seem to be especially
immune to this concern. The word "love" hardly enters the
historiography of America. It may occur as "love of one's country", or
in an oblique quotation from a poem of Walt Whitman, who was a
great lover of persons, people, and democracy, and a
poet whom the ordinary American feels uncomfortable with.

A certain prize-winning and prestigious American

colonial history book of the past generation,
although giving itself ample space by
largely eschewing warfare and governance, does not
carry within its fine index the words:
love, affection, marriage, or family; it does not
treat them, and has only several paragraphs on
women's activities.

Actually, European America was born in a crisis of love.
The shortage of males was acute, and here we speak
even of the Puritans and then more emphatically of
the Virginians, Carolinians, and other settling-ins
that landed more like war parties than family gatherings.
Sexual, social and racial disturbances resulted.
With exceptions in the case of families and cults arriving
as affectional groups in the first place, people
who arrived were largely male - males, too,
whose early American experiences with affection often
took the form of whoring, homosexuality,
rape, and bargaining for or purchase of women.

Since males had so often been thrown upon their resources,
often in their early teens, they had only experience with a
mother, often a bad one, with kind strangers,
and women of the streets. Thereupon, landed in the colonies,
they were mostly bereft of the company of girls and women.
They were taught that sex and concubinage with Indians,
Africans, or any combination of races was
taboo, even against the law, and punished.
Love was tied to vile sexuality and prohibited objects.

In sum, the average American male throughout the sixteenth century
and into the future was mal-conditioned in sexual affairs,
affection generally, and severely deprived. Furthermore,
he was conditioned to treat Indians, Blacks,
foreigners and any others available as if inferiors,
unworthy of his deeper affection, though often as objects of lust.
Seeking out a Black woman for sex, a White man might say
superstitiously and to deny his lust,
it was *"to change my luck"*.

❖❖❖

Quakers, who professed love as the basis of love and religion, were
few in numbers, though influential. Their concept of
love had heavy platonic overtones, despite
the example of Benjamin Franklin, reputed to be a womanizer.
Still, brotherly love was more like the true and full
article than the love that the Puritans loftily discussed,
which was essentially the insensible and condescending
love God spared for erring Mankind, and,
too, an affection that almost entirely assimilated into
relationships of respect.

The Quaker personal and private love for God and
for mankind, including even Indians, their preachments of
absolute peace, their method of making group decisions
by consensus, and then particularly their evangelism:
all this was too much for the Puritan oligarchs.

When Quakers came to Massachusetts, whatever standing they might
have had in Pennsylvania, they were banished.
If they returned, as did four such Friends, they were caught
by hostile locals and hanged; one was a woman.
Thirty were roughly treated and jailed.
This was by the law of May 1661, but
on September 9 of the same year there issued a
mandamus to the Colony to cease corporal punishment and the
execution of "vagabon Quakers", ordered by
none other than King Charles, hardly the democrat.
Still the persecution of Quakers continued.

Puritan colonists, often *en famille*,
cultivated affectional attitudes and relations that tended to
be formal and conditioned upon respect of elders,
propriety of women in respect to their men, secure
worldly goods, and godliness.
Children were authoritatively and gruffly treated;
physical punishment was severe and normal. Although the
breakaway rate for Puritans was high, the guilt and shame

syndrome did not break away with the escapees,
but continued in not very sublimated ways,
in literature, science, education, and
social relationships.

The novel *Manon Lescaut,* that I referred to earlier,
exemplified in the next century and in the Louisiana Territory,
not only the sale of "women of ill repute" to New Orleans males,
but typifies in the character of Manon the perpetual and true
ambivalence of the American male who must love a woman,
but cannot make up his mind whether to love the
"good-bad girl", like Manon, or the *"good-good girl",*
the morally unambiguous creature that his mother,
teachers, preachers, and all the rest of the authorities
insisted he must prefer.

The Puritans had also a bad record in regard to witchcraft.
A long time after Calvin's Geneva had stopped burning
so-adjudged witches (in one year 34 had been burned there),
Massachusetts took up the practice.
It was about the time when Ludwig van Beethoven's
Great Grandmother had been burned at the stake for being a witch,
fortunately after parturition. In 1692,
20 women and men were put to death for
dealing with the Devil and putting the
hex on persons roundabout.

The basic cause was the corpus of Christian belief itself,
of the late Renaissance and Reformation variety.
Immediate causes may have been the ingestion of
large amounts of spoiled rye bread, which
produces a drug not too different from LSD in its effects.
Psychologically witch-hunting blended well with the Puritan ethic,
which regularly promoted a high level of paranoia in the population.
Too, the proverbial sexual repression of the Puritans
protruded from the welter of claims, testimony,
confessions, and accusations..

Being handled by the accused was sexual molestation.
One student of the subject has gone back to the plague of syphilis,
which would bring about a general misogynism,
which would then be projected onto women as witches,
causing several kinds of trouble.

Puritans were superstitious, perhaps excessively so,
possibly because of the paranoia of a God-watched culture:
"It's vain.. for Men to cover the least iniquity:
the Judge hath seen and privy been to all their villainy".
thus one of the most famous poems of the time called
"God's Controversy with New England", by Michael Wigglesworth.
Until the twentieth century, there occurred cases of digging up coffins
in order to rearrange a relative's bones when the corpse
was suspected of sucking the life force from the living,
or another such vampirish offense.

Basic literacy skills were esteemed, and New England was always ahead of the other sections of the country in this regard. Its boats carried more men who had studied at Cambridge and Oxford, too, though it must be borne in mind that these places were less immersed in the real world than a Bible College of today. Harvard and Yale were started up in the latter part of the 1600's, and though not much to begin with, became within two political generations sources of a ministerial, professional and political elite. But a proper full-scale elementary education system had to wait
another three political generations and more:
state intervention did not go so far as that.

The New Englanders kept a great many diaries and published more items than the rest of America put together. The Reverend Cotton Mather alone authored 400 religious tracts, one-fourth of the regional production of all books, almost entirely theological and preachy rubbish. Playing music was practically forbidden, composing it impossible. (A contemporary of Mather, Alessandro Scarlatti of Palermo, Sicily, was meanwhile composing 115
operas, and bringing up Domenico and several other
gifted children there and in Naples.)

The Rev. Edward Taylor wrote poems of obscene innuendos,
one might infer, about his relationship to Jesus,
as asking God to put Christ's nipples in his mouth
as the Virgin drawing him the lover unto a pure baptism.
Still, literature must begin somewhere in an
outcaste society.

A literate father or mother breeds literate children.
A literate pastor has literate children who become
teachers, doctors, editors, writers, poets, and
conscientious civil officers, if they are not
pastors themselves or missionaries. A relatively
small number of people of this sort form a
large proportion of the elite of the land. There is a
hereditary quality to the elite demography of
de-celibated Protestantism, that Catholicism of
that age, castigated for its nepotism
and bastard favorites, hardly approached.

However, education and the kind of education
(liberal religion and pragmatism were New England inventions)
are not the only explanation of the unquestioned
prominence of the Puritans in American history.
First of all, success: they and their descendants
ended up on top of the heap. If ,
like the Indians, they should turn out to be
no longer on top with the passage of time, then
other groups will be invited to rewrite history - Quakers,
Mennonites, Jesuits, Mormons, Jews, Catholics, etc. - just as would
have happened if the sacred geese had not alerted the Romans to the
Gauls scaling their ramparts: we all might be studying Gaelic, and
memorizing the details of this great night of the capture
of Rome to recite at the Feast of the Honking Geese.

It took six biological generations for the New Englanders
to make it and they gave up many dreams on the way.
But whereas in 1670 practically nobody
owned knives and forks, or glassware or any

tea or coffee equipment, by 1720
two or three out of a hundred did so, and
by 1774 in Massachusetts about half
the households owned knives and forks, glassware, tea
and coffee equipment and a third possessed china ware.
Only the "wealthy" were likely to have some mahogany
furnishings. Practically no household
possessed a musical instrument.

With the growth of their material possessions, the Puritans,
now Yankees, did manage to gain and hold
lots of money, respect, education and science,
political power, and power over the country's imagery,
especially when relieved of the Southern competition by the
Civil War and of the Middle Northerners by the latter's
industriousness. They wrote and published many books,
that others had to read for lack of better.
They had a high birth rate when children could count on
obtaining land to farm, ships to build,
money to lend, insurance companies to organize, and so on.
They discovered what whale oil could bring, and
timber, and slave-trading, and gadgets, and furs.
They became inventors when industrial revolution was in
order. They financed railroads. They were hosts and masters of a
continual steam of immigrants who could be used as
domestics and laborers, before losing them and
going on to exploit the next wave.

Many of the most famous and long-lived and richest
families of Rhode Island, Massachusetts, New York,
South Carolina, and Virginia were in the process of becoming so
by participating profitably in the slave trade,
the internal and foreign rum trade, the fur trade,
and land speculation. Smuggling, profiteering,
double-dealing the Indians, privateering, and
buccaneering were all part of the picture.

The poorest half of the population gained nothing from
any occupation except a precarious subsistence,
this, too, often denied in infancy and old age.

Women were universally subordinate in law and in fact.
Not until one gets toward the upper echelons of the
population pyramid, among the top twenty per cent,
does one encounter decent material
standards of living for the times.

New Englanders embraced a melancholy culture;
it would have remained so even if dancing on
the green were permitted. When the Great Awakening was
brought to New England, many felt no need for it:
they were already in the habit of consulting their soul and
finding it wicked. They learned earlier than other Americans
to portray themselves from the start, mostly correctly,
as a suffering lot, who had the right to ask themselves a
and their descendants and the whole world to suffer in
commemoration. They learned that philanthropy in
religion, education, in charity, and even in business could pay
profits directly or indirectly. They never ceased
to profess a higher level of morality than ordinary people.
They cultivated hypocrisy, a useful trait,
in that it let them misbehave secretly, and to
make money hand over fist while professing sanctity.

One more bit of luck, for which they scarcely had
major responsibility, befell the Puritans
with the writing and adoption of the U.S. Constitution.
This, as we shall be seeing, was in many ways perfectly
suited to the ideals and machinations of the Puritan elect.
The general Puritanical elite thereupon developed
as the largest and most significant component
of the elite in the United States; it survived until the
mid-1900's before coming apart at the seams.
And, further, as elites are rated in history,
it might have been among the better ones.

It may have been unfortunate for America, this idea that an
omnipotent God labored in its interest, that its actions, if gainful,
were god-blessed, and if injurious, divinely mysterious.

The so-called savage Indians had no such ready reference
to their God with every action they took.
Yet anthropology books have been full of statements to the
effect that, unlike the western world, the savage world
was at every moment superstitious and prone to explain
everything as the work of spirits and gods or devils.

By quickly resorting to God in happy or unfortunate circumstances,
the ignorant clergy, no matter how filled with *docta ignorantia*, as
Erasmus said, can avoid naming names, the
real names of those responsible for good and evil in the world.
The Pilgrims in prayer upon arrival, and
the Priest carrying the cross alongside Columbus in landing,
united to deprive the New World of at least one promise that
could justify it: a truly new start.

The Pilgrims were only the first of the most. It is erroneous to
believe that American Puritanism, a source of wonder,
amusement, contempt, and anger around the world was
a product of the Pilgrims, Puritans of Massachusetts, and
a few individuals here and there. The essential
vices and virtues of Puritanism were inherent in and
derived from a number of Protestant sects who came to
America shortly after the New Englanders:
Quakers, Pietists, Moravians, Lutherans, Huguenots,
Anabaptists and Baptists, and later on the
Scots-Irish Presbyterians and Methodists, all
conveyed an essentially Puritanical ideology.

The New England Puritans took the lead, because they were
Anglophone, directly connected to England and the English
Universities, had the most prestigious intellectual apparatus in America
and met aggressively (abetted by their motley Marblehead types) the
wide world, up and down the coast and overseas.

When all the less prestigious cults and sects prescribing the
Puritanical formulas for the good life came to the country, and
met up with the New Englanders who had moved South and west,
whether in person or by word of mouth and the press,
they were much encouraged to insist upon their

reasonable facsimiles of New England Puritanism.

Tight-lipped Yankee bankers would lend tight money to tight-lipped pastors of poor but tidy churches. Thus the conglomerate of attitudes usually termed American Puritanism came into being. Backsliding Protestant ministers and worldly Catholic priests might get into the swing of things by dusting off the Puritan idols they had been keeping on their back shelves.

Despite the deism that the names of Franklin, Washington, Jefferson and the rest bespeak, and Tom Paine's atheism, a majority of immigrants to America came believing that God was crossing with them, further that the kingdom of God could be set up here after failing in Palestine and Rome and Country X. And, in due course, whatever the law of the deists, promulgated in the Constitution's First Amendment, might demand in separating church from state, the preponderant sentiment would work its way through onto the dollar bill where it says "in God we trust", and onto the Great Seal of the United States of America likewise.

———————————

Boatpeople all…

Chapter Fourteen

Pluralists

Pluralism as a type of culture characterized the many different Indian groups that occupied the region from New York State, through Pennsylvania, New Jersey, down through Delaware and Maryland. Both great nations, the Iroquois and the Algonquin, were represented by a number of tribes. By the end of the

eighteenth century, they had been reduced to small units,
clinging precariously to lands begrudged them
by European newcomers.

In upper New York State, New Englanders moved in,
and in lower New York, Dutch took hold and ascended the Hudson River.
They also followed the marshy coast and sands of New Jersey
to where they encountered, at the mouth of the Delaware River,
settlements of Swedes, mostly Finns, which were taken over.
The English defeated the Netherlands in the 1660's
in struggles over trading rights here and there in the
wide world, effectively enlarging the new British Empire.

Dutch remained in strength in New York, and
their property rights were recognized by the English.
Well-connected Englishmen tried to shape their own estates
according to the patroon system, semi-medieval in nature, that
bound tenants to the plantation. But the system
encouraged many tenants to flee West as soon as they could,
and others to stay and plot assassinations and riots.
Because the colony lacked the abundant excellent soils and
highly motivated farmers of Pennsylvania,
New York developed less rapidly.

I use the word "farmer" here to mean a
reasonably free cultivator. No one is quite free.
Americans have always called the farmers of Europe
"peasants", using the French term for "country-dwellers"–
Mexican and Spanish "*peon*", Italian "*paesano*".
Less commonly the French use "*fermier*".
Since Americans think that the farmer is something better
than a peasant, the practice sustains a myth about the farmers of the
two regions. Hence I avoid the use of the term
"peasant", knowing how irritated American readers would
become if the word "peasant" were to refer to the American farmer,
who has benefitted by lyrical praise in media and myth.

There have been ten types of American farmers:

the Indian free part-time hunter-gatherer-farmer;
the Indian collective farmer of the Southwest;
the plantation owner;
the plantation slave;
the indentured farm worker;
the farm laborer;
the share-cropper;
the tenant farmer;
the independent landowning farmer;
the partnership; and
the large corporate farm run by a manager or owner.

The European peasant did not become a farmer by crossing the ocean; he became so in name only. If he took to the land, some of his skills and customs would be used, others abandoned and new ones taken up. Often the abilities and affinities of one wave or type of immigrant would be superior to those of the American farmers he would encounter, sometimes not.

Since Englishmen began now to arrive in some number and other nationalities skipped ship frequently, New York City became an early example of American pluralism. By 1643, if we may credit a Jesuit missionary, *"On the island of Manhate there were men of eighteen different languages"*. The population was 5,000. Its government was corrupt and since the colony's government came directly under the Crown without the intervention of a proprietor or corporation, responsibility for the archetypical mess could not be assigned elsewhere than to the royal officers.

The Governors were without exception thieves over a hundred years of time. One, Lord Cornbury the Transvestite, gave a group of speculators two million acres of public land for a pittance. In the next generation, Governor Clinton complained that he had too little land, yet managed to retire to England with 80,000 pounds sterling, equivalent to at least $4,000,000 today. In all, some thirty men were

granted three-fourths of all the land of the
huge colony of New York.

The early English Governor Colonel Fletcher was a model of the type.
He was under orders to halt the use of New York Harbor by pirates;
piracy had become so inconvenient to the several European
governments that they one by one declared war against it. Wealthy
merchants, who had hitherto sold to privateers (buccaneers, pirates -
the terms were loose to fit the practices) their outfits and bought their
goods for resale, were taking disagreeable losses from their sometime
clients. With his stern manners and continual resort to prayer, Fletcher
at first frightened the Dutch, English and other sponsors and their
pirates who had found haven in the spacious port of New York.
Fletcher governed with the advice of a Council, composed of wealthy
men in cahoots with the Board of Trade in London and with
local piratical rings.

The New Man caught on quickly, the good word went out, and the
pirate vessels standing offshore sailed into safe harbor.
Soon New York became a flourishing center for illegal traffic.
The Fletchers lived magnificently, collected gold and silver,
invited pirates to dinner, and Mrs. Fletcher
rode in a carriage drawn by six horses.

Where the demi-mondaine flourishes, the arts are sown.
By the time that President George Washington arrived to
administer the new USA briefly from New York City,
he found that he could enjoy himself greatly with the
plays being performed. He learned there, too,
to read serious books, especially about agriculture.

The key to American pluralism was not New England
nor the South, not New York or other colonies.
It was Pennsylvania, and the man who named it
for himself, William Penn, the Younger.
His father was a politically powerful admiral, whose extensive
estates in Ireland he allowed his son to manage.

The son gained business experience and a love for rural life;
he also became a religious radical, a devoted friend
of the Quakers. He became a Trustee of West New Jersey
in 1674 and sought then a proprietorship,
which he obtained in 1681.

This gift of Charles II is a peak action of
American history, an act equal in material consequences
to the Massachusetts and Virginia foundings and in
moral consequences greater. It became the cement of
the union, for if the Yankee and Slave Cultures had arisen
cheek by jowl, a united front for independence or
federation would have been most difficult to organize.

William Penn did not think of his Quakers as
the chosen instrument for the future of America.
He admired their doctrine, the preachments of J. Fox,
praised their way of life, and pitied their poverty.
Their fervent belief that the God was within one,
their close familial ties, their intense sense of community
of friends who believed alike and resolved all issues
by the collective emotion of consensus,
their pride in their poverty and devotion to toil:
such were the traits that drew to them this quite
remarkable man who could
live in baronial style yet work diligently to
create equality of standing and opportunity.
He thought they were the sort of people who could realize the
dream of rural paradise. What luck for them and the world:
he received from the debauched monarch a bit of land to the
North of Maryland and South of New York,
extending then Westward five degrees of longitude.
This was enough to give a farm to all Quakers
who then lived or would ever live.

Actually, Pennsylvania was a capitalist enterprise.
Even though he gave every advantage to Quakers,
Penn did not give them their land but sold it to them,
5000 acres for a hundred pounds sterling.
He expected that several Quaker families would

get together, buy what they could, and divide it up
into workable farms. They did so.

He had another fine idea, that there should be a city,
which he called Philadelphia,
"City of Brotherly Love, or of Loving Brothers" -
he was not afraid of the Classics (though his clientele
were as far from Oxbridge Englishmen as you could get) -
and in this city, provided that you had bought a sizeable
rural area to farm, you would receive a
large city lot dirt cheap.
Quakers received preference, but others,
regardless of religion, could also buy into Pennsylvania.

Here was pluralism: a leader who realized that country and city,
agriculture and commerce, should be two sides of the civilized coin,
a planner who could lay out a region and bring in his people,
a leader who could legislate for diverse religions and ethnic groups.
He compares favorably with Moses and Aeneas.
Economically and familially, the Society of Friends
acted the prototype of millions of households
that immigrated to America, with modest yet rare qualities.
Thomas Jefferson later coupled them with Jews
as two international sects who could live in the foreign world
of society while remaining apart from it.

They were originally lodged in the Northwestern corner
of England and in Wales for the most part,
just about the poorest part of poor old England
of the seventeenth century. Most were on long leases or
owned a little land. Their large broods
could not possibly live off the land, but somehow
had to be placed as apprentices or tenants somewhere.
They hated to send their offspring to distant places
where there were no Quakers, among people
who gave them this ridiculous name.
(True, sometimes they quaked, as when you are
tremendously excited by the sensed presence of your God,

who enlightens you on matters that would otherwise
be all too perplexing. You shiver, you
shake [there were Shakers, too],
you quaked in awe and pride, that you should be of a
stature, despite your poverty and lowliness,
to be at one with Jesus.)

It was a Quaker idea that all men are brothers -
an ancient idea that could be traced through Greco-Roman
Stoicism and then through the Gospels of Jesus,
an idea that had lost its way many times, to be
rediscovered and applied by cults like the Quakers.
A radical group, threat to both church and state, they were
determinedly, obstinately egalitarian,
pacifist, anarchistic, anti-statist,
anti-ceremonial, anti-all that most people
seemed to want out of life.

As if to assure that other people would know
how different they were, they affected
different dress and speech, so that they could be detected
coming down the road. Remarkably, although
consistent with their pacifist and fraternal philosophy,
Quakers were tolerant of other sects and nationalities.
With all of this, they were persecuted
everywhere they went, beginning with their ancestral haunts.
So when Penn put on his hard sell, as if they were
sophisticated metropolitans, they assembled
in their neat hovels and in their meeting houses
(if their hostile neighbors allowed them) and
considered whether Mr. Penn had presented an
altogether promising offer, that they should accept.

Penn composed promotional literature, which he had circulated into
the Quaker corner of England-Wales, and elsewhere.
Within a few years, the little communities
where they congregated were depopulating.
The biggest city of the whole area was Chester
(to be bigger in the New World as Chester, Pa.)
with 7,000, prettier than most towns of England,

and always to be prettier than its American namesake.
They left Chester and the region around, but, too,
departed from their Quaker circles elsewhere
in England where they had carefully maintained their ways
despite inducements to stray and persecution.
The main body of Quakers began to arrive
in 1675 (in West New Jersey) and
continued until 1689.

Non-Quaker Welsh and English came.
Then came Palatinians, Swiss, Moravians and
other German-speaking nationalities. There were
Amish, Mennonites, Pietists, Anabaptists, and Lutherans,
all of these Germanic (I do not say "German"
because we must wait until 1870 for German
unification, and meanwhile the religio-ethnic components
thought of themselves as Germanic in dialect and customs,
but as special cultural and political entities.

And after them came Scots-Irish, Anglo-Irish, and Scots.
French Huguenots came. People from other
colonies migrated in, and a pot-pourri of
nationalities as individuals.

In 1682 William Penn journeyed through
Germany advertising Pennsylvania for its
religious and political toleration and bountiful nature.
In 1683 Mennonites from the Rhineland arrived,
led by a Frankfurt lawyer. William Rittenhouse
built the first paper mill in America in the same year.
Next year there arrived a Christian communist
commune from the Rhineland which settled in Maryland,
then broke up after a few years. But heavy
Germanic settlement occurred there, founding
towns like Frederick and Hagerstown.

In the same decade some Germans had reached the Hudson

Valley, where the Dutch Patroon system commanded society,
and where shortly a revolt of tenants and the poor broke out,
organized and led by a German named Jacob Leisler,
from Frankfurt. They called themselves the People's Movement and
in 1690 called for a
"First Congress of the American Colonies".
Leisler was soon captured, then drawn and quartered.
His partner in treason, Jacob Miloure, was also executed.

I referred earlier to the 3000 Palatinians
who ended their complicated journey on the
Hudson Valley frontier next to the Mohawks.
Between 1720 and 1770 about
2000 Germans a year came to America,
most to become indentured servants.

A Lutheran Pastor Brunnholtz in 1750
decried the frauds committed by shipping agents and the
brutality of conditions aboard the boats, of
the ruthless disposal of the sick and dying at sea.
He tells how the people arriving in debt or without resources
were penned up like cattle in huts and on straw
to await the sale of their labor for the years to come
to whoever would pay for them.

So powerful was the dream in the Germanies,
"that everyone could become as rich as a nobleman, etc".
that no amount of information sent back
seemed to penetrate the heavy veil of delusion. In words that
would be repeated for two centuries without effect,
*"the province is crowded full of people and living
becomes continually more expensive".*

In the 1760's a number of Germans emigrated to
Catholic New Orleans. Pennsylvania, however,
was the paramount Germanic establishment.
By 1775 nearly half the quarter-million population of
the colony was of Germanic origin. That would be 10% of the
population of the thirteen colonies. Before the century was
out, there would occur through desertions and discharge an

accretion of perhaps 10,000 Hessian
mercenaries from the British Army of the Revolution.

As the best of the land - and it was indeed the best
to be found in America - was taken up,
the later Germans of the 1700's bumped
against Indian territory, and halted, for the
Quaker Proprietor and elected legislature would not
on principle commit acts of aggression
against the natives. The Quaker government meant to
observe its treaties. So the German colonists began to
move along the Eastern rim of the Allegheny
Mountains Southward.

Some of the first to arrive obtained large and
rich farms that they worked with a diligence and science
unknown to the English, and they brought with them
schoolmasters and books and a more literate and artistic
culture generally than the Anglophones around them.
Classical musical culture in America was a German
importation, through their own teachers and
performers and choirs.
Superior church music was of German origin, too.

Germans of the early 1700's were not well-off
and well-prepared as immigrants. The majority were
wracked by wars, economic dislocation, and
religious and political persecution before coming to
America; they were told the usual lies about
conditions there; they arrived as bonded servants or
with no money after having paid their passage.
The miracle of location and adaptation operated for
some. They found a job and could buy a parcel of land
soon afterwards. Or a Quaker group or preceding
Germanic group would hire a batch and
put them to work on a farm.

Those who worked their way West and then South,

for lack of any other possibility en route,
might found some tiny village a day's walk
through wilderness to the nearest settlement, where their
shacks were protected by a stockade and the largest building
served as a meeting house for daily prayers and singing
and as a last refuge should Indians break into the compound.
Meanwhile they scratched the ground for
tubers and raised a few animals.

In 1710 650 Germans made their way
to New Bern, North Carolina. Two years later
they were nearly wiped out in a war with Tuscarora Indians.
Nevertheless, by 1750 Germanic settlers had
gotten down to Savannah, Georgia. To the North,
in Maine, they established the town of Waldoboro.
From here they sent a force to join the British
in attacking the French at Louisbourg. Whereupon
in the following year, Indian allies of the French
attacked and destroyed Waldoboro.

The Germans of Pennsylvania generally supported the
Quakers in politics. Their religious principles and behavior were
more akin to these, than to the Presbyterian culture
of the Scots-Irish who had arrived in large numbers and
mostly moved West. When these came up
against the Indians, they, too, moved Southwards
via the Cumberland and Shenandoah Valleys,
as far as North Carolina. The Scots-Irish
tended to be domineering and
congenitally hostile to Indians.

Current conditions at mid-century found them,
as usual, riled up against the Indians blocking their
way West (as per Treaty) and even
shooting and scalping invaders, and against the Quakers,
who would not vote money for arms nor declare
open season on Indian scalps.

Because they, too, coveted Indian lands and
were indignant at the Indians for forcefully fighting back at

trespassers, the Germanic settlers switched their support to the advocates of a war policy and the Quakers partly resigned from government and partly were electorally defeated. This was the year 1756.
It denoted the end of Quaker domination of Pennsylvania; war policies would rule the Colony and State for a quarter-century to come.

Some scholars say that the Quakers failed at governing. This is nonsense. Would that every government could organize a large territory, admit diverse and sometimes hostile groups, and be conducted with so little corruption and so equitably for a hundred years. That most Quakers chose to be just in foreign relations with the Indians, rather than to break treaties and wage an aggressive war to exterminate or dispossess them, and that they should resign power rather than alter their position should elicit commendation.
One can only say that evil government triumphed over good government, but that is the way that one America won over another - so let those who will, be thankful for sundry fruits of evil.

The Scots-Irish formed over a dozen congregations of the Presbyterian Church in Pennsylvania; several more congregations were of English or other stock. They preferred the term Presbyterian to Congregational, the two designations by this time meaning relatively little, parish members and ministers determining the degree of democracy in church affairs and the extent of deviation or conformity with respect to the continual doctrinal disputation. This was in 1730, when Scots-Irish immigration was heavy.

The immigrants preferred Pennsylvania. They were treated better than in New England or the South, or upstate New York, for that matter. They enjoyed the free-wheeling movement and variety of life-chances that came with the pluralism of the region. They developed,

too, that kind of frontier adaptation that
would characterize many of them for over a century to come.
They were quite poor, and did not do as well
economically as the Quakers and Germanic groups.

A problem they had now and always would have
was that they were inordinately individualistic - like the others,
true, but without the deftness to wrap a shell of
communitarianism around the personalism.

Quakers made up an oligarchy in Pennsylvania;
there is always an oligarchy and they composed most of it.
Putting aside the question whether it was the God
in their soul that illuminated their lives and work,
we can nevertheless understand that, given excellent land,
dutiful children, hard work, and thrift over time,
plus land in town and city that rose in value steadily,
plus freedom from persecution by their
neighbors or the government, and a refusal to go chasing
after Indians and Frenchmen, very many Quakers prospered.
Over half the merchants, entrepreneurs and professional men of
Philadelphia, then competing with Boston
for title of the largest American city, were Quakers.
The average Quaker owned more land, buildings, cattle,
and personal property than the average non-Quaker.
And far fewer of the Quakers were poor.
A third of the Quakers could be termed affluent.

Half of these lived from rents and investments.
It would be useful to know how many of the top hundred fortunes
of America, say in 1760, were held by Quakers;
an unreliable "guesstimate" might give 25,
one-fourth, another fourth being held by Southern planters,
another by New England shipping fleet owners, and
the final fourth by New York's great land-holders and
miscellaneous individuals from other colonies.
I have no information as to who might be joining this group
from Puerto Rico, the Southwest, or New Orleans.

At the same time, the average Pennsylvanian was probably better off than the average of any other colony. The land was fertile and affordable. The laws were benign. Religious and political and therefore personal freedoms were ample. Taxes were low. Prices were rising. Cultural activities were increasing rapidly. Probably not more than 50% of the population could be counted as materially poor, orphaned or distraught by abandonment or excessive mobility, overworked, illiterate, or diseased; this would be the highest level of well-being of any colony.

In the first part of the 1700's the movement known as Freemasonry took hold in England with the founding of a Grand Lodge in England by Dr. James Anderson and Dr. John T. Desaguliers, with others. They devised a general program combining a zeal for social and political reform, a set of ancient symbols - some of the order of masons, some from Egyptian antiquity - a philosophy of the Enlightenment just beginning in France, and an internal structure of ritual and government, some of it secret.

The Masons advocated brotherhood, equality, religious toleration, civic responsibility, and the pursuit of science and rationality in the universe. They were anti-Catholic, anti-royal, freethinking progressives who supported other Masons elsewhere.

Within two years, the Grand Lodge established 64 lodges in the British Isles and by 1732 102 lodges. Simultaneously, lodges sprang up around the world, including Philadelphia, Boston, Savannah, and New York.

Freemasonry was vigorously attacked from the start. The Roman Catholic Church condemned it and forbade Catholics to join as members. Many leading Americans joined the Order, among them Franklin, who had at first

lampooned it in his newspaper. The Masonic
lodges became a powerful force behind the
liberalization of American religion and government,
centers for free discussion, means for the advancement of
secular youths, a secret yet effective pressure group
for the modernization of American laws, and an instrument for the
assimilation of otherwise unattached thinkers,
politicians, and merchants.

Divided between Loyalist and Revolutionary sentiments,
Freemasonry received a setback in the Revolutionary Period,
when Rebels won over some lodges and Loyalists held others.
After the Revolution, the movement resumed its
momentum, and became as important a factor
in the economy, politics, and social life of a great many
American communities as any one of the many
religious denominations. Freemasonry also
provided a model for the numerous American fraternal
orders that much later enlisted millions of
men (often with auxiliary female sections), frequently
providing a substitute for church affiliation.

That Benjamin Franklin became an active Mason
is not surprising. It is hard to find a worthwhile idea or
activity of the times that he did not put his hand to.
A principal founder of the University of Pennsylvania
and the Academy of Sciences, a self-made millionaire in printing,
publishing, and other ventures, an experimental scientist, and a
political adventurer par excellence, who also
organized the U.S. Postal Service, was one of the
top five leaders of the Commonwealth of
Pennsylvania, represented the American colonies
in immensely important diplomatic relations with France
and Britain, and was a top Revolutionary and
Constitutional leader, he has had no peer in
American history as a Renaissance character,
excellent at many things.

If one were to compare him with Leonardo da Vinci,
who lived four mnemonic generations earlier,
one would say that both possessed a multiple excellence,
but, besides being sexual opposites, and the one
being preponderantly artistic and the other being
preponderantly political, Franklin was the fuller moral man.
Leonardo would have sold a bridge design to the Turks,
fortifications to the tyrants of Milan,
advanced weaponry to the French.
"I serve anyone who pays me", he declared.
He lived comfortably and died at a French royal castle,
the same that Jean Calvin lived in but fled in disgust.
Franklin would never had said or behaved so.
He was pragmatic yet moral.

He managed to combine high competence with
sensitive moral judgment in science, business,
politics, and personal life. He bravely defended
peaceful Indians from massacre by a mob of
armed Scots-Irish moral fools, and denounced them
for their other atrocities. He helped Germans get their
publications into print. He gave freely of
time and money, to education and science and public
affairs. His type of philanthropy, which might be generalized as
typically Quaker, had merits lacked by the typical
New England philanthropy, aside from its greater generosity.

It was more truly voluntary welfare in that it was not
part and parcel of the deliberate scheme for the compulsory
and controlled morality of others.
Franklin's philanthropy was thus more modern,
more public, more open-handed.

It needs be said that he made a profit on his investment
in German publications. Also that he enjoyed
fully his role as the exciting "natural man" among
the ladies of France, and he did not stint
in his personal comforts - perhaps explaining the gout
that tortured him in his last years. He resisted
Quaker arguments that the frontier with the Indians

should not be guarded by force. He realized that there was
no stopping the aggressiveness of the Scots-Irish,
Germanics, and others, pushing across the frontier.
He encouraged hypocrisy among Quaker legislators,
who finally voted for provisions, destined for an armed force,
but not for weapons and ammunition.
He was aiding another exuberant Quaker, Wharton,
to obtain an immense land grant from the English Crown offices
when the Boston Tea Party squelched the scheme;
it would certainly had resulted in the
dispossession of many Indians.

He compares unfavorably as philanthropist with
the saintly Woolman, who went to live among the Indians,
a modern anthropologist, to discover what motivated their lives
and what they might have useful to tell
to the paleface world. Franklin came ultimately to denounce
slavery and the slave trade, but he carried advertisements for the
sale of slaves and indentured servants, and occasionally
dabbled in the buying and selling of slaves and redemptioners
through the medium of his Pennsylvania Gazette.
He helped set up a school, but wanted it used
only for anglicizing the children.

His position emerges clearly: he was an assimilationist;
he believed in a single culture, a single language,
and a single economic-social class for all,
regardless of race and previous condition of servitude.
He was a rationalist and wished to do as little as possible
to help organized religion. The poor little immigrant boy
from Boston had gone straight through Quakerism
into deism and enlightened rationalism, and
become an all-around big man in history.
After asking oneself the question, one may ask it of Franklin:
In a continuous effort to be good and effective in the world,
how many close moral shaves and bloody cuts
can be tolerated, and
how may their number be minimized?

Impinging upon Pennsylvania to the Southeast and
influenced heavily by its people and ideas for much of
the time was the colony of Maryland.
Maryland stands unique among the colonies for its original
attachment to Roman Catholicism. A Sir George Calvert
bought from another cavalier adventurer in
1620 a patent or rights to a part of Newfoundland.
Although Minister of State to King James, he attached
himself to Catholicism, and was forced to resign.

Failing to discover upon a visit to Newfoundland any large
promise for settlement, he sailed for Chesapeake Bay and,
with backing from England, secured a concession from
Virginia of the Northern section of the Bay region.
He became Lord Baltimore and was made Proprietor
in 1632, or, more accurately,
inasmuch as he died, his son,
Cecilius, signed the charter papers as Proprietor.
The new Lord Baltimore sent a group of Catholic
gentlemen and 200 Protestant laborers to
found St. Mary's in the following year.
Religious toleration was extended to all sects.

The Catholics, however, were swamped by their own Protestant
work force and by hostile migrants from adjoining Virginia and
Pennsylvania. These took the first opportunity,
after Lord Baltimore's patron, Charles I,
was beheaded, to call in friendly forces from
Virginia to overthrow the government, summon a
stacked Assembly, and exclude all Catholics from office.
Priests and congregations went
underground for awhile.

Calvert-Baltimore, however, made a deal with
Oliver Cromwell, Lord Protector, who repealed the
laws of the Maryland rebels, reinstituted
the Act of Toleration, and reconfirmed
Baltimore as Proprietor. He died in 1675, and

his co-religionists suffered persecution off and on from their Protestant neighbors.

Maryland imported slaves and became part of the slave culture with some strong dissident elements who came to the fore in 1860.
(Delaware, now in British hands, also developed a prominent slave culture overspreading the flatlands between Chesapeake and Delaware Bays.)

Few Catholics entered Maryland afterwards for three mnemonic generations. In 1756, there were approximately 5,000 Catholics in Maryland and 2,000 in Pennsylvania nearby. The Sulspician Order settled in with a monastery. Even by 1790 there were only 35,000 Catholics in all of the United States, guided by a mere 34 priests, who administered an average of 12,270 miles of parish territory.
That is, one per cent of the American population was Catholic; adding New Orleans, the Southwest and Puerto Rico would bring the number up to a quarter of a million, about 8%. A large but unknown number of Catholics got to America unrecognized, and abandoned any hope of pursuing their faith, so joined another sect perforce, or merged with the irreligious multitude.

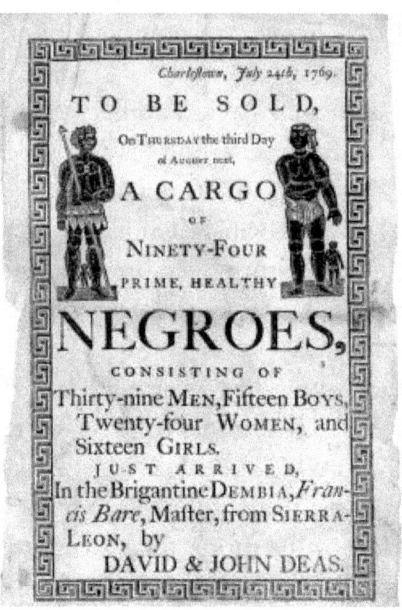

Chapter Fifteen

Southerners

There was to be no tropical paradise readied for
blessed sinners, no gold nuggets along the paths.
The Virginia Company, essentially a corporate board of
well-connected Dissenters sweetened by members
of the nobility and venture capitalists, obtained the dream-charter of
multi-national corporations from the Crown.
To remind you, it was given a two-hundred-mile stretch of the
Atlantic Coast and inland for a hundred miles and
full powers of economic development of every
conceivable kind, together with all powers of
government over the inhabitants of the area, and
tax forgiveness for a number of years.

It was too good to be true.

Dissenters had a strong voice for a while
but then were turned out - in fact, the whole
company was dissolved in 1624 for behaving corruptly.
But a few years later, the Dissenters came into power in
England and the King's clique was evicted. The results
were strange, for a gang of the King's cavaliers took up
refuge in Virginia, while the Commonwealth government
replaced the Royal Governor. The situation changed
again with the restoration of the monarchy under
Charles II, and Virginia carried on as
a royal colony, but still and always with its House
of Burgesses that claimed and received legislative powers,
subject to gubernatorial and royal approval.

Every effort has been made by historians to discover the
true nature of these first inhabitants, without complete success.
Some have claimed that there were as many as
15% gentlemen in the arrivals of the first
half century, but gentlemen and gentry were words covering many
pretensions and offenses. And some question exists as to
how many of the gentry fled elsewhere
as soon as the nature of the country was disclosed to them.
The first boats docking in the inlets of Chesapeake
Bay have been mentioned: leaders & workers to begin with
(a number of *"idle and dissolute adventurers,
attracted solely by the hope of speedy fortune"*
as part of what Captain John Smith of the first
successful beachhead also listed as *"poor gentlemen,
tradesmen, serving-men, and libertines"*).

These were succeeded by similar arrivals, and the special
loads of the first slaves in a Dutch boat,
then a boatload of women and children of
the streets, then a shipment of convicts.
Succeeding years brought their several thousands,
1622, 1277 passengers; 1625, 1202

passengers, 1628, 3000; 1629, between 4 and 5000; 1630, 2500; 1634, 5119; 1649, 15,000 plus 300 slaves. The passengers might be divided into those who paid their way and those who didn't.

Given the circumstances, those who paid deserved to be called gentlemen. The rest were indentured servants (bondsmen or White slaves in fact) for a limited number of years. These were probably the basis for a two-class system, though with later arrivals the class system got more complicated. Only one bondsman out of that large majority succeeded in becoming civically prominent in Virginia in the seventeenth century, Adam Thoroughgood (a Puritan pseudonym, possibly). Some experts adjudge that five of six arrivals during the first thirty years died in short order. In 1649 there lived only about 15,000 Whites and 300 Blacks in Virginia, but the number of livestock was 20,000 and of horses 200.

The Company was distressed by so many deaths and at the number of arrivals who lacked every resource - skills, money, physical capacity, or material goods - and who *"...greatly hindered the Progresses of that noble Plantation"*. It distributed a bulletin in 1622 *"for prevention of the like disorders hereafter, that no man suffer, either through ignorance or misinformation"*... Perusal of this list of about one hundred items gives us roughly and remarkably the same list as one would put together today for a long stay in a lonely stretch of the Rocky Mountains: pickaxes, grindlestones, *"nails of all sorts to the value of"* two pounds sterling, *"One long peece, five foot or five and a halfe, neere {narrow?} Musket bore"*, and *"Sixty pound of shot or lead, Pistoll and Goose shot,.. Two bushels of Oatemeale, One gallon of Aquavite, One gallon of Oyle, Two gallons of Vinegar..., One Rug for a bed 8 s. [shillings]*

which the bed serving for two men"..,
numerous canvas things, four pairs of shoes,
the usual few basic tools, a pot, kettle and
frying pan, *"spoones of wood",* etc.
in all estimated to weigh half a ton, with the
suggestion that if a party of half a dozen is attempting the
passage they bring a tent, fishhooks and lines, and
several pigs.

All of this was estimated to cost 20 pounds,
including 6 pounds for the boat passage - one way.
Anybody who manages this all is given 50 acres of land
upon arrival with another fifty acres at some future date.

One cannot read through the document without assigning
its creation to some land-locked clerk in England dreamily
imagining the perfect safari for the equally imaginary
self-financing gentleman adventurer.
Two hundred years later, he would send the gentleman
emigrant to the Army and Navy Store in London,
which was set up for such a clientele.
The absence of any medicine save Aquavite is notable;
about a third of the passengers would die before their time,
of fever or malnutrition or infected wounds.

The Virginia Colony had to make do with what the upper
classes and Scrooge's clerk and public health authorities
would call *"people of the poorer sort".*
Historians, giving up the old tradition of
calling them cavaliers and gentry, have promoted
them to people of the *"middling class"* or *"yeomanry".*
Sir Josiah Child, a man of vast experience and wealth,
writing in 1693, would put it differently:

*Virginia and Barbados were first peopled by a sort of loose
vagrant People, vicious and destitute of means to live at home, (being
either unfit for labour, or such as could find none to employ themselves
about, or had so misbehaved themselves by Whoreing, Thieving, or*

other Debauchery, that none would set them on work) which Merchants and Masters of Ships by their Agents (or Spirits, as they were called) gathered up about the Streets of London, and other places. cloathed and transported, to be employd on Plantations; and these I say were such, as had there been no English foreign Plantation in the World, could probably never have lived at home to do Service for their Country, but must have come to be hanged or starved, or dyed untimely of some of those miserable Diseases, that proceed from want and Vice; or else have sold themselves for Soldiers, to be knockt on the Head or starved in the Quallerels of our Neighbours, as many thousands of brave English men were in the low Countries, as also in the wars of Germany, France, and Sweden, etc. or else if they could, by begging, or otherwise, arrive to the Stock of 2 s6 pd. to waft them over to Holland, become Servants to the Dutch, who refuse none.

But the principal growth and encrease of the afore-said Plantations of Virginia and Barbados happened in, or immediately after our late Civil Wars, when the worsted party, by the fate of War, being deprived of their Estates, and having none of them ever been bred to labour, and others made unfit for it by the lazy habit of the Soldiers life, there wanting means to maintain them all abroad with his Majesty, many of them betook themselves to the afore-said Plantations, and great numbers of Scotch Soldiers of his Majesty's Army, after Worcester Fight, were by the then prevailing Powers voluntarily sent in thither.

Another great swarm, or accession of new Inhabitants to the afore-said Plantations, as also to New-England, Jamaica, and all other his Majesties Plantations in the West-Indies, ensued upon his Majesties Restauration, when the former prevailing part being by a divine Hand of Providence brought under, the Army disbanded, many Officers dis-placed, and all the new purchasers of publick Titles, dispossest of their pretended Lands, Estates, etc. many became impoverished, destitute of employement; and therefore such as could find no way of living at home, and some which feared the re-establishment of the Ecclesiastical Laws, under which they could not live, were forced to transport themselves, or sell themselves for a few Years, to be transported by others to the foreign English Plantations: The constant supply that the said Plantations have since had, hath by such vagrant loose People, as I before-mentioned, picked up, especially about the Streets and

Suburbs of London, and Westminster, and by Malefactors condemned for Crimes, for which by the Law they deserved to dye and some of those People called Quakers, banished for Meeting on pretence of Religious Waorship.

Sir Josiah concludes that whatever had been the case, Plantations or no, England would have lost all these people - and all for the better.

Counting the early immigrants as the first generation, the third political generation, within a century, that is, saw a class system formed up.
We mean by this a system of groups having more or less fixed life-chances at obtaining our half-dozen major desiderata of existence. (In the several parentheses that follow, I have placed a guess of the percentage of the total population attained by each group over the whole South as of the middle 1700's, including in each the women and children belonging to the group.)
These consisted, then, of a group of large planters, with ever-larger holdings, owning hundreds of acres at the least and an increasing number of slaves. (under 1%)
The second class would consist of small farmers operating what we would call family-sized farms. (10%)
A third class would be the professionals, the merchants and the factors who managed the sales and purchases of the planters. (2%) A fourth class would be the Black freedmen whose occupations would give them a certain independence.(2%)

Then would come a White poor class, living by manual labor or tenantry of a farm. (20%)
African-Americans, many of them first generation Americans, would constitute a class which, though every attempt was made to set it apart, seeped over the edges of several other classes (30%).
Next we would discover a class of bound servants; although from several points of view, planters preferred

Black slaves to White covenanters, ship
masters could make money by fitting as many of
these as possible to fill out their cargoes (10%).

Both the poor free Whites and the White
covenanters were supplemented then by men and
women who were convicted by English courts and transported,
again a transaction pleasing to the shipping interests and
local authorities of England (5%).
The leading colonists hardly complained of the practice
until the eve of the Revolution; until they were
comfortably established, *faux de mieux,* they invited
as many bodies as could be brought over.

Finally there were the numerous Indian tribes,
retrenching but often formidable (20%).
Possibly, women might be considered as a class in
themselves, as they related to each of the above elements.
(They would not yet equal half the population;
they would be a minority among the poor White,
bound servants, Blacks, and convicts.)

We can set the population of the South in this period
at about a million souls.

The ten thousand planters would by this time,
four political generations from Jamestown,
have acquired larger homes than they lived in even over
the past generation. Instead of two to five rooms in
all - with outbuildings for washing and toilet,
for servants, slaves, relatives, livestock, special
workers such as candle makers, shoemakers, and
storage, all looking together like an adobe village of
Mexico or of Russian serfs before 1860,
their house would have had additions, sprouted columns, and been
landscaped. They would have acquired furniture of some
elegance from the North or abroad. One planter
could only know a few others, of course,

for we are talking of an area of about
1500 miles by 70 miles.
And it would be easy to understand how any typical planter
would probably be a big shot in his locale.

Chances are high that a given planter would be growing
tobacco, rice, sugar, or long-stapled cotton.
He would own upwards of 500 acres and thirty slaves.
He owned two or three pairs of shoes, his slaves
went barefoot. He would be overjoyed in the next social
generation to hear of the invention by Eli Whitney
of the contraption called the "cotton gin",
that could comb the seed even out of short-stapled
cotton many times faster than a human could do it.
This could stimulate a huge planting of cotton,
for all of which there seemed to be an ever-expanding and
never-ending demand at the textile mills of
Britain, and, if not there, elsewhere.

Rarely had an elite developed, achieved such heights, and
degenerated in so short a time. The planter was often busy
ordering his help about and deciding what purchases
to make of land, slaves, and goods from abroad.
Still he had so much personal help that
he also had leisure and enjoyed it to the utmost.
This, from all we can make out, consisted, in
their order of preference: social drinking and partying; riding;
hunting; sex, flirtation and sexual harassment;
gambling at dice and cards or anything at all;
horse-racing; politics and quarreling; and, though it hardly is
preferred at all, religious gatherings.

More often than most social types, the planter was personally
generous, affectionate and not money-minded. Very few had
intellectual interests, and he hardly treated the teacher of his children
more respectfully than his shoemaker. As plantation culture
moved west, there were thrown up more opportunistic and
speculative types, planters became more mercenary,
less cultured and more grimly determined to
keep the slave system going.

The planter hobnobbed with other planters,
a few nearby suppliers of professional, political,
material, and financial services, his family, and
his dependents - overseers, servants and slaves. He had
little in common with his counterparts of the Yankee and
Pluralist elites to the North and even less with the
frontier types. He was political and belonged to the
"Old Boy School of Politics", expecting
that he could obtain whatever he needed for himself
of government from his pals, or himself as member of the colonial
assembly or an acquaintance among the
Councillors of the Governor.

Legislation was not at all feared by him as a rule,
for it would almost always be in his interest and
one of the never-ending string of regulations and constraints
directed at the other classes of the population,
without exception, one should stress. He had as great a
faith in laws and rules (for others) as the
Puritan masters of Massachusetts.

He was ready to accept corruption in government
and practice the same. The reason for this,
contrary to its reason at other times and places,
was in large part because it was the simplest and ordinary way
to get things done. English laws affecting his
interest adversely were promulgated from time to time,
but he ignored them, paid to disobey them, or
disobeyed and let the officials try to catch him and
put him through a friendly court to his disadvantage.
None of the terrible penalties attending the misbehavior
of other orders was applied to him, except for
heinous crime, such as sadistic physical abuse and
repeated attempted rape of a slave who was his daughter.

Corruption, as here implied, was business as usual
in Old Virginia. Captain Samuel Argall
rode his boat into Point Comfort as the newly appointed
Governor of Virginia a few years after the first settlement,

but before long he was accused by persons he had cheated in the Virginia Company of having amassed 80,000 pounds sterling. This was the time of Pocohontas, the happily kidnaped Indian Princess, and the invention of Bourbon Whiskey. It was also the time of the great Indian massacre of Europeans, disposing of 400 of the all too few invaders in a single day.

In 1623, an even more important "First" occurred when King James, who had virtues as well as grave faults, by-passed the House of Commons, 49 of whose members had been reputedly given free stock in the Virginia Company, and set up a Royal Commission of Inquiry into the affairs of the Virginia Company. Led by a Justice Sir William Jones of the Court of Common Pleas, a report after five months of hearings castigated the Company, and in the following year the Court of Kings Bench transferred the Company's charter to the King. However, as an old expression goes,
*"The conductor may change in name,
but the music is always the same".*

Women of the Southland followed the bi-racial model, the same as affected males. I have already pointed to the distinctive character of Black women, to their unusual independence before and during slavery, in the tribal and slave households. White women of the South came early under retarding pressures. They were almost entirely illiterate and gained literacy much later than the men and in smaller proportions. They became planters' wives, plantation managers' wives, farmers' (yeomen's, peasants') wives, the wives of poor Whites, the wives of professional and mercantile types, and perpetual servants, and in all cases more securely bound than in the northern American sub-cultures.

Culturally deprived in a large sense, they had two areas where they might develop an unusual outlook:

one, but confined to the wealthier class, was learning the arts and skills of the slaves and a century later learning the arts of interior decoration, music, painting, poetry and literature, where, over time and with the destruction of the social system, they might take charge of the muses and accomplish a modest something of originality in literature and drama overall.

The second was in relation to Black women, where the caste system had to give way to regular contact on matters of hygiene, child development, kitchen and household management. In this latter connection, the most bound females in America met with the singularly liberated ones. In consequence, Southern White women were highly developed by, but less fixated by, the slave system than their White consorts. Because the plantation system was a hacienda system, that is, a work-residence complex, larger farms and plantations (hardly distinguishable except in proportion of work performed by slaves) afforded opportunities in household management of considerable scope, and involved large familial and social networking.

Where the planter male is assigned a powerful role generally and has ample leisure, he will not need the strong-armed, rough-cut female partner usually found in agricultural settings, as was typical of Northern areas. (Comparison with similar classes in the haciendas of Spanish, Portuguese and French plantation cultures is suggested.)

The cult of femininity and beauty was supposed to obsess the women of the Southern planter-professional-managerial class. The myth of the Southern "belle" - beautiful, well-spoken, courteously mannered, socially omnicompetent - was bandied about South, North and Europe.

We may accord some validity to the belief, and seek reasons. For one thing, the upper-class roles just described act to create beauty of the type described. And, by imitation of the upper class, the cult of beauty and therefore beauty itself may have introduced the "belle" to lower and broader social reaches. *"Beauty is as beauty does".* Perhaps, inasmuch as Southerners came from the more mixed royalist English types (Norman, Celtic, Saxon), as against the Dissenters (more likely to be Saxon), a certain beauty would have often accrued. French Huguenots descended upon the Southern shores in some numbers; there might have been a beauteous element coming from the gracile Latin type therein. There may also have occurred some small admixture of Indian and Negro genes, especially in earlier freer times and in the poorer classes, although such mixed types were likely to follow the frontier. Too, the early arrivals included many women of the streets - a great many, to believe certain writers. These have always been on the average prettier girls to begin with than the average "virtuous" female, and therefore more likely to be led astray and, if poor, better able to earn money on the basis of their looks. Their descendants would carry their beauteous genes. Besides these potentiators, the "belle", if numerous and persisting as a type, had to depend upon and emerge from her own social and psychological role-playing.

Families were set up in haste very often. Over half the population had to ask someone else for permission to marry. Fornication was even more common than to the North (except for Delaware and Maryland.) Nearly a third of all first birthings occurred from pre-nuptial pregnancies. Illegitimate births were common - although the concept legally existed among whites only; it was assumed by them that Blacks were naturally promiscuous. Women bondservants were punished cruelly - by public whipping and added terms of compulsory service (when the master felt aggrieved). Adultery, common among men, was disallowed and often punished under the law among women. Prudery was less evident in the South than in the North; the climate invited nakedness for one thing.

In most of seventeenth century Maryland, for instance, in a colony that had turned from Catholic to Protestant by immigration and revolt, the women came or were collected from all over England. The vast majority (75%) were indentured or otherwise indebted to work. Fearful though they might be of the New World, they might at least (or was it a good?) count upon a man and marriage forthwith; the ratio of men to women was three to one.

An ordinary problem of the White planter's woman was her man: he was frequently a philanderer. Nor were his sexual tastes confined to his class, who were all too few, all too similar. It was the servant girl or the African girl who caught his eye. Evidence of this type of behavior comes not only from the few diaries and letters that have come down to us, but from some social statistics. Most notorious of sexual pursuers was the author of the famous William Byrd diaries, of a family standing early and long in Virginia elite annals. He seems to have set upon any girl who moved across his field of vision. And to hear him out, his circle of acquaintances was playing the same "tally-ho". Intercourse on demand, or call it rape.

A figure of 50,000 is often used to estimate the number of mixed Afro-American ancestry in 1750. This is far too small a figure. The U.S. Census of 1850 will give 500,000, ten times as many. And this is believed by experts to be half the true number. I guess it to be 1.5 million - 500,000 correctly assessed, 500,000 who were not recognized because counted as Blacks by the census caller, and 500,000 who were passing as Whites and Indians.

About half the Eur-Africans and free Afro-Americans, between whom there is a high correlation, lived in or in connection with "The Big House", the central structure of the plantation where dwelled the master and his immediate family. They were household slaves or in some cases free servants, and in many cases they were related by blood to other residents of the house, but required to play the role of slaves, such as not joining the guests at formal dinners and denying any blood relationship with the members of the European household.

The illegal sexual intercourse represented by the number of Eur-Africans is extensive. For every survival of birthing there would have been required probably some fifty copulations, which would have amounted to about 175,000,000 Eur-African sexual acts in the two-decade biological generation ending in 1850. Southerners often realized this, and the thought drove some of them wild, because they were Puritanical, sexually deprived, and fiercely racist - with this last reason relating precisely to the oncoming wave of privileged and well-connected Eur-African Americans. The agitation would be particularly of the class of poorer Whites, who had no slaves, and their womenfolk.

(Their imaginings were not too bizarre; slaves have sometimes risen high because they were more to be trusted than the free men of the society. Slaves rose to top Ottoman circles when the now-Turkey was the greatest and a highly civilized power in the world. In Northern India the heads of six Muslim dynasties had been slaves.)
No elite can afford for very long to defy the public opinion of the lower classes. Thus it was that the planter class and its upper class associates of the service class could not but bow to the clamor for strict laws against miscegenation, even while the laws would be observed in the breach. The interracial sex conduct of the upper classes moved down through the ranks of the smaller farmer-slaveholders, and excited both envy and consequent rapist tendencies throughout the male White population. This, too, the planters endeavored to stop, but trapped by their own practices, they could only bring about a hypocritical system of justice, one law for the rich and another for the poor.

The bi-racial culture as a whole entertained high constitutional law in the abstract but a low regard for justice and the law in everyday life. Considering the origins of the people, that found them often at odds with the system of civil and criminal justice in Europe and the earliest colonial practice, their later attitude toward law and justice, conditioned by the continuing inequalities both formal and informal, was bent toward lawlessness and violence.

Practically everyone who has studied the South, and by every methodology, has attested to a much higher penchant there to the use of personal and collective force, lawful (proper force) or unlawful (violence), for the resolution of individual and social conflict. From the very beginnings of colonization rates of violence and crimes of property were higher, much higher than in Europe, even higher than in

England, Scotland and Ireland, that had especially high rates already explained in terms of the disorders and internecine wars of the century before and after the waves of emigration occurred. Besides the reasons just adduced, racial in nature and by the class origin of settlers, there were reasons that shall be taken up in the next chapter,
on frontier culture.

Southern culture began immediately in 1607 to suppress freedom of thought, speech, press, and action and never gave up controls of wide sections of freedom. To speak of liberty in the South would be ridiculous. Even North and West there were many limitations on liberty until the 1970's. Personal liberty in America enlarged in proportion to the growth in national power over the states.

No less and more than their American cousins to the North, Southern Americans tore up the land and decimated the species. The newcomer - call him and her by name, by class, by ethnic origin, call them "pioneers", or "forefathers" or "invaders" - it would take eighteen biological generations to change environmental attitudes, which meanwhile would infect with the inconscient practices of biocide all who intermingled with them and came afterwards.

The plantation crops were hard on the soils. Valuable minerals were leached out without replacement. Improper crop rotation was common. The clearing of timber, partly for firewood, partly burnt to clear land for planting, partly for construction of buildings and boats, and finally for export abroad - all without thought of replacement - got rid of most of the valuable timber in the first six political generations.

To obtain new soils for the voracious crops, the planters and farmers went upland and west, pursuing the same practices as they went, stopping only when they had achieved Eastern Texas. Grave political problems ensued with the incorrigible practices, which moved the population, instead of caring for its resources where they stood. Families, slave and free, were broken up casually to follow the human locusts.

Talk of the small independent farmer or yeoman, as historians please to do, deserves a horse-laugh, then as now. Uninterruptedly the independent farmer, the family-sized farm, was pushed into the boondocks and mountains, the children scattering to the winds upon coming of age. Factories and home industries did begin to operate and sell to the market in the South. It was not originally and always completely rural, with each plantation constituting a self-sufficient economy. As soon as people could get away from this system they did. The plantations and centers of settlements without owners both deserve to be lumped together in counting the village life of the South. What happened to the villages and the industrial processes needs to be told in a later context.

We would not wish to turn away from the planter and, indeed, all social life without resuming the subject of drug consumption. I have spoken enough about the miseries of early American life to let the reader understand an apology that I would like to make for the consumption of alcohol and tobacco. Both commodities make life for the nonce tolerable. In moderation, they are not harmful. They were not harmful then, when a person drank down a shot of whiskey before heading out for a day's hard work on a wet dawn, and when he drank beer or wine or even rum with his dinner. And a glass of beer or wine, even two, for a wedding or at a funeral, seems beyond reproach. That is not what we are discussing.

We are contemplating whole classes of people, men three times more than women, who had a powerful whiskey or rum when they awakened, another at breakfast, a third or beer at midmorning, more at dinnertime and afterwards. We speak of 20% over the whole period - perhaps a quarter million of the million adult White males who lived at the time of the Revolution - who were drunks in this sense or worse, often incapacitated for the performance of their duties. The Blacks, forbidden alcohol on pain of whipping or starving, could not so easily succumb. The Indians did, with dreadful effects, as recounted earlier.

The British population and its descendants might have drunk and smoked themselves into extinction were if not for the greedy corporate staff back in England who were continually shipping over new cargoes of unfortunates.

Alcoholism was and is, of course, a symptom of heavy despair and misery, social as well as individual. The alcoholism rate in the Soviet Union, always bad under serfdom and Czarism, jolted up by terrible warfare, increased under communism until, in retrospect, it would appear to have been a barometer of the collapsing of the regime, and when communism gave way to capitalism even more persons were driven to drink.

Visitors from Europe or Latin America were surprised and shocked by the heavy drinking going on everywhere and at all times; the American Anglican minister of the South was notoriously bibulous. Nor was he encouraged to be sober or solemn, considering the lawlessness and immorality (by his professed standards), of his parishioners (the more wealthy and influential of whom appointed and paid him).

When a delegation sought help from Attorney General Seymour in 1692 to obtain a charter for the College of William and Mary, intended to prepare clergy for the salvation of souls, he exclaimed,
"Souls! Damn your souls! Grow tobacco.".
Most Southern planters, and many others, liked their priests this way. Less than 20% of Southerners attended church services regularly before the Revolution. Yet it would not be long before the South, notably influenced by the Great Awakening of the mid-eighteenth century, would become more and more devoted to revivalism and evangelism.

With huge areas of fat soils and a large, reliable work force, the Southern colonies grew a special sub-culture and with this a special speech, humor, religion, dance, music, ways of dealing with people, attitude to law and order, an outlook on the rest of the country and on the world at large. When Southern Editor Cash wrote his famous 1940 book on *The Mind of the South,* he declared, *"Negro entered into white man as profoundly as white man entered into Negro, subtly influencing every gesture, every word, every emotion and idea, every attitude".*

In all of the regards I had just named, African-Americans have been a primary creator and receptor. The African was so Southern that even Southerners descended from the few early survivors seemed un-Southern by comparison.

The European elite of the bi-racial culture set itself impossible tasks, especially considering its lackadaisical characterology. One was to maintain a "pure" blood line of the motley crowd from Europe in a society that was composed 42% of a motley crowd from Africa and an unknown but motley host of Indian tribes. This madness practically destroyed the nation as well as the South and still contains that fearful potential.

Another madcap idea was to suppress Christian and really all religion among African-Americans. Christianity was a religion suited to equals: *"All of God's children are equal",* etc. News of conversions of Indians, East Indians, Africans, in place, plus all the slaves and Indians of Hispanic America would carry the idea that all or some were going to heaven. One would think that the elite could not be so megalomanic to think otherwise, but many did. They could only expose the contradictions of their personal behavior with their beliefs by joining the Blacks together with them in a church; so they felt and it was so, of course. But there was an overwhelming need for religion among the African-Americans and many devout clergymen and planter wives heard a call to be missionaries.

There was to be no African-American church, South or North, save a solitary congregation, until the Revolution, although African-Americans were fed into the churches as second-class converts throughout the colonial period and even thereafter practically everywhere in America. Except in the totally African-American sects and branches of Christianity, which were expanded in due course.

When they came in, African-Americans had to leave much of their ritual and conduct at the doors. Their thoughts could not be suppressed, of course, but some religious vigor was lost. Most were unhappy in the Anglo-Christian congregations. Outside of Christian churches and even Christianity, they had been developing spirituals, chants, modes of singing and dancing sacrally. The Whites watched them from time to time, as impressed as they were scornful.

What they could not realize was that Africa was entering their culture perforce, a universalized African set of superstitions, gods, ceremonials, magic, poetry, music, and dance. They did not realize that before their very eyes, a gigantic amalgamation of disparate African and Caribbean cultures was taking place; nor did they appreciate the extent to which a new kind of Christian thinking and role-acting was developing.

As they joined Christianity, the African-American fervor, their religious superstitions, their magic, their gestures and dances, their songs squeezed through the arches with them. Liturgically they represented the most striking development since the Latin Mass reached its fulfillment in the Late Middle Ages. So stiff was American Protestantism and so imitative of this stiffness was American Catholicism that much of the originality and quality of the African-American religious ceremonialism had to be abandoned as heathen survivals - as if much of Christianity were not a survival from paganism and heathenism.

It has long been considered that American country music survived the overseas passage from Scottish and English villages to blossom once again in the backs and hills of America. A movement has sought to recapture the purity of the original. Generations passed before the search for purity (which had a racist tinge to it) merged into a search for creativity.

African-American dancing combined elements from ancestral Africa, from the Caribbean and from the plantation slave quarters, and a beat and music, and all three tended to infiltrate and be captured by European song and dance forms. The roots of the greatest American contribution to music and dance were thus in the slave quarters, sometimes imitated demurely or "for fun" by plantation and other Whites.

The White elite also had the weird concept of maintaining slaves in some kind of celibacy except on the occasions when the masters needed to breed them. This was attempted and stud farms for humans were advertised. But the masters had too obvious a contradiction on their hands; people, even slaves, were not horses.
Furthermore, it became obvious that the Europeans had to play the husband's role or turn it back to the slaves on a disorganized basis. Hence, more and more, the masters came to separate young girls and boys and recognize couples, to the point, when associated with the need of planters' wives and disemployed clergymen for a *raison d'etre*, that marriage according to Christian principles was invited and sanctified. No promises could go along with marriage and the *"until death do you part"* phrasing had to be dropped, because families could be torn apart by irritable masters, bankruptcy proceedings, and estate disposition - not to mention a disharmony of the married couple.

Who taught whom Southern English dialect will be argued for a long time. Long ago become the subject of table talk and farce, it has only recently become a scholarly and political question. American historians, although they are skittish around the so-called value-free sociology of elites, will fall into naive elite theory in due course. They will take for granted that whoever runs the society runs its language and everything else. Not so. The elite is especially vulnerable to the language of the masses, witness the way in which Teutonic forms recaptured the English language from the Norman French, until the language of Shakespeare and science reversed the trend.

Bantu immigrants and their descendants coined an American dialect called Gullah, using many African words, syntax, and intonations, ecumenicalizing English and several African languages. The Gullahphones were and are located on islands off of the Carolinas. They cannot be understood by an untrained American from elsewhere.

More general is the Southern sub-culture's dialect itself. An outside American can understand it rather easily nowadays because of television, the movies, and the high mobility of Americans, including Southerners. Understanding did not come easily between 1680, perhaps, and 1920. These were the periods of growing apart from somewhat common roots and developing along different lines and in isolation, both of Whites and Blacks, until the advent of the motor car, the radio, industrial demands for Southern labor, national wars of grand scope, national universities, and television. All of these familiarized the nation with Southern speech forms, both Black and White.

There is a possibility in unrecorded history that historians should attend to. The underground communication system of African-American slaves may have been more effective, continuous and universal than among Southern Whites. Slaves were frequently transferred by sale, by family divisions of the masters, and by achieving freedom; they were not fixed and culturally static.

One has only to see how dance forms of the Caribbean are repeated in Arkansas and Virginia to appreciate that language could proceed readily by the same means and lines of dance diffusion. One will recall, too, that masters and overseers frequently, even regularly, traveled with their slaves, and that the slaves had ample opportunity to communicate with others, as well as with free men along the route and at the meeting places of the masters.

The very fear that the Eur-Americans had of slave revolts betokened an awareness of how, sometimes eerily, slaves in one part of the country knew what was happening that had to do with slaves across the country.

Language is transacted like business and disease; it is catching and transactional, effective as it goes along. And the elite would talk more like the slaves than would the sub-elite and hoi polloi. This is because the common people of the free classes are constantly aware and suspicious of the potential influence of the slaves upon the upper class, and reject slave influence, believing that they can thus cut these influences of language or of any other kind
on the way up the social ladder.

But they cannot. For there are good sociological and psychological reasons for an elite to listen to the most deprived section of the population; there is no threat to be perceived there,
unless one is excited into panic by the poor Whites,
who are much more ready than the top elite to see
a slave revolt where there is none, or even
perceive it earlier when it happens than the top elite,
out of their very paranoia.

In time, the developing language of the South, with its soft accents, lilt, and modulation, seeming absence of rage and aggression, and politeness of expression, cannot have come from the poorer White classes, but must have come from the willingness to please and meekness, willy-nilly, of the slave, and gone directly into the minds and speech, first of the planter class, and then worked its way around and down. Southern manners and demeanor, that were so remarked and appreciated by many people as a contrast to the ever-harsher and more nasal tones of Northerners, were quickly lost in the free Northern African-American, who believed that he could get along faster if he demonstrated his no-nonsense, rough-spoken equality to the Whites whom he encountered.

In some cases the free African-American tried also to recapture his African name or an unmistakable version of it. Here, too, the planter had insisted that his slaves bear a Christian name of his the planter's choice, and not only that, but bear the family name of the planter, although commonly the slave was given no family name officially until

the occasion arose, as it did upon liberation.
Thus came Blacks to be called by French names
in Louisiana and British names elsewhere. (The situation was
comparable to that in Western Europe, when family names became
convenient and required by law and were called "sons of" or named by
place of origin, lords of the manor, objects and biota.)

But the freed slaves faced White opposition and scorn in many official
quarters when they attempted to assume African roots or names for
themselves. Name-restoring bureaus were not established to help out.
Much later, African Muslims, so-called, rendered their names in
Arabic, hardly historical or even deserving, for the largest most
enduring region of slavery was Islamic. (The Black Muslim
movement in America succeeded greatly -
anti-white, anti-feminist, anti-drugs, orderly - and
marched nearly a million supporters around Washington, D.C.
in October 1995.) Champion boxer Cassius Clay
became Muhammad Ali as a clear act of defiance of nomenclature that
had been derived from an age of helplessness in creating one's identity.
He received jeers from the press and boxing fans and
attempts were made often to continue his old name,
but he persisted and won out.

At the same time, with wider knowledge and research, a large variety
of African names and roots became available, and a few bold African-Americans
decided to add this way of capturing comfortably their
antecedents. Thus, Stokeley Carmichael, a champion of Afro-American
civil rights, changed his name to Kwame Toure. Leroi Jones, a leading
spokesman for Black artists in the 1960's and 1970's changed
his name to Amiri Baraka. The President of the National
Association for the Advancement of Colored People (NAACP)
in 1999 was named Kweisi Mfume

The half-million Africans who landed in the continental United States,
plus perhaps another half-million Europeans whose genes became part
of the mix, produced today's thirty million African-American
population who are in some part African. (This may be compared with

the seventeenth century Puritan migration to Massachusetts of some 20,000, whose descendants in some part may reach about one-third the number; these had a longer breeding period and have mixed even more with other groupings.)

South Carolina received 91,591 Africans between 1700 and 1808 (official figures: smuggling brought in many more until 1865); in the process, they became the majority element in the State. Most came from Senegal and Gambia, the Mandes, and from Angola and Zaire (using today's names), these being of one of the major Bantu cultures, Bakongo, Ovimbundu, and Luba Lunda.

The Bantu alone may have constituted half of the original source of African-Americans, as many as all Americans wholly or in part of Italian and French origin taken together. Before the great urban migrations of the twentieth century, three major Bantu centers existed, the Sea Islands, the Virginia Tidewater, and the New Orleans area.

In Louisiana, whereas the Bantu shone in folklore and the arts generally, religion (the Voodoo cult) was Dahomean. In the matter of musical instruments alone, there, the Bantu produced new types of drums, the diddley bow, the mouth bow, quills, washtub bass, jugs, gongs, bells, rattles, ideophones, and the five-stringed harp. The Bantu also added many words to the American language and hundreds of place names, the best of cuisine of American origin (united with the French Creole cooking), iron-working techniques, rice cultivation, and folklore of wide scope. Dance and musical forms were forcefully introduced and became finally the American (and world) artistic vanguard of the twentieth century.

The Mande people of Senegal and Gambia, speaking a score of related languages, were the heaviest contributors to skilled trades and household management in South Carolina and throughout the South generally. Again, their folklore was rich, some of which has gone into and out of the American mainstream: for instance, Brer Rabbit, Sis' Nanny, and other animal and trickster stories; these often carried an ironic vein critical of the White population.

Bi-racial slave culture began with a variegated string of boats from England, received at its edges on the frontiers groups of Germans, took in individuals of some consequence from time to time, such as wandering Jews and French Huguenots, but by the receipt of large numbers of Africans as slaves, became in many regards a bi-racial culture. By "bi-racial" is meant a culture containing two distinctive but inter-dependent sub-cultures, each feeding the other along the whole range of values at stake in society.

In our judgement, the culture was based upon immoral premises racially, economically, and philosophically. Its appealing aspects were accidental, peripheral, and/or tinctured with tragedy and melancholy. Still they account for much of the greatness of American culture today. But the territorial and demographic success of the bi-racial culture in expanding over much of the United States signaled and indicates, not a national good, but national troubles.

A word of genealogical perspective would not be amiss at this point. It has been shown that, statistically, the average French person has inherited the genes of Charlemagne from eight sources. Using the same method of demographic computation, the average French person would have roughly the same number of genes coming by way of any ninth century prolific Frankish camp follower.

By 1776 a typical American had as many of the genes of a convict and prostitute in her as genes of a proper Puritan or any other early class she might have preferred. For every nice and proper person of that time, there was living a smuggler, a prostitute , a murderer, a convict, a slave driver, a slave trader or mariner, or a hopeless drunkard. Double the ratio for sadistic wife or child abuser or heavy drinker. Triple it for illiterates. Quintuple it for hereditary slaves and bonded slaves.

The Southerners' bi-racial culture contained in it the means of taking over an exorbitant amount of the land and a large portion of the popular mind and imagination. It has been the source in scope and intensity of perhaps 90% of the invidious and persistent religious, ethnic, and racial prejudice of the country as a whole. The Southern population had the least auspicious beginnings of the three major cultures. It was constituted by the most deprived and depreciated of all major immigrations that have occurred from 1607 to the present time. It suffered later a devastating war that reduced all of its achievements and value ratings without exception, and then worsened even this position by a guerrilla war of a hundred years against Afro-Americans and Northern interests, until finally, overtaken by external economic and demographic forces, it accepted an ambiguous truce or surrender. But we have much yet to say about such matters in chapters yet to come.

———————

Cultural Minimalism

Chapter Sixteen

Frontier Folk

The frontier has always existed in America and still does.
When a federal bureau declared in the 1890's that
the frontier had ended in 1890, giving
as reason the unavailability of free land,
everyone seized upon the idea as momentous,
holding up this fact as a fetish,
marking the end of an innocent age,
the beginning of real problems for the nation.

The myth of the frontier was succeeded by
the myth of the end of the frontier.

The educated crowd now knew what the frontier crowd knew on many occasions all the way back to the German pastor explaining to his seventeenth century fellow immigrants: land has gone up in price and so, too, the cost of living: go back to Germany if you can.

Thenceforth, after 1890, the concept became the tool of publicity: *"Vote for the New Frontier"*. *"Electronics are the new frontier!" Etc.* And *"the end of the frontier"* became the *"Shucks!"* and dismay of the nostalgic schoolboy.

If the notion were conveyed to the prehistoric Indian, he would indicate that the frontier was where his tribal territory ended and another tribe's began, or where his tribe and another were quarreling over territory. British-Americans early on came to consider the frontier as where they encountered strange Indians, or, less often, where Spanish or French territory began. Often people considered the frontier to be unoccupied land and squattable, a concept foreign to the Indian, who believed that land could be people's stamping grounds without their having to be camped upon it. The boundaries of other English colonies would not be regarded as "frontiers", although there were laws forbidding ingress and egress among colonies, more often ignored than not.

To us, the frontier is depicted by certain criteria. Its area was being newly occupied by strangers, and was on the edge of territory even more foreign to them. The newcomers were in a high ratio of male to females, five to one or more. Many men were alone. Others were in pairs or small groups, never very large unless we speak of a frontier fort, in which event there may have been fifty or more of military and civilians. Living conditions were primitive. Incomes were low. A state of disorder existed, with a high incidence of personal and social violence, and of drunkenness. Property rights were ill-defined and often contested. Religion was in abeyance. The people viewed the economy of the area in a highly exploitative way, dreaming of wresting riches from its resources.

A strong belief in personal and social equality pervaded the frontier. This was natural under the chaotic conditions of every sphere of life in frontier regions, and did not occur because the denizens had read Rousseau and Locke on natural rights. A traveler in the back country of Massachusetts as late as May 1771 spoke of the "spirit of equality", everywhere prevailing, with "no notions of rank or distinction in society", alluding unhappily, also, to the absence of law and order and civilization.

Equality, we venture to say, ought to be the practice of continual delicate mutual perception and adjustment of qualities of the self and others which deserve respect and support. There is no reason to take the trumpeting of "equality" in frontier areas as signifying more than a special loosening of physical bonds. The frontier population was a volatile mixture of social types: adventurers, land speculators, surveyors, fugitives, malcontents, soldiers past and present, trappers, traders, peddlers, Indians, African-Americans, "loose women", ethnics of various nations - English, Scots-Irish, French, German, Welsh, Spanish, mixtures of various races and creeds - thinking that they might stay here and send for someone to join them. They were often at odds, knives close by.

A few of the newcomers planted crops. Except for an occasional scholar or learned preacher, intellectual life was nil and so-called higher culture was held in fear and contempt, occasionally in awe.

Almost always, these were the elements of the first stage of the frontier. But usually a frontier passed within a political and social generation into a second stage. The second stage saw the persistence of all of the first stage traits, but in a dwindling form, except that soldiers, surveyors, speculators, and would-be farmers increased.

The ratio of females increased and families became more frequent, concentrated in a tiny settlement or scattered far and wide because the man of the family believed he has gotten a great bargain in land and is optimistic that the Indians and Caucasian thugs will let him be. He was often wrong.

Ministers of the Gospels - raggedy-Ann preachers –appeared, but could hardly find sustenance and wended their way begging and praying among a population generally uninterested in religion. He administered the sacraments of marriage, baptism and last rites wherever welcomed to do so. Sometimes he built his own congregation by finding a promising spot, and going back and forth recruiting and leading people to his "diocese".

News of his presence would be passed along by word of mouth. Families seeking to settle would come and find him. Speculators did the same thing, sometimes in cahoots with the pastor, advertising the virtues of a place and offering land for sale. Surprisingly soon, people would descend upon the frontier's primary settlement by the road that was more and more safe and traveled (like the Wilderness Trail that Daniel Boone blazed from North Carolina to Kentucky through the Cumberland Gap, following the Indian way,) and then spread out laterally, until a full-scale second-stage frontier culture was operating.

In both the first and second phases, conditions were not good. Every value was in short supply. Money incomes of most people were insignificant. The people lacked political power. They were out of touch with the power elite. Health conditions were bad, never mind the pure well-water and river-water; diseases still spread, there was almost never a medical doctor when you needed him.

Food was not as abundant as the hunting-and-fishing enthusiasts would let one believe; one had to be skillful at these occupations and spend plenty of time at them to eat well and feed others, but, if so, then what did one do to further his fortunes? Fresh vegetables were scarce and disdained. He was a rare frontiersman who ever picked and ate a dandelion. Pork, Indian corn, and game were available with some fish. Wild berries were picked and acorns ground into flour. Dried cereals and jerked beef came from a trader.

Respect was not organized. The dispossessed of the world have little chance to cultivate respect, or affection, for that matter. People had much bad to say about everyone else it would seem - on religious, ethnic, racial, social grounds and personal habits. Enlightenment was supposed to emerge from communing with nature and reading the Bible. Very little else for the time being.

Frontier folk lived half or more like Indians, but hated Indians all the more for this; in the circumstances of their own lives, the Indian's life was enviable, and envy projected into contempt and hostility. The Indian had all the land in the world, while he, the self-anointed superior being, cannot be sure he could hold on to any land that he squatted on or paid for in dubious sale. Affection was wanting for the same reasons as respect, and the lack of women hardly helped the situation. Most likely no parson was around to preach love for Christ and one's brethren.

Numerous frontiers arose and transmogrified in American history, and it would be well to allude to them to show the importance of the phenomena, prior to picking them up in their own time and place. The frontiers that have been of most concern to us thus far, or that will be under further discussion here number six: the Hispanic Spanish-Indian borderlands from 1492 to the events that will bring them to conclude their typical behavior - well into the 1800's; the French-Canadian borderlands from 1604 to 1763; the Yankee Colonial Frontier; the Pluralist Colonies Frontier; the Southern Frontier; and the Revolutionary War Frontier from 1607 to 1790.

To be dealt with later are the Trans-Allegheny Frontier, the Old Southwest Frontier (Greater Louisiana), the Old Northwest Frontier (also Greater Louisiana), the Great Plains Frontier, the Pacific

Northwest Frontier, the Far Southwest Frontier, and then some special frontiers: the mining towns and camps, the Indian enclaves frontier, the cattle-age frontier, the farmers' frontier, the Hawaiian frontier, and the Alaskan frontier. We might even speak of city and suburban frontiers, but these lose the meanings defined above.

Perhaps the extensive world of piracy on the high seas should be considered a frontier. Pirates formed a social order of the destitute and abandoned; they recruited members from the abused of the navies, privateers, and merchant marine; they developed a code of behavior, rules, and customs, through a network of communications, for men went from one gang to another and pirate boats met at sea or in safe harbors; in the 1720's the naval and shore authorities intensified efforts to get rid of them, and executed hundreds. A desultory and near-futile fly-swatting.

By their nature, frontier boundaries are not clear, and they are always in motion. For example, Pennsylvania was a proprietary colony, with vaguely stipulated boundaries that hardened with time, and treaties that gave it ultimately its present seemingly logical rectagonal shape. But its people often seeped into other areas and other colonists impinged upon it.

The Virginia Tidelands, Chesapeake Bay, Southeastern Pennsylvania, the Appalachian, Delaware Bay, North (New England) and South (Swedes, Anglican, and Quaker) New Jersey elements constituted sub-cultures of the Pennsylvanian Region, which was the centerpiece of the Pluralist Culture Region.

To its West, its people moved down into Northwestern Virginia (later West Virginia); its most vigorous frontier was there and directly West where it was infiltrated by the New York and New England cultural elements essaying to move around the Southern edges of the Great Lakes.

Here and not so much with the Eastern sub-cultures, the Indian nations, depleted and reduced at the end of the French and Indian War in 1763, were still a formidable obstacle to the variegated horde and gangs of invaders. They were unreliably joined to combat Europeans, and often abetted the very processes that were killing their own kind. Abandoning their former principle of "production for use", they traded skins and furs in numbers so large that the animal populations reduced beyond the support level and this in itself caused many individual clans to shift away from the frontier. At the end of the century of the 1700's, Indian tribes of the vast area East of the Mississippi accounted for 125,000 persons, while the Europeans reached three millions.

When the Indians discovered in 1763 that their French allies had been defeated and had turned over the Indian interest to the British, they were dismayed and angered. Chief Pontiac of the Ottawa Nation came to the fore and organized a group of tribes, primarily Algonquin, but also Iroquois and others from as far as the Mississippi River, to expel the Europeans from the vast area outside of the colonies.

The war was vicious. A British commander was told to treat the Indians not as enemies but as sub-humans to be exterminated. Despite numerous small victories, Pontiac's forces were unable to conquer Fort Pitt (at Pittsburgh) and Detroit. His allies grew disheartened and abandoned him. He made peace.

The uncertainty of land titles, the high value placed upon geographic points of value - inlets, heights, hardwood groves, rich soils, those distant from swamps, or near to other settlements, and the absence of forces of law and order, brought on many a deadly quarrel. Puritans fought Quakers in Central New Jersey. Where the Delaware Bay people met the Chesapeake Bay people, fire-fights erupted. British Northern Border immigrants fought with Yankees in Northeastern Pennsylvania and the Connecticut Valley.

The most combative and intransigent of the newcomers were the Scots-Irish, who had immigrated with a burning hate spurred from depression of the linen trade and the rapacity of Anglican landlords and clergy, and English-Scot Borderfolk who, after having been rendered quite destitute by the four depressions between 1717 and 1770, arrived in several waves. Most were males; 4 out of 5 were young males in the English and Scottish immigration of 1773-76, and they were supplemented by their kindred folk from North Ireland.

Most headed directly for the border areas. A kind of leadership was provided by kin of clan chieftains, or by someone from a better family: ethnarchs, we can call these; they often kept their leadership in the New World. The Scots-Irish frequently forced out earlier settlers, not to mention Indians, by their obnoxiousness. Quakers and Anglicans would move away from the hill country to escape them. A Pennsylvania land office official declared, *"the settlement of five families from Ireland gives me more trouble than fifty of any other people"*. (These were Scots-Irish of course; when the Irish Catholics came they were shepherded by priests and gave less trouble - to begin with.)

At first the Quakers thought to lay a head tax on immigrants, which would rebuff the impoverished undesirables. Penn vetoed the idea for being against humane principle. So the local authorities decided upon ushering the newcomers rapidly West and out of the way; there they could constitute a buffer against hostile Indians.

Unfortunately the buffer, a defensive concept, was used for aggressive purposes. Indians were incited to violence. The settlers hollered that they were being attacked and that they should be armed and reinforced. The Paxton Boys, leading a gang of them, massacred a number of Indians, including friendly Christians, and, after scalping them, vowed to march on Philadelphia, there to do the same to the Quakers.

Treaties were signed by British officials and the Indian Tribes. Proclamations were issued. British troops were ordered to bring about respect for the boundary lines. All to no avail. George Washington railed at the parcels of "banditti", who were roving the frontier. The powerlessness of authority has never been so manifest in American history as in the violation of frontier agreements. At least 60,000 people moved into the frontier beyond the lines. Similar movements were occurring far to the North in New England and New York, and far to the South.

Promoters were ready to try any device to buy land, bring in people under indenture, and gain a hoped-for enormous profit. With the queer first phase of its communitarian history over with, and settled upon a solid slave culture course, Georgia had an enormous frontier area North and South. The latter bordered upon East and West Florida, which were transferring from Spanish to British to Spanish to American title as time went on, but remained for a century and more the empire of the Seminole Indians, a haven for all the frontier characters listed earlier above.

St. Augustine on the Atlantic and St. Marks on the Gulf of Mexico were small settlements of barely noticeable growth. Escaped slaves abounded in the colony. Many entered the Indian tribes and assimilated. Georgia slave masters were usually frustrated in their search for runaways, once the Florida border was crossed.
The same intermingling of Indians with African-Americans was occurring at many points to the North even beyond the slave colonies. Also, tribes could be counted that had become mixtures of Indian, African and European. Nobody offered an acceptable logic for treating this unique type of person. None other than the distinguished Patrick Henry and John Marshall supported legislation in Virginia to give a bonus to every White person who married an Indian; it might have passed into law if Henry had not gone out of town on business.

Virginia, it should be recalled, almost allowed slaves a century earlier to serve out their bondage after a limited period and would have abolished the inheritable status of slave. It is votes of this type and of the type that showed a large proportion of Virginians disfavoring secession in 1861 that make us seek to avoid over-generalization. People are both good and bad everywhere, and are found to act both ways during their lives.

In one of the periods of English occupation of Florida, a promoter thought how fine it would be to indenture not his fellow-countrymen, who knew nothing of Southern agriculture, but Mediterraneans who could work miracles with the soil. He inveigled some 1,500 Italians and Greeks in families to come settle down some 35 miles South of St. Augustine on a sandy waste with a ten-year work-lease contract, the land then to revert with improvements to the owner. They were treated as badly as the indentured servants to the North. Supplied mostly with corn and a bit of pork, and forbidden to fish, dissatisfaction grew into insurrection in 1769. A regiment of troops arrived to put them down. . .

The poor rarely won in any of the riots, rebellions, insurrections, demonstrations, violent attacks, or group escapes that lit up the pages of colonial history. At best they might receive some small concessions following upon exemplary punishment, or disperse and make their fortunes individually in the highly mobile great society, with its many niches, or into the wilderness.

Some of the most famous Americans were speculators in land, besides whatever else made them famous. Daniel Boone is 300-year old myth: I've mentioned before this misty personage in a coonskin cap, who led the first settlers along the Wilderness Trail in 1775, who was a resolute and crafty fighter of the Indians, who founded the State of Kentucky, and disappeared into tradition that spun out in numerous volumes, giving more and more exaggerated accounts of his prowess and achievements, like Davy Crockett two political generations later.

He was real. He could read enough to let him carry Gulliver's Travels (not the Bible) in his pack sometimes (showing that he was nostalgic, too). He did probably tell his wife Rebecca when someone moved to within two days' journey from their cabin, *"Old woman, we have to move, they're crowding us"*. But he founded a settlement, Boonesboro, too, with a bow to fame. He was the agent for Richard Henderson, perhaps the largest of land speculators in the immediate pre-Revolutionary period. The settlers he led into Kentucky earned him commissions from Henderson.

Despite how the Indians had killed his sons, he liked Indians (granting that there were friendly and hostile Indians), lived with the Shawnees and considered himself one of them, with an Indian Godfather; he even conspired with the Shawnees against the White settlers. "Worse", he did some jobs for the British during the Revolution, and was tried for treason afterwards. Whereupon he fled to the Missouri frontier, ran a tavern, farmed a little, and reminisced to frequent awed visitors until he died at the ripe age of 86.

I have already mentioned, too, that Benjamin Franklin was in London, engaged (he always had several things going) with others in an enormous speculative venture to obtain from the Board of Trade the land of Vandalia, a fat slab stretching from Pittsburgh, then a frontier collection of huts, down to the West of North Carolina. Just as it appeared that the grant would be theirs, a gang of ruffians dumped a load of British tea into Boston Harbor.

Washington always had time for business, too, and, being originally a surveyor, knew the lay of the land. Like Franklin, he was one of the richest of Americans, but who says that the rich may not want more? He was as devious as the next man. One time he is writing his surveyor associate, William Crawford, don't tell anybody what you are up to, nor that I believe the King's proclamation about the new boundary of the frontier will not be in force for long. And after his veterans have been given some land, he writes his brother Charles to kid them along in order to discover what value they set on their land.

Even speculators longed for some sort of stability - not too soon, of course. They could be frustrated by squatters, endure violence at the hands of border ruffians, find themselves before judges and officials more crooked than themselves, and be constrained by hostile ordinances and rules of a new division of government - state, county, municipal, or a special district. The more responsible leaders began early in history to voice a despair that civil society was disintegrating before their very eyes. The frontier expressed their worst fears. They pleaded for family, order, controllable compact settlements, and the control of expansion. They asked for an end to irresponsible individualism. They wanted *communitas*. In vain.

What changed the Frontier Phase I to the Frontier Phase II? An excruciating process by which the uncontrollable elements spun off out of control, by which those who owned before sold to those pressing in, so that they had nothing to do but move elsewhere, by which -

as with the cocoon and the butterfly - the unrecognizable community metamorphoses into something resembling - all too clearly - the older places from which the disorganized pieces originally came.

In the long-stretching back country, an indigenous elite was forming. They would usually be born leaders in the Old Country, in the American coastal lowlands, or be descended from Old Country parents. The third biological generation would be found heading movements, militias, courts and legislatures. One study found that most of the back-country elite of a North Carolina region were of families that had been of substance in the North British borderlands. They carried the names of Henry, Calhoun, Polk, Jackson, Houston, Bell, Graham and Bankhead. The influence of such families would grow with time, as their kin multiplied, and as the population and power of the western states grew.

Once more, the evidence supports the view that even under the most chaotic conditions of the frontier, customs, status, and influence - no matter how measly - move across the seas and with the transportation of laws. America, the greatest land of opportunity for the wretched of the world, nevertheless gave a more cordial helping hand to the immigrants who had been advantaged in their Old Country environment. I doubt that we shall find an exception to this rule down to the present time.

Nor will we find here or in any other frontier community that certain something which is so often declared to be the quintessence of the frontier: democracy.
Reckless individualism and chaotic change, yes.

Political cartoon by Benjamin Franklin

Part Four

REVOLUTION AND CONSTITUTION

An army of principles can penetrate where an army of soldiers cannot.
Thomas Paine

Half a dozen major causes and several minor ones
brought on the American War of Independence,
the Revolutionary War, it is often called,
or else the American Revolution.
If a cause is major enough, it becomes effectively a war of its own.
So it is with the American Revolution, in which at least
seven major causes are to be recognized, mingled in struggle.
More of this later.

The successful termination of the Revolution,
from the standpoint of American leadership generally,
boosted the useful art of constitution-making
that had already attained sophistication in the individual States,
and would now go through a trial by one constitution,
the Articles of Confederation,
before culminating in 1791, with promised Amendments,
in the Constitution of the United States of America.

The significance of a political generation lies largely in this,
that a group of men of political age
- usually in their thirties and forties -
command power and policy in such a way as to
turn the bend of the river of history, shaping events, then
steering along the changed course. A new historical
generation, a new period, will arrive and be named, but it is uncertain
and even unusual that 33 years later a new group of men will grasp
the helm and straighten the course, or bend it backwards, or even more
in the direction toward which it has been
swung by the older generation.

There is in every culture, and sub-culture -
indeed, in the processes of every group over time -
the phenomenon of the agglutination of traits and behaviors.
When there is a large change, a quantavolution, all changes.
For example, in fifteenth century Florence, the parts of
every institution were changing rather in the same way under the
same impulses, including the character of people. When the
Renaissance, as this concatenation of events is called,
spread North to Germany and France, new practices moved
in concert, except of course that Italy and most Italians and most
Renaissance culture remained more or less in place. When the
Renaissance arrived in England, it lent its traits, ideas and conduct to
the last Tudor monarchs, especially to the
Age of Queen Elizabeth I, and thereafter.

When examining the events of American history, we define a *period*,

in contrast with the three types of generation,
by the noticeable change in the total agglutinate of culture.
We speak, for instance, of the Revolutionary Period
and of the Constitutional (or Federal) Period.
This latter Period can be cut off with the advent of a
Jeffersonian Period, mainly because of a change of governing
political parties in Washington, D.C. But if most
other significant areas of life changed little, the
Constitutional Period could be seen to end only with
the second term of President James Monroe, by which time,
around 1821, many indications of a new Period were consolidating
amidst the sealing of the effects of the old Period.

This shall be our way of dividing the material, but,
be assured, it makes little difference. Coincidentally,
two geniuses of the Revolutionary and Constitutional Periods,
John Adams of Massachusetts and Thomas Jefferson of Virginia,
allies, then foes, reconciled in old age,
veterans of four biological generations,
two political generations,
and a single memorial generation,
died during the same hours of 1826.

Battle of Lexington

Chapter Seventeen

Prelude to Rebellion

By 1763 the American Colonies had
achieved so substantial a population and "Gross National Product",
so far away from Britain, that we can ask the question
in retrospect: "What could have held them to the
British Empire?" Our answer would probably be,
"Nothing besides armed force or mutual regard".
To many Americans, England was a drag.
It oppressed typical American minds, their peculiar vision,

a rampant American craving for equality and mobility.

No better reasons could exist for getting rid of the connection,
no matter what the circumstances. And,
so far as losing the Loyalists was concerned, these,
by their very circumspection with regards to the bonding,
were an additional load on the drag of the parent.
Few people in America could go back to unbrutalized
progenitors or recall happy times in the Old Country.
Moreover, half were only step-children anyhow,
non-English by descent.

Yet, before fracturing, relations between the nations
underwent severe contortions, energized by unconscious
psychological drives, and rationalized in terms of ancient
civil rights, high taxes, and severe despotism.

The colonies reached a take-off speed before rebelling.
Back 33 years from 1775,
1742 and thereabouts, the
colonies, as such, could be said to have achieved an admirable
equilibrium bordering upon the Enlightenment
that was now spreading out of France:
Glass-making factories were set up in 1739-40 in
New Jersey by Caspar Wistar, using German and
Belgian craftsmen. In 1740, Parliament
legislated to permit citizenship to
any person resident in the colonies for seven years,
upon taking a loyalty oath; what's more, it allowed
Quakers and Jews to be exempt from oath-swearing,
and let any citizen of the colonies carry his or her
citizenship from one colony to another,
significant of a sense of togetherness of the colonies and
foreshadowing the Constitutional provision that extends the
rights and immunities of a citizen of one State to all States.

In 1741 the number of fishing boats operating out of
New England alone approached 2000.

The American Philosophical Society was
established in Philadelphia in 1743 for the purpose of
scientific inquiry, with Thomas Hopkinson as President and
Benjamin Franklin as Secretary. In Bethlehem,
a Collegium Musicum was founded for the production of musical
concerts by Moravian churches. (Moravian John Antes
composed the first American chamber music,
trios for strings.) In 1747 the
College of New Jersey, now Princeton University,
opened its doors at Elizabethtown. And so
colonial culture followed upon the heels of Europe.

The British government had its own way of behaving. It had been
having a jolly successful time in the world by the standards then
prevailing: winning wars, cashing in on heathen loot of the true Indies,
luxuriating, reveling in memories of a century of revolutions thankfully
completed - acting overall as if it would live forever.

The London mob was a nuisance, it is true.
In 1768, for instance, numerous
crowd demonstrations, riots, and strikes occurred,
usually protesting against high prices of necessities of life.
The lessons of such events were not lost
upon American agitators.

Remarkably, the elite, when they had to consider American problems
at all, were almost unanimous in believing that the Parliament, and the
King when the Parliament was not offended, had sovereign rights over
the colonies. That the Americans spoke a kind of English should only
make it easier to get the message across to them. The elite - titled,
rich, or both - and respectable upper middle class had a
condescending interest in the colonists, who were generally of the
poorer class of people, who provided a great lot of raw material - as
any third-world country should - who bought greedily more than they
could afford from the merchants of England. There was no higher
culture to import; an occasional Indian in regalia was fun.
We have treated the Americans very well, they thought.

Until now the colonists had experienced no great problems coming out of Britain. Royal governors had been increasingly running affairs; there were more of them, too; but the colonial legislatures were gaining in experience, corporate confidence and power. Nor was there even much reason to concern themselves with the Old Country except as a giant "Post Exchange" and a depot for receiving their exports and crediting their accounts at the going rate. They bought English books and other printed material in large quantity, yet, here, too, they were publishing too much to be readily controlled by authority, religious or political. Whatever legislation and customs duties applied to them were not onerous or could be evaded. Also, giant Post Exchanges existed in other countries.

Was it then success that spoiled imperial harmony? Certainly the fatter the chicken, the more solicitous the farm wife. Every index of American economic growth rose rapidly. Could not the Home government now reap a reward for its patience? What good is a colony unless there was some government revenue to be obtained from it? History at this point could become a tale of a score of attempts to extract funds and obedience from colonials and an equal number of tactics to ward them off. In the end would happen the Revolution.

But Revolution, at least this one, that ushered in the Modern World, requires a thoroughgoing explanation. Indeed we need to go into abstruse considerations of psychology and sociology to explain what happened.. There comes first the traditional causal sequence of highly visible causes marching along from 1763 to 1776, boom, boom, boom. Attached to these, but extending farther and deeper, come perceived and unperceived but reasonable explanations. Then I would point out the kinds of tactics used in pushing the revolution forward - quite extraordinary, even brilliant - and the responsive tactics of the British authorities - these being stupid and torpid on the whole and exhibiting a contemptuous disregard of what might be motivating the colonists.
Finally I would offer an overall explanation of how it flared up.

Until the very end of this third type of explanation, it will simply not be conclusive that there should have been a Revolution. No causes seemed to have been sufficient in themselves or in combination to bring it about. The Revolution, I think, had to come out of something peculiar about the American people at that time, something that we will understand better because we have laid the foundations for it in earlier chapters.

Already familiar with most of the background factors that tended toward independence by revolution, we need only allude to them briefly in order to understand how they worked. The fiercely individualistic, almost anarchistic, Leveller influence of the mid-1600's revolts in England spread their contagion to the New England and Pluralist colonies; *"every man a king"* in his own ego-circle. Colonial governments had not given into the directly and fully democratic government that these ideas implied, but the pressures were being felt all along the line.

Locke, in his well-read *Second Essay on Government,* developed the notion that government was a social contract among individuals, and this idea too played into the already developed idea of written constitutions being the basis and authority of government; Locke also developed beautifully the value of personal property (preferably lots of it) in perfecting human happiness and fulfilling human nature. There occurred the "Glorious Revolution" of 1688, which affirmed the right of Parliament to have the last word on legislation and verily on the person who should be King, and promulgated encouraging words about individual liberties. (Actually, this Revolution was the self-serving work of a gang of military men seeking to preserve their careers, elevated during the Protestant rule.) Britain's behavior, as well as its philosophers, was setting a momentous example for the colonies.

In the middle 1700's, the philosophers continued their work of eroding the basis of British authority: the New Radicals picked up where the Levellers had left off, and added the big idea of
"Happiness of the Greatest Number"
(an idea of Giuseppe Beccaria that was developed in political science by Jeremy Bentham, whose *Fragment on Government* occurred in the fateful year of 1776). From France came the justification of a government such as the English, whose

departments - executive (monarchical), parliamentary, and judicial - are separately independent and capable of balancing off one another, with excellent effects, according to the author of the theory, Baron de Montesquieu; his theory was exaggerated and therefore dubious, but sales of his Bordeaux wines to flattered English customers picked up markedly.

In a very different way, Jean-Jacques Rousseau was promoting revolution by advocating a return to nature, with books of anthropology, *The Social Contract,* and on education, like *Emile*. He gave man natural rights to liberty and gave legitimacy only to governments formed under contract or something similar thereto. (He also advised mothers to nurse their own infants, which so affected the upper class that they could be seen at the Opera suckling their babes; and his return to nature appeal was heard by Queen Marie-Antoinette, who took to farming, and milking her own cows in the Versailles palace gardens.)
One can appreciate how Benjamin Franklin, *très chic* in a beaver cap, wooed the ladies of the French court; but he never kept his eye off the main chance, which was to get the French government to come out openly in alliance with the Americans rather than to feed the Revolution unofficially. Together Locke and Rousseau provided the natural state of man as the blank tablet on which to write the Declaration of Independence and the numerous constitutions of 1776 and thereafter.

Hardly had the year 1776 begun than Tom Paine, a trouble-making New Radical, who had left his native England for America only two years before, published *Common Sense:* the book swept Americans off their feet; a hundred thousand copies were quickly sold. The War was already on, even without a complete weaponry against the King, so Paine's breathtaking propaganda tract against the institutions of monarchy and colonial dependency mobilized thought, and incited many ordinary people to action.

By the mid-1700's the Enlightenment was in full swing in France and spreading around Europe and into England and the Colonies. Diderot and D'Alembert were furiously preparing their *Encyclopedia* of how to do everything in science and society. Voltaire, the scourge of religion and bigotry, who may have been the world's premier social critic, was in full vigor. People like Franklin and Jefferson were all ears to these superb noises. No one could well avoid fetching notions of the rationality and perfectibility of mankind, the possibilities inherent in science and invention, the need for reasonable arrangements of the machinery of government instead of the hodge-podge of institutions that had come down from medieval times. In the forefront of Enlightenment ranks were the Freemasons, multiplying rapidly all over America. Although spawned in Britain, they found American waters deliciously energizing. Through Jackson, excepting John Adams, the Presidents were Masons, and later on, too.

Thus we had fighting for the independence of the Colonies some fresh major ideas of the modern age quite up to the moment: the urge to egalitarianism and individual rights to life, liberty and the pursuit of happiness, the doctrine of popular consent to government, the justification of resistance to tyranny and the value of a republican government of separate and balancing branches, the need for a real elective rather than an elite's "virtual" representation of a considerable part of the population.

I shall merely mention the American pamphleteers who belabored these points. Their big job was to relate all of the world-shaking ideas to the proximate needs of the American colonists. They began with James Otis in 1764 speaking of the rights of the colonists as British subjects. Daniel Dulany, publishing a year later, was intent upon obtaining full and equal representation for the colonies. John Dickinson, a Philadelphia lawyer, aforementioned, published in 1767 his "Letters of a Pennsylvania Farmer". James Wilson, also from Pennsylvania, published a similar pamphlet, as the crisis deepened. John Adams, in Massachusetts, the same who defended the British charged in the Boston Massacre, turned ponderously into a Patriot with his own pamphlet.

No worthy theorist should ever have disputed that the power to govern includes the power to tax, and that the power to tax is the power to destroy. These are sacred principles to even a moderately observant politician. Yet both English and American advocates wasted much ammunition in banging away at these statements, as if the smithereens would compose an answer to what ailed British-American relations.

To cap the propaganda process, Thomas Jefferson joined with Benjamin Franklin and John Adams to write a *Declaration of Independence of the United States of America in Congress Assembled* of July 2, 1776. (The two-day difference from July 4, when it was published, could be called an administrative delay. The names of the actual signers from the Continental Congress were not made public until some months later.)

In the context of revolutionary propaganda, the Declaration was a masterpiece. It made the signers feel it worthwhile to put their lives and fortunes on the line; it ennobled the whole rebellious operation; it made the British King, Parliament and officialdom appear to be a heinous crowd; it made armed rebellion seem to be the only way out for a large oppressed population. It provided so many accusations that anyone who proposed to defend the British cause would be overwhelmed by the charges at the start.

But once again, we must remind ourselves that the War was already on at this late date, and return to its intermediate-range causes. For many historians, the rise of the merchant class in the colonies and the restrictions put upon them by the Crown adequately explain the Revolution. I would say yes to the first and no to the second. The Revolution would not have occurred if the merchants had been few, poor and weak. Instead they were numerous and increasingly wealthy and powerful; more than that, they were not a particularly peaceful class, engaging, as they did, in privateering, the slave trade, and wholesale smuggling. Too, they had acquired worldwide experience and profit. They were not country bumpkins.

Indeed, many a merchant feared more than anything the strict enforcement of the laws against smuggling, entailing confiscation of his boat, fines, and possible imprisonment as the alternative to paying a tax that might be several times the cost of the bribes for smuggling safely. But the corruption of British officials - almost down to a man, they had to be paid off - created as bad a situation as the thousand American jurisdictions where pay-offs have been *de rigueur* in contemporary times. So did their procedures - red tape, delays, sneering at all and sundry. Most annoying, but hardly ever a *casus belli*: substantial merchants usually could send minions to wait in line and be snubbed.

Could the merchants and their media of opinion have been so indignant at the smaller sums that they had to pay in bribes of customs officials and all the others, that they were ready to pay an honest tax honestly administered? There is no sign of that. Could some of these Americans have been so devious that they wanted Independence so that they could have for themselves and their own friends the customs and tax collection jobs and the proceeds of bribery?

However, rather than answer this question, we might go on to ascertain the other nodes of discontent. On the frontier, more than anywhere else, there was an ethnic dislike or at best a tolerant indifference to the British. I speak of most Scots-Irish, many Germans, and various other nationalities who had poor memories of the British at home and who were expecting the British to side with the Indian tribes "in preference to their own people" on issues of warfare, land rights, and civil rights. The land speculators got a big scare in 1763 with the Royal Proclamation that took all of the land West of the mountains into Royal hands and put it under the jurisdiction of the unreliable Quebec authorities.

The evangelistic and independent Protestant sects were numerous and often small, and they feared that one day the Crown would decide to build up the Anglican Church in America, send over a horde of priests, and make the Church of England the official church of America. The same elements had aroused large sections of the American people to heights of religious ardor. A "national" spirit had developed. Now, if those with this ardor and spirit were tired of revivalism and looking for another exciting experience, and if those who had not received the religious message but wished they had received any kind of message at all were also looking for excitement, what better than a resistance movement and a revolutionary movement to provide a second Great Awakening! The religious spirit was in abeyance in much of the population.

The age of veneration of elders was passing, too. Patriarchal authority had began to attrite upon its New England landings. The population was now not only in large part long divorced from Old Country ties, but composed of brash youth - with most of the population under the age of 16. The Revolution was to be of youth against age. Family relations had undergone a fundamental change in America, and to a degree in England. Tie-ins between parental and political authority are close. When the one moves, the other follows.
Such has been known since Plato wrote *The Republic.*

One may wonder, however, at the increasingly sophisticated and powerful planter class, firmly in control over most of the South. Why should they be inclined to resent the British? Here the evidence is striking, though rarely brought forward. The planters as a class were near bankruptcy. They owed a great deal of money to their British agents and bankers. They had splurged on gadgets and consumer items. They had suffered, as farmers always will, years of insects and droughts and floods, during which they ran up debts, and, being premature Keynesians, they had borrowed so as to spend during the bad times in anticipation of the good times, but, of course, as all the Keynesians should have known, in good times they spent even more.

They were not savers; to the contrary, they had run up by 1775 total personal debts with accrued interest, according to the main group of British merchants reporting in 1791, of 4,137,944 pounds sterling and of this amount, 2,305,408 pounds were owed by Virginians. The Southern personal debt came to five-sixths of the total all-American debt of 4,930,656 pounds owing to British merchants. The planters' homes, lands, slaves, and forced laborers were mortgaged to a small number of British merchants. Nor could they protect themselves against dispossession, as, say, they might have done if they were truly feudal lords operating under the English feudal code of laws.

The merchants were of the class of religious Dissenters who had thrown some of the planters' Cavalier ancestors of the previous century out of England.

Speak what one will of the necessity to pay one's just debts - and the planters were not the best audience anyway for such moral righteousness - the conditions of survival personally and as a class dictated that the planters enter upon a revolution to separate themselves and preserve themselves from Britain.

Thomas Jefferson, as he composed the Declaration of Independence, owed a Glasgow firm and a London firm a total of about ten thousand pounds. This could have been a reason either for or against his amending John Locke's natural rights of man to life, liberty, and property in favor of "Life, Liberty and the pursuit of Happiness". Half a dozen considerations becloud the issue from either side, and I would warn both the naive and the cynical reader against a thoughtless conclusion.

The crisis of the revolution lasted from 1763 to 1774 and the War from 1775 to 1783. The Royal Proclamation of 1763, giving the western lands back to the Indians and forbidding settlement (with perhaps a hundred thousand Europeans already scrounging around the vast region) marked a big split in the interests of the American and British allies. Although the Proclamation was soon amended, a hostile suspicion was aroused. This could be called the first of various measures that were taken by the British government and considered in the end so evil that all the rhetoric of the Declaration of Independence would be justified. In 1768 and 1770, British officials concluded new treaties much to the disadvantage of the Iroquois and Cherokee Nations, taking from them most of the Near West.
The colonists of course were pleased.

In the year 1763, the British government decided that it ought to enforce the Navigation Acts for a change. These measures were typical of the authoritative economics of the age in Europe: "keeping all profits to one's own nation" by directing all trade to pass internally and be taxed before being allowed to move into international commerce. Americans could not ship directly to France, but had to pass through English customs and often unload and sell in England for transshipment, with or without processing, to France. The system called for blocking imports from foreign lands as far as possible, whether to the colonies or the motherland. The amended Acts also set up a Vice-Admiralty Court at Halifax to try cases of smuggling. Even though this meant trial without jury, there was nothing unusual then or now about the procedures.

Not only were the Navigation Acts typical of state conduct generally, but the extent of smuggling and bribery were already so great as to return to the British Treasury in a given year no more or even less than was spent on setting up and carrying on the system. While one American trader was complaining at the corruption, another was engaged in corruption. One searches practically in vain for American pamphleteers urging Americans to obey the laws against smuggling and bribery - or, for that matter, against any criminal activity to the disadvantage of the motherland. One must wonder, in the great war of 1756-63, whether the colonies traded more with Britain than with France, Spain, and Holland. Yet no sooner had the War ended and the British government begun thinking about reducing the national debt, and taxing also the colonies for their part in a War that benefitted them greatly, than a great hullabaloo arose.

In 1764, as part of a Revenue Act, Parliament cut the duty on molasses in half, in order to compete with the lower charges for bribery, and to collect more money. It imposed new duties on textiles, wines, coffee, indigo and sugar. The express purpose of the tax was to raise revenue; hitherto taxes were considered incidental to the regulation of trade, not levied for general governmental revenues. The distinction incited a long bitter debate, which to this day is incomprehensible, no one having been able to make a clear or even a useful distinction.

Again in this year that so annoyed many colonists and gave them an inkling of the privileges of Big Brother Abroad, the colonies were ordered to cease to print paper money. Naturally this resulted in a deflation and depression. It also kept the colonies from building enormous debts, from causing a heavy inflation, and from going bankrupt.

In 1765, we had the Stamp Act. This foolish kind of tax, much favored by many nations up to this day, sells stamps to put on documents of all kinds, and playing cards, chewing tobacco and other items. It was a sort of a "value added tax", or "sales tax" on consumption. The colonists raised such a row that one would think the world was coming to an end. To this day the history books speak excitedly about this invasion of the sacred rights of British subjects. The Massachusetts Assembly called for an all-Colonial Congress. Some 27 delegates from 9 colonies appeared and denounced the law and the purposes imputed to it. The Stamp Act was repealed by a baffled British government.

Also in 1765 Parliament passed the Quartering Act that required all colonies to feed and house British Army troops. (Note that the soldiers need not be lodged under the same roof with your family; your town could provide a barrack for them; rent would be paid for private lodgings.) Rumor had it that a total of 10,000 troops would be permanently stationed in the colonies. Many colonists wondered why.

In 1767 Prime Minister Townshend, who was quite learned but considered to be one of the more stupid statesmen of the period, instigated the Townshend Acts, which a) provided three new admiralty courts (not until the 1920's would special courts against smuggling have so much business); b) raised taxes on several colonial imports; c) created a strong Board of Customs Control at Boston to keep a tighter rein on sea traffic; d) declared that Customs would pay the salaries of top colonial officials instead of the assemblies, which had been doing so hitherto but often withheld money, paying too little and otherwise seeking to restrain and direct official conduct by their power of the purse; e) finally, New York's Assembly, which had refused to provide quarters for troops, was suspended. Townshend was cracking down.

Elements of the population were giving the British soldiers a hard time. "People of the better sort" hardly cared, or even encouraged the "bad sort". In 1770, pestered seemingly beyond endurance by a few ragamuffins, citizens, and, who knows, "patriots", a British sentry called for help, was reinforced, and amidst flying snowballs and jeers and curses, let fly a volley of real bullets, producing from the five dead and several wounded the infamous "Boston Massacre". Notwithstanding that the ringleader, named Shattucks, shot dead, was an escapee from slavery, the South as well as the North declaimed indignantly at this killing of Americans.

Several soldiers were tried in local courts under due process of law, and acquitted, with the exception of two who were found guilty of manslaughter and branded lightly. They had a good lawyer - John Adams! In the Gaspée incident, two years later, when a gang of Rhode Islanders boarded a stranded British coast guard cutter and burned it to the waterline (ostensibly in revenge against the inequitable application of a licensing law to a shipper), the British sought in vain for a jurisdiction and a court and jury suitable to arrest and try suspects.

One waited, now, while the clock of crisis ticked away, for two years.

In 1773, the British Prime Minister, in a diabolically clever mood, decided how to help save the huge East India Company that was going bankrupt and had enormous tonnage of tea on its hands. He would have it transported to America, there to be sold at a price that would wipe out all the smugglers, at the cost of a few honest traders, alas; at the same time, he would ingratiate himself with the colonists, who would relish buying tea at a small fraction of its former price. (This is a typical ploy of an unrestrained monopoly to destroy competition; the price could be raised later when the enemy is destroyed, the tea is disposed of, and the East India Company is saved.) Moreover, he would use the opportunity to sell the tea through friends of the government, rather than employing the usual distributors.

Here was perhaps the fatal error. Historians are prone to explain that the colonists recognized the whole arrangement for what it was: but what was it? Nothing terrible; rather good, indeed. But definitely not good for two groups who were rapidly becoming most Patriotic: smugglers and regular tea distributors. Just the people who, in the name of the people and liberty, could set up a "Tea Party".

First, throughout the land, newly appointed receivers of tea were intimidated and resigned their commissions as sellers of tea. At the docks, captains and crews were threatened until they sailed off. In Boston, the three boats carrying tea waited for a propitious moment to land and dispose of their cargoes at the warehouses of persons rewarded with contracts to receive the tea for resale - two relatives, it happens, of the Royal Governor, Hutchinson, already a hated man, whose house had been burned down by a mob in a previous incident.

Gangs of Mohawk Indians appeared out of nowhere - although some said that they could recognize Sam Adams and John Hancock, two influential and notorious troublemakers, among the "Indians", and other locals as well - and dumped 75 tons of tea, all there was of it, into the sea. (The true Mohawk Tribe, led by Chief Joseph Brant, sided with the British when war came.) The "spontaneous" gang was none other than the old "South End Mob", reinforced.

There was rejoicing throughout the colonies (but we are far from hearing a unanimous voice of the colonies yet). The British government soon came up with several Coercive Acts (1774-5) designed to bring the Yankees and everyone else to their senses. The Port of Boston was closed. Any trials of British officers, high and low, for offenses in the colonies would henceforth be conducted in Britain. Troops were to be lodged in private homes where the colonial governments would provide no other quarters.

Local government in Massachusetts, that had been conducting elections and flourishing with some vigor for over a century, was suppressed in favor of appointed officers of the Governor, and this man would now be a military governor. Enter Governor General Gates. Enter also a large army and fleet. These laws were referred to by many colonists as The Intolerable Acts. In most of the colonies, a general boycott of British goods was engineered.

With the dissolution of the Massachusetts legislature, the representatives formed a Provincial Congress to agitate further. The Virginia Assembly, itself dissolved for treasonable activity, reconvened informally at popular Raleigh's Tavern, and called for a Continental Congress of all the colonies to organize and carry on the resistance. The call was generally heeded. The end of the Crisis was nearing and the War about to begin in earnest.

Half the War for Independence was over. The Colonials had won it. A comparison of the tactics displayed by the British Empire and by the Americans will reveal how it happened.

The Home Government needed funds and peace on the borders of the colonies. It had guaranteed peace in the North and South, in Canada and Florida, and had made excellent treaties with the Indians in the West. There was plenty of room for colonists to engage in a controlled expansion over the mountains and to the South and North, so that this vast frontier should have been manageable. But its management required troops and money.

It all came down to a reasonable need for money, most of which, if not all or more than all, would be spent to keep law and order in the colonies, and assure peaceful commerce and law enforcement on the seas. We note that taxes were assessed that were not at all burdensome. The colonial elite was rich and getting richer in the North and Middle Colonies. The personal possessions of more and more people were extending; wealth was trickling down. In the South, reckless spending made a difference; the planters were indebted and putting pressure on their own debtors, but the Southerners below the top were as well off as the Northerners.

We are still, of course, talking about the upper classes, a slim percentage of the total around the colonies. But it was some of these or aspirants thereto who were apparently seeking trouble with the British, not the vast majority living at the subsistence level.

The British sent troops from time to time, but hardly so many as to give reasonable grounds for threat. They as often acted to appease the colonists as to punish them. They asserted various arguments, legal, logical, economic, authoritarian and fraternal. This was their counter-propaganda. Parliament argued that its authority was supreme and binding over the colonies "in all cases whatsoever" (1766, after repealing the Stamp Act). No precedents or laws forbade its powers. They protested against the part the colonists played in smuggling, and the corruption of the customs and other services of the Crown. They attempted reorganization of the courts and services. As the crisis matured, the government, supported time after time by heavy majorities in Parliament, warned and threatened and cajoled, then ordered colonial assemblies to disband. Other late tactics of suppression were detailed above.

What had His Majesty's Government not done? It might have instituted a merit system in the choice of Governors and other officials. It might have given its troops instructions in manners and deportment in regard to the civil population. It might have urged on and subsidized the potential loyal element in some form equivalent to the rebellious associations. It might have bought up some of the colonial newspapers and used them as mouthpieces, as many a democratic government has done. It might have imposed a larger censorship, never mind the precedent of the Zenger case.

It might have distributed titles of nobility to some of the more famous men of the colonies, who would then serve in the still powerful House of Lords. It might have allotted seats in the House of Commons to the colonies, but then a quarter of the House might have come from America and more as time went on. Unless a mere quota of seats were granted, soon Britain would have been torn apart by domestic and overseas factions and the monarchy threatened once again. Anyhow, it would take another two political generations before the English rationalized the apportionment of the Commons and extended the vote to a larger portion of the middle class; the Great Reform Act of 1832 was achieved only after prolonged debate, many riots, petitions, demonstrations, and group pressures on Parliament and King.

I have used some modern terms here, for ironic contrast, but none of these steps were impossible and several were vaguely attempted, even the election of members to Parliament..

Meanwhile we have only to review the tactics of the independence element to understand their victory, and to see why the next century would be the age of the bourgeoisie.

They were superior propagandists. Not only were their pamphlets very well tuned to middle class aspirations, but they were couched in symbols that at the same time in some cases - freedom, liberty, equality, fair trials, anti-militarism, etc. - held appeal to all classes. They simulated loyalty from time to time, and up to the last minute hypocritically pleaded with the King, whom they already had converted into a monster, to make peace.

Their proclamations were often superb: the Virginia Resolves (Patrick Henry et al, 1765), the Massachusetts Letter to the Colonies of the same year and of 1768, the Stamp Act Congress Declaration of Rights and Grievances of the Colonies and its petitions to the King and to Parliament; etc.

They used the docks, the multitude of taverns and newly originating cafés, the town squares, and all other places, official and informal, where people congregate, to agitate. Achieving a critical determinant of who is to win a revolution, they took control of the streets.

They were experienced in all these ways of getting people organized to influence others and use their economic, psychological and ultimately forceful pressure to gain their ends. They intimidated the opposition by threats and by force. Already early in the crisis, they were beating up opponents, burning houses, looting warehouses, and marching about in gangs. They were heckling the enemy at every turn - British and Loyalists alike. They used the law to try British soldiers for minor offenses. They burned boats and dumped cargoes overboard, what would be called propaganda of the deed. It is notable that assassination and murderous terrorism were not practiced.

At the end of the crisis, however, they frightened the British governors and officials into flight abroad and this was sufficient to send many thousands of Loyalist Americans into exile. This incredible feat was the equivalent of winning several major battles. We stress that, far from the myth of history, it was not the rural guerrillas that caused the imperial power to shrink from sternness, so much as the urban guerrillas.

The American rebels were experienced and clever at organizing conferences, assemblies, crowds, and conventions. They also organized permanent groups: Committees of Correspondence, beginning in 1772, that maintained contact with rebels all over the continent, and sent information and suggestions. They organized the Sons of Liberty, a perfect name with a double meaning, friends of freedom, but also freedom from England.

They despatched envoys and hired agents in other countries to obtain intelligence, cultivate friends of colonial rights, and finally to inveigle these nations to enter the fray on their side. Years before the struggle at arms began, the French and Spanish governments let it be known that they were favorable to American independence.

They organized major economic boycotts that hurt English trade badly, with the Sugar Act of 1764, the Stamp Act resistance the year after, at the time of the Townshend Acts in 1767, and at the time of the "Intolerable Acts" in 1774-5. Public mass boycotts, whether by consumers or producers, were strikingly original forms of aggressive resistance. Just as the they were well ahead in the use of propaganda by print, the Americans were avantgarde with their boycotts. In the nineteenth and twentieth centuries, the boycott would often be tried and occasionally worked in England, France, and India, for instance, and became part of the populists' bag of tricks.

As the crisis progressed, the colonial leaders doubled the training of their colonial militias and stocked arms and munitions here and there. They began, then, the second and fighting phase of the Revolution with troops and supplies. For a century and more they had experience with the militias in the field, in Indian conflicts and with European opponents and allies. No nation in the world then had a people so adept at force of arms as the American colonials. They did not have to depend upon the treason of professional troops or some disaster occurring in the Home Country.

The American War of Independence burst forth at a time when the Empire was in excellent shape in most regards, with a stable government, an experienced king, cabinet and parliament, a fleet second to none in the world, and securely-held peripheral lands and overseas colonies. England also had four times the population of America.

Britain even had its public opinion on the side of its governmental policies. (Very few voices favored the colonials, although among them was eloquent Edmund Burke; his was a double-edged sword inasmuch as he also advocated persuasively the theory of "virtual representation", not only because he proved the theory by siding with the colonists, who cast no votes for him, but because he represented, in Parliament, a "rotten borough" and was responsible to only one man, who "owned" the seat.)

Yet the winning of the propaganda, economic, and insurrectionary war, the first phase of the Revolution, effectively set up the victory that would come with the second phase.

I have been using a "they" for the revolutionaries and probably should define more clearly the elements composing them. For perhaps the first time in modern history, a thoroughly secular and socially mixed aggregate organized a large-scale revolution. From what we have said of causes of the discontent, one should have little difficulty in recognizing these groups and their place. The mix was composed, first and foremost, of the merchants and shippers, with the lawyers and employees who were tied to them. This large mercantile element, perhaps the largest and certainly the most prestigious of its kind of any land, with the exception of the Netherlands (which had a semi-monarch), was intra-communicative from Canada down to Florida and into the wilds of the trappers. It had few aristocratic ties and could hope for none, nor particularly sought them, for it had a low regard for the feudal class.

It supported a vigorous lot of newspapers, as readers, owners and advertisers, and with common needs for more information on every subject that affected trade and commerce. It supported the militias, as guarantees against riots. It lived in the environment of incipient industry and mechanics; it could sense the Industrial Revolution, and what it would mean in production for sales and profit.

The mechanics and artisans, in turn, wanted to obtain, with slight compensation, and by hook or crook, as many devices, inventions, tools, and industrial processes as they could from the Old Country and Europe, and resented the laws and officers of England that sought to forestall and frustrate them.

Next, the politicians of the day found their votes among the people of means, and only these could vote in many places; politicians also waxed strong when the power of the royal governors waned. Other groups who supplied leadership were the militia officers, anti-Anglican religious sect leaders and secularists, real estate dealers and speculators in land, and the planters - for reasons that I mentioned earlier and because they had more to gain by political power vested in the local and colonial governments than a government supplied in large part from London.

Despite its multiple competencies, the potentially fully-empowered American elite was a small minority of the population. This is to be expected; no political movement is conducted by a majority or even a large minority. It always devolves upon a small minority. If we were to consider the stance of various elements of the population in relation to activating and fighting the Revolution, we would arrive at the following estimates in percentages of the total population :

Active "patriots" & direct supporters	5%
Loyalists (Tories) Active	5%
Pacifists	3%
Non-political, apathetic	6%
Indentured servants, convicts	2%
Slaves	6%
Indians	3%

Women and children under 14   70%

I have set aside woman and children to strip down the elements to
their realistic numbers. There were notable women and many opinion
leaders among women generally. They are counted within the two
categories of Patriots and Loyalists, but not in the other categories.
Boys and girls over fourteen were capable of working and fighting for
a cause, usually that of their parents, unless they were already
out in the world.

Noteworthy are the equal proportions given to Patriots and Loyalists.
Given a population of 2.5 millions, each group would number about
125,000 men. About a third of the Loyalists fled before the fighting
began, fearing for their lives; a third stayed to agitate or fight actively
for the British cause; a third became tacit supporters or underground
helpers on occasion. They included at least half of the professional,
ministerial, and well-to-do classes of the towns of the pluralist middle
colonies, and nowhere were an insignificant number.

About as many Loyalists volunteered for service in the British army as
there were Patriot volunteers in the American army. But Loyalists
were less energetic, less skilled at organizing, agitating,
propagandizing, improvising, and financing illegal operations.
Very few had a "fire in their belly".
Generally they called for law and order, and relied upon the British government and
armed forces to put down the rebellion.

To examine the causes of the Revolution and events leading
up to it is to be impressed by the solidity and mildness of British rule.
Of stupidity there was abundance, but hardly enough to
generate and justify warlike passions. Taxes seem to have been
reluctantly, belatedly, imposed, and to have been affordable.
Freedom of assemblies and of the press were very much
in evidence except in dire confrontations. Few suffered in dungeons
or under a false arrest, nor were people beaten, tortured, or sent into
exile. No one's property was confiscated without trial. Impressments
of sailors occurred unjustly on occasion. Most measures of the British
government were slow reactions to provocative

conduct of colonial groups.

Therefore, when one reads the Declaration of Independence in the light of what had been actually transpiring in the American colonies, one can divide it into a theoretical statement of the sources of human governance and authority, which one can hopefully agree with, as do I, but which was fairly hypocritical on the part of most of the signers of the Declaration, and then into a statement of 28 generalized grievances that are incredible. (Jefferson initially thought even to put in an allegation that King George had forcibly transported Africans to become slaves; considering the heavy participation of Americans in the slave trade and the indispensable part of the Southern economy and culture that slaves had become, this would have been idiotic; anyhow, slavery advocates in the group refused it.)

With respect to the long list of grievances, if they are accepted as truths, they are a just cause for rebellion, unless one is a pacifist or hopeless optimist. But if read as gross exaggerations or premonitions of what might have occurred or might occur, they are a marvelous catalogue for purposes of propaganda. It is particularly notable that no item in the catalogue is tied to a specific incident. All items are generalizations of types of events: quartering troops upon the people (the British tried not to put soldiers in homes), burdensome taxes (no worse than in England), etc.

Returning, now, to a thought that occurred to us at the beginning of this chapter, we wonder once again at the strength of the emotions generated among a large number of colonials calling themselves "Patriots".
We mark in this regard a single passage from the Declaration of Independence, that "when a long train of abuses and usurpations, pursuing invariably the same Object evinces a design to reduce them under absolute Despotism, it is their right, it is their duty, to throw off such Government, and to provide new Guards for the future security".

Here occurs the key word "design". It suggests that we look for an underlying psychic system at work among the accusers, that some might term an ideology, but is one level more obscure than an

ideology. Call it perhaps a paranoiac system, paranoia; a considerable number of influential and active Americans thought that the British elite was conspiring against their rights, their persons, their liberties, their property. (The elite is personified late in the Crisis and in the Declaration strikingly as the King himself, not the Parliament nor the ruling class nor the Anglican Establishment - whereupon we remind ourselves of how Tom Paine's book a few months before had shown how to strike directly at the devil King and Monarchy; as the modern journalist professor would say,
"personalize your target")

Civilized Christian men almost never wage a war positively, but must persuade themselves that they are victims or about to become victims of an evil force. "Right and proper" people never wage a war until they have convinced themselves that they are the victims of aggression and despoliation. The themes are pounded into people's minds, their own minds: There is a British elite conspiracy against the American colonists! The British government is utterly corrupt! The King is about to make slaves of us!

Remember now, that we are dealing with people who not too long before were burning witches, and who very recently were participating in incredibly great mass religious revivals at which they were called to account for their sins and to take Jesus onto themselves. Now we are speaking of prosperous Christians who deal in rum and slaves and smuggle goods of many kinds. We are treating with slaveholders who are heavily in debt. We are speaking of untutored frontiersmen rightfully afraid of their Indian enemies and the mysterious friends of the Indians. We allude to the finally and just recently experienced wave of consumerism, which brought luxuries to people who had hitherto lived in a hand-hewn culture.

Here they are, conspiring by all means, fair and foul, against the British establishment. Recall how lowly the origins of so many, how discriminated against were the religious practices of many of them,
how tough a time so many had in finding a foothold in a land few wanted really to enter. More than ever, too, the British ruling class was as foreign in manner, motive and interests as
Chinese mandarins.

There are too few rational material reasons to explain the full Revolutionary fervor; unconscious motives must be introduced to blow them up to life size. It is then that one begins to smell and taste the Revolution. The unconscious gives the seemingly "understandable" and "sufficient" motives their initial character and enduring drive. The paranoiac formula is that guilt and sin and bad feelings about oneself are displaced to other people or objects or ideas in order to alleviate one's inner sufferings. What one has been feeling about oneself becomes what one asserts that other people are like and other people are doing. And, finally, of course, these other people are wicked and should be punished. We Americans are not the conspirators; we are not the corrupters; we are not the enslavers: You are conspiring to steal our liberties and property; you are corrupt; you are going to make us your slaves; you hate us! Therefore, in the name of all that is good and holy, we resist your aggression and declare ourselves freed of you.

The War is on!

———————————

Surrender of Cornwallis (Sculpturally depicted)

Chapter Eighteen

Seven-fold War

To help in testing schoolchildren, the American Revolution
of seventeen-seventy-six to seventeen-eighty-three,
also called the War of Independence,
which sounds more respectable, or the Revolutionary War,
is stated to have begun with a
Declaration of Independence of July 4, 1776 and to have ended with
the Treaty of Paris of 1783. Adults may understand it as a conflict that
began substantially with the Crown Proclamation of 1763 giving the
western lands back to the Indians, and a shooting war was well under
way before the Declaration. I am apparently
thinking of a twenty years' war –
twelve years of restless peace and conflict, followed by

eight years of continual warfare, beginning with the British march to Concord in 1775.

The causes of conflict are themselves conflicts, wars peacefully pursued, and wars, like this one, are conflicts pursued by violent means. It must have a name in order to be discussed, so let it be called here, anyhow, the Revolution.

The Revolution encapsulated seven various long-term conflicts contributing directly to bloody exchanges:

1. The War of Independence, the violent attempt to separate from Britain by beating off British forces despatched to preserve British rule, is the conflict that holds all the others together.
2. The warfare between Loyalists and Patriots can be distinguished for having its own life and meaning. Also participating in this conflict were those who felt and acted as if they were at war against the religious establishment; Anglican ministers were presumed to be Loyalist and hunted down, imprisoned, and exiled.

3. Indian warfare in two large regions of the frontier, North and South, constituted the continuation of traditional warfare and an inflamed newer struggle for territory in the west.

4. To many it was a war of republicans against the institution of monarchy. Embedded in this conflict was a struggle between the young and old, even if no group could legally declare war in the name of youth against age.

5. For many it was a war, though they may not have fully realized it, of the merchant and manufacturing class - the bourgeoisie - against the feudal class and mercantile state of England.

6. But there was a war, too, occurring, begun before now, of the populists against the rich elite (whether Royalist or Patriot).

7. There was a formal international war, declared by France and Spain against Britain, and by Britain against the Netherlands for helping the Americans.

❖❖❖

Perhaps the best way to intelligize this multiplex conflict is to narrate the course of the War for Independence plainly, interspersing and following with enough comment on the associated conflicts to give them their autonomous due. The beginning of the proper War might as well be fixed at the incident on the Lexington green, where a British contingent of 700 soldiers on the way from Boston to destroy supplies and make arrests at Concord encountered a company of militia or minutemen who seemed drawn up for offensive purposes and refused to withdraw upon command. Arrogant and presumptuous Major Pitcairn, who led the British, ordered a volley of fire and a bayonet charge, leaving a score of casualties. The British reached Concord, could make no arrests of such as Sam Adams and John Hancock, who were supposed to be hiding out there. The munitions of the Massachusetts militia had been removed.

Thereupon the British marched back under a continuous gunfire from indignant farmers and militia in ambush along the route. Hundreds of casualties were suffered.

The Battle of Lexington-Concord was one of some 1331 military conflicts on land during the war. The next large encounter occurred in Boston itself, where the Massachusetts militia had mobilized to encircle a large British army and naval force which had come to occupy the town and put down the rebellion. Here, at Breed's Hill, near Bunker Hill, entrenched colonials were driven off only following several costly attacks by the British. The two battles mightily encouraged the Patriots and informed the British and Loyalists of the difficulties lying ahead.

Washington arrived shortly after the battle, from Philadelphia, where the Continental Congress, of which he was a member, had named him to be Commander-in-Chief of the Continental Army. This was to be composed of an all-colonial force under the Congress' direct control, supplemented by the colonial militias.

The siege of Boston continued through the winter, until the British decided they ought to proceed to Halifax, Nova Scotia, where far fewer rebels existed, transporting with them a large number of correctly fearful Loyalists.

Later on, heavily reinforced, they descended upon New York City, where the Loyalists were strong and where they might best coordinate the job of suppressing the rebellion, with Southern and Northern regional headquarters. So the army and fleet set up a permanent headquarters in New York, there remaining comfortably until the end of the War.

As is common in warfare, everyone's plans failed and whose plan failed last determined who in disgust would sue for peace and who would be the victor. The initial plan of the British, to suppress the worst rebels, the Yankees, failed, whereupon they sailed away. Meanwhile the Continental Congress had been in session most of a year. Mutual slanders and threats between the Congress and the King assured that there was to be no peace without war. The King proclaimed a total blockade of the Atlantic Coast. At great cost this was continued from year to year. The Congress authorized any possessor of a boat and crew and guns to prey upon British shipping.

At least 4000 entrepreneurial Patriots took to the sea as privateers with licenses to capture and sell British ships and their cargoes. It was a major wartime industry, a private enterprise navy, employing 100,000 crew members. Shares as small as 1/96 of a single enterprise could be purchased on the market. Thousands of prizes were seized in the course of the War, several times more than the British captured. Many Loyalists engaged in privateering as well, on behalf of the British. Still it was a continuously losing battle, and when the French, Spanish and Dutch got into the act, the British hurt as if by a perpetual cannonading of the Thames docks.

Congress also thought to conquer Canada, with the hoped-for help of a French-Canadian uprising. Two American columns worked their way toward Quebec, and besieged the City throughout the fall. In December their combined assault failed; one commander, Richard

Montgomery, was killed on New Year's Eve, 1775; the other, the yet to become notorious traitor Benedict Arnold, was wounded. The French-Canadians were unmoved.

Indeed, the Revolutionary cause appeared to lack appeal in many places. Newfoundland and Nova Scotia were saved for the King. So was the rich Island of Bermuda, although numerous sympathizers of independence dwelt here. The Caribbean possessions - Barbados, Jamaica, the Bahamas, Honduras, remained Loyal or apathetic. The Floridas, that had become a haven for Georgia slaves, and were making a beginning in fishing and agriculture, did not take the rebellious leap.

Congress did not neglect the seas. It found two small boats and called into being the American Navy: It despatched the boats to Bermuda, where with the help of friendly (treacherous?) islanders, they could make off with a load of munitions. (Not hearing of this, Washington sent a boat later on for the same purpose, and it barely escaped destruction by the alerted Bermudian forces.) Nassau, in the Bahamas, may have been the first official American amphibious operation, carried out by a Congressional raider.

The only true gunships that the Americans possessed were captained by John Paul Jones, a Scottish-born former rum-runner and slaver (who quit the trade in disgust), a thorough professional fighter who fought everybody, including his associates. His first sloop knocked off a number of British craft. Benjamin Franklin in France bought him an old larger boat that he fixed up. On this "Bonhomme Richard", he engaged the "Serapis", a first-class English ship, in a furious battle, left his sinking ship, and boarded the "Serapis". He brought this to France to repair. (After the War he could not receive command of the American Navy, he found no employment for his talents in France, and finally sold his services to Russia, where once more he was rejected by the gang of Admirals, mostly incompetent, and sent off to the Black Sea to fight the Turks in 1788. He won there a great battle, had the credit snatched from him by Prince Potemkin, a favorite relative of Empress Catherine, and returned to France, there to die a pauper.)

While Captain Jones went his dogged way, many an American merchant was making his fortune on the seas, first by smuggling and bribing his way past the British authorities and thereafter by smuggling and bribing against the rules of his new country. He would also be running a privateer or two. His main object was to get rich by selling to the armed forces of the United States, then to the State militias, both of whom insisted that he take at least most of his payments in continental paper money or state notes; and then to such of the civilians as had hard money in gold or silver at least in good part, then to the British for hard money, then over the seas to buy products with hard cash or partly on notes, then back to the United States to repeat the performance.

Very likely there was no such animal as a fully honest American merchant in those 20 years of which we speak. It is not impossible that the famous Robert Morris of Philadelphia, who had charge of procurement for the nation and ran an import and export firm on the side, who has been proven to have mixed up his moneys with the government's moneys to his own advantage, stood in the first rank of men of (partial) integrity, besides which he was a Patriot who did work hard to win the War and would have been hanged if it had not been won.

A noble fiscal gesture of the war was the gift of the King of France of one million pounds of credit even before the Declaration of Independence was proclaimed. This hard currency and credit was used to buy and ship munitions to America. Without it, the Americans could not hope to fight a major engagement. As the war went on, other means were found: including making one's own materiel of war and buying, yes, from British quartermasters and traders. Although they could print thousands of pieces of paper called money, the Continental and State governments could hardly put their hands on a coin of value: *Gresham's Law* was working with a vengeance: "Bad money drives out good money".

Farmers exhibited typical human conduct: given a starving army of Patriots nearby to whom you mouth allegiance, given a crop of beans and a head of cattle, given an American army purchasing agent with paper money and a lawful right to ask you to sell these to him, given a British purchasing officer willing to pay the same or a better price and gold and silver to pay it with, to whom would you convey your goods? Hint: British soldiers rarely went hungry. Hint: the American soldiers often looked like scarecrows and went A.W.O.L. (absent without leave) at the sound of a dinner bell. The surplus fertility of American soil and a nimble needle and thread helped to keep the American troops going.

Students tend to become angry at the Continental Congress for *"making a mess of the new nation's finances"*. This is unfair. Money is vital to all public operations. War is a public operation in large part and is expensive. The people with money hated to be taxed; they were fighting (so they said) against British taxes. So the Congress borrowed. But it could only do so if people believed that they would get their money back. Most of the time, there was not enough confidence to borrow very much. Money could be printed on paper; sellers would be required to accept it. This was done, but as soon as there was too much paper or too little confidence existed in the paper, the paper lost its value and became
"not worth a continental".

The States had similar problems and often competed with and were stingy with Congress. The States sold Loyalist properties, which the rich bought. They sold public lands (which the rich also bought). They even gave over their claims to Western lands as the War drew to a close but could not properly organize the sale of these for hard cash, which was in short supply. So the troops camped, marched, and fought on too little food and wore wretched clothing and ported not the best of arms. They went off from camp and stole and looted, but this also was not enough.

The primary American force turned out to be the Continental Army, under Washington's overall command, but divided up in various ways as the theaters of war developed. Its men were supposed to be Patriots, representative of the citizenry as a whole, volunteers for a year or more, regularly paid, dressed in proper uniform, and armed with standard equipment. They were in fact none of these. They finally achieved a full uniform as the war came to a close. They were poor men of the unsuccessful or proliferate farming class, or of the underclass; many had been forgiven a term as indentured servant, or freed from slavery, or let loose from criminal conviction, or had newly immigrated to the colonies.

The first "Emancipation Proclamation" was proclaimed by Lord Dunmore, Governor of Virginia, in 1775, who announced freedom for all rebel-owned slaves and indentured servants who quit and reported in to the British forces. Some thousands responded; the slaves ended up in the West Indies for the most part, the indentured servants in England or in flight to the frontier. Virginia offered the bondsman freedom for enlisting. Later Virginia granted freedom to slaves who had served the Revolutionary cause. An estimated 5% of the American forces at any given time were African-American, about 5,000 volunteers.

A few American soldiers were literate, and even wrote home on occasion. Some had fled home or sought adventure. Some of all types were inspired by the ideas of independence and equality. All were promised land and bonuses. All had to soldier under badly-selected, poorly trained officers. Each State was supposed to supply a quota and the regiments were maintained by State origin, but sometimes the States did not fulfill their quota, and no man no matter where from was likely to be deemed unfit for service. The militias of the colonies, then States after July 4, 1776, had hardly improved over time. These were supposed to defend their States, but would also be sent to join the Continental Army and assist its operations under its command.

Actually the question has often been asked and it is a major one: what did keep the Revolution moving? What did keep the Army going at all, miserable as it was a good part of the time? Much analysis has ended in bafflement. There are those who would say that things could not be so bad (even while every decade of research shows that the whole war was that bad and worse). Others try to prove that this pathetic force was genetically, mentally, and morally so superior that it could stand any kind of deprivation and defeat. Still others say that there was nowhere else to go, notwithstanding that the actual soldiers composed only a small fraction of the total number of men of military age and were physically competent, with plenty of places to go - like the hills and the frontier and even into the British Army, for that matter.

More likely than any of these theories is one that can be carried back into history from World War II. The small regular Army of the United States before 1940 consisted largely of men low in education, social background, and life expectations generally, and of pessimistic and negative temperament - remarkably comparable to the rank and file of the Revolutionary militias and Continental Army. Many were rural Southern and many others were of recent urban immigrant stock. They were paid relatively less than the Revolutionary War soldiers ($21/month less deductions vs. $6/month), but regularly, and were fed much better and had sturdy uniforms. A caste system divided officers and men. Often soldiers were called "riff-raff". Yet these men, along with the Philippine Scouts, put in excellent performances against fanatic highly-trained Japanese on Bataan and Corregidor in the early weeks of the War, nor were their later contributions negligible.

The psychological components of such morale were explained later in the War. Hundreds of controlled and scientifically composed interviews were conducted, both of German and American soldiers, who had been in battle under circumstances where only some major fraction would be alive and unhurt after a month in action. The major conclusion was that the men stuck it out because they were among other men who were sticking it out. Men, many of whom had no other friends left in the world but these around them, lately acquired, nevertheless found their end in life in the maintenance of their spirit of cohesion. Once this feeling establishes itself among a core of men in a squad or platoon, there is no dispersion of the group as a fighting unit except by annihilation or by discharging the core members. Probably this is the bond that kept together American Revolutionary troops, who, by other calculations, should have scattered to the winds.

On the frontier, the American forces were more irregular. Often they were not English, but Scots-Irish, German, Dutch, French, and others. They included local militias. They were opposed by Thayendanegea (Joseph Brant) Chief of the Mohawks, who sailed to England there to sign a treaty of alliance between the Iroquois Confederation and Britain. The Onondagas were struck by smallpox and lost their capacity for war. The Oneida and Tuscarora tribes sided with the Rebels.

By 1778, the British and Indians were burning and killing along the Pennsylvania frontier, so a punitive expedition of 4,000 men under John Sullivan was despatched by General Washington. Following his instructions, they killed whoever could be found and burned forty Cayuga and Seneca villages and their fields. The Iroquois persuaded the Southern Indian tribes to go on the warpath as well. In consequence, South Carolina troops and a Virginia-North Carolina force destroyed hundreds of small Cherokee settlements, with their crops, and killed whoever fell into their clutches.

In the same year George Rogers Clark led a small expedition by boat down the Ohio to the Mississippi River, entered the Francophone town of Cahokia, opposite St. Louis, where he recruited enough French to double his force of under two hundred men, and captured the town of Vincennes on the Wabash River from its Anglo-Indian defenders. In 1782, the British told the Iroquois, who were still fighting ferociously, to quit the war.

When the British cause was lost, Sir William Johnson, Indian Commissioner and friend to the Indians, husband to several Indian wives, a speculator in great land tracts, left the United States with Mohawks and Highland Scot Loyalists for Canada. (His family name had been MacShane.) Chief Thayendanegea lived into the nineteenth century.

All was set for the next great land rush.

The British armed forces contained four elements, each making up about a quarter of its numbers. About one-fourth were regular troops, of about the same social composition as the Americans, but constrained by a system of discipline and training much more severe and effective. Not enough men, even given the mass of poor unskilled males of the British Isles, volunteered for service. Recruitment was heavy in Ireland. American Loyalists also joined in some numbers.

The Army turned to Germany, there to recruit another quarter of the British Army, typically from Hesse, whence all Germanic troops came to be termed Hessians; they were also called mercenaries, but all regular troops were paid; moreover, it is unlikely that the rank and file of home troops were more patriotic than the foreigners, that is, not at all so. A third of the German survivors took advantage of American propaganda and deserted for money and land, or retired in the colonies: instant patriots.

The Indian tribes allied to the British believed, properly so, that they stood to be better treated by the British from London than by the colonial governments, especially should these be freed from the Home Country. The Indians were also better compensated by the British than by the Americans. Scalp bounties were commonly paid. An unknown number of Afro-Americans were freed to fight with the British and many were impressed for labor - as indeed, were Whites everywhere and by both sides.

The fourth quarter of British troops was made up by Loyalists, organized as militias or special troops. They contained more men of a higher social class than did the American troops and British regulars; they had been threatened with or had experienced dishonor, beatings, and eviction from their old homes. The Highland Scots of the back country of the South also volunteered to fight for the King in some numbers; they had come to America on Royal land grants. Yet Loyalists generally presented some of the problems of the Revolutionary militias.

We should count, alongside the Americans, the French army and naval armada that were sent over and helped to deliver the decisive blows against the British. At the siege of Yorktown there were as many

French soldiers as Americans, and the French fleet defeated and chased off a British fleet that could not have been opposed at all by the American forces. Also to be counted on the American side were certain friendly Indian tribes, enemies of the pro-British Iroquois nation.

Neither the Continental forces nor the state militias were adapted to disciplined frontal confrontations in battle, and the militias were employed tactically by placing them center up-front where they could be relied on to fire once or even several times before retreating. Then the Continentals would step in to reform the caving line. Most of the time the men had not enough to eat, and during at least two winters, those of 1777 and 1778, suffered gravely from malnutrition and cold. So many deserted or took sick at Valley Forge in the winter of 1778, or quit when their short term was up, that the Army could hardly muster a few hundred men. If the British had left Philadelphia to attack it and pursue it, the Army would probably have vanished into the snows.

It is extraordinary that so few mutinies occurred, and these were so mild. On the first day of 1781, a body of Pennsylvania troops, many with booze under their belts, killed and injured officers standing in their way and marched on the Continental Congress in Philadelphia. Washington sent troops to deter them, but ordered that they not be fired upon. He sent off to New York to obtain some of their back pay, and in subsequent negotiations, the men were allowed discharges from the Army. Not long afterwards, some two hundred New Jersey soldiers set off for the State Capital at Trenton to demand compensation and reforms. They were surrounded. Two of their leaders were quickly executed by firing squad. Once, after Yorktown, a group of about 80 soldiers invaded Philadelphia, demanding pay, whereupon Congress adjourned and fled.

Washington's Army, come down from Boston in 1776 to engage the British in New York, first met its enemy on Long Island, was defeated, and retreated to Harlem. Washington suffered a second defeat on Manhattan Island and withdrew Northwards, crossed the Hudson River, and headed South until he arrived with his army in Pennsylvania. Getting the Americans to fight a major engagement was not easy.

Washington won striking minor engagements meanwhile. Meanly, on Christmas night, while the Hessians of Trenton were in a drunken stupor, Washington's force crossed from Pennsylvania and slew or took prisoner most of them. Later he won a sharp battle at Princeton, then had to retire in the face of superior numbers. But the British then also retired, to New York City. These engagements had an enormous morale value. Americans had shown themselves far less able to provide for an army than to celebrate victories vociferously. This trait continued for a long time.

The British Generals had an excellent but non-binding idea. If an army from Canada could journey Southward along Lake Champlain towards Albany and the Lower Hudson Valley, and if a second army could march up the Valley, and the twain should meet, they would defeat any minor opposition on the way and split the enemy between New England and points South. So, during the summer of 1777, General John Burgoyne's Army began trudging South.

Several small American forces ultimately under the overall command of Horatio Gates, with strong assists from Benedict Arnold and others, cleared his routes of potential irregular supporters and a small relief force of regulars, and fired upon his columns incessantly. He arrived at Saratoga, far short of his goal, turned this way and that, and settled down beleaguered. Sensing the kill, every day the American Army grew larger. Before long his situation was hopeless. He surrendered the 5,000 survivors of his original army of 10,000 men in October.

The news shocked and thrilled the world. The French were so confident now that the Americans were not a lame duck that a treaty of alliance was promptly drawn up and, with the ebullient Franklin in

attendance, France agreed to go to war against Great Britain in aid of the United States. The two events sealed the verdict of the Revolution: the United States would be independent.
The English should better have quit then.

Because General Sir William Howe fancied the idea of capturing the rebel Capital, the British Army of New York that should have gone to meet the Burgoyne expedition sailed South to the Chesapeake region and up the Bay and marched on toward Philadelphia, defeating an attempt by Washington to stop it at Brandywine.
The British captured the capital city without difficulty, and pondered what next to do.
America was so vast that there could be no thought of marching everywhere. Unless the Loyalists could take over and hold vast stretches without British army and naval help, the war would last indefinitely.

Another battle was lost by Washington at Germantown.
He was trying to pry his way back into Philadelphia.
Washington did not wish a guerrilla war.
He simply had not enough men and equipment to face the enemy's main body. This was probably just as well because whenever the major forces met one another in pitched battle, the British cannonading would be more ample and destructive to begin with, the brilliant scarlet formations more depressing, and then the British lines would hold and the American lines break. It may have been beneficial to the cause,
that many American soldiers operated on the axiom,
"discretion is the better part of valor", and
"he who fights and runs away will live to fight another day".

If Washington and most other American generals had won their heart's desire, they would have neatly lined up their men to fight against much better trained and equipped professionals - with potentially disastrous results. On the occasions when Washington was caught in the middle of a retreat - as at the Battle of Manhattan-Harlem, and the Battle of Monmouth, he would swear and curse at the retreating men (up to the rank of General) and beat them upon their heads with his sword to turn them back.

Nobody was more favored by him than the wily Prussian Baron von Steuben, who presented himself before Washington with a title and military rank that were both fraudulent, but with a letter from Franklin, and was appointed Inspector General and drillmaster, and who turned out the troops in neat close order drill after a while, and introduced a proper system of hierarchical relations into the confusion among the ranks. (He was a homosexual, who was said to have enjoyed the favors of Frederick the Great.) Washington's personal bodyguard troop was composed of Pennsylvania Germans, who were more docile and trustworthy than the rank and file generally.

With his expensive handsome wardrobe and other *accoutrement,* whose cost was reimbursed by the Continental Congress upon vouchers scrupulously tendered, with his dashing young subalterns, Marquis de Lafayette and Alexander Hamilton, with the aforesaid spit-and-polish household troop, Washington was a reassuring figure to the formal French, whose support was essential to victory.
They could let themselves believe in an America.

While the outlying reaches of the Anglo-American Empire stood for the Empire or at least within it without too much revolutionary agitation, they were sorely disturbed by the coming of Loyalists exiles, quadrupling the population of Canada, for instance, and flooding in upon the Floridas and the Caribbean island possessions. Naturally, Spanish, Dutch and French opposition forbade using their possessions for refuges.

In the course of the War, the Spanish captured East and West Florida with Mobile, Pensacola, and St. Augustine, Honduras, the Bahamas, and blocked British entry of the Mississippi River. The Dutch lost St. Eustatius Island, where the first American boat anywhere had received a national salute, and where an enormous traffic in war goods was taking place. Admiral Graves, the Briton who captured it, became rich in consequence.

The colonies, now States, could count on a certain hostility in the areas such as Ontario that received Loyalists, enduring long after

Americans of a later day, confident of their national virtue, assumed that anyone speaking English in the Americas was "just like them".

Virginia's royal Governor called the Loyalists to arms as soon as the Continental Congress acted to war against Britain. He was defeated but managed to burn down Norfolk. In North Carolina, the Highland Scot settlers, donees of land by the Crown, joined with Regulators, who, we recall, hated the Coast people who had frustrated their demands for representation, and attempted resistance to the rebel takeover, but were soon defeated by a Patriot contingent.
They had intended to join up with British regulars coming up under the leadership of Cornwallis and Clinton. The British resorted to Charleston, but were met with heavy and successful resistance to both army and navy units.

In 1778 heavy British forces landed near Savannah and with the help of Florida Loyalist irregulars captured Savannah from its small American garrison. They then marched up to Charleston, destroying and looting plantations and settlements on the way. They found the city ready to fight them and suffered through a heavy siege before they triumphed over the bottled-up American army of General Benjamin Lincoln. The surrender of about 5,500 men was comparable to the loss of the British at Saratoga three years earlier, but no one any longer could take the outcome of a given battle as a prognostication of the victor in the War.

Congress now appointed the Hero of Saratoga, General Horatio Gates, to command the army of the South. He moved from one disaster to another. He ventured to confront a section of Cornwallis' army at Camden, South Carolina and was trounced. His command did not stop retreating until it reached Hillsborough, North Carolina, 160 miles away over hill and dale.

Just when Cornwallis thought that he had pacified South Carolina, two of his lieutenants, not the nicest of men,

who had been leading an army of Loyalists
on a vengeful rampage of the back country, encountered
difficulties. An army of Patriot irregulars and populists,
that was composed, led, and manned in large part by
second generation Scots-Irish and North English Borderers,
descended upon them. One part of the army under Ferguson was
annihilated; prisoners of war were killed offhand.

Tarleton of the second part had his come-uppance
two months later after a new Rebel commander for the
Southern Theater, Nathanael Greene, had arrived.
Daniel Morgan, despatched to harass Cornwallis, was
attacked by Tarleton's force, and backed against the Broad River.
With nowhere to turn, his militia stood like rocks and inflicted
crippling losses upon the onrushing Loyalists and British.

Upon the next round, Greene's army, pursued by Cornwallis, was
made to stand and fight a pitched battle at Guilford's Courthouse: here
Greene posted his militia in the front rank and ask them only to fire
three shots before withdrawing. As they dodged off,
the British rushed in and were subjected to heavy fire from their flanks.
Then Greene broke contact, and Cornwallis departed for reinforcements
and supplies. Greene marched up and down,
losing more than winning, yet holding his army,
and inflicting painful damage upon the enemy.

But, meanwhile, Cornwallis had decided that Virginia would be a
profitable arena, and there was joined by General Benedict Arnold.
Arnold was now a British commander, after having been a brilliant
American officer and Commander at West Point. (In the most famous
episode of treason of a war burgeoning with treasonable acts, he had
tried to sell out West Point to the British; the capture of an
intermediary disclosed the plot and he had fled.)

Cornwallis, feeling a need for continuous support from abroad,
chose Yorktown on the Chesapeake as a fortifiable location
where he might receive the expected English fleet.

Meanwhile, far to the North, Rochambeau,
relieved from a British naval blockade, marched his

6,000 hitherto largely inactive French
troops Southward to join Washington's force
for an attack upon New York City.
But before they launched their attack, word came from the West Indies
to leave a force at New York to dissemble a siege, and
hurry their major forces South to Virginia to
unite with De Grasse and converge upon Cornwallis.

On August 30 De Grasse landed his 3,000
soldiers in support of Marquis de LaFayette's small army,
which had been skirting around Cornwallis' force.
On September 5, Admiral Graves and the Royal Navy appeared, and
the next day, De Grasse gave battle. Graves withdrew, leaving
command of the sea approaches to the French, and sailed to New
York to repair his damaged ships. Cornwallis had nowhere to go and
prepared for siege. De Grasse sent ships up Chesapeake Bay to ferry
the armies of Washington and Rochambeau to the Yorktown area, and
now there were a total of 16,000 men besieging the British army of 8,000.
This was not an impossible disparity to give battle, but Cornwallis held
off. When a French force captured a major redoubt, and a second task
force under Alexander Hamilton, Washington's most trusted staff
officer, captured a second redoubt, Cornwallis thought
that he must sooner or later admit defeat.
So, only eighteen days after the siege began,
on October 17, 1781, he gave up.

He asked to surrender to the French, with some reason, but the French
graciously (or meanly, depending upon your point of view)
insisted that Washington do the honors. When Cornwallis
pleaded that he was too ill to appear for the ceremony, Washington
turned over the task to another as well.
His mortification eased by time,
Cornwallis went on to become Governor of India, where he
established a fine record for reform of the administration of
that great civilization.

Not much combat ensued thereafter.

Acts of madness and vengeance would continue for some time. Many prisoners of war had yet to be brutalized, to take sick, to die.

Painstaking research has offered us some conclusions on the casualties of the septuple war. Before citing and analyzing them, we figure that they were insignificant in relation to the increase in the American population that was occurring. Like women of North Vietnam and Viet Cong, two centuries later, living amidst terrible loss of life and destruction, women of Revolutionary America were far out-breeding the killing rate of their enemies. During the 20-year Crisis and War, the population of the thirteen colonies and States grew from about 1.7 millions to about 3 millions, by nearly two-thirds. Obviously the War was not occupying all of people's energies nor forbidding immigrants. Nor was there any shortage of manpower for the armies and navies.

In a total of 1331 military engagements and 218 naval engagements of the Revolution of which there is record, a total of 7,174 Patriots were killed, 8,241 wounded, and 18,572 captured. An unknown but large number deserted. Unromantic death came not only to many of those reported killed, but also to 8,500 of those taken prisoner, and to 10,000 more who died of disease in their own American camps. In addition to the 5,674 dead, many deaths occurred aboard the hundreds of privateers which prowled the seas for eight years. There were uncounted murders all over the country, and many deaths from hardship of those in flight or deprived of sustenance. Too, a large but unreported number of Loyalists were killed in battle; moreover, their camp death rate and prison death rate were as bad as the Patriots' rates.

Hence, on the one hand, the casualties appear unimpressive; probably four million Americans lived during this period, which would give us 1% dying as a result of the War. (In the five years of World War II, the Soviet Union lost 12% of its immense population.) On the other hand, once a person was touched by the War, survival without death or injury was very much less likely. If one considers solely the Patriot deaths in relation to the estimated 200,000 men who served at one time or another, the resulting 12.5% rate is typical of eighteenth century warfare. (One does not know how to fit in the 100,000 crewmen of the privateers.)

Records were not kept for German or Royalist casualties by the British army. Since the British maintained larger forces under arms than the Patriots generally, their casualties may have been higher, and their casualty rate perhaps would be nearer 15%. Indian casualties were heavy in relation to the numbers engaged, often because Americans took no prisoners.

Nor for the people "unengaged" was it a comfortable war. Most things were in short supply, even those such as furnishings that had for a few years been coming on the market. Many soldiers, all too many, had wives and children. Often these became camp followers, along with others whose fathers or husbands were not soldiers. None had adequate means. They cared for the men and earned money by helping others without women. Philadelphia and other places boasting of "brotherly love" expelled the women and children of men who were fighting with the British enemy. At Wilmington, the British evicted 21 patriot women with their children. When the town was retaken, the same order was given to Tory women, but a petition of Patriot wives objected on grounds that the women had not been ones who had expelled them earlier.

Women moved around a lot, and were often suspected of conveying intelligence. In 1780 in Albany County, a Board for Detecting and Defeating Conspiracies gathered cases against 32 women and over 400 men.

The two most famous women of the Revolution, she who manned a cannon, Barbara (Hauer) Fritchie, and she who conveyed intelligence, Molly (Maria Ludwig) Pitcher, were German-Americans. Elizabeth Burgin of New York managed the smuggling of 200 American prisoners out of New York; her husband died in patriotic service; a bounty was placed on her head; she was reduced to poverty afterwards and could obtain no help. In 1779 the women of Philadelphia solicited from door to door and collected $300,000 in paper currency. They wanted to give every soldier several dollars to use as he wished. Washington objected that they would spend it on liquor, and would lose their respect for the paper money. Finally they produced 2200 linen shirts for the soldiers.

When he received the news from Yorktown late in 1683, Lord North, Prime Minister, realized the game was up and resigned. Four months after Yorktown, the House of Commons voted to end the war, and a peace-making ministry of pro-Americans was sworn in. Now the English tried for a separate peace with the Americans in order to divide them from the French. This succeeded in part, because the general treaty was so long in coming.

The Spanish wanted Gibraltar back: but the British position was: anything else, yes, Gibraltar no. The Americans had promised the French not to make a separate peace; the French had promised the Spanish not to make a separate peace. Finally Spain was temporarily at least appeased by getting back the Floridas instead of Gibralter. That this meant another wrenching move for the many Royalists who had taken refuge in Florida disturbed the British negotiators and King not a little - but not a lot. Involved Indian nations were not party to the Treaty. They were by now too weak and divided to demand a voice.

The American negotiators, Benjamin Franklin, Henry Laurens (freed from the Tower of London where he had landed after being captured at sea), and John Jay particularly, suspected that the French, in their efforts at compromising the parties, might give away America's western lands to the Spanish. Jay's suspicion was probably not justified. The French Minister Vergennes was angry with the Americans' failure to stick to their treaty, but the Americans excused themselves, saying that they wanted to get their terms down on paper, and the treaty would not be finally effective until the French and British came to their own final accord.

Not until September 3, 1783, was the Treaty of Paris finally signed.

Great Britain recognized the independence of the United States of America. The whole of the land West to the Mississippi was conceded to the United States. Distortions of all boundaries marked the best maps - such as the Mitchell Map - of the day. The United States agreed to recommend to the States that they turn back to the Loyalists confiscated property, and to place no legal obstacles in the way of British merchants trying to collect on debts owed them at the start of the Revolution. (Little was done on either score.) The United States might be quite pleased with the Treaty of Paris.

That the Revolution was a social war is agreed by experts but conveys little meaning to the average American. Possibly this occurs because the disgusting aspects of the War are rarely exposed to public view or in schoolbooks. I mentioned in the last chapter that in the preliminaries of the war there were frequent episodes of mob violence and that gangsterism was common throughout the colonies. Nor need we be reminded that the governors, officials, and half the rich and cultured families of thirteen autonomous colonies did not abandon their precious possessions and friends and neighbors and flee because they lost a pacific election. They were terrorized by a great many incidents of destruction of property, of threats, of beatings, of the agony and ignominy of tar-and-featherings, of shots in the night, of menacing graffiti, and they were expecting an intensification of all of this, including jailing in loathsome places without any of the rights of Englishmen that the Patriots were vaunting.

Many of the ruffians and vigilantes of these days were youths and boys, who were being born and growing up in the twenty years of the Revolutionary cycle. The baby boom was unending, even if the flow of immigrants was temporarily diminished. A great many of the legions of young felt that they were beset by their elders. Frequent declarations went to reveal that this was a war against patriarchy, against the father-figure of the King, against the old order of the world, against the repression of the disadvantaged younger generation in favor of the old, against the highly privileged elders.

The printed and oral propaganda that had deluged the young from birth, stressing the worth and sanctity of age, was heard now as so much blather. The young fought the war. Early demands for a younger voting age, for abolition of the laws of primogeniture that gave all property to the eldest son, and for more respect and power in general, increased as the war went on.
The young formed a larger proportion of the population.
The egalitarian manners of the Americans,
noted everywhere by everybody,
were not a simple function of the political philosophy
of Paine and Jefferson, but were engendered by the
preponderance of young of free and equal, if low, status.

Withal, there was a loss of the higher culture in America.
Many of the cleverest Bostonians were forced to depart.
The colleges were weakened. So too with the other colonies.
The youth movement of those times had too little
background in the arts and sciences to search out and
work at a new and promising culture .

(Nor did the youth movement, nearly two centuries later, do much better).

"The Intolerable Acts" incited the First Continental Congress. This vicious British cartoon from *The London Magazine*, 1774, was promptly copied and published by Paul Revere in Boston.

Chapter Nineteen

Continental Congress and Confederation

As if to model itself upon its people and territory, the Revolutionary and Confederation government was fly-by-night. Before it moved to Washington, D.C. on November 17, 1800 at the beginning of the second session of the Sixth Congress of the United States, the all-American government's Capital paused at eight different towns: Philadelphia in two places, Carpenter's Hall and the State House, 1774-6; Baltimore, Henry Fite's House, 1776-7; the Philadelphia State

House again, 1777; the Lancaster (Pa.) Court House for one day in 1777; the York (Pa.) Court House, 1777-8; Philadelphia first at College Hall and then the State House, 1778-83; Princeton (N.J.) at Prospect House and Nassau Hall, 1783; Annapolis (Md.)at the State House, Trenton (N.J.) at the French Arms Tavern, 1784; New York City, at the City Hall and then Fraunces' Tavern, 1785-89; and, finally, under the Federal Constitution, New York City 1789-90 and Philadelphia, 1790-1800.

The USA preserved its secularity by never meeting in a church, but found taverns compatible with the affairs of state.

The members of these first Congresses may have made them the best in American history. Processes of government between 1774 and 1789 were so varied and seemingly transient that they have been passed over or misunderstood. Yet these fifteen years introduced much of the subject-matter and important structures and precedents of subsequent times. For example, the debates over representation that followed the Declaration of Independence addressed the issue of State representation in the Congress, rehearsing the arguments for equality of States, of apportioning the vote according to population numbers, or relative to a State's riches.

The Continental government operated between 1775 and 1781 by means of a Congress of thirteen independent States. It could be called government by mutual State nudging. It could also be called government by consensus, since very little could be done without the consent of all the States. President of the Congress of the "United States of America" was the top executive of the whole - there were sixteen Presidents in the 15 years - with as many powers as he could coax out of the thirteen States. To achieve specific objects such as to feed the Army, negotiate with France, or carry the mails, Committees were formed, which either carried on their business themselves or appointed others to do so.

The accomplishments of government in this period were extraordinary. Were it not for the fact that its actions so often had to contradict its *raison d'etre*, it would no doubt have written more brilliant pages of history. That is, in order to win the Revolutionary

War, the Continental Congress and its successor after 1781, the Congress under the Articles of Confederation, were compelled to commit some of the very "crimes" that the colonies had named as the reasons for demanding independence.

Nor do I refer alone to the corruption rife during these years and the glaring inequalities of all values between the high and low levels of the people. I refer also to the legal complaints, that the rights of citizens of the USA were practically whatever the military and the States would allow them, and that laws and rules of the central government were commonly observed in their breach rather than their enforcement. And that, no sooner had the Revolutionary nation been born than it began, because it was compelled by circumstances, to commit the kinds of offenses that were listed as the causes of rebellion against England in the Declaration of Independence.

All officers of the government were named by delegates named by State legislatures who were elected by a minority of the people. They had to get all the States together to levy compulsory charges and taxes. They had to set prices on basic necessities. They had to devise a number of penalties and punishments for disobedience to the laws and rules that they set forth. They maintained an army during the War and afterwards. Changes in manners and culture possibly accounted for most of the perceived improvements achieved by the Revolution; the new Americans were governed, not in the Congresses, but in their States by their own kind. Still, the pulling and tugging of the Congress on numerous matters kept the individual States from *"going to Hell in their own way"*.

When the Second Continental Congress met in 1775, it acknowledged and provided for hostilities, and urged the States to reconsider and rewrite their constitutions in keeping with the objectives of the Independence movement. The States did so. The main results were several.

Although they paid lip-service to the separation of powers and checks and balances among the Executive, Legislative, and Judicial branches, the Revolutionary State governments headed straight for legislative supremacy. The executive was weak. In Pennsylvania, it was a plural council of thirteen members. Elsewhere it was a Governor and council (cabinet). The Governor was elective by the qualified voters in five Northern States including Massachusetts and New Jersey. Elsewhere, he was elected by the State legislature. Mostly his council was also appointed by the legislature.

He was concerned largely with "execution of the laws", commanding the militia, and pardoning pardonable convicts. His veto of legislative action all but disappeared. He was mostly elected for only a year, and in the South he could not run again for the office. He might appoint employees of the government only with the consent of his council or the legislature. One notes the heavy trend toward constructing a direct democracy, but there was a ways to go - for example, in broadening the electorate.

Only in Pennsylvania and Georgia was the legislature single-chambered. Otherwise it was bicameral. The Pennsylvania experiment with a single chamber and a plural executive should have had a longer experience so that its lessons might be learned, but it was one of the victims of the democratic principle of "reduction to the most common denominator" that makes experiment in government practically impossible - save by serendipity, i.e. accident. The bicameral assembly imitated the colonial form where the Governor's council had been a legislative body akin to the House of Lords in England, he the Governor imitating the King.

Now this upper house became elective, but usually with a more limited electorate than the lower house and with longer terms of office. In the lower house, on the supposition that short terms discouraged the onslaught of despotism and also allowed the instruction of members frequently by the voters, annual elections were ordinary:
"where annual elections end, tyranny begins" -
how nice a slogan!

These lower houses exercised practically all the formal powers of the State government. They alone could initiate bills to raise and spend money; thus did the "People" finally come to control the purse strings. They often appointed even minor officers of the State.

They were elected by a variety of means of balloting, usually not secret, by the plurality quota (the winner is the one who gets the most votes, not necessarily the majority, should more than two men be running). The suffrage was confined to a fairly numerous group of White males, making the total electorate a minor fraction of the population. Voting was voluntary, and often participation was low.

The judiciary was hardly the imposing institution of today. Its first instance was the justice of the peace. Then came an appeal court. Judges were sometimes gubernatorial appointees, sometimes legislative. They applied an Americanized version of the English common law and such laws as the legislature of the State passed. There was as of yet no national or confederational law. There would not be until the federal judiciary was set up by the Constitution. This meant that in practically all cases, a conflict between two states or parties of different states would be handled
by a court in the state where it occurred, or
by an agreement between the two states, or
by Congress under the Articles.

The concept of "judicial review", whereby a court can fault a state law or action for violating its own constitution, was yet unborn. Each State, however, carried a Bill of Rights or its equivalent in its Constitution. Due process of law was guaranteed in governmental actions taken against persons and their property. Complaints at abuses of rights, familiar under British rule, were taken care of explicitly.

I have mentioned some of the achievements of the Continental Congress. It was composed of representatives of the more prosperous seaboard sections of the population, selected by the State legislatures. A number of them were freethinkers, non-religious freemasons, or their sympathizers. They feared "the people", meaning the

assemblages, ruffians, and earnest mechanics who appeared in
threatening gangs on occasion, but they were one of the most stable
and competent revolutionary assemblages of modern times.

They did not hire counter-gangs, once the Revolution was underway,
or try to centralize power by violence,
even though more central power was needed to run the War properly.
The State governments were another matter.
They were often instigators of the persecution of Loyalists by
legal and illegal means.

The Congress operated from the beginning by appointing Committees
such as drafted and came back conveying the Declaration of
Independence, and later with the Articles of Confederation.
Other Committees were executive in nature,
administering functions, such as finance.
Still others acted as negotiators with individual States.

After the British had seized Philadelphia and Congress reassembled at
York, its members felt an urgent need to go about preparing for a true
confederation. The great victory at Saratoga enthused them and they
knew that they must put up a solid front to the French to win an
alliance. It could not be thirteen sovereign states presenting themselves
for recognition; it had to be a United States of America based on the
legitimate authority of a constitution.

For fifteen months the Congress had on hand a draft
that it had authorized John Dickinson to prepare;
now, in November 1777, it adopted one change and
recommended immediate ratification by the States.
The one change was proposed by Thomas Burke of North Carolina,
newly arrived: it affirmed that the States were sovereign
and that the Confederation could exercise only
those powers that were expressly delegated to it.

The Articles were ratified by all the States except Maryland, which
insisted as a preliminary to her approval of the document that the
States should turn over control of the lands of the West to the new
Confederation. The obstacle was overcome early in 1781 when
Maryland asked for the protection of the French fleet

against British marauders and was told by Admiral De Grasse
that the State had better sign the Articles of Confederation
and come back to him later on the matter. Here
was one more French contribution to the edifice of America.

The Articles called the new government "a perpetual union",
established by the States, not the People.
Its single and supreme organ was the Congress.
It consisted of delegations from each State,
numbering from two to seven members depending upon population.
A member served an annual term but could not be designated
by his legislature more than three years out of every six.
His salary was to be paid by his State.
In voting on Congressional issues, each State had one vote,
which was the majority of the vote of its delegation.
Were the delegation to be tied, its vote would be null.
Passage of a law required approval by nine States.

From 1775 onwards, the Congress exercised
certain powers that had been those of the British Imperial government.
These were important, if not new, powers of the central government
and the States were used to not exercising them.
They included the conduct of foreign relations -
comprising diplomacy, declarations of war, negotiations for peace,
and the exchange of ambassadors. A single unified system of
Admiralty Courts to adjudicate cases arising out of
sea-borne commerce and vessels at sea had
also to be provided.

Further, the Congress was designated to establish standards of
weights, measures, and coinage. It might borrow money. It could
create a postal service. And it managed the armed forces of the united
colonies. All of these powers were exercised.
They proved to be significant.

The performance of assigned tasks was constrained, however,
beyond the point of efficacy and efficiency.

The Congress had no power to levy taxes,
regulate commerce internally or externally, or issue money.
It could not insure promises to foreign nations about commerce,
nor guarantee any State's currency,
nor truly represent the States in many areas
where foreign nations demanded responsibility.
It could not prevent a State from organizing a navy and
taking to the Seven Seas. It carried little weight
with foreign governments therefore, and, lacking an
impressive central officer, it had no one to represent it
vigorously in a world much impressed by monarchs.

The absence of an executive branch meant that the Congress would
continue to operate by means of the committee system.
Schoolchildren hear that this was fatal to good government,
yet are told - or should be told - that the later Congress
under the Constitution came to operate through
a small oligarchy of Committees and Committee Chairman,
some of whom within their own sphere became
more powerful than the President.

So it is possible that with the passage of time,
the Confederation Congress would have developed a
stable and efficient means of governing executive offices
by committees, and using a hierarchy of committees
to allow conflicts and problems of integration to rise to
the top hierarchy of committees for resolution, as indeed came to be
the situation in the Constitutional Congress, where an exceedingly
sophisticated system of bringing together and deciding the
parts of complicated questions evolved.

We should also note that the Revolutionary and Confederation
government was politically proto-Federalist, that is, run by a
national network of financial, media, social and political leaders.
Therefore policies might be developed and executed
with this informal government pressing upon
the reluctant formal government.

The governments did not slump fatally despite the separatist, private, selfish and often corrupt management of public affairs. A populist government, lacking experience, membership, and rule by an informal power network, would have gone berserk under the circumstances and likely end up in Jacobinism, purges, and Bonapartism. For example, Roger Morris, directing the Office of Finance (and his private business affairs, largely centered in Philadelphia), operated cavalierly. Highly energetic in his first years, less so before retiring a decade later, the "Financier of the Revolution" achieved marvels of money-scraping, mixing, plastering, laundering, and painting. He was avant-garde in his appreciation of social statistics, and prepared a set of proposals for obtaining by personal interviews nationwide a detailed social and economic report on how people lived and worked; action on the concept waited for two centuries. When the War ended, he wanted to fund debts of Confederation and States through the central government, but failed (and this would be done by Hamilton and company later). Still, surprisingly he left office on a balanced budget.

At one point, in 1784, facing a Dutch bill of exchange which could not be paid and which, if tendered, would have exposed America's deplorable financial condition, he urged the even then disreputable technique of "kiting". That is, with the help of John Adams and Benjamin Franklin in Europe, he would arrange the issuance of bad government cheques (notes) that would hopefully be made good by other bad checks, betting on collecting the necessary cash before the final check was submitted for payment. But before the conspirators carried out this trick to parry the Dutch threat, John Adams was able to obtain a straight short-term loan, and soon enough the cash and commodities came in to pay off the obligation.

The lack of a potent executive power was probably not the reason for the major troubles of the two confederational governments. Most of their actions were severely constrained by the state legislatures. And they were born in the midst of war. But, comparing what was done on their initiative with what was done by the first Congresses of the United States under the Constitution, it is not at all apparent that the country was governed badly in the first instance.

The absence of a judiciary is notable. But this, too, need not have become a matter of great concern. Granted there would be a confederational law developing. Still, it has been always a principle of sophisticated as well as crude legal systems that, *"Given a case, a law can be found to apply to its adjudication".* Of both Roman and English common law systems this is so. As for the lack of a Bill of Rights in the Articles, certain protections were actually afforded and others were guaranteed in the constitutions of the State governments.

While running the war, making peace, and laying the foundations for a new constitutional framework, the Confederation Congress collected all the lands of the West into a territorial form of government and made provisions for them to become States in time. It passed the Northwest Ordinance of 1787 (following earlier partial versions of 1784 and 1785) that in one grand simple formula provided land grants for setting up public schools and colleges throughout the Northwest. This put the new Territories well ahead of the old States in support of education.

The same Northwest Ordinance showed that the Congress was perfectly willing and eager to have new States join the Union. It divided the new frontier lands into Territories, and declared that they would be governed by an elective legislature and a governor appointed by the Congress. When any one of them had achieved a population of 60,000 it could apply for admission to the Union as a State, presenting a Constitution that it had drafted for the approval of Congress.

The Confederation government wasn't all benevolence.
The Articles, so stingy on powers for the government,
harshly commanded that any runaway servants be returned
to their owners in their home State.
There was to be no refuge for the White slaves.
And, of course, not for the Black.

A post-war depression occurred, and in 1785-86, farmers were
generally in bad straits. In Massachusetts many thousands of debtor
suits were filed in the courts. Conventions of debtors were held,
petitions were sent to the legislature, to no avail.
The courts ground on, crushing one family after another.

Now Daniel Shays came to the fore, a war veteran. He and his
comrades mobilized thousands of farmers and closed the courts of
Western Massachusetts. Alarm bells rang all over America. The
Confederation government was appealed to but, without troops
to send, was helpless. As it turned out, the Massachusetts militia
was more than adequate for the job of breaking up the
insurrectionary force, killing several rebels, sending
Shays fleeing across the State line.

But the episode was turned into a conservative's horror story, and
those who wanted a stronger national government replayed the story
incessantly, to indicate what would happen everywhere unless there
were a strong government to keep debtors going through the courts
like sheep through the slaughter pen. Thus Shay's Rebellion.

The main problem of the Confederation did not lay with the
requirement of a top-heavy majority to pass legislation. Given the
diversity of states and their interests and the prevalence of a potent
regionalism, it was inevitable that the government could move slowly
or not at all in certain areas. And, in fact, it moved as slowly in the
decades to come, with only majorities of a bicameral legislature to
satisfy. The single-organ, neatly trimmed-down government could

have gone on indefinitely and competently. The problem was not one
of structure. It was already inventing forms of policy deliberation and
administration to take care of its needs.

What was lacking were the several powers which, as mentioned
above, were deliberately withheld from it -
power to levy and collect and spend tax monies,
power to regulate interstate and foreign commerce, and
exclusive power to issue paper money as legal tender -
these and other powers that could
not be dreamed of at the time.

But even these could have been provided,
if amendments to Constitution could have been by a majority,
or a two-thirds vote of the State legislatures. For instance,
all States but Rhode Island at one point favored an amendment
to allow the Congress to levy a tariff, and it therefore failed.
Then, when Rhode Island acceded to the idea,
New York State vetoed it.
Too, we shall see that precisely these powers were not
so clearly stipulated in the Constitution to come.
Whereupon it did require a dubious reach-out for power
by the Supreme Court, Congress, and the President
at different times to add
new powers to the federal government.

In the end, we begin to wonder whether the principle
of amendment by unanimity was not the problem -
but only because so many kinds of "ordinary" legislation
were needed and these would require unanimity.
It isn't as if the Constitution-to-be was easy to amend.
Indeed, the huge powers of the federal government
today in regard to taxes, commerce, and currency
were not obtained by constitutional amendment,
but through a stretching of the Constitution and by
ignoring the very language that was interposed to restrict it,
and before it the Congress of the Confederation,
insisting that only the powers expressly delegated be employed -
for this was the same language to be used in the
Tenth Amendment to the Federal Constitution as part of

the Bill of Rights, an amendment like the others whose immediate
passage was a condition of acceptance of the
main body of the Constitution.

We also wonder whether the real change
from Confederation to Federation would not occur
because of something quite apart from all issues
of this or that power and right.
Perhaps the real power that made the country
into a federal republic under the Constitution. and
later into a centralized federal republic was
the creation of the Presidency.
People and state governments under the Confederation
could not feel that they were dealing with
a "True Central Government",
for, where was the king? where was the head?
the commander-in-chief?

Both in this period and in the next,
the glamor of the President,
especially of General George Washington,
was effective in making nationalists of the American people
and in paving the way for the acceptance of powers
residing in and exercised by the central government.
In a way, then, there was too much of the Enlightenment
and the Radical in the Confederation structure,
not enough of the Primitive and Monarchical.
The marriage of the Father of His Country
with the Constitutional institution breathed life into the structure.
One need only look at the French Revolutionary process
to see that the stage of radical Jacobin collective leadership
descended into Bonapartism, Emperor Napoleon I.
The more modest, but in the end just as pompous,
American solution allowed a fairly smooth transition of
constitutional forms in the critical period under discussion here.

Informal moments of the Constitutional Convention

Chapter Twenty

The Framers

"Some men" wrote Jefferson in a letter,
"look at constitutions with sanctimonious reverence,
& deem them like the ark of the covenant,
too sacred to be touched.
They ascribe to the men of the preceding age a
wisdom more than human, and
suppose what they did to be beyond amendment".

He could say this all the more nicely since he had been

enjoying the fleshpots of Paris and the *"gay face of nature"* in the
countryside thereabouts with the lovely Madame Marie Cosway at a
time when the Constitution was being drafted.

The sacred documents of the American creed became the
Declaration of Independence of 1776, the
Constitution of 1789, with its
Bill of Rights (Amendments I to X).
The documents are kept in a 55-ton bombproof vault and
can be viewed only through bullet-proof
ultra-violet-filtered glass. Elaborate examinations by
microscope are conducted every several years to
see how many iotas of ink have blanched.

When the most powerful and rich, and perhaps culturally
most productive people in the world
worships a creation document,
just like the most "primitive" of peoples, and refers all manner of
good and glory to the Framers and their
Constitution, a historian of the people may properly
ask why. Have other peoples been unlucky?
Incompetent? Unworthy?

Two centuries of scientific progress have occurred since the
Constitution was ratified by the States in 1789 and the
first elections took place under its provisions.
In all this time in all the world, no document,
no movement, no plan, no philosophy, and certainly no
constitution has shown itself to be rational and correct in its
expectations of its future. We should be suspicious
therefore of claims that the American Constitution
arose to quite another level of achievement.

Our job here is to bring into focus and
interpret the tribal dreamtime.

The Constitution was not perfect for its day,
it was not highly original,
it was not popular,

not much was expected of it,
it acquired ten immediate amendments
(out of 200 proposed)
as the price of ratification,
it lacked foresight of several great developments of history,
and it collapsed into a frightful Civil War within
two political generations.

Patched up and carried on the barrels of guns,
it became an offensive weapon not of the oppressed
but of an oligarchy of economic power.
Finally it allowed just about everything that "needed" to be
done by whoever could put through a winning combination of
the political forces of the nation.

In the years after World War II it was used as a
verbal instrument to humiliate professors into taking oaths.
Eschewing heroics, a Professor of Constitutional
Law at Harvard explained that he had no objection to
swearing his support for the Constitution,
inasmuch as it had supported him for many years.

The Constitution was elegantly drafted by a man who
hated the people. Some of the greatest Revolutionary
leaders rejected the document. It was not democratic.
It preserved and protected slavery.
Its amendment became so difficult, after the first
special burst of eleven amendments, that the
Constitution changed mostly by slippages and distortions of its
language, by hypocrisy,
by *coups d'etat* of courts and executives,
by economic disaster, and by war.

Amendments to push up a date have been ratified quickly;
amendments to declare women equal in rights to
men have lingered for decades and failed.
Every institution that it provided for is today
almost unrecognizable in its base, powers, and functions.
Many of its provisions are defunct;
if they are not unused, they are not employed

as intended but in devious ways.
Its most beautiful and humane passage was in the very process of
ratification given conveniently the name of "Preemble",
and declared to be legally inoperative., until a judicial change
of mind two hundred years later.

Nonetheless it is to the Preamble that one must go to begin an
understanding of the role and therefore the glory and prestige of the
Constitution. For there we read that
"WE THE PEOPLE of the United States,
in order to form a more perfect union, establish justice,
insure domestic tranquillity, provide for the common defense,
promote the general welfare, and secure the blessings of liberty
to ourselves and our posterity,
do ordain and establish this
Constitution for the United States of America".

What is said in this passage is that the People,
not God, not a Monarch or Dictator,
not a Class of Society, not Nature, nor the Bible,
nor Right Reason, nor These Contracting Parties of Interest-
the People,
containing within themselves the force and legitimacy
of all these foregoing powers,
here ordain and establish how they shall rule themselves.
No sooner had this magnificent statement of the
People been expressed, when the Constitution
proceeded to limit the People.

This was inevitable, for the People does not exist,
never has existed, and never will exist,
except in a statistical sense, if one wishes to
count live bodies - and, most importantly, as a delusion
that lets a normal person feel united with a massive identity, and
that guides his behavior as if this collective identity were
real and cognitive. As soon as one goes beyond
mere enumeration - a meaningless exercise in itself -

one divides the people, and as soon as that happens,
one is in the realm of stresses and strains,
of differences of treatment, of restraints and freedoms.

Since the People as such does not exist,
we must regard the awe, deference, love, and pride
with which the Constitution is viewed and worshiped in
America as precisely the same primitive regard that
would be granted to any other form of legitimate authority -
divinity, reason, a charismatic leader,
a legendary law, a traditional monarch or elite.
Most people require that they be ruled, psychically and
more or less materially, by an awesome power.

What is to be made of the fact that Authority for the
Constitution was a mythical "people"? But all such
legitimating authorities might be called mythical.
Those who believed in the myth would behave more
enthusiastically in regard to whatever was tied to and
prescribed in the name of the myth. Moses claimed that his
tablets of the Law were dictated to him by Yahweh;
those who scorned his announced authority and
worshiped the Golden Calf, Moses massacred.
Early Puritans of Massachusetts and Connecticut
also believed that God guided their covenant-composition and
constitution-drafting.

The republican Romans, closer to the deist American
Framers, used as their legitimating
authority the double myth of *SPQR*
(*Senatus Populusque Romanus* -
the Senate and the Roman People). The English people were
expected to believe in the traditional legitimacy as
well as the godly unction implicated in the
Divine Right of King James I of the United Kingdom.
So with the kings of France.

At this point in history, "the People" was in ascendency and the
authors of the Constitution, its Framers, knew that no
considerable objection would be heard if they put everything they were

empowering on the backs of the People. Furthermore, they had no alternative. They were already in the historical age of democracy, when no antique symbol could be brought forward for any new government, at least not in any socially, religiously and economically advanced nation.

Although the Constitution became a primeval creation dreamtime myth, it was also a creature of an age of rationalism, the Enlightenment, and it carries the intrinsic logic of an applied scientific creation. It proceeds: In order to do this, we must do thus: whence instruments, powers, restraints, demands, etc. The Constitutional State - the ideas of a rule of law, and the devising of an ideal structure attracting habitual conformity in all governing procedures - is a form of applied science. The premise of an authoritative legitimacy - the People - is a geometrical contrivance, to be followed by applications of the premise and its needs to political reality. This applied science conforms to the Enlightenment ideology, and to basically similar constitutional forms that were also generating in France.

Several of the influential supporters of the Constitution - Hamilton, Madison, Franklin, used quantitative metaphors of the science of the day. They thought of balance and equilibrium as in the lately developed field of mechanics. They counted people and divided them into numbers for this or that purpose - a census, representation, votes in the legislatures. There was a tendency to make human operations in politics exact. And to make of people numbers that can be manipulated in different combinations for political reasons.

And the concept that they had of society as a congeries of groups was not only an advance in scientific sociology, but also effective in prescribing for such a society.

The Framers did achieve a number of rational controls, because their theory - that society was composed of competing groups, and that the economic factor was important in the settlement of human conflicts - was justified by the events of the time in Western Europe and by the tsunamis moving out upon the other continents from Europe. This interest group theory of government, the best in the history of political philosophy until then, occurred in Madison's *Federalist* paper number 10.

The Framers were not thinking in terms of evolution, which would come heavily into science and politics a century later. Nor in religious terms. And the question might be raised, whether in avoiding religious contamination, they did not evict morals, throwing out the baby with the bath water. They did not think consciously and seriously of the value of those human beings, in the vast majority, whom their constitutional prescriptions would govern.

They were blandly, calmly, easily in favor of a certain elite portion of the population, "people of the better sort", whose game of free and assisted commerce they wished to be played, and whose arena they wished to smooth and prepare for action, and whose rules they thought they might refine; they thought their main function might be to get rid of various old physiocratic and mercantilist ways of messing up the game by statist rules.

They pondered the contrivances that the free enterprise class would find handy: a modern unified system of weights and measures, of coinage, of copyrights and patents for protecting advances in ideas and inventions. And they wanted to prevent any hooliganism that would come from the crowd if it were not guarded against by such devices as a standing army, a guarantee to the States of a republican form of government, and a right to interfere anywhere in order to protect federal law and authorities.

There was not a large confidence around the country
regarding efforts to bring about a closer union.
Pessimism persisted to the very end of the operation,
especially from the change-weary "inside dopesters" of the country.
Washington gave the Constitution twenty years
on the outside. Madison also thought that his
baby wouldn't breathe for long.

Endorsement of the Convention by the Congress of the Articles
followed two conferences previously held and aborted, and from the
failure of various commercial meetings. Madison's
resolution in the Virginia legislature came out of the
Committee on Commerce and urged all states to send
commissioners to Philadelphia : *"to provide
effectually for the commercial interests of the United States"*.
Congress endorsed the Convention and in a resolution of
February 21, 1787 limited its
scope to *"the sole and express purpose of revising the
Articles of Confederation"*. Was it worried about rumors of a
forthcoming newly constituted government?
Or was Congress attempting to avoid irrelevancy?
Art. 13 of the Articles required that any amendment be
"afterwards confirmed by the legislatures of every state".
This was evaded. An unusual majority was provided instead,
so that nine states would have been enough
(not counting Vermont, that came in just then)
but actually all approved - only six without
reservations demanding or requesting amendments.

Records of the Convention are unsatisfying. Only sly
Madison's notes tell us much of what transpired, and
these were not available to the public for another political
generation, after all of the participants
had passed from the scene.
So they could not be contradicted by eyewitnesses.
The secrecy of the proceedings was hardly calculated to set

an example for a democracy. It is improper to excuse the men by
saying that it was *"the way things were done in those days"*.
They knew very well that what they were doing
had to be kept under wraps, and released as a
timed capsule under the right auspices.

Framers, Founding Fathers, Authors -
they have been called, nor were these called so
at the time but more properly members of the
Convention at Philadelphia, which,
we remind ourselves, was not supposed to
compose a new constitution but to strengthen the old.
The Framers were formally the seventy-four men
selected by the legislatures, which were operating under
plurality procedures on the basis of small, male,
Caucasian electorates. Only 55 reported in
(of which 31 were lawyers, not much different from the
25 lawyers among 56 signers of the Declaration of Independence).
An average of 30 attended the proceedings,
18 were vigorous participants in the convention processes,
and 40 finally signed (including
Secretary Jackson who was a delegate - who took bad notes),
but BARELY A DOZEN - IF THAT MANY - ORGANIZED AND RAN THE SHOW.
A typical elite phenomenon:
from 4,000,000 people, one in twenty electors,
to 1,000 legislators of the 13 States,
to 74 nominees, to 55 check-ins,
to 30 typically in attendance,
to 18 centrally involved participants,
to 10 controllers,
and then back out and up again, with 40 signers,
the hundred-plus members of the Articles Congress,
to the 1,000 State legislators,
to the 1000 men elected
to the ratifying conventions in the 13 States
by the 120,000 electors,
to the 100 or so managers of the Federalist cause,
to the 4 million inhabitants.

Moreover, in most of the cited numbers there were
elites-inside-elites-inside-the-total-number; for example,
a few men controlled the attitudes and procedures of the Congress
and of the State legislatures.

And of the 120,000 potential voters, a third cast no ballots. *"We the
PEOPLE"* in the end consisted of the number of voters, say, in
Chicago's Fifth Ward (of Fifty Wards) today.

Getting to the Convention was difficult, and to the ratifying
conventions and to the First Congress was just as hard, and
explains the frequent delays in arriving at quorums to
commence proceedings. There was a chance in six that
you would have an accident, a shipwreck,
a stagecoach incident, a storm or wash-out that would make an
improbable journey practically impossible. Roads were
unpaved and often mere paths.
Facilities along the route were minimal.

It took a few days to assemble the quorum and more,
but finally, at Philadelphia, Pennsylvania,
on May 25, 1787, some fifty-five men from
a majority of States assembled, a plurality of them
eminent, all well-connected or well-to-do,
not exactly filled with brotherly love -
brotherly love being mostly what poor people and
Quakers spoke of - but polished in dealing with human affairs.

Gouverneur (a proper name, not an office or a
misspelling) Morris of New York, a principal figure at the show,
positively detested the people at large.
He was largely responsible for the dry elegant style of
the Constitution, and its concise, logical, and formal progression;
he personally made much law in the process.
Throwing his weight around and venting his illiberal views
at every turn, with an arrogance that shows clearly

through the only records we have of the proceedings,
he obtained the dislike of historians, who unfairly downgraded him.
One story is told: he bet colleagues that he would
slap George Washington on the back in greeting.
He did, too, but said afterwards that the look he
got in return made the bet not worth winning.
(*Nota bene:* then, before, now,
a typical American was a born bettor.)

The group as a whole would of necessity reveal here
several fundamental unbrotherly attitudes,
that would presage significant problems of the future.
We have, unfortunately, too little of the interplay
occurring, as delegates arrived and departed. No one
expected mere honeyed words, because those who stayed were
still going to perform major operations on the
Articles of Confederation, the ongoing constitution of the
young Republic, even while the Articles were alive,
if unwell.

Philadelphia was a good convention town and an
experienced Capital of the country. Largest of American cities,
though well down the line today,
it was nicely situated in the middle of the 13 States,
moving from North to South. It was not committed to the
ideologies and life styles of the New Englanders and Southerners,
between whom little love was lost but much business was done.
New York had not only been a Loyalist hangout, but
it was not ready to strengthen the union.

Philadelphia had boarding houses, and friends, and
friends of friends, with whom delegates could stay.
General Washington, who arrived punctually from Virginia,
had reserved rooms at a boarding house, but was
prevailed upon by the Robert Morris'es to stay
at their house, nearby the Hall. The streets were not safe:
some delegates carried weapons against ruffians;
they rode and walked together;
some had bodyguards.

The delegates, chosen by their state legislatures,
acted with varying degrees of tight instructions from their
home bodies. Some could do as they pleased,
and this was because they did not want to do too much.
Attendance was not compulsory, and some arrived late,
some came and went, while some left before the work was done.
It was not a strictly disciplined operation.
Nor were the ordinary delegates awed by
the task and responsibility tendered them.

No one came to the Convention who was determined to break down
such unity as the Confederation had provided, or primarily to
guard against change. They all believed that "something
has to be done" to bind and control matters
physical, military and especially fiscal that
appeared to be getting out of hand.
The active and well-to-do were running scared.

There may have been guilt and nightmares for what the new upper
class had done to the Loyalists - and in collaboration with this
same "riff-raff". (Nor had they carried out their
promises to compensate the Loyalists for their property
loss, much less the physical harm and terror.)

Present was a clutch of proven human relations operators,
led to begin with by Alexander Hamilton,
still the young whippersnapper under the protection of the
august George Washington, whom he later called his "aegis",
(probably a reference to the ancient shield of Zeus that
Athena was permitted to use, possessing magic powers,
including a Gorgon's head the sight of which
would cause people to freeze in fright). Formerly the
brilliant aide-de-camp, he carried now a
new role as an intermarried member of the
power elite of the State of New York, with expansive
theories of economics and finance. His birth as a West Indian
bastard and his orphaning at 13 was fairly forgotten
in a country where it took a wise man to know his own father.
However, Hamilton was to leave the Convention because the

other members of the New York delegation quit,
disgusted with the prevailing nationalist spirit, and
Hamilton had to depart with them. He stayed in touch;
he was a top propagandist over the country and
a top manipulator of the difficult
ratifying convention in New York.

Washington's reputation as a General and patriot of
all the colonies had been enhanced since the Revolution,
his famed reserve grown, too, annoyed by
infirmities like ill-fitting dentures and arthritic limbs,
but with a critical role assigned him by unanimous consent,
President of the proceedings; there he might cast his shadow
continuously over everyone and not have to say much
except through his reliable agents, and in fact,
in the torrent of words that eventuated in the Constitution,
he is recorded to have spoken only once, and that
to make a small point at the close.

Without exception the delegates - who one day
when things seemed to be working out well would be called
Founding Fathers - were of the top one per-cent of the
population of 4 millions in regard to
property, education, positions of authority and
power, and a group on the whole healthy.
Eldest of the group, now octogenarian, reminiscent
of the Albany Plan of Union of a political generation past, was
Quaker, scientist, inventor, womanizer, printer,
writer-publisher, Indianphile, land speculator,
industrialist, Revolutionary leader, diplomat,
Masonic Freethinker, and first Postmaster General,
Benjamin Franklin.

The two broadest social class aggregates present were the
Northern financial and mercantile interest and the Southern
plantation interest. Among the 55 men who
attended the convention, there was no shopkeeper,
laborer, or small farmer, although these made up the

overwhelming number of Caucasian males in the population. More than half had been to college. About two-thirds owned State or Confederation bonds, which would incline them to provide the fiscal means to repay them. Almost a half had lent money at interest; they would presumably wish the value of the money to remain stable, and would want protection against any takeover of law-making by the debtor class, which was huge. A fourth of the delegates owned slaves. Most were involved in large landholding deals.

A perennial debate among historians concerns the extent to which their personal economic interests determined the motives of the Framers and thence the Constitution itself. Extreme positions have been advanced by Marxist economic determinists and idealistic rationalists. On the whole the Framers and the Federalists-to-be of the population were a fearful and anxious group, but more nervous over social disorder and uncertainty than over the value of their property. That is, they were more afraid of losing status, position, and their group identity than of giving up possessions or pursuing profits greedily.

They were also more narrow than they were selfish in their view of government, or, rather, narrowness let their selfishness stand out. The Constitutionalists, the Federalists, tended to be cosmopolitan in psychology and outlook, whereas the anti-Constitutionalists, the anti-Federalists, tended to be parochial. The former felt at home in an enlarging world of ever-differentiating occupations, whereas the latter felt most at home by his fireside in a clannish bucolic locality.

Both groups had enjoyed political experience. A fifth had participated in State constitutional conventions. Over two-thirds had been members of the Confederation Congress. Over half had been State legislators. A few had been State governors or judges.

Still, among those who signed the Constitution were
only six men of the surviving 43
who had signed the Declaration of Independence,
eleven years earlier.

Though painstakingly studied by hundreds of scholars in their every
aspect, the relative influence of every member of the
convention cannot be known. It would seem that a dozen men
could be named who were responsible for assembling and agreeing
upon 90% of the Constitution; they would be
James Madison, George Washington, James Wilson,
John Dickinson, George Mason, William Randolph,
Alexander Hamilton, Elbridge Gerry, Roger Sherman,
Gouverneur Morris, Benjamin Franklin, and one more man
whose name presently slips my mind. Jefferson,
to repeat, was not present; he was Ambassador to France.
John Adams was also abroad.

James Madison of Virginia, all of five feet in height
(the same as Lenin and shorter than Napoleon),
slender, pained migraine sufferer, thirty-six years
old and looking even younger, wealthy of family,
conscientious slave-holder, Princeton College
graduate, unlucky in love, a heavy reader who
arrived with trunk upon trunk of books: he was to
be the hero - so unlikely a hero that it makes one
superstitiously favorable to the Constitution to
learn that he was its Father. His theory of interest-group
checks and balances, in society and government both,
pervaded the meetings and the end-product.

Those in effective charge at the Convention wanted a
Constitution with several features. One and all knew that
they were to strengthen the bonds that would tie together
profitably the individual States while
leaving them their liberty. (More and more,
liberty of a government to do as it pleased was called
"sovereignty" since Jean Bodin had glorified the idea and the word.)

They hoped for a government with a tidy purse of its own, refilled periodically by modest taxes. This income was to be used to pay off the existing debt and run up new debts from time to time; it was to maintain a small standing army to enforce the government's laws, fight Indians, and other external enemies; it would sustain a small independent establishment of judges, Congressmen, and an executive; it would support a navy to fight smuggling, pirates, and possibly an enemy.

They wanted to get rid of the rule of unanimity and extraordinary majorities in decision-making, but recognized the need to limit strictly the national government, and were ready to recognize the need for a two-thirds majority on a few matters. They wished to reconcile the principle of the equality of states with the principle of relative riches and population (riches were acknowledged to correlate statistically well enough with the population of a State).

They were interested in a balanced constitution, which to them meant a separation of powers into the judicial, executive and legislative branches, and various checks of each upon the other to keep any one branch from infringing upon the others. They had two other balances in mind, although not referred to as such: they wished to balance the federal government with the states, and they wished to balance the rights of the small states with those of the large states.

The structure of the document exhibits the separation of powers, for the Congress, the Executive, and the Judiciary are taken up in separate major sections. Thereupon each branch has ways of checking the others. Thus the President might veto (the word was not used in the Constitution) a bill of the Congress, in which event a special majority of two-thirds was needed in both houses to override. Thus, too, the Supreme Court was independent, chosen for life, and could smooth and chip away at the acts of the President and Congress when adjudicating.

(Its power of declaring executive, legislative, and
whoever-else's bothersome actions unconstitutional came later
by a *coup d'état* of a sort and several subsequent
repetitions of the same).

The legislature, with the power of the purse, could impoverish both
judiciary and executive; it could appoint or approve the
designation of justices and judges. Its power to impeach,
try, and remove members of the executive branch
including the President and Judges, too, was a judicial
function of consequence. A clever critic might have said to
all of this, that the power to check, if exercised
forcibly and extensively might quite upset the balance of
powers and the separation of the branches, and
one would be correct to say so.

There were other kinds of balances and checks -
like a complicated trapeze act it all was.
The Senate was there to check the House
And vice versa. The Federal government
was to check the States and vice versa.
The people were to check the government and the
government the people. The Framers wished to prevent a
majority of the electorate, even a limited electorate, from
having a direct voice in the government (only several
would not have hated public opinion polls)
beyond the House of Representatives. Nor did they
tolerate the notion of the "great beast", the people -
in Hamilton's off-the-record language -
breaking into the law-making, law-execution, or
law-judging processes. They were afraid to write a limited
national suffrage qualification into the Constitution for the
election of members of the House of Representatives.
Instead, relying upon the niggardliness of the States in
handing out the right to vote, they let the states
define each its own qualifications for
casting a federal ballot.

They wanted Congress to be the most important branch of
government. They still had faith in representative

government through the legislature. They wished the legislature to have the power to vote money, and inscribed a system for controlling all tariffs, but no export duties (this to allay the fears of the Southern exporting states). The essence of republican government must be the legislature.

The word "republican" occurred only once: the federal government guaranteed each State a republican form of government. The word "democracy" did not appear at all.

How to elect the legislature became the hottest issue of the Convention. The Virginians, well-prepared, came into the Convention with a scheme that provided two houses, one elected by the voters, the second to be elected by the first house from lists of nominees provided by the state legislatures. New Jersey delegates counter-attacked with a plan in favor of the small States and States' rights. It provided for the State legislatures' electing an equal number of representatives to a single-chambered Congress.

In concluding debate on the subject, a compromise coming out of the Connecticut delegation was approved. This created one chamber elected by State legislatures with equal representation for all States, and a second chamber elected by the voters with seats apportioned to the States in relation to their population. The Virginia plan had let the two houses of Congress elect a chief executive. The New Jersey idea was to have an executive council elected by the single house of the Congress. The Connecticut version employed the Electoral College in choosing the chief executive.

Most delegates wished a real executive branch headed up by a real executive, to wit, a President chosen in his own right. They wished the executive to have the power to conduct foreign affairs,

except when it came to making war or writing
his own treaties. Although tempted to
make him popularly elective in order to make him a
truly national figure, they gave his election over to
a national Electoral College under State influence.
And so they provided. Members of the "College"
would be chosen as the States saw fit, whereupon,
in a single meeting, they would vote for President and
Vice-President, the latter being the runner-up
among the several candidates for President.
A majority of votes would be needed to elect the President;
lacking such, the House of Representatives,
voting as States (with equal voice to every State)
would choose him from the top two candidates.

The Framers wished their handiwork to be durable,
so they made the document difficult to amend.
Two-thirds of both Houses and three-fourths of State legislatures
was one of the four difficult methods of change.
But there it was, the method of change. It had to be there.
It was in all the State constitutions.
The provision in constitutions for their amendment was
itself an invention within an invention. For it
confirmed that there was truly an origin of the Constitution
in the people; they might, not easily to be sure, change it.
It implied, too, that the proper method to change the
basic structure, powers, and functions of a government was by
peaceful and legal means, not by violence,
royal marriage, or voodoo.

They wanted to make the country safe and indulgent for
business, and therefore included various clauses that
forbade the States from impairing the obligation of
contracts, issuing currency, imposing any
import or export duties,
interfering with interstate commerce, or
making engagements with foreign powers.

To assure uniform rules of the game, full
recognition was to be given each State's acts

by every other State. Privileges and immunities of a
person in one State had to be extended to citizens
present there from any and all States.
The Framers protected patents and copyrights
nationally (but ominously did not protect
the creations of foreigners).

They wrote up other benefits to business in the course of
providing benefits to everyone, and vice versa:
such would be a prohibition against denial of the writ of habeas corpus;
a provision for a national bankruptcy law;
a power to fix and control the currency;
a power over citizenship, immigration and naturalization;
jurisdiction over the post offices and standards of
weights and measures; and the prohibition
of legislation that would increase the penalty for a crime
ex post facto (after the dastardly deed was done).

They provided for a jury in all criminal cases of
any consequence, and allowed it in civil cases.
They tightly defined the requirements of proof of treason and
they forbade bills of attainder to restrain executive and
Congressional persecution of a man's family..

They liked the existing system of handling the territories
and admitting new states and kept the jurisdiction in the
hands of Congress. They did not ask opinions from the
vast frontier areas.

The several tiny cliques within the top elite of the
Convention managed to get together on all of these
matters and then went out to the hustings and legislative
halls and achieved national agreement. Yet the
leaders of the convention were almost continuously pessimistic.
In retrospect, their victory does appear to have been miraculous.
Most Americans, even of the limited
electorate of the day, really did not want
the Constitution, or wanted it only with some singing clauses
that they believed such constitutions were designed to carry.

❖❖❖

A number of things happened that they did not want,
most of these coming later. The matters that escaped their
attention, or were deliberately avoided, or that they took up
gingerly and dropped as explosive, were numerous and
revealing in their entirety. For instance, once they saw
how heated an issue it was, they gave up any interest in
a reform of the electorate that would have made it
more democratic.

The electoral college did not work at all as expected;
all too many candidates for the offices of President and
Vice-President appeared after the first round.
Political factions began to narrow the choice
of the "best men" of the country. The Electors had little to commend
them as sage nominators; they were ordinary politicians or their
friends. Worse, two men running together were
likely to tie or emerge with the wrong man, that is,
the Vice-Presidential candidate of the group getting
more votes than the Presidential candidate.
(So this was changed by the Twelfth Amendment in 1804.)

Still, very soon, Electors were entirely bound by
public promises to a given Candidate.
So the complicated machine became
practically valueless.

The Framers did not foresee the extent to which democracy
"in spirit" would take over the executive branch, or the
extent to which the interest groups would not coalesce
even when the public interest would seem to demand unity,
as in the case of a foreign threat, or the
extent to which State powers, relative to the
Federal powers, could become greatly reduced.

On the other hand, they built the defenses of the States of
small populations so firmly into the Constitution
(in the Senate, for example), that it became impossible to readjust an

imbalance of representation. The Framers could not, of course, foresee some social changes - the reduction of agriculture to 2% of the work force from over 90%, the many difficulties in local government that came from letting these be the creatures of the States solely; the Frankenstein's monster of the President's war powers; the growth of governmental employment to one-sixth of all jobs; the power of sectionalism in the Senate to keep the country eternally divided; and more.

The Constitution was to change markedly by means other than formal amendment. Several of the amendments were adopted, too, in order to help get the Constitution itself adopted in the first place, while other amendments were imposed upon the Southern States under duress and had to wait for political changes to be enforced. Various amendments were adjustive and technical. Such was the changing of dates for assumption of office. A couple of amendments were responses to the obstinacy of the Supreme Court on social issues, permitting a federal income tax, for example. One, prohibiting most uses of alcohol, was repealed after a dozen years. Late in these pages, we shall reveal more fully the futility of the amendment process.

Whereas the Framers were sensitive to the potential interests of merchants, large planters, and politicians, they seem in retrospect to have been calloused in regard to the poor, the debtor, the small farmer, the widow, the illiterate, the aged, the prison inmates, women, children, Blacks, Indians, indeed just about everyone else in the population except the top five percent or so. Their perspective on the population was narrow. If, as political animals, the Framers had sympathetic feelings for the aforesaid 95% of the people, they would condense into a wishful theory that whatever they might provide for the five per cent would trickle down to the rest.

Hardly any section of the Constitution was directly and intentionally beneficial to the lower majority of the population. A long list of serious problems, most of which were continually flaring up, were not engaged. Among them would be:

*

The continual destruction of Indian nations
*
The inevitable visibly approaching direct egalitarian democracy
*
The halting of slavery and indentured service
*
The conservation of the union against potential State nullification and secession
*
The growing real inequalities of States, yet the equal national power given them
*
The great land frauds and conspiracies going on at the time and foreseeable.
*
General discrimination against the western regions of the States
*
The epidemic corruption at all times everywhere
*
A mechanism for preventing continual land and sea free booting and gangsterism
*
The suppression of freed Blacks
*
The suppression of free workers by wage fixing, strike-breaking, and political disabilities
*
The advancing deterioration of soils and forests in old and frontier areas.
*
The high incidence of personal violence and crime

*

The symbiosis of special interest groups with every political office

*

The lack of uniformity of state laws on common problems like waterways, and crime and punishment

*

The conflict of libel law with freedom of expression

*

The neglect generally of public education, scientific study, and cultural development

*

The rampancy of factionalism, parties, and mafia-like conspiracies, ranging up to treason

*

Ignoring of all problems of women and their very existence (Among the 85 Federalist papers was only a single mention of women, in #6, where the intrigues of courtesans and mistresses were raised as a warning beacon.)

*

Absence of a federal general police power to back up the given general powers

*

Rapidly growing unplanned cities and urbanism (Tammany Hall was founded within a month of the effective adoption of the Constitution.)

*

Little concern with the development of inventions of the approaching steam age (a group of delegates ventured to a demonstration by John Fitch of his newly invented steamboat.)

*

Corrupt election processes in the States or need to provide clean elections for Congress

*

Apparent unconcern with potential corruption of ordinary federal employees

The Framers who were slave-holders or connected with the slave

trade were not the worst of the lot;
still, the three provisions that dealt with African-Americans were
contemptible. One called specifically -
in a document of General Principles -
upon the States to return to each other any
refugees from slavery or bondage.
A second permitted specifically (again) the
slave trade to go on for another twenty years
before permitting Congress to ban it.
(This guaranteed another biological generation of
Americans to be born and raised in the endorsement of the
slave trade and of profits for the New England and
South Carolina slave-traders, and a cost-cutting
supply of humans for the Southern plantation.)

The third was inserting into the method of apportionment of
Congressional seats and direct taxes a provision,
that all the free and bound population except
untaxed Indians, be counted, but only
"three-fifths of all other persons".
James Madison in Federalist #54
justified this compromise between North and South,
and explained that the Constitution considered them
"as debased by servitude"
so that they were not truly persons;
they were *"inhabitants",* but *"divested of two-fifths of the man".*
Thus the Framers went out of their way to
appease the Southern delegations - yet, ashamed
perhaps, or wary, they did not mention the word
"slave" in the Document at all.

The Constitution that came out of Philadelphia
helped the collected ruling elites of the thirteen States
to hang on to most critical powers of government and
to prosper economically. The Framers did not
speak with the specific voice of Adam Smith, but
they were similarly inclined. They felt for the most part that
by guaranteeing the success of the well-to-do
through the control of the power of the commonwealth
they would assure the same class, which they saw clearly as a

small minority, of high standing on the other value indices of
respect, education, and personal well-being.

To put a good face on the Document and their work,
the Framers discussed how to go about presenting
it to the public. An indication of unanimity was important.
Yet it had not been unanimous at all.
Some of the members refused to sign their names.
With Gouveneur Morris instigating him, Benjamin Franklin
suggested that the form declare:
*"Done in Convention,
by the unanimous consent of the States present"....,*
and with this, all but three of the forty-two members then
present signed the Constitution. Five hundred copies of the
document were printed and distributed to those with
"a need to know" around the country.

The Framers believed that they might get the Constitution
adopted if they could avoid the stipulation of a unanimous approval of the
States. They probably could not do so if they turned it over to the
existing Articles of Confederation Congress to
vote on (as States, not as free representatives),
or if they asked the Congress to give it over to
the mercies of the State legislatures, most of
whom were under the influence of localists,
independent farmers, and debtors.

Hitherto, in violation of their instructions,
they had reconstituted the government;
now they by-passed an important faction of both the
Congress and the State legislatures by asking
Congress to ask the States to call special conventions
to debate and vote on ratification. Remarkably,
both institutions dutifully responded, and the conventions
were called under special elections. This by-passed the
existing networks of statehouse politicians;
it allowed the Federalists to bring to bear all of

their social, financial, political, and propaganda forces in a one-time-only battle for ratification.

Furthermore, by voting to pass along the Constitution to the States, the Articles Congress in effect was granting the right of the Constitution to be approved by a vote of nine of the thirteen States (soon fourteen with Vermont, which had been playing a semi-treasonable game with the British to become Canadian), foregoing the principle of unanimity that was part of the Articles constitution. Moreover, the States, by setting up their individual ratifying conventions, were agreeing that the Constitution should take force by a vote of less than unanimity.

Now the battle was joined. The arena was immense, the whole of the United States from Maine to Georgia, in town and country. Every weapon of propaganda and agitation could be employed. Every interest and individual could enter the fray. Every kind of social issue could be introduced as relevant to the approval or rejection of the Constitution. The economic division between poor and well-to-do was important enough to bring defeat to the Constitution had it not been for the limited suffrage. For example, in 123 counties where the average dwelling house value was $100 or more, 69% or more turned in a "yes" vote, whereas 158 counties where the average dwelling value was under $100 provided "yes" votes of 47% or less.

Generally, those eligible to vote were such as voted for the State legislators, a minority of White males. It is astonishing how close the anti-Constitutionalists came to victory, even among the delegates chosen by these voters. Study upon study has shown that a majority of adult White males in the country were against the Constitution. A plebiscite even among the restricted suffrage-holders would have defeated it.

The first ten amendments may be said to owe their existence to oversights and faults of the Framers, who were impelled by a fear of public opinion in the upcoming conventions. Their very existence shows how unpopular was the work of the men at Philadelphia, regardless of Washington, Franklin, and Company. In the privacy of the Convention hall, they talked about a Bill of Rights, but persuaded themselves that a government of strictly delegated powers lacked the power to destroy liberties and rights: ergo, there would be no need for them. It was a case of men reasoning themselves proudly into a hopeless position. Even before they exited the hall, they had the uneasy feeling that they must acquiesce to some set of amendments if the Constitution were to be ratified. James Madison, always careful, carried a list of possible amendments with him.

Polemics of ratification were fairly narrow, but also informed, and on a high practical and legal level on both sides. The most famous disputatious material consisted of the 85 *Federalist* essays composed by Hamilton, Madison and Jay. Richard Henry Lee's *Letters of the Federalist Farmer* were an able presentation of the position of Anti-Federalists. Innumerable tracts and posters appeared - not so reasonable. Dirty tricks abounded in the election and organization of the convention delegates. Bribery was common - whether of legislators, voters, delegates, or press.

Professor McMaster wrote a century ago during a peak period of corruption and reformism, *"In all the frauds and tricks that go to make up the worst form of politics, the men who founded our state and national governments were always our equals, and often our masters".*

False promises were made; John Hancock,
whose handwriting was so conspicuous among the signatures to the
Declaration of Independence, was inveigled to
change his stance by assurances of support to be Governor
of Massachusetts, or Vice President, or, who knows,
President, in the event that Virginia failed to
ratify the Document. With men like Patrick Henry
against it in Virginia, the Federalist situation there was critical.
So was it in New York, where five weeks of
all-out efforts turned a hostile assembly into a
barely favorable majority.

Within a year of its adjournment, the Constitutional
Convention's work won approval, first of the requisite nine States,
then quickly of Virginia and New York, then the
laggard, North Carolina, and finally Rhode Island
(May 29,1790, under threat of economic sanctions).
Seven States ratified while either
requiring or demanding amendments -
called "Bills of Rights", though not entirely such.

In no State was there a resounding victory for the Constitution.
It was very much a minority document.
The *"if..then proposition"* is sometimes justified, sometimes heuristic,
often entertaining - so we may present it occasionally:
If the total population had been represented
in the Convention, then a monumental struggle
would have occurred, but, if the Convention had held
together to the end, the results would have been vastly different and
possibly large segments of the tragedies of the nation -
social, military, economic, cultural, affectional -
over the next two centuries would have been avoided.
Perhaps the USA would have become a
welfare state a hundred years earlier!

Doubts of the intrinsic ability of the Constitution
to survive its infancy were assuaged by the public response.

In all the towns, parades were held to celebrate the ratification.
(Americans cherished every opportunity to parade.
The United States was already a public country, wide-open
to crowd behavior. That the people were largely of lowly origins
heightened the need and pleasure at public displays of
their collective identity as "the People".)
Federal processions and celebrations followed
the approval of the Constitution in the several states.
The bannered "Ten Toasts of Philadelphia" symbolized all.
Actually obstreperous, hostile, and vituperative elements
marched in counter-parades in every State.

Parades continued to be a major part of every
voluntary civil manifestation for 150 years,
then began to diminish when newsreels, radio, and
television took over and people spread out
over the countryside and the world on holidays, and
more of them became skeptical and derisive.
Furthermore, the demands of all kinds of groups,
some of them highly controversial, for their own parades,
put the whole idea of parade at risk.
To which add the recent unpopularity of military might,
the staple of traditional parades, as the
symbol of the public mood and national prestige.

America's Constitution was imitated around the world.
It was progenitor of all national constitutions.
Efforts at revising generally or rewriting the Constitution
have never been able to get off the ground. Were they to
succeed, considerations such as those
appearing in the last chapters of this book
might help set the agenda.

The Constitution, and all laws and treaties pursuant to it,
were declared to be the *"supreme law of the land"*.
Any law or action or judgement of a State
contrary to these would be null and void.

As law, it induced compulsion and habitual behavior in leaders and people. As compulsory habit it fostered similar and imitative behavior of many kinds - in its domestic habitués, in other governments, domestic and foreign. It emerged from and gave its color to the broad stream of Living History. It carried forward its influences more than most other habits, laws, practices, ideas, and processes that took place earlier or later. Compared with most other actions and processes, it became a behavioral constant of large scope and domain. Considering the Americans' penchant for willfulness, unlawful behavior, violence and disorder, the Constitution, with all its faults, helped the center to hold.

A living historical process affects national character. It is most important that people believe that they are living under a constant faithful regime and such has occurred with the Constitution. All of its harrowing experiences, including the Civil War, were forgotten; it remained a kind of perpetual virgin. It has changed a great deal - evolved, some say, who would like to make the slightest questionable change a product of the wonderful immanence of nature.

The Framers would be shocked and dismayed to observe the operative significance of their words today. Perhaps amused. (Eastern Seaboard respectable types did not laugh then as they do now. The pandemic American *haw-haw* probably originated with people unrepresented among the Framers.)

James Madison presents the Bill of Rights to the First Congress

Chapter Twenty-one

Constitutional Government

George Mason and Luther Martin had sought to place a Bill of Rights in the Constitution, but others, including James Madison, would have none of it, arguing that rights were already well-protected in the Constitution; since the government-to-be had only explicit powers, it could not go out of the way to curb rights. They quite underestimated popular feelings on the subject.

The term "rights" was a slogan, of course, in that any number of items could be included as negative interpositions of possible acts. Rights had been popping up since ancient times. Athenians had rights;

Socrates was put to death by due process of law (unfortunately guarantees of academic freedom were lacking). Since English common law was supposed to apply in America, English rights, and the limitations thereupon, were supposedly part of American law. The writ of habeas corpus, if you had a lawyer, was generally available. So was trial by jury in criminal cases, the jurors consisting of one's "peers" or equals in a whimsical way, and coming from one's neighborhood (often actually not the defendant's, but the court's and prosecution's neighborhood, where the offense was committed).

The right to speak through an attorney was on and off, appearing quickly in colonial Massachusetts. The rights of assembly, free speech, and free religious practice were often limited. The states were generally active in coining basic rights for their own constitutions and people.

Some two hundred proposed rights came into the lists before the pruning process began - some new, most of them discussed publicly hitherto, some out of context. New Jersey, in its first Revolutionary Constitution, gave the right to vote to qualified women; it was to be withdrawn in 1807 even though most other signals seemed then to read "Go" toward direct democracy.

The most prestigious source of lists was the Virginia Declaration of Rights adopted in 1776. Much of it was the work of George Mason. Nine were regarded as the statement of principles for a republic and seven were said to be the rights of citizens. Basic to republican government were declared to be the equality of men, the sovereignty of the people, the right of revolution, the rule of the majority, the separation of powers, the subordination of the military to the civilian authority, and the practice of referring systematically to the fundamental principles of government, The power to suspend laws was denounced. However, one of the "fundamentals" that was slipped in declared that any movement to set up a government in addition to the Virginian already functioning would be illegal.

The individual's rights included an entitlement to suffrage, for all who possessed evidence of an interest and attachment to the State. A person was entitled to know the cause of his arrest, could not be compelled to testify against himself, and must have a speedy trial by an impartial jury of the vicinity. Excessive bails and fines, cruel and unusual punishments, and un-specific warrants of search and seizure were banned. Freedom of the press was guaranteed. A final article allowed that all men were entitled to the free exercise of religion according to the dictates of conscience.

The example of Virginia, most powerful of the States, was fetching. The Northwest Ordinance of 1787 gave the Congress of the Articles of Confederation a chance to display its sentiments, for there it could, as it could not for the whole country, invest the territorial residents with a set of rights. Habeas corpus and trial by jury, freedom of religion, reasonable bail and moderate fines were guaranteed, whereas cruel and unusual punishments were prohibited. Private property and contracts were guaranteed inviolable. Finally, in a surprising development, slavery in the Northwest Territory was prohibited.

Nathan Dane and Manassah Cutler, an Ohio Company land speculator, were responsible for the bulk of this work, including the prohibition against slavery. The Massachusetts Constitution and laws furnished inspiration for the content and style of most of the articles.

In no State were the guarantees promulgated in Bills of Rights and Constitutions fully effective. The press, for instance, was often bullied, suppressed, and censored around the country, especially as bitter controversy developed over slavery. States extended guaranteed rights often reluctantly, and the Federal government obtained finally a Bill of Rights that protected people from Federal encroachments, not State hindrances. Therefore federal courts could not reach into the State Constitutions or interrupt State conduct either.

Conscientious James Madison brought the matter of a Bill of Rights to the floor of the House of Representatives as the First Congress went to work. (He had been defeated for the Senate and barely elected to the House, so irritated by his influence on the Constitution were his district's voters.)

At first, he, Vining, Gerry and others thought that they could insert the

Rights here and there in their proper place in the Constitution, but then they saw that they were opening up the Constitution to relentless amendment and that the Bill was a simplistic *idée fixe* and would be in the end added anyhow. So they concentrated upon reducing the rights in number until twelve were approved by the Congress with the requisite two-thirds majorities, then sent to the States, where, *mirabile dictu*, two insignificant amendments were evicted, and the famous ten remained to be approved by the requisite three-fourths of the legislatures.

The United States had their (it took many years to begin saying the singular "its") Bill of Rights! The First Amendment forbade a religious establishment and protected the free exercise of religion, and banned any abridgement of freedom of speech or press, or of the right to assemble peaceably, or to petition the government. Next, a well regulated militia was said to be necessary to the security of a free State, meaning literally the individual States, and therefore the right of the people to keep and bear arms must not be infringed. The Third Amendment restricted the government's right to quarter soldiers among the citizenry.

The Fourth protected people against unreasonable searches and seizures, and directed that a court warrant be the basis for any such action against persons and places. The Fifth Amendment guaranteed a proper indictment and trial, precluded a person's being put twice in jeopardy for the same crime, protected any person refusing to testify against himself, guaranteed compensation for private property taken for public use, and forbade the deprivation of life, liberty or property without due process of law. The Sixth defined a number of aspects of trial procedure in a criminal case that helped the defendant to a "fair trial". The next provided for trial by jury in civil suits. The Eighth forbade excessive bail or fines or cruel and unusual punishments.

The Ninth Amendment declared that the rights proclaimed in the Constitution were not exclusive of all the rights of people. The Tenth Amendment announced that powers that were not delegated to the federal government, nor prohibited to the States by the Constitution, were reserved to the States respectively, or to the People.

The First, Fourth, Fifth, and Sixth turned out to be the most important and controversial. The others either were progressively outmoded or - Ninth and Tenth - strangely inactive. The Eighth enjoyed a revival. It originated at a time of horrible penalties - lopping off ears, branding, enchainment, etc. - which it had little to do with halting; it has been lately invoked in attacks against capital punishment for being cruel and unusual, with some success.

Regrettably, Madison's efforts to include, among the amendments to the Constitution, an application of the rights of conscience, freedom of speech and press, and the right to a jury trial in criminal cases, to the State governments, as well as to the Federal government, failed.

I must note in passing the tragic irony that while the new Republic was honing its liberties, the great French society, in the throes of *its* Revolution, was sharpening its guillotine, readying it to sever the heads of hundreds of savants who would have been welcome to America.

This all happened while the new government was establishing itself in Philadelphia, following its start-up in New York City. As first President, George Washington made the proper appearance in a fine coach, and gave an inaugural speech redolent with praises and rosy predictions for the United States under the Constitution. His election came about practically unanimously. Congress rewarded him and his successors with a very high salary of $25,000. (He was already second richest man in America after one Elias Hasket Derby who possessed about a million dollars in assets, 0.16 of the wealth of the country. He was not paid during the War, except for expenses, but his expense account was meticulously kept and self-indulgent.
By his last will, Washington's great estates were split up and his 300+slaves guaranteed freedom upon the death of his wife. He thought slavery inefficient and possibly wrong, but did not agitate the subject.)

His Vice-President was John Adams. His protégé, Alexander Hamilton was named Secretary of the Treasury, Thomas Jefferson Secretary of State, and General Henry Knox Secretary of War. Inasmuch as the spirit of the times seemed to call for a "non-partisan" government, and parties in their modern sense were unknown to the world, one could not call Washington's administration a coalition government, but such, in fact, is what it was, represented by a Hamilton and a Jefferson faction. That finished off the positions within the Cabinet, which could be called by the name because Washington was in the habit of convening the small group to discuss issues from time to time. Later posts introduced an Attorney General , a Postmaster General and a Secretary of the Navy.

Washington was already referred to in 1787 as "Father of his Country", though he would have liked to be the father of a son. (R. Marion's recent study assigns this to a genetic defect, the Kinefelter syndrome, a chromosomal abnormality that correlates height, facial structure, poor impulse control, risk taking, poor judgement, and authority problems with infertility. Others earlier had blamed the sterility on childhood mumps or Mrs. Washington.)

The cult of Washington assumed fantastic proportions, like that of Napoleon and Mussolini and Mao Tse-Tung. His "paternity" coincided with the cult of youth taking over the country, for he was old but epitomized the revolt against the old forms of authority and embodied the sense that the whole world was new, a feeling pervading the popular mind at this time. They agreed when he said in his inaugural address that America would now exhibit to the world the virtues of a great republic.

Washington suffered gladly a removed and boisterous popularity. Nonetheless, as his first term advanced into a second term, and the in-fighting of his administration became intense, his adherence to Federalist as opposed to "anti-Federalist" opinion became more pronounced, and he caught his share of verbal brick-bats from the press, pulpit, and legislatures. He was sick and tired of the business when he retired after two terms, but put together a fine *"Farewell Address"*, in which he invoked Americans to eschew partisanship and permanent alliances with foreign powers, and otherwise to work hard and save their money.

The country continued its rapid peopling and development during his years as chief executive. The War crisis and Revolution had not stopped this; in the 20-year period 1763 to 1783 its people grew by one-third, and its agriculture, industry, and commerce, uninhibited by hostile gunfire and legal restrictions, in fact spurred on by the same, grew by leaps and bounds, illegally as well as legally, of course. Immigration was heavy. The country now consisted of the following demographic ingredients (ca.1790):
about 25% of English ancestry;
25% German-descended;
25% of "Celts" from Wales,
Scotland, France, Ireland, and significant
other minorities; 20% of African origins;
and 5% Indians. This was old stuff for Americans.

The wealth of the nation was distributed as it had been from the beginning, no less skewed for the fact that the richer Loyalists had lost all, because their wealth had gone to capitalists who could buy up their property or to the State governments. A few received compensation after the War. Nor had the Revolution any general effect upon equality of wealth in America.

One might think that the vast tracts of land being distributed almost for nothing would tend to equalize the wealth of the country; it is true that about half of the households in the country owned real estate; but what usually happened is that large speculators were favored in the organization of the selling and then resold in large sub-divisions or else the land was subdivided into ever smaller parcels and worth little. Recently it has been shown that the distribution of wealth in frontier areas was no less unequal than in the older settled areas.

Moreover, every mile of distance of a township from a major city correlated with an increase in inequality of wealth to the disfavor of the rural area. It had been claimed, too, that the distribution of real estate was more equal in America than in Europe, but here again, land in America was more unkempt than the European land and comparisons in size or in supposed value are deceiving.

When Lee Soltow applied the Gini Index, which at 0 has perfect equality of distribution of an item, and at 1 has everything in one person's hands, he found a Gini coefficient for wealth in real estate in 1798 among all adult free males at .80, a highly inequitable figure. He also discovered that the effect of the distribution of Loyalist assets might have been to diminish inequalities, but that it was more than compensated for in the direction of greater inequality by the fact that no more than 8000 individuals profiteered from the repayment of $32 millions in federal debt.

A remarkable estimate of the number and value of the people's housing was made in 1798 by the Federalist administrator and statistician, Oliver Wolcott. Sampling heavily from the total of 577,000 dwellings of America, Soltaw found the mean value of people's houses to be $262, the median (50% more, 50% less) to be $96, and the mode (that is, the commonest value of a dwelling) to be $80. Some 50,000 dwellings, hovels really, were worth $9 or less. The Gini Index gave .706, indicating that the kinds of homes that were painted for future picture books were extravagantly priced and few. Nor are the shacks of the 20% slave population even considered here.

The average wage was 50 cents a day. Literacy was still the gift of a minority of the people. Few public schools had yet started up. The prisons of the country were foul beyond comprehension, some like slave ships, others like torture chambers. There was almost no conception of a nation dedicated to the general welfare as had been proclaimed.

The old, now that the young were in the ascendancy, were lucky if they had a hut with a cot to die in - I am here speaking of free White men and women. It was symbolic that Thomas Jefferson was to vacate in his old age his cherished Monticello, that he himself had designed and constructed, as it had to be sold for his debts. Disease was rampant though less virulent than before. (Washington died of pneumonia after returning from a cold rainy ride.)

It was the Federalist period, too; the votes in legislatures and in the hustings show that an ideological division existed between rich and poor in the sense, at the least, that the poor felt themselves kept down by the Federalists, and the Federalists felt that they should stay down.

John Jay, a key figure in Revolutionary and Constitutional activities, with many high-placed relatives and friends, said *"Those who own the country ought to govern it"*. He was one of those nationalists, who, in these times, were pushing Americans toward a keener sense of the country as a whole. Like Hamilton, he believed that the mercantile and industrial rich, and the exceedingly rich in general, were the vital elite that would unify the nation.

John Adams, Revolutionary, diplomat, Vice-President and President, thought that the rich would grow richer and the poor poorer, but naturally sided with the *"gentry"*. He said that
"the moment the idea is admitted into society that property is not as sacred as the laws of God and that there is not a force of law and public justice to protect it, anarchy and tyranny commence".
(He was not leaving much in between the extremes.)
He believed society worked by corruption and spoke resignedly of
"the cohesive power of public plunder",
one of the most trenchant and continually valid comments on American history.

The policies of Alexander Hamilton as maestro of the Federalist legislative program and Director *de facto* of executive management were integrated, on-target, and workable. The members of the First Congress, battered by storm, shipwreck and coach-wreck, had hardly assembled a quorum before he was belaboring them with reading material, brilliant reports on what the country needed. The Framers, he among them, may have talked about the legislative and executive branch and the separation of powers, but he had nothing but powerful legislative proposals coming out of the Executive.

Just as Madison had an obligation of conscience with the Bill of Rights, Hamilton had a pressing obligation to the moneyed interests of the country. Wherever they and their better-class dwellings were located, their townships voted more heavily Federalist, at least so far as Pennsylvania is concerned, and there is no reason to think matters were much different elsewhere. They had worked hard to get the Constitution adopted, and results were expected, and forthcoming.

The aggressive nationalist Hamilton proposed that the federal government fund the national debt inherited from the Confederation and the War at full value. This delighted all those who held these lowly rated bonds, most of which had passed from their original purchasers at ridiculous prices into the hands of speculators. But no price is ridiculous which is at the market's intersection of supply and demand, intimated the Secretary of the Treasury, and he had a point, but so did Madison, who said, why not divide this shocking repayment so that the earlier holders would collect some of the inordinate gain. Congress agreed with Madison.

What can you do with such a collection of crooks in Congress, commented Jefferson, and there does seem to have been something fishy-smelling about the yea-vote for funding the debt and the fact that half the Senators and Representatives and their family and friends held large amounts of the "worthless" bonds.

Proof of this was secreted in the Treasury and was let be known only after a century, but the information had been leaked to Jefferson. Many records were destroyed in a fire before Jefferson took office, and another suspicious fire occurred in the midst of a scandal involving the Secretary of War, Timothy Pickering. In charge at the Treasury was Samuel Dexter, and when the same Dexter was transferred to Treasury, a second fire destroyed many records. It was the early equivalent of "shredding" damaging evidence by machine, rather like the inefficient original Chinese recipe for roasting pig by burning down the cottage with the pig inside.

Not content with this victory, Hamilton speeded on to the next, and proposed that the Federal government assume the war debts of all of the States. This was shocking, when you consider that the States were supposed to lose, not gain, by giving over powers to the Federal government. Here Hamilton had a problem in that the Southern States, for all that their planters were deeply in debt, had seen to it that their governments had paid off the bonds that they held. (Had they been calculating that public money used to pay debts would be returned as private loans to themselves?)

So it was the Northern States, where the theories of thrift that became mythical originated, which still had not repaid their debts. Naturally they were pleased with Hamilton for pushing their obligations onto the new Federal government.
There seemed to be no way out of this.

But Hamilton had an idea. There was no problem that he and his enemy Jefferson could not solve together if they put their minds to it. He invited Jefferson out to dinner and there, with Madison, they concocted a worthy scheme. The government had already decided that it needed a place that it could call home, but a sectional quarrel erupted over whether the home should be in the South, or in the North, or in-between. Southern hospitality won out.

Hamilton suggested that if a certain few Southern Congressmen would support the assumption of State debts, the Federalists would not be adverse to letting the new Capital nestle against the warm flanks of Virginia. He further sweetened the deal by agreeing to pay bonuses to those virtuous States that had repaid their debts.

Proceeding briskly, Hamilton advanced a program of tariffs on numerous goods from abroad to protect and encourage the growth of American industry and agriculture. He wished to give bounties and subsidies to stimulate needed activities. He wished to begin an extensive program of internal improvements, such as roads and canals, and to encourage inventions and discoveries. Only his proposals for some protective tariffs were passed. Otherwise his program remained

an inspiration for federalist and federaloid thought in
American economics.

All the money for such generous provisions would extrude from that very modern way of paying debts, by borrowing more money. He believed that *"a national debt, if it is not excessive, will be to us a national blessing"*. This was in 1781 during the War and means, correctly, that a national debt is a unifying force. Thus Hamilton was practically the first government financier who understood that your credit can improve if you owe money, and sometimes the more money owed the better. (This principle has lately been extended to many a high-roller in the world's financial markets, and to credit-card holders, much to their amazement - for they had been reading *Poor Richard's Almanac* instead of Hamilton's reports to Congress.)
In truth, Hamilton did learn much from the manipulative genius Robert Morris of the Continental Congress and Confederation (who died, alas, in a debtor's jail) and taught something in turn to his close Assistant at the Treasury, William Duer (who died also in prison for debts). But he was *sui generis*, honest in the formal manner, and anyhow was not yet involved in any financial scandal in the strict sense of the term, when he was foolish enough to accept a challenge to a duel from a serious killer, Aaron Burr, who mortally wounded him.
(Possibly he thought Burr, fearing political disgrace, would not take deadly aim.)This was to be in 1804.

Hamilton was not disposed to watch his tongue or spare his enemies. In 1800 he was writing to John Jay that Jefferson was "an *atheist* in religion and a *fanatic* in politics", and the anti-Federalist Jeffersonian party was *"a composition of very incongruous materials but all tending to mischief - some of them to the overthrow of the Government by depriving it of its due energies, others of them to a Revolution after the manner of Bonaparte"*.

However, we are still admiring the virtuosity of Hamilton in the Treasury, from the age of thirty-four on. Madison had introduced the first revenue bills, modest duties, and a tax on incoming ships (like an airport tax) based on tonnage. Modified by Hamilton and others, these passed. Hamilton wanted a true excise tax to exercise the long-sought-after power to tax for revenue.

He chose a tax on whiskey, which passed in 1791.

Now then he asked for the creation of a Bank of the United States to issue a uniform paper currency for the country, backed up by government bonds. Gold and silver coins were in short supply, and could not in themselves serve all the need for cash exchanges. Private capitalists would pay in 8 out of 10 million dollars and the government the rest in bonds. The capitalists could use government bonds for 3/4 of the stock, but must offer gold and silver for the balance. They would name 20 Directors, the government five. The Bank, argued Hamilton, could serve numerous functions for the government and the economy - hold funds securely, float loans, stimulate industry and commerce, manage the currency, etc.
Madison in the House objected that the Constitution had made no provision for such a bank, but the Federalists passed the bill through Congress, and Washington, after hearing out the division of opinions in his cabinet between strict and broad constructionists, the Jeffersonians and the Hamiltonians, signed in favor of Hamilton, nationalism, and loose or broad construction.

Under the microscope was Article I, Section 8 of the Constitution that granted to Congress the right to *"make all laws necessary and proper for carrying into execution the foregoing powers"*. Jefferson cited the Tenth Amendment reserving non-delegated powers to the States and people, and warned that there would be no end to federal powers if this first step were to be taken now. Hamilton showed that the word "necessary" was itself of several meanings, like "useful", and opined that, if the end is clearly set forth in the Constitution, then a measure clearly intended to further that end as a means, and not forbidden by the Constitution, is safely constitutional.
The Bank was opened in 1791,
its stock was gobbled up, and it served its purposes.

Paper currency could now be printed, and the famous dollar bill appeared, carrying the countenance of the Father of his Country and replete with the symbol of the American bald eagle, which is an endangered species (Franklin suggested the useful and peaceful turkey as a better national bird) and the Freemasonry symbolism of Franklin on the other side of the great Seal of the United States: the pyramid or supposed architectural principle underlying the universe, the all-seeing eye that supposedly represents the Mind of an impersonal God who designed and oversees said universe (which is also originally the Eye of Saturn). Numerous Congressional committees discussed its design before it was passed into law. Did they know it was Masonic? - of course, they did.

The dollar emulated the worth of the famous Spanish "pieces of eight", the metal peso, and was named after the German Reichsthaler or Imperial Thaler which had originally been the Joachimsthaler of Bohemia's silver mining area called the Joachimsthal, and became in English the "rix-dollar". The $ symbol was Spanish.

It was the world's first decimal monetary system. Unfortunately, the Federalists stuck with the English system of measures instead of going along with the French Revolutionary metric system.

The times were not religious. The sects were happy enough to have the federal government renounce any religious establishment and were actively encouraging the States to go do likewise; the last of them did in the early nineteenth century. But in the Revolutionary period only 4% of American Whites and therefore only 3% of the population belonged to a church. They were not so tolerant as they were indifferent. Nearly half the signers of the Declaration were freethinkers.

In 1783, President Ezra Stiles of Yale University observed, "It begins to be a growing idea that it is mighty indifferent , forsooth, not only whether a man be of this or the other religious sect, but whether he be of any religion at all; and that truly deists, and men of indifferentism to all religion, are the most suitable candidates for public office".

A successor President of Yale, Timothy Dwight, changed the tune to chant against foreign conspiracies and atheism. Paranoid attacks stepped up toward the end of the 1700's, against, for instance, a harmless association of freethinkers, not Masons, but rather called

Illuminati, who were, while admittedly anti-Catholic, deemed also atheistic and conspiratorial against public virtue and order. Founded in Germany, the order had succumbed in Europe before perking up in America. Here, too, it expired, but not from the horrendous accusations directed toward it.

The excise tax on whiskey flew home to roost in 1794. The mountain counties of central and western Pennsylvania, according to alarming reports, were aflame with rebellion. The revolt had spread through the back country of Maryland, Virginia, the Carolinas, Kentucky and Tennessee. The farmers had been growing grain and, lacking transport facilities, were condensing and distilling it into whiskey. Large frontier areas depended upon the cash return. But it was more than just whiskey.

The rebels were largely of Scots-Irish and North Borderer English origin, of the poorest and most aggressive class. They were anti-Constitutional and anti-East. They played rough with Federal officers, beating, torturing and killing them. They brought government to a halt by robberies, terrorist bombings, and invasion of the courts. Their leaders tried to get backing from Britain and Spain, hoping to set up a separate nation of the West. (Later there would be similar conspiracies, with the names of Blount, Wilkinson, and Burr to call them by.)

Reaction by the national leadership was prompt and decisive. First, of course, panic had to occur. And exaggeration of the danger. Then an army larger than any General Washington had commanded in the Revolutionary War set off to quell the rebellion, with General Henry Lee at its head and Alexander Hamilton alongside, eager for battle. He had visions of himself leading a conquest of the Far as well as Near West and of binding into the U.S. the Spanish possessions. Although in his early twenties during the Revolutionary War, his staff work and field soldiering had indeed been brilliant.

However, the rebellion dwindled in the face of overwhelming force. Several score prisoners were taken; some were marched in their rags through Philadelphia before being cast into dungeons. Two nitwits were found guilty of treason, but pardoned by the President.

A more terrible struggle with ominous overtones
for the United States was meanwhile occurring on the
Island of Saint-Domingue (our old acquaintance,
Hispaniola or Santo Domingo,
grown already by then to carry half a million Africans
and a tenth that number of Europeans).
Toussaint L'Ouverture, a self-educated slave, with
Jean-Jacques Dessalines and Henri Christophe,
led a slave revolt in the name of human liberty and rights, that
won Haiti's independence from France and sent its Europeans
for the most part fleeing to Louisiana and elsewhere.

Toussaint beat off assaults by a British fleet and conquered the Spanish Eastern region of the island, ruling it all. In 1802 Napoleon sent an expedition to recover the Island, but this French army, decimated by guerillas and fevers, surrendered in 1804 to the revolutionary government. L'Ouverture was seized while negotiating, sent to France and there died in prison.

Haiti retained its independence, however, until, in the early twentieth century, the U.S. sent in marines to occupy the island on behalf of its creditors in America and Europe. Franklin Roosevelt ended the "protectorate" in 1937. Haiti , with a remarkable music, literature, dance, and spiritualist Catholicism, stood all the while as a perceived threat to racists in nearby America; over time, too, scores of thousands of Haitians immigrated to the States.

A new federal customs collector wrote Hamilton at the end of 1789 that the great majority of vessels evaded customs laws. It had always been done, and new habits were difficult to instil. Administrative management at the end of the century was rudimentary and inept, not only because the Republic was new but because the science itself was new. America had not yet benefitted from the Prussian or the Napoleonic models. Further, there was no old bureaucratic tradition, no practically hereditary official class as one would find in France, the Kingdom of the Two Sicilies, Turkey or China.

Hamilton was almost alone in perceiving the future of the arts and science. He made strong efforts to obtain integrity, permanence, coordination, planning and rationality in the Treasury, largest of the Federal agencies. For instance, he insisted that the collectors of revenue must not write their own opinions of a matter, but must follow the course set forth by Hamilton's office. He was not loath to intervene wherever he could perceive a fault. He was not popular.

Exemplary businesses were rare. There was then little for the government to learn from them, and vice versa. A Northern carding mill employed 900 persons, a giant enterprise. The Aera and Aetna Iron Works of North Carolina had ninety workmen. An important shipyard employed fifty men. The Massachusetts Bank had three employees in 1789. American practice favored committees for administrative work as well as for policy decisions; and Americans were much more prone to argue over their work routines than their English, French, German or Dutch counterparts.

War had been, as usual, a teacher, and had improved administrative skills, as well as work discipline, control of functions, and planning. Lawyers were into everything, and anybody could become a lawyer, so that pragmatism and functionalism gave way to legal quibbles and deductive decision-making. There were no textbooks, manuals, or essays until Necker's *Executive Power* appeared in 1792, a prompt English translation of a famous French official's ideas.

Postal service, begun under Franklin, was handicapped, as was all travel, by bad roads. Jefferson and the anti-Federalists insisted upon county construction and local maintenance of right-of-ways, an impossible situation. Madison was more flexible than Jefferson in having the federal government undertake road building. Yet little was yet done. Between certain points, service was rapid: New York to Philadelphia in one day by the time of the Revolution, Boston to New York in 3.5 days in 1793, Boston to Savannah 22.5 days and $70 in

1802. From Philadelphia to Mount Vernon would take four or five days, Philadelphia to Lexington, Kentucky, 19 to 31 days. The Supreme Court justices had to ride the Circuit to preside over lower courts, a bruising experience, regularly repeated. Official documents were sent in various ways, the most important by messengers, some by trusted friends, often in a chain of several recipients and forwarders. Though complaining, Jefferson nevertheless maintained a flood of correspondence. So did many others. It was an epistolary era. Early in 1790 Jefferson wrote to William Short at the Hague that he was informed only up to October 7 of the previous year; he merely knew that the King of France, a captive, had been removed to Paris; he also complained that Short's handwriting was illegible.

Reports of Congressional and court proceedings were let out to private printers, who sometimes made politics determine content. The Governor of Mississippi Territory, a huge area of few people, was given a modern schoolgirl's allotment of stationary, quills, and pencils for administrative use; included in the paltry supply was "Tape - red - for tying papers...20".

European governments were regularly printing and binding together copies of all pronouncements under one cover. John Adams wished this for America for Presidential proclamations, notices of appointments, legislation, etc., and he found the *"present desultory manner of publishing the laws"* etc. *"infinitely disgraceful to the government and nation, and in all events must be altered"*. But he was 130 years ahead of time in projecting the *Federal Register*, as it is called.

When one speaks of the Federalists it is, of course, of Hamilton and at first Madison, Washington, too, then of John Adams, Oliver Wolcott, Timothy Pickering, Ames, William Smith, Boudinot, Robert Goodloe Harper, Rufus King, Ellsworth and Cabot. If they read like a roster of the fallen, it is pathetically near the facts. As will occur now, they are to be replaced, uprooted, their philosophy of an integrated, progressive, nationally centered, executive-led government rejected, their administrative structure peppered with holes and fiscal policies damned.

The Federalists should have succeeded in foreign politics as well as in the domestic sphere, given their experience, their prestige abroad, their wide education, and their wealthy connections. They did not. Indirectly and directly, their foreign policies brought them down, almost entirely in 1796, quite so in 1800.

No myth is more unrealistic and injurious than that America has habitually restrained from involvement in foreign affairs. Only a continuous propaganda from important news media over the history of the country, followed by gullible text writers, could have let this idea become entrenched in so many American mentalities.

Naturally one will encounter often in politics wishful expressions to be neutral, to keep out of trouble, "to speak softly but carry a big stick", etc. But wishing and propaganda does not make it so. The country has been entangled in foreign affairs and engagements from beginning to the present.

This to said to introduce several brief paragraphs on the Federalist period. I mentioned earlier that conspiracies were brewing to separate the West from the nation, to become independent and imperial, to ally with Canada, with Spain, with France, with England, even with the Indians, and/or to conquer all their lands. Not to mention plots to descend upon and invade the Eastern States in retribution for many wrongs. The frontier was for visionaries of all kinds.

Besides, there was a real Indian War in 1794-5, or perhaps one should say the usual Indian War. For here there were battles and campaigns : "Mad Anthony" Wayne and the Battle of Fallen Timbers, the defeat of 12 tribes and the Treaty of Greenville with them, extracting for a $10,000 annuity Ohio, Indiana, and parts of two other Midwestern states. This disgusting business was destined to go on and on.

Abroad, a great and prolonged conflict was waged in Europe, beginning with the French Revolution and the attempts of the several monarchical countries to put it down. The French republican armies were trouncing all armed forces who came their way. The British fleet was trying to keep supplies from reaching the French and began to capture and confiscate American ships doing business with the French. A cry for War went up in America.

Washington was reminded that the United States was pledged to go to the aid of France by Treaty, but ignored his advisers and the Treaty, declaring ambiguously that the country was a neutral and Americans should not violate the rules of neutrality. So much for the observance of treaty obligations.

But the English remained a problem and Washington sent John Jay, sensing no conflict of interest, although Jay was Chief Justice of the Supreme Court, to negotiate with the English. Jay returned in due course with one of the more unpopular treaties of American history. He had been told by the British that they would in their own good time abandon the frontier forts that they had promised to give up a decade earlier, that they would let Americans trade in the West Indies under obstructionist conditions, that they would pay for the ships that they had seized, that they would pay nothing in compensation for the slaves they had removed in the Revolution, and that, thank you, yes, they would accept a payment by the United States government for the debts of private Americans owing Britons since time immemorial.

New England disliked the trading provisions, the South disliked the slave non-settlement, the anti-federalists wanted to pay nobody's debts and hated England anyhow. The Treaty barely scraped through the Senate. The House got into the Act, though lacking an express role in foreign affairs, because it had to be the originator of all money bills, and money was needed to implement the Treaty; ever since, it has been clear that the Constitution failed in this aristocratic pretension.

At the same time, the House demanded from Washington that he show them the documents dealing with the Jay Treaty and he refused, citing what has since come to be called "executive privilege".
It is a right to preserve the separation of powers
by shielding the operations of the presidency.

The Spanish were much more amicable when it came to dealing with the greater Florida territories, and gave up to the Americans, represented by Charles Pinckney of South Carolina, their claim to the large stretch of land between Georgia and the Mississippi River, holding onto only the broad coastal Florida strip and peninsula. The Treaty of San Lorenzo was signed and ratified in 1795.

The French were already making difficulties. Citizen Genet, he was called, arrived full of plans to run the French Republic's wars from an American base, and began outfitting and licensing privateers, and engendering anti-British propaganda. President Washington had him recalled in 1793 as too much of an embarrassment (besides which the French Revolution had gone beyond the "clean" stage into a Reign of Terror, turning off any French sympathies the Federalists may have still possessed. Genet stayed in America and married well; he was due to be guillotined if he returned.)

The French now began to plunder American shipping, taking 300 ships by 1796; their reasons: Americans had been unfaithful allies; Americans had given the British promises to remain neutral and carry on commerce with English possessions.

By now, John Adams had become President. He was not bellicose. He sent over a committee to treat with the French authorities and they dealt with the three agents, referred to as XYZ, of the notorious Talleyrand, who suggested that a payment to the Directorate of a quarter of a million dollars to grease the skids might be in order and that a loan of $12 millions would also help their cause.

When word of this reached America, enraged slogans such as "Millions for defense, not one cent for tribute!" rent the air, this despite the fact that several years before the Father of his Country had paid $100,000 to a Cree Indian Chief and made him a U.S. Army General to pave the way for a giveaway treaty, and had done the same for the Bey of Algeria who had been holding some American sailors prisoner.

In 1800, to cap the poor Federalist foreign affairs record, a Convention was signed with Napoleon that stopped the French raids on American ships but got nothing back for the damages suffered earlier. By staying unwarlike, however, Adams did the country a service and made himself more unpopular than ever.

He still had a way to go, however, and to enhance his unpopularity took upon himself the support of the
Alien and Sedition Acts of 1798
Only Federalist and other paranoids could explain them - perhaps driven mad by the sight of so many French agitators running around the country. A comparison of the vote of Congressmen from Districts with higher dwelling values and greater equality in respect to living conditions with those from Districts of lower values and greater inequality shows the former voting more heavily for the Alien and Sedition Acts. Evidently the respectable Americans favored "McCarthyism".

The Alien Act allowed the President to expel "dangerous" aliens or have them tried and imprisoned. The waiting period for citizenship was lengthened from five to fourteen years. The Sedition Act made it a high misdemeanor to combine or conspire against any activities of the government; further, it forbade writing, speaking or publishing anything of a "false, scandalous and malicious" nature against the government or its officers.

The Federalists were making a crime of what everybody in the country had been doing as part of their American heritage. Fifteen indictments were brought, convictions were obtained, fines and imprisonment of editors occurred. There were no terrifying round-ups. Still, in view of the Constitution's First Amendment, not to mention several of its articles, the conduct of the Federalists was deranged and politically suicidal. It put them squarely up against the Bill of Rights.

The courts were not then in the business of correcting the constitutional judgement of the executive and legislative branches of government, so that legal defense against the Acts would not work. However, in a foreshadowing of evil events down the years, Jefferson and Madison wrote resolutions to be presented by the

Virginia and Kentucky legislatures, which passed in December of 1798. They professed to regard the Constitution as a compact among the States, such that, when Congress exceeds its powers under the compact, the State may interpose itself and nullify the action.

The Madison-drafted Virginia Resolutions declared that the States *"have the right and are in duty bound to interpose for arresting the progress of the evil,"* when Congress exceeded its powers. The Kentucky Resolutions, answering opposition from Northern States, declared that the State had the right to adjudge violations of the Constitution: *".. a nullification by those sovereignties, of all unauthorized acts done under color of that instrument, is the rightful remedy"*. Thus were coined two legalistic doctrines that were to have a rebirth in the debates prior to the Civil War.

Both States called upon the other States to help, but got scant support. Here the anti-Federalists were threatening to destroy the Republic. Jefferson advised against violence. The Act was repealed upon a change of administration.

Meanwhile, a certain amount of armed insurrection did take place with the armed band of John Fries that promoted tax strikes against a Federalist excise tax, the same that produced the great statistical count of the some 700,000 dwellings in the United States. Fries and two others were sentenced to hang for treason, but along with others involved, were pardoned by the President. The history of treason trials in America, like some other types to be mentioned, partakes of the absurd.

Thomas Jefferson had been Vice-President in the administration of John Adams, though of anti-Federalist persuasion. This had happened because Hamilton outsmarted himself in the elections of 1796. He disliked Adams, and thought to get Adams' Vice Presidential candidate elected President simply by persuading several Carolinian electors to vote for Pinckney and Jefferson. They did, but others up North voted against Pinckney when they heard of the deal, and the result was that

Adams received most ballots of the electors, but Jefferson received the second highest number and therefore became Vice-President, leaving Pinckney out in the cold.

In 1800, though, it was the real thing. Jefferson and Burr were chosen - how so will be explained in the nonce - and Adams and the Federalists were out. It would be a long time before they could light all the fireplaces in the White House again. They left the federal government a thriving enterprise, bank and all, with sixty different functions created under legislation of the Congress.

They also left the government with scores of new judicial offices created at the last minute by the "Lame-Duck Congress" that held its session following the November elections with many defeated members. Changeover of offices would occur in March. Naturally Adams promptly filled the offices with loyal Federalists, including one most important choice, John Marshall, to be Chief Justice of the Supreme Court.

———————

www.ingramcontent.com/pod-product-compliance
Lightning Source LLC
Chambersburg PA
CBHW081123170426
43197CB00017B/2731